STALIN'S
PROSECUTOR

STALIN'S PROSECUTOR

The Life of Andrei Vyshinsky

ARKADY VAKSBERG

Translated from the Russian by Jan Butler
With a Foreword by Robert Conquest

GROVE WEIDENFELD
New York

Published by Grove Weidenfeld
A division of Grove Press, Inc.
841 Broadway
New York, New York 10003–4793

First published in Great Britain in 1990 by
George Weidenfeld & Nicolson Limited, London

Library of Congress Cataloging-in-Publication Data

Vaksberg, Arkady.
Stalin's prosecutor : the life of Andrei Vyshinsky / Arkady
Vaksberg ; translated by Jan Butler.—1st American ed.
p.   cm.
Translated from the Russian.
Includes index.
ISBN 0–8021–1333–8 (alk. paper) : $19.95
1. Vyshinsky, Andrey Yanuaryevich, 1883–1954.   2. Public
prosecutors—Soviet Union—Biography.   3. Moscow Trials, Moscow,
R.S.F.S.R., 1936–1937.   I. Title.
LAW
345.47'01—dc20
[B]
[344.7051]
[B]   90–22239
CIP

Manufactured in the United States of America

Printed on acid-free paper

First American Edition 1991

10   9   8   7   6   5   4   3   2   1

Acknowledgements

This book could only have been written with the help of those who, striving to restore the truth and spread it as widely as possible, provided favourable conditions for me to work in, either by helping to collect material by all available means or by generously sharing their memories. I should like to express my sincere gratitude to the following: the Party Control Committee at the CCCPSU; the Procurator-General's office of the USSR; the Chief Military Procurator's office of the USSR; the Supreme Court of the USSR; the Central State Archive of the October Revolution; the Moscow City Party Archive; the Foreign Policy Archive of the USSR; the Central State Film and Photographic Documents Archive of the USSR; the All-Union Lenin Library.

Dr Valentin Berezhkov; Valentin Cherkesov; Sergei Gromov; Dr Genrikh Ioffe; Dr Piotr Krupnikov; Professor Vladlen Loginov; Klára Mácsay; Dr Vladimir Naumov; Dr Boris Pyadyshev; Yevgeny Smolentsev; Dr Oleg Temushkin; Vladimir Terebilov; Mikhail Shatrov; Professor Sigurd Schmidt; Mavrik Vulfson; Galina Yerofeyeva; Ambassador Vladimir Yerofeyev; Ambassador Leonid Zamyatin; Erik Zhagar.

The British Library; the GB-USSR Association; the US Library of Congress; the Kennan Institute (USA); the George Soros Fund (USA); the Soviet-American Cultural Initiative Fund; the Hoover Centre (USA); Stanford University; the Harriman Institute; Columbia University; Harvard University; Yale University Library.

Robert Arsenault (USA); Lord Bethell (GB); James Billington (USA); Alexandre Blokh (France); Dmitry Bosky (USA); Ambassador Sir Roderick Braithwaite (GB); Antonina W. Bouis (USA); Professor Robert Conquest (USA); Ellen Dahrendorf (GB); Martin Dewhirst (GB); Professor Victor Erlich (USA); Professor Lazar Fleishman (USA); Cornelia Gerstenmaier (W. Germany); Professor Israel Getzler (Israel); Professor Eugene Hoski (USA); Professor Geoffrey Hosking (GB); Professor Peter Juviler (USA); Edward Kline

(USA); Professor Leon Lipson (USA); Sir John Lawrence (GB); Sir Fitzroy Maclean (GB); Dr Nadine Marie (France); Jean-Jacques Marie (France); Ambassador Jack Matlock (USA); Kathleen Berton Murrell (GB); Geoffrey Murrell (GB); Professor Alexander Nekrich (USA); Professor Peter Reddaway (USA); John Roberts (GB); Sir Frank Roberts (GB); Professor Peter Solomon (Canada); Lord Shawcross (GB); Professor Richard Shupbach (USA); Nicholas Verte (France).

At their own request some sources prefer to remain anonymous, hence the absence of precise references.

If I have failed to name someone, I would ask them to forgive me. So many immensely busy people gave me the kindest and most generous co-operation in writing this book—the feeling of camaraderie I experienced will always remain a most cherished and exhilarating memory for me.

Contents

Foreword

In the past three years, one of the most revolutionary developments in the Soviet Union has been the rebirth of truth, and especially of historical truth. Among the figures who have been foremost in discovering and presenting the real facts of the dark age of Stalinism, the name of Arkady Vaksberg ranks very high. Like everyone who is trying to keep up with Soviet revelations about the long-hidden past, I have in recent years become an eager fan of his.

So far, material direct from the archives of the Ministry of the Interior, the KGB, the Ministry of Justice and so on has been skimpy. A small but important selection has been produced (in such periodicals as the *Izvestia TsK KPSS*, under a board headed by Gorbachev and Yakovlev) on the direct demand of the leadership. But in general, these major repositories of fact have remained closed.

So the search for the hidden details has been left largely to a few individuals with an eye for the possible locations of copies of documents, or a genius for following up clues from survivors of the period. Dr. Vaksberg is one of the supreme examples of this new research.

It is remarkable to trace in this book the way in which, among the professional classes whose positions brought them closest to the most secret recesses of Stalinist reality, an underground tradition carried a scattering of facts down to those of the new generation, like Vaksberg. The old lawyers, doctors, and bureaucrats would occasionally voice the truth, and Vaksberg was there to record it.

But his legal background not only gave him long-standing contact with many who had participated in the secret falsified trials of the Stalinist regime. It also, in one way or another, provided access to the background of those episodes—that is to say, the secret police records of interrogation.

At the center of the vast perversion of legality that marked the whole epoch, we find the extraordinary figure Andrei Vyshinsky, the jackal of the Stalinist jungle. Among those who embodied the fearful

ix

inhumanity and the moral and intellectual corruption of the Stalin autocracy, he takes a high place. In fact, even by Stalinist standards, there is something particularly mean and repulsive in the career of this able and intelligent public figure.

Vyshinsky's past as a revolutionary, even if a Menshevik one, is extraordinary on its own merits, and particularly so if we compare it with the unrelieved servility of his later career. But (as Solzhenitsyn has pointed out) the life of revolutionaries under the Tsars, harsh though it seemed at the time, was a bed of roses compared with the fate of anyone who gave even minor offense under the Communists. Lenin and Stalin and the other Bolshevik enemies of the Tsarist State were exiled to Siberia. But once there, they had allowances, sometimes even a servant, and spent their time in reading, hunting and discussion. The equivalent victims of Communism who were not shot were sent to hard labor in inhuman conditions of hunger, cold and often death. Vyshinsky's Menshevism, and his active participation on the legal side in the Provisional Government, had left him particularly vulnerable when Communist rule was established. In order to survive, to avoid what seemed an almost inevitable fate, he became a leading accomplice in Stalin's crimes.

Vyshinsky became world famous in the 1930s as the prosecutor and producer of the great faked "Moscow Trials," which caused a sensation on a world scale. A great deal of misapplied intelligence went into these week-long productions, and Vyshinsky, at the center of the stage, showed remarkable dramatic and forensic skill. These bloody and revolting farces, in fact, are his major achievement. Vaksberg, as a lawyer with different instincts, is the perfect investigator of his predecessor in the profession.

Vyshinsky served Stalin in other important capacities, as Vaksberg also develops. The present book tells for the first time of the preparation of the Soviet team for the Nuremberg Trial. This was by no means an easy task. For a major charge against the Nazis was that of having launched an aggressive war—a crime for which the USSR itself had been expelled from the League of Nations only six years earlier. Another of the accusations was of Nazi responsibility for the Katyn massacre, which had actually been carried out by the Soviets. Also, the Soviet judge at the trial, I. I. Nikitchenko, had been on the "court" that conducted the fake trial of Zinoviev and others in 1936 and was not by any means accepted as genuine by everyone in the West. (He also appears in this book in charge of many other, less public, faked trials Dr. Vaksberg has interestingly tracked down.)

As it turned out, Moscow need not have worried too much, for the

Western representation at Nuremberg accepted almost all the Soviet positions without qualms—though quietly omitting any finding on Katyn from the verdict.

Then Vyshinsky played another important role on the world stage, as Stalin's Foreign Minister. (I remember him at the United Nations, ostentatiously leaving off his instant translation earphones while President Truman addressed the General Assembly.) And one of his other services to Stalinism is very relevant to the present day and the rebirth of the liberty of the Baltic States. For Vyshinsky was Stalin's emissary in imposing the Soviet regime in Latvia in 1940.

The author has deployed a mass of illuminating detail, not only about Vyshinsky himself, but about almost all the long-secret activities of the whole terror apparatus. His account here of the anti-Semitic "Crimean Affair" of 1952, in which all the leading Yiddish writers were among those who lost their lives, is the first full account of that obscure and horrible case.

Arkady Vaksberg appears in this book as a sane man quietly gnawing away at the roots of paranoid falsification. He is not, of course, the only Soviet citizen responsible for bringing that rotten enormity crashing to the ground. But he has played a unique role in the process. Above all, as I have said, he has shown that extraordinary instinct for the discovery of records which in principle still remain inaccessible, but of which copies exist in the possession of various institutions or individuals.

This book, though it makes no claim to cover more than the career of a single, if crucial, individual representative of the epoch of total terror and total falsification, gives us one of the profoundest insights yet into the whole phenomenon of Stalinism, which has cast—and is still casting—such a dark and deathly shadow over our whole epoch.

ROBERT CONQUEST
Stanford, California
1990

STALIN'S PROSECUTOR

Introduction

I cannot write this book without first explaining how, on two occasions, Vyshinsky came to my aid. Twice he came to my rescue, without knowing anything about me. Both times it had to do with my studies at the Institute of Foreign Trade.

There were two prestigious institutions of higher education in Moscow, the doors of which were practically barred to ordinary mortals – the institutes of International Relations and Foreign Trade. There was no way I could get into the first: the likes of me were just not accepted there. The other, though, remained more democratic for a while. Soon this tiny crack was to be sealed up as well, but not before I had gained top marks in all the entrance examinations and won a place. I was then sixteen.

Young people matured earlier in my youth. I was no exception – and not just in the social sense. Independence, an ability to take decisions – these aspects of social maturity were possessed by many of my peers. But in one respect I was very different from them: my mother had not instilled in me suspicion and fear – the two distinctive elements of the period, and its permanent psychological backcloth. Having suffered the loss of loved ones, Mother shouldered all our anxieties alone – I grew up in an atmosphere in which I could exclaim with absolute sincerity: 'Thank you, Comrade Stalin, for our happy childhood!'

This is how I came to be so defenceless and downright foolish once I had got into the Institute, where completely different ground-rules applied. It was a launching pad for one's career, and many students started immediately to work on theirs. Many but not, of course, all: among the students in my year were some very talented and very decent people who went on to become Academicians and distinguished scholars, professors, ambassadors and prominent figures in the arts and sciences. But the place was also teeming with obvious careerists, schemers and trouble-makers. This, however, only became apparent to me much later on; at the time they were simply students who

I

aroused one's instinctive fear. Those who had been 'recommended to study by the Party's district committees' looked down upon the rest of us, who had got in entirely through our own endeavours, and without this powerful helping hand.

It was not difficult gradually to involve a young man like myself in the internal tensions of the Institute, for throughout my childhood and adolescence I had been completely out of touch with the realities of the time. The in-fighting was for a place in the Komsomol (All-Union Leninist Communist League of Youth) and on trade union electoral bodies – springboards for future advancement, the simplest and by then traditional way of forcing one's way to the top. I, too, was pushing someone forward. He was 'one of us', while each of his rivals was 'one of them'. 'They' won, and 'we' lost.

There was a price to pay for losing: I got off with a stern reprimand, still unaware on what dangerous ground I had been treading. One of the young speakers, aged about twenty, castigated me for having proposed another candidate for a planned organization whose inspiration came from a higher authority and reminded me that 'Comrade Stalin teaches us to fight against any members of the opposition and factionaries.' He ended, I remember, by saying: 'We shall not stand any opposition in our Institute!' I should have been terrified, but I merely laughed: at the time such political bombast seemed quite absurd.

But I laughed too soon. The storm clouds were gathering. Shortly afterwards I was summoned by the head of the student administration, a man called Akaba, who until recently had been the Minister of State Security of the Abkhazian Republic. He was from the same clique as Beria*, only a 'second-rater'. His transfer from the post of minister, albeit of an autonomous republic, to that of the head of an institute's student administration was not particularly impressive; but his new post was in Moscow, and in the foreign trade network, so this could bode well for the future.

In his tiny office the ex-minister made me sit down opposite him, so close that our foreheads nearly touched. He reeked of eau de Cologne and had stale breath. He gazed at me with a condescending smile on his lips, like a snake before a rabbit. 'I suggest you leave voluntarily,' he said. 'Why?' I really had no idea. 'Why?' I repeated, without waiting for a reply. Akaba smiled, examining me closely. 'You don't fit in here.'

---

* Chief of political police in Georgia, later replaced Yezhov as chief of Soviet political police.

'Why?' I repeated. 'Because of your personal credentials ... I shall expect your resignation by tomorrow – not later than twelve o'clock.'

In the evening I told my mother what had happened. I understand now what a shock it must have been for her, but she did not let on. She had always tried to protect my peace of mind. All she said was: 'Don't you write anything of the kind.' I did as I was told. Nobody summoned me again. Examination time came. I sat them all as though nothing had happened and then went off on holiday outside Moscow.

About ten days later I received a telegram from my mother telling me to come home. Waiting for me there was an envelope which had come through the post, enclosing a copy of an order expelling me from the Institute 'for failing to appear at a *subbotnik* [voluntary unpaid work session] to clean the yard'. People used to say in those days that you can always find something to nail anyone for. I recalled this at the time, but it did not make matters any better.

The absurd way in which this order had been 'formulated' made it seem not very serious, and suggested that it might be worth putting up a struggle. At least, that's what I felt. But my mother decided otherwise. 'There's no way back now,' she said. By this time, I think, she had another plan in mind.

Herself a lawyer since the 1920s, and the daughter and wife of lawyers, Mother was on friendly terms with a colleague called Dora Vladimirovna Horvitz, a highly cultured and greatly respected person. A relative of the great pianist Vladimir Horovitz (due to a clerical error her surname in her birth certificate had been spelt without the second 'o', thus she did not have to admit in official application forms that she had relations living abroad), she had found her vocation in the legal profession, specializing in the defence of children and adolescents. She had worked with Vyshinsky at the People's Commissariat of Education and had met him on numerous occasions. After becoming a lawyer, Dora Vladimirovna used to plead with him on behalf of her wards – he was already the Procurator of the Russian Federation (RSFSR), and was soon to become Deputy Procurator-General of the USSR. In short, she suggested to my mother that she should turn to Vyshinsky for help.

Of course, in theory Vyshinsky, now head of the Soviet diplomatic corps, had nothing to do with student affairs – especially since the institute in question came under the Ministry of Foreign Trade rather than the Ministry of the Interior. But in practice Vyshinsky could have a bearing on everything if he chose to. And this time he did. He received the two women in his office on Kuznetsy Most: two colleagues, two women lawyers who had come to see a fellow-lawyer. If Mother had asked for the order to be revoked, I am sure he would have said 'no'. The ridiculous 'reason' given in the order expelling me from the Institute suggested to him at once that the real reason lay elsewhere. However, the Ministry of Foreign Trade was under special management: Beria was in charge of personnel there, just as he was at the Ministry of the Interior. Nobody knew this better than Vyshinsky.

But Mother's request was quite different: that her son should be allowed to finish his education and not be left 'out in the cold'. As it was, the militia could simply have deported me from Moscow as 'a person of no fixed occupation', without even waiting for me to get fixed up with some kind of job.

This is what Mother told me years later:

Vyshinsky saw us late in the evening, at about eleven o'clock. He was sitting at a huge desk lit only by a table lamp – there was no other lighting in the room – and writing something. When we came in, he went on writing without looking up. We stopped by the door, expecting to be invited over to the table. He went on writing in silence, taking no notice of us. Perhaps this lasted only a minute, but to us it felt like an eternity. At last he looked up, got to his feet, and said by way of a greeting: 'I am listening!'

We walked up to the table. He neither sat down himself, nor offered us a seat. He looked at Dora, recognized her and nodded slightly. He gave me a sharp look and did not glance at me again. It took Dora literally three minutes skilfully to explain the crux of the matter. He interrupted her only once to repeat the surname [I carry my father's surname. My mother's is different]. I remember Dora saying: 'We know you always help lawyers in trouble.' Outwardly he did not react at all. Towards the end of her explanation, Dora took the account of our request we had written up beforehand and put it on the table. All this had taken about four minutes. Five at the most.

Vyshinsky did not say a word. He pressed a bell. A man appeared instantly: later I learnt that his name was Kharlamov. He stopped next to us and waited because Vyshinsky was writing something, standing with a blue pencil over my letter. Then he held it out to Kharlamov, and nodded to us: 'You will be notified.' The audience was over.

Two weeks later I was summoned to the rectorate of Moscow University and notified that I had been enrolled as a fourth-year student in the law faculty on the condition that I sat all the examinations for the past three years before the end of the term. In an office, where a dossier had already been opened on me, I read and committed to memory Vyshinsky's momentous instructions on my mother's letter: 'To the Rector of Moscow State University, Professor I. S. Galkin. Comrade Galkin, I think you could remove the obstacles which do not appear to me to be significant. A. Vyshinsky.'

Professor Galkin, it goes without saying, did as he was told and enrolled me without daring to ask how I had deserved such high-ranking patronage. The instructions worked like magic: the rector could not take his eyes off them. This safe-conduct appeared to guarantee me total immunity. But it only appeared to: there were other powers besides the rector of Moscow University, and they were a good deal stronger.

Once I had been expelled from the Institute, I lost all my friends. None of them associated with me again – which did not surprise me: why ruin one's life for no reason? There was only one 'exception': a man who had been in my year, and had never been a particularly close friend, suddenly displayed unusual comradely solidarity towards me. Not only did he not turn away from his disgraced friend, but he took to visiting us, sometimes hurrying over to my house straight from the Institute. A day apart made him miserable. He used to suffer like someone madly in love who had been parted from his beloved.

I took all this at face value, but Mother, seasoned by experience, sensed danger. This friendship, which was becoming rather a bore, could not be based on friendly feelings alone. As an experiment, Mother stopped leaving out a meal for him. He used to arrive hungry from his lectures and stay until the evening without getting any supper: as soon as she returned home from work, Mother used to shut herself away in her room ('to finish off some work') without giving us anything to eat. But it did not prevent him from showing up – he simply brought his own sandwiches, neatly wrapped in a starched napkin.

Mother became increasingly alarmed. I began to feel the same way, though at first I cracked jokes about her fears. After a small row I gave way to her, told my 'friend' that I was busy, and stopped seeing him for a few days. Then he started ringing every hour, sometimes even more frequently, wanting to know what I was doing, whether I had gone out and, if so, where to and how soon I would be back. 'He's gone to meet a girl,' replied Mother in a flash of inspiration, squeezing

5

my arm in case I accidentally burst out laughing. 'Who is she? Is he at her house? Couldn't I telephone her?'

Then we had the brainwave of saying that the girl I was going to see was my cousin. We phoned my aunt and asked her to say that her daughter had gone to the cinema with me. All evening he kept ringing my aunt, who had to pretend that instead of going back there after the cinema, we must have gone for a walk.

There was no way we could keep this up for long, and we ended up by letting him back into the flat. He had been trying to get in for at least ten days, and when at last he did so, he didn't know what to talk about. 'Let's play chess,' he finally suggested. We played a long, boring game in silence. Then he asked if he could make a telephone call. What he didn't know was that there was a second telephone, in the next room, which Mother had no scruples about picking up. A man's voice answered. 'I'm here,' said my friend, without calling the person by name, introducing himself, or greeting him. 'Well done!' came the answer, and that was the end of the conversation.

We went out for a walk. There was nothing to talk about. I was overwhelmed by a feeling of despair. I felt as though I was walking along Gorky Street for the last time. On the slope that led down towards the central telegraph office he suddenly stopped, looked up at the new houses which had been built and said, 'What revolting houses! I ask you – Soviet architecture! They've disfigured the whole centre of the city, don't you agree?' 'It's not very good architecture,' I agreed – whereupon he patted me cheerfully on the shoulder and hurried off to his trolleybus stop.

When I told my mother about our conversation, she shut her eyes in horror. 'You criticized the Party's town-planning policy. The construction project on Gorky Street was approved by Comrade Stalin.'

Once again she telephoned her friend, but Dora Vladimirovna said, quite reasonably, that 'on this issue' it was not convenient for her to go to Vyshinsky herself. But we should still go, and only to Vyshinsky. And, what's more, we should do so without delay.

The husband of an elderly Bolshevik, Yekaterina Gordeyevna Karmanova, under whom Mother had once worked, was now employed at the Procurator-General's office and had been quite closely acquainted with Vyshinsky for some time. He agreed to arrange a meeting for Mother without even asking the purpose of her visit. A few days later, Vyshinsky received her once again.

Here is what she told me years later:

Again, it was in the evening but not so late this time – around eight. And once again in his semi-circular office on a corner of the second floor – from its window you could see the gloomy Lubyanka building. This seemed symbolic to me at the time. Sort of bad luck ... I felt I could not control my agitation, especially as this time I was alone. And I had to wait nearly an hour in his reception before I was let in.

When I finally went in, Vyshinsky was standing behind his desk. I thought he would be looking down but he kept his eyes fixed on me. His stare pierced right through me. I found I could not explain things in a clear and coherent manner. I lacked Dora's calmness and iron logic. My legs kept buckling under me, but he did not invite me to sit down. He listened with his lips tightly compressed. After a few minutes he interrupted me with the phrase: 'Kindly be more concise.' This knocked me completely off balance, but somehow I managed to get my most important points across. I had just begun to say something I had prepared beforehand about why I had come to him with such an unusual request when he interrupted me with: 'That's beside the point,' and then exclaimed, 'Dilettantes!' This unexpected word stuck firmly in my memory. Not fools, not idiots or something of the kind, but dilettantes.

'Address your enquiries to Karmanov,' he said and sat down, which meant our conversation was over. I said goodbye – he did not reply – and left.

Unable to contain myself any longer, I rang Karmanov next morning with the excuse of thanking him for his help. He said, 'You were in the nick of time. Your son was born lucky.' Meeting me many months later, Yekaterina Gordeyevna whispered, 'Sima, dear, you're a genius! God Himself gave you the idea of seeking my help.' Nobody has ever spoken about this to me again.

This is how the story ended. In the evening of the same day on which Mother had spoken to Karmanov, my 'bosom friend' phoned again. Mother answered the call. I was standing nearby, and I can still remember, word for word, what she said: 'You're a monster, forget this number and the way to our house.'

A few years later I met a graduate at a party. Hearing my name, she asked in surprise: 'Have you been back long?' 'Where from?' 'The camp.' 'The camp? What camp?' I honestly had no idea what she was talking about.

Her story did not take long to tell. She had been invited to the birthday party of a mutual acquaintance, and my 'friend' was among the guests. Out of the blue he had suddenly mentioned my name and suggested that I should be invited along. When everyone agreed, he immediately dialled my number. He said who he was, and then his face fell. A few seconds later he put down the receiver. 'What's wrong?' everyone exclaimed at once. 'He's been arrested,' my 'friend' said. 'His mother's just told me.'[1]

This is perhaps a suitable moment to recall another occasion on which Vyshinsky influenced our destiny. Not mine this time, but that of a close relative: my father's brother – my uncle, in other words.

My father was already dead when the Great Purge, that mass extermination of people, began in 1937 – which was the only reason why the blades of the gigantic 'meat-grinder' failed to hack through our family. But to make up for it, they had already, by the spring of 1936, struck down my Uncle Genrikh, an eminent economist, board member of the People's Commissariat of Finances, and department head of the State Workers' Savings Banks and State Credit. He was branded a 'Trotskyite', a 'spy', a 'saboteur' and a 'terrorist', and then shot. A year and a half later his chief and friend, Grigory Grinko, the People's Commissar of Finances, was convicted on the same charges, along with Bukharin and Rykov, in the so-called Third Moscow Trial.

After Genrikh, my father's other brother, Matvei, was convicted. A professor of economics and law and a prominent public figure, he was the Academic Secretary of VARNITSO – the All-Union Association of Workers of Science and Technology for the Assistance of Socialist Construction. (In current terminology this would be called the Association of Scientists in Support of Perestroika.) Matvei's only crime was that he was his brother's brother – indeed, the sentence pronouncing his deportation actually spelt this out: 'for being the brother of an enemy of the people'. His mother, my great-aunt, who was seventy at the time, was also to be deported with him.

Professor Vyshinsky had also been a VARNITSO presidium member since the early 1930s. My uncle and he had sat together on the presidium and on the editorial board of the journal *Science and Technology Front*. I suspect that, when he asked Dora Vladimirovna Horvitz to repeat my surname, he must have been thinking of my uncle.

The President of VARNITSO was the world-famous biochemist and ex-Narodnaya Volya* member, Academician Alexei Nikolayevich

---

*An organization set up in the 1880s by proponents of terror who advanced a Socialist programme and whose main objective was the assassination of the Tsar.

Bakh. On 2 December 1936, he sent the following letter to Procurator-General of the USSR Vyshinsky:

Dear Andrei Yanuarievich,

Dramatic circumstances compel me to turn to you for urgent and effective assistance. On 23 December of this year Professor Matvei Abramovich Vaksberg, with whom you are well acquainted, and his mother were sentenced by the NKVD [People's Commissariat of Internal Affairs] Special Board to five years of exile in Kazakhstan. Judgement was passed in their absence. Nobody brought any charges against him or cross-examined him.

I know Comrade M. A. Vaksberg as one of the leading representatives of VARNITSO and a key member of our journal's editorial board. He is an exceptionally valuable and conscientious worker, unquestionably dedicated to the cause of socialist construction. He has never been expelled from the party or faced prosecution. Considering M. A. Vaksberg undoubtedly to be a good and honest Soviet worker and public-spirited man, I hereby ask you to review the Special Board's sentence.

I do not know how this letter was sent to Vyshinsky, but that same day the Procurator-General prevented the sentence from being carried out. For seven months nobody touched my uncle: it looked as though the trouble had passed and a miracle had been worked.

But Grinko's arrest, and the preparations that then began for what was to be the most ostentatious and important of Stalin's murderous trials to date – the trial of the 'Bloc of Rights' – significantly changed the situation. Yezhov, the People's Commissar of Internal Affairs, confirmed his decision to exile my uncle, and Vyshinsky decided it was better not to get any further involved in the matter, on the grounds that only so much could be done for people, especially in such an insidious and dangerous area as this.

Nevertheless, eight years later he again responded to a request for help – very warily, and again without success.

After serving his sentence of exile in Semipalatinsk, my uncle settled in Alma-Ata. Expelled from the Party as an 'enemy of the people', stripped of his academic title, branded the brother of a 'terrorist', he was helped along by courageous, honest and generous-spirited people in Kazakhstan. Work was found for him at the university and in the People's Commissariat of Trade, where he immediately became a department head. His intelligence, wide-ranging knowledge and professionalism proved more important than his past convictions. The

9

Vice-Chairman of the Soviet People's Commissariat of Kazakhstan, Omarov, the People's Commissar of Trade, and the Rector of Alma-Ata University sent petitions to the Procurator-General, who was then Konstantin Gorshenin,[2] to have their colleague cleared of his previous convictions. A similar petition was written by one of my uncle's ex-colleagues, Klavdia Mikhailovna Moshchinskaya, a senior lecturer at the Chair of Marxism-Leninism at the Moscow Institute of Law, who decided to seek Vyshinsky's protection, just as Academician Bakh once had. World War II was drawing to a close; and the screws were beginning to be loosened slightly. Although the wave of mass arrests was over, other issues were causing the 'leadership' concern: the genocide of entire peoples – the Ingush, Chechen, Kalmyk, Balkar, Karavayev, and Crimean Tartars – was under way. From this mass production line it proved possible to withdraw a single human 'unit' who, even by the standards of those days, had nothing marked against him. Vyshinsky instructed his assistants to 'make inquiries'. It was meant as a hint, an exercise in good relations and nothing more, and the hint was taken.

Two colleagues of the Procurator-General's office, Paté and Serebryennikov, compiled a draft protest calling for the Special Board's sentence to be revoked – an extremely rare event for those days. Beria was informed, and immediately intervened. Vyshinsky might have stood up against others, but not against Beria – neither would Procurator-General Gorshenin, even less so. On the draft protest Gorshenin wrote: 'For these things Paté and Serebryennikov should be dismissed from work.' What 'things'? Nobody asked. The chief's instruction was carried out immediately.

Another twelve years went by before the Supreme Court rehabilitated both brothers. One of them was already dead; however, the other lived to see justice triumph and, totally blind, went on working at the University of Kazakhstan until his death at the age of ninety-two.

I apologize to the reader for this lengthy introduction. The point of it has not been to conjure up personal memories, explain deep grudges, or explore episodes of my life, all too insignificant in comparison with the tragedy that befell millions of people – an entire society, and an entire country.

The point of it lies elsewhere, and is particularly important for this book. Everything I have just related is completely unknown. I could have concealed it, on the grounds that nobody need ever have discovered that Vyshinsky had twice saved me from disaster. But I believe this would have been dishonest.

1

'Fifteen minutes before I was born I still had no idea that I was about to come into the world. I am making this seemingly trivial observation because I want to get a fifteen-minute headstart on all the other remarkable people whose life story begins with tedious monotony from the moment of birth.' So begins the tongue-in-cheek auto-biography of the well-known Russian humorous writer Arkady Averchenko.

I very much doubt whether Vyshinsky could have written like this about himself, even jokingly. He did, however, have an astounding ability to foresee everything, not just fifteen minutes or fifteen months, but fifteen years ahead. Ironically he was born on 10 December, and nearly a hundred years later this same day, which few remembered as Vyshinsky's birthday, was declared International Human Rights Day by the United Nations. This paradox is made less bitter by the thought that the birthday of one of the world's greatest henchmen, who abused human rights and destroyed human lives, should now be a day of solidarity and hope, a day of struggle for dignity and freedom.

In 1883, in the town of Odessa, which has given the world so many excellent writers, actors and musicians, an auburn-haired boy, whose name was destined to resound around the world, was born into an unremarkable family, recently arrived from Poland.

It is known for certain that Andrei (Andrzej, to be absolutely precise) Vyshinsky was descended from an old Polish family, and even, it is said, through some side branch of the family, distantly related to an illustrious Polish cardinal. It is even claimed that, at least until the end of the 1930s, some of his not-so-distant relatives held very high positions in the Polish state's political hierarchy. However, Vyshinsky is among the most common surnames in Poland, so quite possibly these people were not relatives at all.

According to another version – it would probably not prove difficult for Polish historians, should any of them feel like tearing themselves away from more topical problems, to check this out – the father of the future 'celebrity', Yanuarii Vyshinsky, first held anti-Russian views (nationalistic views, as we would call them these days), and then did a sharp about-turn, and became a loyal supporter of the Russian Tsar, Alexander II, even earning himself an Order of the Russian Empire, before fleeing from his incensed countrymen to the shores of the bounteous Black Sea, where hospitable, cosmopolitan and mirth-loving Odessa welcomed all refugees, regardless of their ideas and positions.

However, the young child did not stay there long: he was not yet five when his family set off in search of happiness to Baku, another town which was then renowned for its tolerance of foreign tongues and beliefs, origins and personal background. It was also renowned for its heated revolutionary struggle and for the political passions which permeated its social and cultural life.

An experienced pharmaceutical chemist, Yanuarii Vyshinsky began by working as the manager of the Baku branch of a Caucasian company trading in pharmaceutical goods, before starting up his own business – a chemist's shop in what is now Gubanov Boulevard – which brought in a sizeable income. Everything went well and the family had no material worries, but obviously the couple were not getting on, because the mother, a pianist, suddenly took the children and moved away to Kharkov, where she earned her living by giving music lessons and running a canteen from home at which impecunious students and clerks could eat for a modest sum.

The family only moved back to Baku three or four years later, and Andrei, already eight years old, started at the classical gymnasium. He received a brilliant education, proving himself an outstanding pupil entirely through his own endeavours. Many years later, in a letter to 'dear Andrei', a Baku lawyer by the name of Grigorii Melik-Shakhnazarov recalled their schooldays together in the third, fourth and fifth years, when the bloodthirsty prosecutor-to-be was 'well-known for his biceps. It was quite dangerous to start a fight with him.' His biceps did not, however, prevent him from having a great feeling for the arts: the Vyshinskys regularly hosted literary, musical and singing evenings and dances, at which the children of their circle used to gather.

At a gymnasium ball – he already displayed an exceptional talent for the waltz – Andrei Vyshinsky became acquainted with the young and beautiful Kapa Mikhailova, who had a long train of admirers. Only he, however, succeeded in winning her heart, and a few years later they married and lived happily together for the rest of their lives. Kapitolina Isidorovna Vyshinskaya died at a venerable age after outliving her husband by nineteen years.

The town's revolutionary spirit proved stronger than his prosperous family's innate conservatism. By the time his father sent him off to study law at Kiev University, Vyshinsky had acquired rebellious convictions and a rebellious past. No gymnasium gathering of anti-Tsarists took place without him. No revolutionary speech was made by the workers without his support, albeit moral: he sided with the oppressed and the downtrodden rather than the powers that be, and firmly resolved to fight for their rights.

Kiev was another city with strong revolutionary traditions, and the first-year student at once began to take an active part in the work of illegal Marxist circles. The consequences were soon forthcoming: a few months later those students who had taken part in the 'disorders' were expelled, not just from the university but from the city as well. Andrei returned home to be greeted by a loving but disapproving father. When it came to questions of ideology, most families in the Russia of those days were divided.

Instead of drawing the conclusions the authorities – and his parents – had hoped for, the expelled student became even more deeply involved in illegal activities. He registered his choice by joining a party: the Social Democrats, rather than the Bolsheviks-Mensheviks. His name became known throughout Baku, for in those days the entire town was on one or the other side of the revolutionary barricade. Given his temperament and his gift for oratory, he was swept upwards on a sudden wave of workers' and students' disturbances. In the autumn and winter of 1905 he took an active part in a mass railway strike, which other workers then joined.

Forty or so years later, in a letter to Vyshinsky, one of the strikers, Vaso Odzelashvili, a canning factory worker from the Georgian town of Gurdzhaani, gave a colourful description of Vyshinsky during this strike. Although his motive for writing was to get his pension raised 'in view of his active revolutionary past', and although he was obviously keen to flatter the friend of his youth, he seems not to have taken too many liberties with the truth, since the same or very similar details appear in letters from other people unknown to one another:

Comrade Vyshinsky, remember the armed detachment you organized which was made up of workers [Vyshinsky was twenty-one at the time]. We were all armed. . . . You were then living on the corner of Armyanskaya and Gymnazicheskaya Street – your entrance was through the yard, and first on the right. I often dropped by your house to collect political leaflets.... Remember, in 1905, that big strike you led. The armed detachment played a big role then ... Comrade Vyshinsky, you were working as an accountant at Dorozhnov's linen shop, and you were lying low there.... Members of the 'Black Hundred' [an armed anti-revolutionary group active in Russia between 1905 and 1907] were after you – your house was raided by the secret police and everything was turned upside down, but they didn't find anything – three or four days before we'd taken away your gun, leaflets and typefaces....

Remember Alexandrovsky Cathedral, and the subversive printing-office opposite which used to print leaflets – you sent us there to pick them up, and I threw a sackful over my shoulder and carried them over to you, but only your wife was in, and I said to her: 'Give this to Comrade Andriusha.'

Remember when the members of the 'Black Hundred' killed Piotr Montin and a large funeral was organized under your personal leadership, all our detachment was there.... You walked about ten steps ahead of us, in your student cap and summer coat. When we reached the castle, something came crashing down, people started dashing all over the place, and we reckoned that members of 'Black Hundred' were after us. But you turned round and said sternly to us: 'Detachment, keep together, be prepared.' And we replied: 'We'll die together, Comrade Vyshinsky!' ... You mounted the railway carriage's steps and made a speech. You spoke for a long time, there was a sea of people, and we, the detachment members, were by your side all the time. I remember your last words as though it was yesterday. You said: 'The time will come when we shall revenge the enemy for everything.' And sure enough it has.

Either because he did not know about it, or because he did not want to remind Vyshinsky of the other work he was involved in, Vaso Odzelashvili made no mention of what Vyshinsky's armed detachment did most of the time. So what were they doing?

Let us listen first to Vyshinsky. Early in the 1930s, in light of the changes of direction being planned in his rapidly advancing career, he wrote a biographical note for his personal dossier. He described this period of his life as follows:

Influenced by the horrors of the February Armenian-Tartar massacre, the monstrous police carnage organised by the Baku police force and by rich Tartar aristocrats under cover of the Cossacks of the Labinskaya Squadron and the soldiers of the Salyanskii Regiment, who for three days shot down the undefended Armenian population in the streets of Baku and burned women and children in the blazing houses of the Armenian districts, I resolved to concentrate entirely on organizing the Party's armed forces. I was involved at this time in the organization of an armed detachment comprising several hundred Baku workers – Mensheviks and Bolsheviks. [In the mid-1930s Vyshinsky changed the last part of this text to 'mostly Bolsheviks'.]

It seems that Vyshinsky also kept quiet about this armed detachment's main function, which was to assassinate suspected police collaborators. He personally organized and carried out – along with others, of course – the assassination of the provocateurs Alexander Grigoriev, Movsumov and Plakida. For this, or perhaps for his activities in general, Vyshinsky was allegedly attacked while in the company of his wife, the charming Kapa, by a member of the 'Union of the Russian People'* in 1907 – at least according to an account which was even recorded in the old reference books.

One has to say 'allegedly' because apart from the words 'was attacked', which appear in one reference book after another, there is not a hint anywhere as to how or when this attack occurred, or what its consequences were. The newspapers usually reported on the attacks of members of the 'Black Hundred' – the Social Democratic press tended to carry detailed accounts of such episodes, demanding that the culprits should be brought to trial and punished. And later on, after the Revolution, the victims themselves were generally only too happy to exaggerate the details. Yet in this particular case there were no details. None. Anywhere. For the time being I can find no explanation for this bizarre fact...

24 May 1950 – this is the date at the top of the letter that Aliovsat Guliev, a senior lecturer at the University of Azerbaijan, sent to Andrei Vyshinsky:

---

* A right wing group founded in 1905 which tried to appeal to a large section of the people, denouncing bureaucracy as a barrier between Tsar and people and attempting, with some success, to divert social discontent against the Jews.

Dear Andrei Yanuarievich!

During archive research in Tbilisi I came across certain documents concerning your revolutionary activity in Baku in 1905, of which I have made copies.

If these documents are of interest to you, I could hand them over to you *at a private meeting.*

Such a meeting must have taken place, because among Vyshinsky's personal papers are copies of documents from the Central State History Archives and Museum of the Revolution Archives. On the one hand, these documents cast light on some incomplete pages of his life story, while on the other introducing new mysteries yet to be solved.

From representations made by the Baku district court's prosecutor to the Tiflis city court's prosecutor on 30 January 1906, it is clear that fifteen people were brought to trial over the railway strike, and that Andrei Vyshinsky was third on the list. They also indicate that custody was used as a means of suppressing the action, and that Vyshinsky was taken into custody on 21 January.

What became of the investigation? Nothing, obviously, for it is known for certain that in 1906 and 1907 Vyshinsky was safe and well and at liberty, and involved in much more dangerous work as far as the authorities and the law were concerned than taking part in a strike – and was even, if one is to believe the version mentioned earlier, wounded by a member of the 'Black Hundred'. This means Vyshinsky was not detained for long. Why? I do not know the answer.

To this period also belongs a denunciation of 20 January 1906, kept in Vyshinsky's personal archive, by a secret police operative working under the code name of 'Southern', in which he states that during the strike 'people destined to play an extremely important role in the workers' local movement came to the fore'. These people were named by the police agent as the Shendrikov brothers – Lev, Ilya and Gleb – and Andrei Vyshinsky, whose speech 'against Dr Sorokin, who had played a sinister part in the October massacre, acquired vast significance and caused an extremely powerful upsurge of revolutionary feeling.' (Among Vyshinsky's other actions reported in the press of the day were his public lecture on '1848 in Europe', and his fund-raising efforts to organize a canteen for the striking workers.)

Meanwhile it soon became known that the Shendrikov brothers were actually police abettors, local 'Zubatovites'[1] and organizers of the 'Union of Baku Workers', which was run with the authorities' silent approval in order to keep union members out of the political struggle.

18

At various meetings in which the Shendrikovs were accused of acting against the workers' interests, Vyshinsky made thunderous speeches in their defence. He played a prominent role as secretary of the Baku council, which the police had also succeeded in infiltrating with their spies. Bolsheviks were very much in the minority on this council: of the 225 deputies, only 10 were Bolsheviks, but instead of being formally divided between Bolsheviks and Mensheviks, they worked here as a single group of Social Democrats.

However, at the end of 1907, just as the Shendrikovs' careers as political figures came to an end, the armed detachment's terrorist activities stopped, and the revolutionary wave began to subside, Vyshinsky was suddenly back in prison again because of the same railway strike, which had happened over two years before. What's more, he was charged this time merely in connection with a single not just minor, but very minor, episode: 'In December 1905 at one of the meetings at the railway workers' theatre in Baku he made a speech inciting railway personnel to join in the general political strike.' In February 1908 a special session of the Tiflis court sentenced Vyshinsky – for this alone – to a year's imprisonment in the fortress.

There are at least two mysterious facts that draw themselves to our attention here.

Firstly, if there is a document covering the instigation of criminal proceedings and the course of action selected in 1906, there must also be one on the closure of the case. Or at least on the custody being cancelled (or changed?). A person in custody cannot be released from prison without a document authorizing his release. But where is this document? There can be no doubt that it once existed.

Senior lecturer Guliev compiled a selection of police and legal materials from the archives and gave them to Vyshinsky. There is no document among them explaining what happened after Vyshinsky's arrest in January 1906. Is it because there was no such document in the archives, which is really strange? Or because this is what Vyshinsky decided to remove from the selection – which is even stranger?

Secondly, Vyshinsky's personal dossier contains three biographical notes which he wrote in the twenties and thirties (files were kept in every personnel department on the progress of each person's career). His conviction and imprisonment in the fortress are described in only a few lines, and, what's more, there is not a word about his detention in 1906 and release from prison shortly afterwards. There is no mention either of why, after being tried first, in 1906, under Article 102 of the Criminal Code ('A violent encroachment on the change of the form of government' and, on top of that, being 'in possession of a firearm' – which were punishable by a life sentence of hard labour) and under 126 ('Participation in an association whose aim is the overthrow of the existing order', which was punishable by a term of hard labour), he was convicted in 1908 only under Article 129 ('The delivery in public of an anti-government speech'). There is a huge discrepancy between what Vyshinsky did and the crime he was convicted of and sentenced for.

Both these mysteries have yet to be solved.

After delays caused by its being submitted for approval to the highest judicial authority, the judgement finally came into effect and was executed. Vyshinsky was sent to Bailovka Prison to serve his sentence.

Still standing today, Bailovka Prison suffered from terrible overcrowding in those days. According to sanitary regulations, it was intended for four hundred, but in actual fact had well over fifteen hundred crammed inside its walls. Conditions were fairly relaxed: the cell doors were not locked and the prisoners were allowed to wander about 'on visits' from one cell to another, and many of them slept in the corridors.

Vyshinsky's cell contained far more inmates than it was supposed to, just like all the others. One of the bunks was occupied by a prisoner who had been sent there several months earlier. In the police documents he was put down as Gaioz Nizharadze, and the other prisoners called him by his nickname – 'Koba' – but his real name was Iosif Vissarionovich Dzhugashvili, or simply Stalin. Huddled in a corner with his legs tucked under him and his back to everyone, wearing a dark blue loose-fitting shirt with a side-fastening collar and a hood tossed over one shoulder, he used to spend hours studying the 'language of the future' – Esperanto. (Thirty years later, on Stalin's orders, all the Esperantists in the Soviet Union were either shot or deported to the GULAG – labour camps controlled by the NKVD – and Esperanto was branded the language of spies and wreckers.) However, he never fully mastered either Esperanto or German, which he had taken up even earlier in Batumi Prison.

Tearing himself away from his textbook every now and then, Stalin would get involved in heated arguments with the Mensheviks and SRs (Socialist Revolutionaries), who were mostly 'politicals'. The criminals looked up to him and never joined in the arguments. Along with the other Mensheviks, Vyshinsky was among his main opponents. It is hard to say who used to win as there were no 'judges' or 'juries', but

Koba, his cell-mates recall, took an active and energetic part in the arguments, working his opponents into a frenzy. One of those who always backed him up – physically rather than verbally – was Sergo Ordzhonikidze.[2]

Passions sometimes reached boiling point; they argued until they were hoarse – they had no other way of occupying their time. However, perhaps only two of them never lost their cool, and they were 'Koba' and 'Yuri'. No matter how much they differed in temperament, accomplishments and manners, they both had nerves of steel. And that was a quality Koba admired even then.

The 'politicals' lived like a commune, sharing out their food parcels in a brotherly manner. Whenever he got an opportunity, Koba greatly enjoyed making *kharcho* – Caucasian mutton soup – and spicy Georgian sauce. However, not many prisoners received food parcels, as most of them came from very poor families who generally lived a long way from Baku. Vyshinsky was among the very few not to be forgotten and to be supplied with top-quality food. There were no restrictions in force, and his loving young wife regularly brought delicious home-cooked meals for him. It went into the shared pot, but as a sign of reconciliation, and with general consent, Vyshinsky frequently gave his own share to the sullen Koba. Koba was only too pleased to eat it, but as soon as he had done so, instead of saying 'thank you', he would start up another argument, cursing the young Menshevik Andrei for all he was worth.

This continued for four months. On 23 October 1908 Vyshinsky completed his prison sentence and was set free the same day. Seventeen days later Stalin was deported to Siberia. Their next meeting would take place nearly ten years later.

After being released from prison, Vyshinsky spent a short while at home, recovering from his stressful experiences (this rest brought him great personal joy: the birth in 1909 of his daughter Zinaida, with whom he was to have a loving relationship throughout his life). Then he set off for Kiev and was immediately enrolled at the University – at the law faculty, of course – where in the middle of the year his student rights were restored, seven years after his expulsion for political unreliability. These seven years had been so eventful and stormy for the Baku Menshevik that they could hardly have made him any more trustworthy. If anything, they had made him less so: an organizer of political strikes, an armed detachment leader, a terrorist, the presidium secretary of an electoral council with pretensions to real power in the town, and, finally, a state criminal who had just come out of prison – what better police testimonial could one have asked for. But, evidently, more democratic times were now underway: the university welcomed Vyshinsky back with open arms.

Perhaps it should come as no surprise that Vyshinsky was an excellent student, and immediately displayed both talent and diligence. He took an active part in student circles, and was equally attracted to differing areas of learning. He was given special attention by the eminent Russian law historian Professor Vladimirsky-Budanov, under whose supervision he prepared a paper 'On the Origin of Law' which paved the mature student's way – by now he was already nearly thirty – into the academic world: when he graduated, the academic council unanimously voted to keep him on in the Department of Criminal Legal Proceedings to study for a professorship.

But just then the university's administration suddenly remembered the former insurgent who over the past five years had done nothing to incur the regime's wrath. So what had this completely loyal law graduate done to incense them so? What had he done wrong? Or was this a clever manœuvre on someone else's part to deflect suspicion of their involvement in a shady deal with the police? This blank spot in his biography still needs to be looked into by someone who will perhaps prove more successful than I have been, and come up with documented answers to these questions.

Once again Baku gave Vyshinsky refuge. But this time he was unable to find work in his field. As the father of a young child, he was forced by everyday concerns to put his ambitions to one side for a while and concentrate on earning his daily bread. Hard work is the key to success, especially if one has brains as well. The youthful but no longer young university graduate succeeded in making a good impression on the rich parents of some recalcitrant pupils, and they were only too happy to engage him for a perfectly decent fee as a private tutor. Hearing of the talented tutor, the headmaster of a private gymnasium, Ananii Pavlovich Yemilyanov, invited him to teach Russian literature, geography and Latin – he could turn his hand to anything. (The headmaster lived to a venerable age; he methodically sent Vyshinsky lengthy greetings on his birthday every year, and always received a warm personal reply.)

However, Vyshinsky was still attracted to the legal profession, for he was a lawyer not only by education but also by calling. When all his attempts to get a barrister's practice in Baku had ended in failure, he decided to try his luck in Moscow. There, too, every practising lawyer had plenty of efficient assistants, yet there was no other way of getting an independent practice: to gain the right of entry to the courts, one had first to serve an apprenticeship in a lawyer's office.

After considerable ordeals in Moscow (where he also made ends meet by giving private lessons and preparing young dunces for their school-leaving examinations) fortune smiled on him: the unemployed thirty-two-year-old was spotted by one of the most eminent lawyers of the day – Pavel Nikolayevich Malyantovich, who had acted as a counsel for the defence at numerous political trials, defending Lev Trotsky, the accused in the trial that followed the December armed uprising in Moscow of 1905, the mutinous crew of the *Azov* battle-cruiser, and many others too. He was a man with clearly expressed liberal democratic convictions, and was impressed rather than shocked by Vyshinsky's political background. He took him on as an assistant, and it was only thanks to him that Vyshinsky was able to become officially registered as one of the lawyers of the Moscow courts. His modest but promising legal practice lasted for about a year and a half.

The possible overthrow of the monarchy drove him once again to take a revolutionary stand. In few other instances did such a large percentage of one single profession put itself at the service of the February 1917 revolution. Hundreds of lawyers and their assistants took up various posts in the new bodies of local government. Vyshinsky first got a position in the Zemgor, the joint committee of district and city unions which had been formed to organize supplies for the fighting army – or, to be more precise, in the editorial office of the news bulletin it published – and then, almost immediately, became a commissar of the first militia division of the Yakimanka district of Moscow. Meanwhile, new bodies of power began to be established, and when the Yakimanka district acquired its own local authority Vyshinsky was elected chairman, once again of its first division.

This auburn-haired official, who was already becoming rather stout, was often seen in shiny trousers and a threadbare jacket (then all the rage) at Menshevik party meetings and, less frequently, at meetings for the electorate, where one of his duties was to distribute pre-election literature: the elections to the district and city *dumas* (councils) were drawing near. He was then elected into the district (Kaluga) *duma* by Menshevik voters, and co-opted onto the city *duma*. His incendiary speeches made an impression on the not very politically aware women workers of the First Golutvinskaya textile mill, but failed to impress those people at Party meetings who had been seasoned by the political battles. However, his most conspicuous work was organizing free canteens for needy workers. The food was handed out under Menshevik slogans, and Vyshinsky used to joke – while actually meaning it quite seriously – that: 'The ideas of Menshevism are being poured into our clientele with every spoonful of soup they take.'

He also poured these ideas into his audiences at district and city *duma* meetings, displaying obvious conformism: whereas ten or twelve years earlier he had approved nothing, he now approved everything. The Bolsheviks, as is well known, were highly critical, to put it mildly, of the Provisional Government's policies, whereas Vyshinsky was highly enthusiastic about literally every government ruling. It is not my intention to discuss the 'pros' and 'cons' of the acts passed during the wave of February reforms. I only wish to register a noticeable change in behaviour of a successful politician: now that he was completely satisfied with the established regime, and regarded it as his own, he began to make energetic propaganda on behalf of its policies. Take, for instance, his hastily published pamphlet *What Kind of City Dumas Do We Need?* in which he claimed that the Provisional Government's municipal reform 'had surpassed one's greatest expectations'.

But a most important event in his short-lived career as district chairman was his signing of an order to which he attached not the slightest importance at the time. And yet this order was to affect the rest of his life and determine the line of conduct he adopted to the very end.

In September 1917, in view of the ominously changing political situation, the Provisional Government braced itself for yet another reorganization. Its head, Alexander Kerensky, until only recently one of the foremost defence counsels in political trials – defending in particular the Bolshevik state *duma* members who had been charged with treason – remembered his Moscow colleague Pavel Malyantovich and asked the Minister of Finance, Tereshenko, to invite him to join the Cabinet. Malyantovich agreed; but whereas all the other Cabinet members were members of various political parties, he belonged to none. Following his own convictions and the advice of the Minister of the Interior – Nikitin, a Menshevik – Malyantovich joined the Menshevik Party (was he at all influenced in this by his former assistant, Vyshinsky?) and took up the post of Minister of Justice and Chief Procurator. He worked in these capacities for exactly one month, from 25 September to 25 October – when, along with the other ministers of the Provisional Government, he was arrested and dispatched to the Fortress of SS Peter and Paul, where he spent two days.

However, his month in a ministerial post coincided with a decree which was to prove fateful for him and for Vyshinsky, albeit with diametrically opposed consequences for the two of them.

Here is the instruction that Vyshinsky, as chairman of the Yakimanka district authority, received along with all the other chairmen in October 1917:

A resolution of the Petrograd Board of Inquiry has called for the arrest and prosecution of Vladimir Ilyich Ulyanov-Lenin in connection with the armed action on the third, fifth July in Petrograd [this was merely a pretext in an attempt to avert the revolution which the Provisional Government now knew was being got ready]. In view of this I ask you to ensure that the resolution is carried out immediately, should the person in question appear within the confines of the district under your authority. You are requested to report on ensuing events.
Minister of Justice P. N. Malyantovich

A similar instruction was issued by Chief Procurator P. N. Malyantovich to the procurators of the district courts.

What should a representative of the lowest rank of executive power have done on receiving an instruction from a representative of the highest rank? Naturally, he ordered it to be carried out immediately, and appropriate posters with a picture of 'the person in question' were stuck up on the walls of houses in his district. He did not, however, manage to report 'on ensuing events' because a few days later the posts of both the minister and the chairman were dissolved. And so Malyantovich's instructions were never carried out by his former assistant and then subordinate, Vyshinsky – much to the latter's chagrin no doubt, at least to begin with. Malyantovich, however, always considered this a sad mistake.[3]

The October Revolution ruined the lawyer's ambitious plans just as his political career had got off the ground. He realized at once that, as a Menshevik, he would not survive for long under the Bolsheviks. He had urgently to look for more stable and promising work. Once again, personal contacts helped.

In Baku, Vyshinsky's parents had been on neighbourly terms with the Khalatov family. When Bagrat and Katya Khalatov had their first child, Artiomy, they all celebrated the birth together, and drank to the newborn baby's health and happiness. Andrei, still a young schoolboy at the time, took part in the family celebrations.

The baby had grown up and become a student at the Moscow Institute of Commerce. When Vyshinsky had arrived in Moscow to seek his fortune as a restive, homeless graduate, his young ex-neighbour, Artiomy, had gladly shared his lodgings with the wordly-wise Andrei. Vyshinsky did not forget this good turn and, when he became an important official in the district authority, he made Artiomy a member of the Zamoskvorechiye *duma* and, far more importantly, a member of its food authority. Immediately after the Revolution in Petrograd, without waiting for the outcome of the struggles in Moscow, the far-sighted Artiomy Bagratovich, who had only just turned twenty-one, joined the Bolshevik Party.

A couple of weeks later the situation changed drastically. Now it was Khalatov's turn to help Vyshinsky – after all, one good turn deserves another. The Menshevik Vyshinsky left his local authority post to become a food inspector. His Bolshevik friend, Khalatov, was promoted to an even higher post and became a deputy of Moscow's special commissar on food and transport. So they clung to each other, these neighbours from Baku.

Soon there appeared on the scene in Moscow a third Baku man who, though not born and bred in Baku, had spent important formative years working there and shared similar memories of the town: Stalin – once a cell-mate, now an influential member of the Bolshevik leadership, and People's Commissar on Nationality Affairs. How could the young Andrei, even in his wildest dreams, have imagined back in Bailovka Prison that his fierce opponent would rise to such heights? The Government moved to Moscow, the doors of the hotel which served as its headquarters were always open to the public – the mania for total secrecy and total fear had not yet begun.

It was at their first Moscow meeting that Vyshinsky took the wisest and most prophetic decision of his entire life – and, to do him justice, he was to take not a few wise and prophetic decisions in the course of his life: he did not say a word about the kindnesses he had done his fellow-prisoner in Bailovka Prison, and from the very start addressed him in a formal manner that one would not associate with fellow-sufferers and comrades-in-arms. The not so distant past – the cell, the disputes, the sharing of food – everything was completely forgotten, or to all appearances it was: life had put an end to it, and Vyshinsky had enough intelligence and tact not to make an attempt to revive it, or to use it for his own ends.

And it was because he did not that things went in his favour, which is a paradox only for people who are not very good judges of human nature and will never make a success of life. Vyshinsky was and did.

Only a short time before he had been a nobody, searching for somewhere to perch himself, but now at long last he had acquired not only a lucrative position but a springboard for his future career. What had already happened to provisions and to the entire system of *supplies* at the end of 1917 presented Vyshinsky with real power and real prospects. Emphasis is put on the word 'supplies' because not even the burden of war had brought significant changes to the normal life of the market, which ran along the simple lines of people with goods selling them for money and people with money buying goods. Then suddenly everything was turned upside down, and people with goods surrendered them to the State and people requiring them received them from the State – but not when they wanted them, or even really needed them, but in keeping with some kind of system regulated at will by the State and responding to some kind of justice interpreted at will by the State. As a result, those who had control over goods – bread, salt, sugar, clothes – ruled supreme. For they had real power – not just over a city or region, but over life and death.

This is the kind of power Vyshinsky now had concentrated in his hands.

His immediate superiors were Artiomy Khalatov and Alexei Rykov, both members of the People's Commissariat of Food responsible for Moscow's food supplies. Their staff were attached to the Moscow Council, which was run by Lev Kamenev. Under these three men Vyshinsky advanced himself in two important ways. In the first place, he became head of the requisition department of the Moscow Railways, a department which took away from the peasants food products which they had brought to Moscow to sell. Secondly, he became the administrative head of distribution at the People's Commissariat of Food: or, to put it more simply, he became a key official, for he was solely in charge of distributing products and basic necessities across the entire vast, famished, poorly-clad and poorly-shod country.

With the friendly backing of Stalin, Rykov and Kamenev, he confidently rose higher and higher. Khalatov was the good genius who had set him on the road to fame.[4]

Vyshinsky not only implemented but strengthened the theory behind the insane 'distribution' system which took over from normal buying and selling. It was then that the outmoded word 'shop' was replaced in everyday language by the word 'distributor'. This passion of Vyshinsky's for finding a way to encapsulate and substantiate continuing political changes, to put words to the whims of the 'top leadership', was to stay with him and make him irreplaceable at every stage of his career.

It is an interesting and bitter experience today to read his arguments in a brochure, published as a 'textbook for district schools', which contained two articles highly indicative of the theorist's approach – 'The Policies of the Soviet Authorities in the Sphere of Distribution and Exchange' and 'The Co-operative and Its Forms'. 'Bourgeois society,' writes the author:

> was unaware of the problem of distribution.... Distribution requires unity, a broad-based guiding principle.... Established on 27 October 1917 [the third day after the seizure of power], the state monopoly of food-stuffs and consumer goods, which did away with the free exchange of such goods and cut down the means of self-supply to the bare minimum, made the State directly responsible for supplying the working population with everything that came under the heading of 'basic necessities'.

Perhaps the State really did assume this responsibility, but to this day the population has never been provided with 'everything' that comes under the heading of 'basic necessities'.

But one of the most brazen and unconcealed pieces of cynicism appears in a passage from Vyshinsky's address at the First All-Russian Conference on Distribution Committees in November 1919: 'Nowadays in distribution one does not have to follow the universal principle of justice.... We are changing over from the principle of distribution on an egalitarian basis to the principle of class distribution.' And to confirm the correctness of this thesis he ecstatically cites: 'Comrade Zinoviev's aphoristically apt observation: "We give herrings to the workers and leave the herrings' tails for the bourgeoisie." ' Seventeen years later he was to demand capital punishment and eternal damnation for the 'aphoristically apt' Comrade Zinoviev, who was by then 'bourgeois carrion' and 'a mad dog'.[5]

Coming into contact with real power for the first time, Vyshinsky could not help but get a taste of it. And it evidently poisoned him for life. However, he was cautious as well as shrewd. There was still no sense of the Bolsheviks having won a complete victory; resistance was still very strong, and he was still perfectly satisfied to belong to the Mensheviks' social democratic movement. On the one hand, this did not prevent him from holding a high official position and even from getting promoted, while on the other hand, should 'anything' happen, he still had a political alibi: should events suddenly change, he could easily and convincingly prove that he had been honestly collaborating with the Bolsheviks, but had not gone over to the 'infidels'.

At the same time the Mensheviks themselves were by no means united. They included supporters of various trends, some of whom were in favour of working with the Soviets, while others were totally against. It goes without saying that Vyshinsky was among the former. Along with Boris Ber, Yermansky, Olga Domanevskaya and others, he was 'for the power of the Soviets but without the Bolsheviks' – much to the dissatisfaction of Martov, whose group they belonged to. (This is the slogan with which the Kronstadt sailors were to mutiny in March 1921*.) At the 1918 May Day Parade he walked at the head of a column of Mensheviks from the Zamoskvorechiye district of Moscow who were carrying a placard reading 'All power to the Soviets!', 'And only to the Soviets!' the column chanted in unison, giving the words 'and only' a meaning that anyone could understand.

Apart from working at the People's Commissariat of Food, he found time for active party work. Already a familiar figure who had caught people's attention, he became one of the organizers of the 'Iskra' Social Democratic (Menshevik) Club, again in the Zamoskvorechiye district, and the representative of the same district on the Menshevik Party's Moscow Committee. With his phenomenal capacity for work and indefatigable constitution, he never shirked social responsibilities or kept aloof from the collective, and was accessible and on equal terms with everybody. V. A. Krauze, one of his colleagues who had also worked as a lawyer's assistant before the Revolution, was to recall much later in a letter to his former chief how the latter had ridden along the Saviolovskaya railway line on top of a wagonload of firewood with the rest of them, and how he had inspired the mobilized soldiers with his 'infectious good spirits, energy, cheerfulness and singing of songs'.

When particularly troubled days came, and nobody was in any mood for songs – Denikin† was swiftly approaching Moscow – Vyshinsky and a group of other leftist Mensheviks, including the then very well-known D. Y. Dalin, elected to set off for Tula and put themselves at the disposal of the local authorities there. Appearing before Grigory Kaminsky, the town committee's secretary and executive committee

* A revolt by the sailors of the Baltic fleet and garrison of the naval base at Kronstadt against the rule of the Communist Party. The fortress was stormed by the Red Army and hundreds, if not thousands, were massacred but no public trial was ever held.

† A General in the Tsarist Volunteer Army that fought the Bolsheviks in the Civil War which followed the Revolution.

chairman, and by then also the head of the Tula fortified district, Vyshinsky made an impassioned speech in which he declared that he and his comrades were interpreting the slogan 'Moscow is in danger' as a summons 'to become personally engaged in the struggle to save Soviet power from the mortal threat'. Kaminsky wrinkled his nose – like all orthodox Bolsheviks of the old ilk, he was not very fond of Mensheviks and treated them with a certain amount of scorn and distrust – but the danger was very real and any support might prove useful. Vyshinsky's support consisted of making incendiary speeches – which apparently had some impact on the Red Army men and mobilized the townspeople – digging trenches (well away from the front line) and generally doing any work he was asked to. And eventually he won a commendable report from Kaminsky himself.[6]

It seems very likely that Denikin's defeat prompted Vyshinsky to define his position at last. There was no longer any point in further hesitation. The routed volunteers' army was fleeing south and their hapless evacuation was being prepared. Wrangel was still to come, as were Kronstadt and other anti-Bolshevik actions, but to anyone with any sense the truth was obvious: the Bolsheviks had won, and anyone who did not wish to be left out in the cold, or somewhere even worse, anyone who was concerned about his career and his future, had to get in line – especially (let us remember this again) when there was a chance of tasting the sweetness of power.

His next meeting with Stalin decided everything: not yet General Secretary but already a Politburo and government member with great influence and authority among Party officials, Stalin could not, of course, decide matters of great state importance on his own, but he could certainly decide unimportant ones. This particular matter – of breaking with the Mensheviks and joining the Bolshevik Party – may have been unimportant for the country as a whole; but for Vyshinsky and his personal future, it was of the utmost importance. In a very short time, however, it would become equally important for the country, for it would enable the new Bolshevik to reach pinnacles of power from which he would not only command millions of people but also be in a position to dispatch them to unmarked graves.

Stalin's word proved decisive: in February 1920 the Zamoskvorechiye district committee admitted Vyshinsky to the ranks of the Russian Communist Party of Bolsheviks and issued him with Party Membership Card No 1219905. At the time he was delighted by the prospects opening up before him. Later on he was to think back to those days with terror. What terrified him was not, of course, that he had joined, but that he had been so late in doing so – that he had waited for nearly two and a half years, and that everyone around was well aware of this.

Of course, other Mensheviks had joined even later than he had: Maisky a year later,[7] Zaslavsky no less than fourteen years later.[8] But this brought little comfort: the fact remained that young Comrade Andrei had hesitated too long, managing in the meantime to acquire quite a paunch for himself in starving Moscow.

2

At midday on 5 November 1918, on the eve of the first anniversary of the October Revolution, in what used to be the Kremlin's Hall of Legal Statutes, a trial began which was historic even by the standards of those days. Until only a short while before the person standing trial had, as a member of the then very small Central Committee, been at the very top of the Bolshevik Party's hierarchy. Unlike other Bolsheviks who were involved in illegal activities and were known only to the police and a small circle of fellow Party members, this Central Committee member was renowned nationwide. He had headed the Bolshevik faction in the State *duma* and had made impassioned and crippling anti-government speeches, which, in keeping with the *duma*'s procedural rules, were then published in the press.

His stormy parliamentary career had lasted two years, but in 1914, after informing the *duma*'s President, Rodzyanko, that he was resigning from his duties as deputy, he had suddenly vanished. Without letting the Central Committee know of his resignation, he had fled abroad – and, just as suddenly, turned up again with Lenin, who was then residing as an émigré in the Austro-Hungarian (now Polish) town of Poronin. He explained this strange behaviour of his as the result of excessive nervous stress.

By now it was being rumoured that this Bolshevik Party Central Committee member and head of the *duma* faction, Roman Vatslavovich Malinovsky, was also a paid police agent, and that far from going abroad of his own free will, he had done so on police instructions to avoid even more dangerous and scandalous exposures. It was strictly prohibited for a police operative to be put into parliament and kept there on a salary – even in this dirty secret organization, which did not baulk at using any methods, they must have had some scruples.

The Mensheviks were the first to release this rumour and spread it with convincing consistency, and for this reason alone Lenin regarded it with scepticism – as, in general, he regarded anything that issued from the Mensheviks, considering any criticisms they made as attempts to denigrate and discredit their political opponents. But it was not only the Mensheviks who considered Malinovsky a police agent: the same allegation was firmly upheld by the Bolshevik Bukharin, and substantial evidence in support of it was also provided by Yelena Rozmirovich, the secretary of the *duma*'s Bolshevik faction. Malinovsky, however, refuted her evidence, which he declared to be the revenge of a rejected mistress. Lenin, who loathed any washing of dirty linen in public, refused even to investigate these arguments: Malinovsky's attempt to slander his former colleague and assistant earned his condemnation on moral grounds – not political ones, and certainly not legal ones, which was, of course, to Malinovsky's advantage.

A Party commission was set up – a kind of court of honour – comprising Lenin, Zinoviev and Yakov Ganetsky, a Polish Bolshevik who enjoyed Lenin's total trust. This commission decided that there was no indisputable evidence against Malinovsky, but that by fleeing abroad he had violated his duty to the Party and should therefore be expelled from it. Two years later, however, after the overthrow of the Tsarist regime, the police archives were opened and documents were produced which fully substantiated the Mensheviks' claim. It appeared that for many years Malinovsky had worked as a police agent under the code name of 'Tailor', and as an informer had earned the colossal sum of seven hundred roubles a month, more than a governor's salary. N. A. Kolokolov, an investigator for the Provisional Government's Extraordinary Commission, questioned Lenin, his wife Krupskaya and Zinoviev on this matter, and they all reiterated that the Party's hearing had been based on the facts then available, and that they had been insufficient to find Malinovsky guilty. Lenin added that no matter what damage Malinovsky had done to the Party, the benefits from having his *duma* speeches published in the legal press had outweighed it.

The tumultuous political events in the wake of October 1917 pushed this bizarre affair into the background. It had been totally forgotten when Roman Malinovsky suddenly and voluntarily returned to Russia, and turned himself in to the revolutionary authorities. His real motives for doing so – psychological or otherwise – have still to be indisputably ascertained, but the fact remains that he returned. Another aspect of this drama was that the Chairman of the Investigation Commission of the Supreme Tribunal at the All-Russian Central Executive Committee was Yelena Rozmirovich, and the prosecutor appointed for the Tribunal's hearing was her second husband, Nikolai Krylenko[1], a Bolshevik since 1904, a member of the first Soviet government as the People's Commissar of Military and Naval Affairs, and the first Soviet

Supreme Commander (with the rank of ensign) of all the country's armed forces. The holder of two university degrees, in law and history, he had written those impassioned *duma* speeches for Malinovsky, which the latter had made even more cutting and provocative.

Such was the trial that opened on the eve of the first anniversary of the October Revolution and was attended by Lenin, who – judging by eye-witness accounts – was appalled by the abyss which had opened up before him. And there, too, among the spectators, who completely packed out the fairly spacious Hall of Legal Statutes, was Vyshinsky. Apart from the sensational nature of this extraordinary trial, which had naturally attracted considerable attention, there were at least three good reasons, three powerful incentives, for Vyshinsky to be there. As a militant member of his party, he must have been delighted that the Mensheviks had been right after all; as a Pole, he must have taken a passionate interest in the fate of a fellow-countryman who had participated in the Revolution and then behaved so scandalously; and as a lawyer who had continued, despite the tremendous pleasure he gained from distributing herrings and herring tails, to gravitate towards legal theory and its practical application, he must have been aware of the unusual nature of a trial which was to serve as a precedent for the future: a new judicial power, with no laws and only its own revolutionary brand of justice to rely on, was trying a man who, in the eyes of the law in force at the time he had committed the acts he was charged with, had done nothing unlawful and therefore, according to legal dogma, could not be brought to trial 'without a formal charge'. Now, however, the dogmas had been destroyed – all of them, not just the legal ones; every single one, without exception. To witness new legal structures being conceived on the ruins of the old was, for a man like Vyshinsky, a fascinating spectacle and an instructive lesson.

Who could have imagined, least of all Vyshinsky himself, that here, in this hall, at this trial, he would begin a brutal and merciless – if initially silent – duel with a man whom he immediately recognized as his rival and exact opposite. This man was also a lawyer; unlike most of his Party colleagues, he was too a well-educated specialist with a university degree and was a superb orator, capable of carrying away his enthusiastic audience. And they had a great deal more in common. However, whereas the latter had the advantage of being a Bolshevik, a 'favourite son of the Revolution', standing at the helm of power, Vyshinsky was a Menshevik and therefore only a 'step-son', someone who was tolerated but not loved. Whether or not Vyshinsky had reason to – and I think, in fact, he had – he considered himself a more forceful lawyer, a more astute politician, and a more eloquent speaker, capable, of course, of making even greater speeches.

This rival was Nikolai Krylenko, and his name will appear many times again in this book.

Malinovsky was shot: legal dogma had been clearly disgraced.[2] The trial had a most powerful effect on Vyshinsky. He was still working on the food front, and would continue to do so for some time to come, notching up points and achieving one success after another, while at the same time watching others making the laws and constructing Soviet justice without him and instead of him. When the New Economic Policy (NEP) was introduced four years later, he was left completely jobless, but by then he had already left a noticeable mark on the theory and practice of 'distribution', and become quite a well-known figure. It was then that he returned to the legal system, which in one way or another, directly or indirectly, he was to be involved in for the rest of his life, no matter what post he happened to hold later on.

Vyshinsky really did love his profession and felt completely at home in it. He became a member of the *nomenklatura*: the system by which in the USSR appointments to specified posts in government or economic administration are made by organs of the Communist Party; such a concept already existed in practice but not in theory. Thus he appealed to the Moscow city committee of his very own dearly beloved Bolshevik Party to find him a legal position.

His request was granted and he was sent to the Collegium of Lawyers, having been 'recommended' (this word, the euphemism for an order, had already arrived on the scene and was soon absorbed into everyday political life) to the post of Chairman. The 'recommendation' was, of course, honoured by electing Comrade Vyshinsky in an open ballot. Nobody dared vote against him.

Some may consider this post unimportant and minor, a sign of Vyshinsky's demotion when compared to his previous job of distributing the country's food supplies – at best, a step backwards. But they are wrong. The legal system had been destroyed and was now emerging on new and primarily class foundations – it gave an illusion of democracy and a sham guarantee of defendants' rights. To create and run this legal institution in such a way that it appeared all-important while remaining totally insubstantial was a highly complex and responsible task. Only the loyal and devoted could rise to it. It was certainly not fortuitous that the choice fell on Vyshinsky, and it did not come as a demotion for him.

Still, in my opinion, this was not his real vocation. Despite all the 'ifs' and 'buts', in the last resort a barrister still had to defend. And this was something Vyshinsky had always done badly. Somehow he did not feel right defending – the other side of the legal battlefield suited him far better.

Two or three months later the lawyer left his post as Chairman to become a prosecutor. He was not just an 'ordinary' prosecutor but one who was attached to the judicial board of the recently formed Supreme Court of the Russian Federation (RSFSR). Having set its bureaucratic and official network in motion, the *nomenklatura* machine found him a suitable post and set him on the right track. It was here he made his first legal speeches, some of which have been preserved for posterity in shorthand reports.

The subjects of the first trials he was involved in sound uncannily familiar: investigators and judges who had accepted bribes from dishonest tradesmen and then let them get off scot-free in exchange; big shots in the ever-expanding bureaucratic departments and unscrupulous Party members in privileged positions who had used their connections to become speculators and black marketeers; high-ranking economists from the legendary Pomgol who had made a fortune out of the common people's tragedy and had been lining their pockets while others starved.[3]

The appalling outrages of the day, which fully deserved the prosecutor's wrathful pathos, could not fail to attract widespread public attention. The prosecutor became a talking-point, a household name. He came to epitomize Justice. He was marking down werewolves and degenerates, and doing so for good reasons: stupefied from drinking binges and card-sharping, the *nouveaux riches* in their leather jackets inspired loathing in any normal person, and in their case no censure seemed excessively harsh.[4]

Only now, fortified by grim historical experience, when one re-reads this blood-curdling 'oral literature', does one notice things that were almost certainly not noticed then. And even if they were, they were most probably considered quite natural – such as the attempt to give sickening but, unfortunately, widespread crimes a political slant, come what may. Having timidly and insidiously crept into ordinary criminal analysis, alien words suddenly started cropping up, such as 'agents', 'spies', 'spiritual wreckers' and 'all kinds of bourgeois stench'. Such combinations of words, which had only just become part of the everyday vocabulary and were essentially an oratorical device, the rhetoric of mass meetings rather than a reflection of reality, did not grate upon the ears: what all this 'anti-revolutionary' scum was conspiring was far too sordid and vile for that.

Vyshinsky tried very hard not only to win the trust of his colleagues and comrades in the Party, but also to show how much better he was at championing people's rights in the courts than Krylenko. If one is objective and honest, his speeches really were more impressive. They combined fervour, logic, sarcasm and conviction. They were designed for judges, spectators, readers, and for different social and cultural strata: they had something for everyone. Krylenko's speeches, on the other hand, were noted for their verbosity, laborious rhetoric, use of virtually unintelligible pseudo-Marxist phraseology and impoverished language. What caused his speech on the Malinovsky case to stand out from the rest was its heightened emotion, for he had concentrated considerable personal feeling in it. Several years later the trial of the police agent and traitor of the Narodnaya Volya party, Okladsky, gave Krylenko his last chance to display his temperament in court.

From the very beginning of this invisible duel Vyshinsky had the look of a sound professional and Krylenko that of merely a garrulous dilettante, but this clear superiority by no means meant that Vyshinsky's prestige increased in Party circles, where he continued to be treated with unconcealed hostility, especially as he differed in every way – in style of dress, conversation and humour – from his new Party comrades.

And so the episode which took place almost immediately after Vyshinsky had been appointed a prosecutor of the Supreme Court of the RSFSR is hardly surprising. His transfer to this work coincided with a Party purge: a commission which had been organized expressly for this purpose called up Communists in turn, after they had first handed in their Party membership cards. On the basis of a long interview (or a short one, depending on how lucky they were) the commission then decided whether the 'purged' member deserved to remain in the Party. If not, that was the end of it.

Here is how one witness described Vyshinsky's own interview in the Supreme Court's Party cell:

'Those who had already been checked out stayed behind for a while in the reception room, talking among themselves. As it so happened, we were sitting there when Vyshinsky came in. ... His face was bright red and he was obviously very agitated. The Commission had not given him his Party membership card back. .... What had gone on during the interview, Vyshinsky did not say. After withdrawing to the far end of the room, he started pacing up and down.

'The next day one of the court secretaries described how Vyshinsky had sobbed hysterically in front of Judge Solts, and how the old man had been so astounded that he had even gone and fetched him a glass of water himself.

'Friends used to call Solts "the Party's conscience" because he was in charge of the Central Control Commission, the Party's highest court. After conferring with the other members of the Control Commission, he gave Vyshinsky his membership card back. A few days later, when Solts was drinking tea with us, Galkin asked him about Vyshinsky. Solts smiled sheepishly and said, "What do you expect of him? The fellow tries as hard as he can. He works hard: one must give him a chance. People are not born Bolsheviks, they become them. If he does not turn out right, we'll expel him again."

'Thirteen years later, in July 1936, I went into the NKVD building and was heading towards my office when suddenly I caught sight of old Galkin. Escorted by a guard, he was leaving Boris Berman's office under arrest. He was a very sorry sight. I went through to Berman and asked him to do everything possible for Galkin. It was from him I heard that Galkin had been arrested on Vyshinsky's orders.'[5]

The author of these memoirs, Lev Feldbin, was a prominent operative in the NKVD's reconnaissance department, and was known to the public as 'General Alexander Orlov'. Written after his escape to the West, and reprinted more than once in numerous languages, his bestselling *Secret History of Stalin's Crimes*, though containing a certain number of inaccuracies and mistakes, may be commended on the whole for its authenticity and thorough, first-hand knowledge of the material. The description of the purge which Vyshinsky underwent in such a dramatic manner and which, one would have thought, left a festering wound in his heart, is indirectly confirmed by the following sentence from Vyshinsky's official biographical notes dealing with the late 1920s: 'During the Party purge I succeeded in proving to the Commission the sincerity of my break with the Mensheviks and devotion to the ideals and programme of the Bolshevik Party.' This sentence is not in subsequent editions.

Vyshinsky proved his 'devotion to the ideals and programme of the Bolshevik Party' not only to Solts's commission but also to a wide reading public in the hope that a small section of this public – the Party leadership – would also glance at his writings. He was a prolific writer, but among his publications a special place was occupied by his *Essays on the History of Communism*, a two-volume edition comprising the lectures he gave at the Institute of Economics and various other Moscow halls. (At the Institute, incidentally, he somehow managed in an inconspicuous way to hold more than one post simultaneously and rose to the position of dean, demonstrating his irrepressibility, his versatility and, once again, his extraordinary capacity for work.)

These essays were only recently removed from the secret list – what an irony that many of Vyshinsky's own books should have been removed from general circulation and kept locked up in special depositories for years and years – and no great insight is called for to guess what they were found guilty of: they profusely and more than deferentially cited the idols of the day, the men at the helm – Kamenev, Zinoviev and Bukharin. And Stalin as well, of course, but grouped with the other three. It is easy to imagine how Vyshinsky longed to destroy this two-volume work of his, and most probably he did so in so far as he could. To a great extent he succeeded, but not entirely. We can now see for ourselves how he tried to adapt a theory – a historical and philosophical theory this time, not a legal one – to fit the needs 'of the moment'. However, let us remain objective – he was not the only one by a long way.

Now that entirely new practices are just getting off the ground in the Soviet Union, and the directors of enterprises and heads of higher educational institutions are being elected instead of appointed, it may well seem incredible to some people that in 1925 Moscow University's academic council, which comprised quite a few old pre-revolutionary professors, could have met to elect a new rector. True, the voting was open, but the nominations were not freely proposed – in fact, there was only one nomination, and that had been recommended from above. But everything was done by the book in a highly decorous and democratic manner: the professors raised their hands all together, and swore in their new rector.

As the reader has no doubt guessed, this new rector was the rapidly advancing Professor Vyshinsky, who by now had a high-powered and diverse career in the public sector behind him. He was being transferred here not only to disseminate erudition and eternal virtues but – more importantly – to be in charge of all the other disseminators at the country's most important and prestigious academic centre.

39

Under his rectorship the sacred cradle of humanism began to get rid of the profusion of class enemies who had penetrated its walls. Students from non-proletarian families were declared class enemies and rejected – 'as a rule'. It goes without saying that there were individual exceptions to the rule, but only the Rector was entitled to decide who was 'passable' and who was not – still more so since, let us not forget, he had been elected quite freely and democratically, and not appointed to this post. The bastion of civilization and culture gradually began to free itself of unsuitable professors. It was, of course, virtually impossible to purge and find suitable replacements for all the pre-revolutionary professors. However, the Rector tried very hard, guided by the principle that it was better to overdo things than to 'underdo' them.

Perhaps he could explain his position and the policy he had adopted more clearly himself? (Perhaps this policy was not to his liking, but it was his duty to conduct it – and who at that time, or even today, could have differentiated between the two?) There follows a most telling excerpt from an article he wrote at the time, entitled 'Topical University Issues':

> The university, like the rest of society, is involved in a class struggle which is intensifying and deepening. . . . Class contradictions, which are hostile to the proletariat, are trying to lean on the authority of university departments, to become consolidated in them and sometimes even, from a defensive position, assume the offensive. . . . The propagation of *kulaks'* [rich peasants], priests' and populist petty bourgeois ideology must be resolutely eliminated from the walls of the Soviet university.

Strictly speaking, it was his not particularly proletarian background and political past that enjoined the new rector to act resolutely and intransigently on this issue, in case anyone suspected him of protecting others from his class. That his actions should have been guided by this simplest of psychological mechanisms is quite understandable, but once he embarked upon his course of action, he found he could not stop: there was no way back – he had sold his soul, and there was no way of retrieving it. Not that he made any attempt to.

Of course, he was not only in charge of administrative affairs, he also taught – his favourite subject – the criminal trial. He tried to prove how bad legal procedure had been under wretched Tsarism (which had nevertheless enabled Vera Zasulich,[6] Beilis,[7] and many others to be acquitted), and how good it was now that it was based on proletarian class principles. At lightning speed he published a thick student text-book on the criminal trial. Today its revolutionary scholasticism makes one positively reel. One passage, however, does draw attention to itself: 'It would be a great mistake to regard prosecuting as the main function of the Procurator's office. The main objective of the Procurator's office is to be the bearer and guardian of lawfulness.' What priceless words! Especially if one recalls what came later. Not in the course textbook – in real life.

As far as his natural talents were concerned, Vyshinsky was first and foremost an orator and only then a 'writer' and administrator. In those days, however, he rarely got the chance to speak, and then, more often than not, at private conferences, sittings and meetings. He never missed an opportunity to dazzle an audience with his elo-quence: he felt at home on any rostrum, no matter where it happened to be. In particular, his heartfelt speech at the funeral of Academician Vladimir Mikhailovich Bekhterev had considerable resonance.

As is well known, this outstanding neurologist, psychiatrist and psychologist, the founder of reflexology and a scientific school, the organizer and head of research institutes, one of which bears his name to this day, died within a matter of minutes under mysterious circumstances. Before this sudden and completely inexplicable attack he had been perfectly fit and well. Rumour immediately linked it to the fact that he had recently diagnosed paranoia in his most distinguished patient, Stalin. He had indeed given such a diagnosis, although, as the ancient Romans knew, 'post hoc non est propter hoc'. There is, it goes without saying, no direct evidence which would enable one to confirm unequivocally that he was murdered by poisoning. (The organizers and executors, if there were any, were bound to ensure their tracks were swept clean.) However, there is an exceptionally large amount of circumstantial evidence, to which a considerable literature has been devoted, and it is hardly fortuitous that this version has withstood the test of time, and remained firmly implanted in the memories of several generations.[8]

The funeral's organization was entrusted to Moscow University, or its Rector, to be more precise: the appropriate authorities looked after the body, while Professor Vyshinsky, a greatly revered figure by now, saw to the funeral ceremony arrangements. He opened the ceremony, after which speeches were made by the 'all-union elder' and 'grand-father' Kalinin, as he was called, and various real academics. The Rector was certainly not sparing in his praise but, after all, one was allowed to praise the dead as much as one liked. 'Academician Bekhterev,' declaimed Vyshinsky bombastically:

'was a giant of human thought. All his life Bekhterev was at the service of humanity, of working people. He died at a moment when the country was transferring on a broad front to cultural construction, and for this reason his loss is exceptionally great. We must raise higher the banner which Bekhterev served, more deeply and strongly infuse the union of science and labour, following the behests of the deceased'.

Slightly later on, as Procurator-General, Vyshinsky and his team – doing just that, and 'following the behests of the deceased' – were to sentence to death the Academician's son, engineer Piotr Vladimirovich Bekhterev, and send all his family to labour camps and into exile.[9]

Vyshinsky, it seemed, had achieved everything he had set out to. In his biographical note – in all three versions I have seen – he confirms that teaching and academic work were his main objectives. What better way of accomplishing them than as Rector of Moscow University? In terms of his career – if one remembers he had started out only ten years before as a lawyer's assistant – he had done staggeringly well.

But evidently he had already been singled out for far greater objectives, for another career. The choice he was given in 1928 was in itself highly significant and telling. This may be asserted with great confidence because it is quite obvious that his appointment at such a level must have been confirmed at the top. By whom exactly? We can easily find out by a process of elimination.

What we have here is a test run, hitherto without precedent and, according to Stalin's design, intended to create one. From information supplied by Yevgeny Yevdokimov, an ex-criminal, then the OGPU (precursor of the KGB) representative in the Caucasus and a close associate of Stalin, a 'wrecking organization' of some sort was uncovered in the town of Shakhty, in the Rostov region. It consisted of a number of Soviet and foreign engineers who, acting on instructions from Paris, had decided to fight against the Bolsheviks by blowing up and destroying the Donbass mines. Fifty-three men were brought to trial – never before or since had such a large number of defendants been tried at once. The whole point of it was to attract as much publicity as possible, so the former Moscow Club of the Nobility, the marbled Hall of Columns in Trade Union House, was selected as the location.

During the preparations for what was to be an unprecedented political show, the most important problem was not so much selecting an eloquent prosecutor – they had just enough forceful speakers to scrape by – but obedient and devoted judges. An excessively precise interpretation of the law, the voicing of doubts any honest judge was bound to have, the rejection of unsubstantiated demagogy, falsifications, assumptions, the stretching of points – any of these could spoil this most important affair. A figure was needed who would combine many different qualities: impressiveness and respectability, erudition and repute (foreign observers and reporters were expected), ingenuity in the event of unexpected and unforeseen turns in the trial, reliability from the organizers' viewpoint, an ability to influence both the accused and the public. In other words, there was definitely no suitable candidate among the official judges, who had all been promoted from quite humble working positions, and were mostly without a legal education and the essential experience.

Vyshinsky, on the other hand, was a lucky find. I do not think that there was anyone else among the performers Stalin had to choose from at the time who could have competed for this role. There was only one obstacle to clear: officially, in the formal sense of the word, he was not a judge, and so could not be put in charge of the Supreme Court, the only body suitable to pass judgement on such major 'criminals'.

At a stroke of the pen a substitute for the normal court was revived. By no means associated with the most glorious moments of Russian history, it had been resorted to in earlier times, before the Revolution, to give a trial particular prestige and to accentuate its special nature – and, of course, to give special clout to the judgement it pronounced. This 'substitute' had the pompous, archaic title of the 'Special Judicial Presence'. In simpler terms, it was an unlawful extra-judicial body, whose legal functions were not specified anywhere. Such was the extra-judicial, extra-legal body of which the leading theorist of the criminal trial and Rector of Moscow University, Professor Vyshinsky, was made head. Moscow University's historic past sanctified him in this post.

So who chose him for such a responsible role, and to carry out such an important mission? Evidently, whoever it was had need of this trial and, what's more, had sufficient power both to set and solve its task. Trotsky was already in exile; Zinoviev and Kamenev had been totally stripped of power, and the trial was implicitly directed against Bukharin, Rykov and Tomsky, Lenin's closest collaborators and key

Bolsheviks before the Revolution. The trial was a personal affront to Kuibyshev (since he was head of the Supreme Economic Council, it looked as though he had harboured wreckers and saboteurs); it is known for a fact that the OGPU Chairman, Menzhinsky, was against the trial. Whom does that leave? By a process of elimination the answer, obvious as it is, becomes still more obvious. And more indisputable. If the idea for the trial was Stalin's, then, surely, so was the choice of its most crucial figure – the Chairman of the Special Judicial Presence.

There was one other circumstance – a small detail which would not be spotted by anyone who did not know about the machinations going on inside Judge Vyshinsky's head – that made this trial a highly important landmark in his life. Sitting to his right at the Procurator-General's table was his old 'friend' and rival Nikolai Krylenko. This was the first time they had worked together in a team entrusted with the conduct of an extremely important operation. Each had been allotted his own role. Naturally, the born speaker wanted to play the role assigned to his rival, for the prosecutor not only makes speeches but leads the examination as well; he is always on view, demonstrating his ingenuity, wit, energy, and a whole range of fighting qualities. The judge's role is far more passive and inexpressive. Vyshinsky agonized, but he also felt proud: after all, he was presiding over the trial, and the final and most important word was left to him.

It was at this trial that the seed was sown which was soon to germinate and produce shoots in profusion: all the court's attention was concentrated not on analyzing the evidence, which simply did not exist, but on securing from the accused confirmation of their confessions of guilt that were contained in the records of the preliminary investigation. At the open trial, in front of a huge public, some of the defendants withdrew their previous confessions. Others changed them several times during the course of the trial, and anyone in the hall, unless he was blind or a half-wit, could clearly see what had gone on behind the scenes the night before: reduced to despair by blackmail, threats and physical intimidation, the victims 'confessed' again and then, recovering their senses, denied the lies, and next day took the oath and slandered themselves again.

Whereas Krylenko publicly mocked the victims, Vyshinsky, on the contrary, wore them down with a taunting logic delivered in a sophisticated and dignified manner. Eye-witness accounts provide us with the most curious psychological portraits of the two pillars of Soviet jurisprudence at the time: while Krylenko emerges from their recollections as an insensitive boor, almost a lout, Vyshinsky is remembered, if not with warmth, then at least with respect – evidence of his displaying such qualities as politeness and responsiveness.[10]

Making use of his right as the presiding judge, Vyshinsky repeatedly interrupted Krylenko when he got too carried away, cooling his ardour, putting him in his place and using sarcasm at his expense. He made a point of patronizing the defence while displaying his contempt for the prosecution. Was he posing in front of foreign observers? Or trying to win popularity? Or was he enjoying a chance to bully his rival a little, having decided there was no need to hide his dislike of him? Most probably, it was a mixture of all three. What particularly irritated him was the prosecutor's political rigidity, his inflexibility, his dreary straightforward method of exposing the accused, his primitive generalizations. 'The intelligentsia,' asserted Krylenko in his speech for the prosecution, 'was never a class or a stratum of the population which had its own clearly defined, distinct political face. By its very essence, as a serving and non-producing social stratum, the intelligentsia was always condemned to be stratified.' Observers noted that these pedantic 'Marxist' revelations brought a wry smile to the face of the Chairman of the Special Judicial Presence.

While Stalin was still unwilling to fall out with the intelligentsia, Bukharin was demanding capital punishment for the intellectuals who were on trial. Vyshinsky avoided taking sides, trying to give the impression of an unbiased, objective and democratic judge.

A few years later the situation was to change completely: Krylenko would be remembered as a taciturn, weak-willed and helpless man who had withdrawn entirely into himself and was expecting a stab in the back at any moment, while Vyshinsky, 'spiritually strengthened in the fray', and fully aware of his power and invulnerability, would be humiliating the people around him, demonstrating a total lack of respect for others, mocking his visitors, and sometimes – in the heat of the moment – shouting at them. But all this was still in the future.

Eleven times the Professor, reading out the sentences to the over-crowded hall, repeated the words 'death penalty'. Five of the eleven condemned to death were shot. The newspapers reported that 'the sentence had been executed', and immediately afterwards announced that Vyshinsky had published a book summing up the trial's results. His thoughts on this score, expressed so soon after the event, are very important for an understanding of the processes, both socio-political and legal, which were nearing fruition.

Some of the accused, it seems, had sincerely shared their anxieties and fears with him: 'I was afraid that the Soviet regime was only capable of destroying and not creating' (engineer Bratanovsky); 'It seemed to me that the Soviet system could not restore the country's devastated industry and economy' (engineer Gorletsky); 'There was, of course, scepticism as regards what was happening in the economy' (engineer Kazarinov). What conclusion did the lawyer Vyshinsky draw from these confessions? They, it seems, 'undoubtedly testify to the fact that these people had consciously embarked on a path of sabotage and wrecking'.

What's more, various combinations of words figured here which in a few years' time were to become catchphrases – 'Moscow wrecking centre', and 'Kharkov anti-Soviet centre'. The model had been invented and tested, and would soon be working at full tilt.

The judge's book contains numerous quotations. Absent, however, is the group of thinkers who had been cited not so long ago by the author of *Essays on the History of Communism*: we shall not find here the names of Zinoviev, Kamenev, and Bukharin – or, indeed, of anyone except Stalin, true without 'wise' and 'great' for the time being, though occasionally we are already encountering 'as Comrade Stalin justly says' and 'as Comrade Stalin indicates'.

However, what is perhaps most important here is the thesis formulated with cynical candour and directness by the author – who had not yet, of course, foreseen the year 1937, but was acutely aware of the order that was being 'dictated by a social class [by Stalin]. The Soviet court, this responsible body of the proletarian dictatorship, must proceed, and always does proceed, from considerations of state and economic expediency.'

It was not yet the fashion to award decorations hurriedly after the event. But he did get a reward, and it was announced in the press: 'Comrade A. Ya. Vyshinsky has been appointed a board member of the People's Commissariat of Education.' Nobody can provide us with written evidence of how much Vyshinsky's zealous execution of this extremely important task had influenced the decision to promote him. But the link between them is perfectly obvious anyway.

From today's perspective Vyshinsky's new appointment does not seem much of a promotion. Of course, on the bureaucratic ladder already in operation in those days, a board member of a people's commissariat was a high position – especially on a board run by Lunacharsky. However, it was still only the Commissariat of the RSFSR, and not of the USSR. And the area Vyshinsky was put in charge of – professional training, or manpower reserves, to use more up-to-date terminology – was dull and offered poor prospects.

That is how it looks nowadays, but at the time it looked quite different.

Professional training was in a very poor state owing to the desperate shortage of personnel. Attempts to combine the uncombinable – a rigid class approach and ideological intolerance with the training of a sufficient highly-qualified work force – suffered one failure after another. The older generation of professors and academics, including the Marxist scholars Mikhail Pokrovsky[11] and Vladimir Friche, helped to provide school education at all levels. Beside them, Vyshinsky seemed like a political commissar: not just another person called in to help, but a 'special supervisor', the implications of which were fairly derogatory: a recruited outsider whom they all feared.

In a letter the eminent musicologist I. Ya. Ryzhkov told me how he had learnt from the poet Valery Briusov's sister, Professor Nadezhda Yakovlevna Briusova, who was then department head of music schools, that Vyshinsky used to carry out regular 'checks' on the contents of the desks, briefcases and handbags belonging to the personnel of the People's Commissariat of Education in search of illicit materials and 'objects not relating to the direct official functions of the person involved'. In comparison with the 'checks' that were to be carried out absolutely everywhere later on, these seem like innocent fun, almost a practical joke – but you can at once identify the author's style.

He used to particularly enjoy the board meetings at which lists of banned books were approved. In those days this noble task was carried out by the People's Commissariat of Education, and the lists previously drawn up by an appropriate commission of 'plain clothes enlighteners' were distributed beforehand among the board members for their approval. The first list was signed by Nadezhda Krupskaya at the end of 1923, and published in the *Herald of the Leningrad Department of Public Education* for 1924. It contained about four hundred titles: Dostoyevsky's *The Devils*, Leo Tolstoy's philosophical and religious works and Jules Verne's novels, which were said to glorify colonialism, were all removed from the library and bookshop shelves. When the new lists were discussed, Lunacharsky, a genuine scholar and true intellectual, preferred to say nothing. Vyshinsky, on the other hand, could always prove with disarming logic why it was better to prevent the undiscerning reader from encountering a dubious book rather than leave him to defend himself against it.

He was not, however, to work long with the People's Commissar, as Lunacharsky soon asked to be allowed to retire. Who knows, perhaps the self-assured Commissar's relationship with Lenin's closest associate and comrade-in-arms, Krupskaya, had something to do with it. It is unlikely that Lunacharsky did not understand the score, and did not know the true worth of his assistant. The People's Commissar was degraded, but this was a mere detail in the general picture: Lunacharsky could not help but see the way the tide was turning and what the results would be.

He was replaced by Andrei Bubnov.[12] The story circulating among Commissariat of Education personnel that Vyshinsky had been surreptitiously placed near Lunacharsky to 'finish him off and take over his position as People's Commissar had not been borne out. Krupskaya was made Deputy People's Commissar and put in charge of libraries. Her predecessor, Professor (later Academician) Otto Yulievich Shmidt, was a friend of Krylenko, and a member of his mountaineering expeditions, which we shall return to later on. Among all these staunch Bolsheviks here was this commissar who had once been a Menshevik, and not just a rank-and-file member of the defeated party but a highly energetic and prominent activist. It was a bizarre situation.

However, they worked in an amicable and well-coordinated manner, although they were already afraid of Vyshinsky. No, not as Stalin's right-hand man – this was hardly apparent to anyone yet – but as a representative of that mysterious surveillance network which had already penetrated all the state machinery and social strata. And as a denunciator who was forever fulminating against someone and causing their downfall.

Take, for instance, the way they discussed the strictly procedural question of whether or not it was necessary for a final-year university student to present a diploma project. Various points of view, it would seem, are possible here, and it is a matter for discussion. For us, that is – but for Vyshinsky it is an indisputable political issue: no diploma projects! Most of the students were poorly educated, semi-literate young people with unsullied class credentials, who were quite incapable of undertaking any serious project: to do so would immediately show up their pitiful potential. The country was being provided with ideologically-sound ignoramuses who had to be spared any tedious extra work. That is why supporters of the project were told by Vyshinsky that they were 'enemy spies', 'concealed opportunists', 'ideological wreckers' and even 'transmitters of *kulak* views'. The 1930s had not yet arrived, and such terms were not yet in vogue: for the time being the name 'kulak' was still being branded on those personally involved in the class war in the countryside. But Vyshinsky displayed laudable initiative by propagating those labels which had already begun to crop up in the field of science and education.

Feelings also ran high over the issue of students' practical training. It is clear that anyone not used to studying and not particularly gifted would experience difficulty mastering theoretical knowledge, so it was easier to show them than explain things to them. The old professors were unanimously against continuous practical training: as true scholars, they wanted to educate qualified specialists, not talentless people gloating over their social origins. They were severely harassed on this score by the 'proletarian' Vyshinsky. At a rectors' conference in 1930 Vyshinsky made a speech in which, as he switched to personal attacks and unconcealed threats, one can already clearly hear his intonations as a prosecutor. After mentioning some of the professors by name (Senevich, Rodionov, and Sirotinsky, among others) who considered that the abolition of diploma projects and transfer of study from student auditoria to shop floors would be detrimental to the economy – there were already twice as many practical as theoretical study periods – Vyshinsky declared their position a 'Trotskyist affect-ation' and the 'work of a class enemy', and promised to 'put into motion all possible means' to make short work of his opponents. And he certainly kept his word.

In one of his speeches the following sentence suddenly appeared: 'We are now compelled to send teams into the areas of total col-lectivization.' I wonder who compelled him (them) to? Of course, it was not 'who' but 'what' compelled them to – a desire to curry favour at a crucial and truly momentous point in history. It was Stalin who was carrying out the collectivization, it was Stalin who was insisting on it, and that, as far as Vyshinsky was concerned, said it all. Others were still putting up a struggle and producing arguments against the set pace of collectivization, against the forms it was taking, but Vyshinsky saw no point in arguing because he had already realized beyond any doubt that Stalin was always right.

What did his envoys – these officials from the Commissariat of Education – do in the countryside? They set up public teams for denouncing the kulaks, kulaks' henchmen, and middle peasants. They instructed village teachers so as to be a suitable influence on their pupils. And they certainly were. They collected children's denunci-ations against their parents, relatives and neighbours. Betrayal was paid for quite generously in those days – with a pair of boots or a

49

subscription to a Young Pioneers'* or Komsomol newspaper. Along with the teams of officials Vyshinsky also sent children into the countryside to help with the dispossession of the *kulaks*. They formed the nucleus of the model children's collective farms: even these existed then, but people avoid discussing them today.

Both People's Commissar Bubnov and his deputy, Krupskaya, gave their wholehearted support to their fearsome commissar, albeit in a less aggressive and vehement style, trying not to resort to the vocabulary and terminology that had quickly become part of his everyday speech. They were in favour of the policy he was conducting but, unlike Vyshinsky, did not call upon people to gloat 'over the old scholasticism and routine, over the old academic style and academic arrogance'; they did not promise 'to tear' the universities, secondary schools and training schools 'out of dead men's hands'. But they were still in favour of it.[13]

Representatives of the Russian teaching profession's truly 'golden age' – Pinkevich, Pestrak, Gosinovich and Gastev – whose positions were very well-known to the head of the Main Board of Professional Training, Vyshinsky, were shortly to face him in court in his capacity as prosecutor. With his blessing, they were all annihilated. Other leading teachers, such as Blonsky, Ventsel, and Iordansky, were dismissed from their posts and doomed to poverty and oblivion. Of course, it was not Vyshinsky in person who initiated the destruction of the Russian teaching profession. It was the age or, to be more precise, the system, working through him. But, fervent and inflexible, he proved an excellent executor.

* An organization for ten- to fifteen-year-olds intended to educate children in the spirit of Lenin.

3

Many thousands served Stalin with religious devotion, but only a handful enjoyed his trust. And not for long.

He had trusted, or, rather, believed in Vyshinsky from the very start, and he was not disappointed. And, more importantly, he realized that Vyshinsky's place in the cataclysmic years to come was certainly not in the field of education, for which, for better or worse, others would be found. In the combat zone to which Vyshinsky was to be sent, he would be peerless. And this was the absolute truth.

A final test awaited him before his great promotion. A new public trial was being organized, no less important than Shakhty. A new psychological stimulant was needed: the campaign to denounce wreckers which had been whipped up by the Shakhty trial was beginning to die down. Arrests were going on all the time but, since judgements were pronounced in secret, behind closed doors, outwardly it looked as though all was quiet in the towns and cities, and that the class struggle had been transferred entirely to the countryside, where the tragedy of forced collectivization was being enacted. Enemies were needed – and not just any enemies, but powerful, respectable, and well-known ones. What's more, they had to be organized into some sort of illegal underground grouping.

This badly-needed trial took place in the late autumn of 1930. The show's production team was the same as it had been two years previously, as were the chief performers. A Special Judicial Presence was again formed, and again headed by Vyshinsky, while Krylenko was once again in the Procurator-General's place. For Stalin it was to be an important rehearsal for what was to go down in history as 'The Great Terror', and for Vyshinsky it was to be an all-important test on which his future career depended.

Compared to the Shakhty Trial and its fifty-three defendants, the dock this time was nearly empty, with only eight people in it. Only eight, but in a different league to the unknown Shakhty engineers: the main protagonist was Leonid Ramzin, the world-famous scientist, a professor in the Moscow Higher Technical School and the founder and director of the Heating Engineering Institute; and nearly all the others held key posts in the State Planning Commission (Gosplan) and Supreme Economic Council. Both these organizations were headed by Valery Kuibyshev, an old Bolshevik, Lenin's comrade-in-arms and one of the political leaders of the Red Army during the Civil War. In effect, the trial was aimed at him. By now, according to the historian Robert Conquest's calculations, forty-eight Gosplan officials had already been executed, giving the impression that the organization headed by Kuibyshev, so vitally important to the Soviet economy as a whole, was riddled with spies and wreckers. Ramzin himself had played a major role in Lenin's plan to electrify Russia (GOELRO), so this was a test run in the sense of prosecuting a person with an impeccable past who had enjoyed Lenin's support. The accused were charged with having had organizational links with engineer Palchinsky, tried at the Shakhty Trial, about whom it was vaguely rumoured that 'he had been shot for taking part in a counter-revolutionary organization' (according to another plausible version, Palchinsky was unable to withstand the torture and had died during the investigation). The 'Industrial Party', as it was called, was linked to another party, the 'Labouring Peasants Party' – which during the trial was referred to as the 'Kondratiev–Chayanov Group', consisting of prominent scientists and writers who had been sentenced to death by a secret court. Ramzin and his comrades were presented as being agents of the President of France, Raymond Poincaré (the prosecutor mockingly referred to him as Citizen Poincaré), as well as of the British 'spy' Colonel T. E. Lawrence, the oil magnate Henry Deterding, and other imperialists. The trial was accompanied by a noisy, almost hysterical propaganda campaign, culminating in an article in the press in which the son of one of the accused, Ksenofont Sitnin, an engineer in the All-Union Textile Syndicate, demanded the death penalty for his father.

A sinister distinctive feature of this trial, making it essentially different from the Shakhty Trial, was that all the accused confessed to the charges brought against them. There was nobody there like old Rabinovich, who two years before had cut Krylenko short in front of the whole hall and declared, 'You can shout as much as you like, I'm still not going to slander myself.' The submissiveness with which Ramzin and his comrades agreed to confess to being spies, wreckers, and saboteurs was totally unprecedented, and caused complete and utter consternation. It had a particular impact on Western lawyers and, in general, on people whose sense of law and order had been cultivated on classical notions of justice: the confessions of the accused, as it were, ruled out the possibility of any argument over their guilt. At that time, and for years afterwards, it did not occur to many people that a confession made in a public court of law had not necessarily been freely and voluntarily given.

This time it was not serenity and uprightness or totally unbiased judicial attention that Vyshinsky epitomized, but the punitive sword of Soviet justice. He self-assuredly assumed the role of the prosecutor who would soon be declaiming at the Great Moscow Trials. In point of fact, he became a second prosecutor actively helping Krylenko to 'unmask' the accused. Whenever he considered that Krylenko was being insufficiently astute, pushing or deft, he would butt into the examination, 'helping' his colleague along and giving him — and everyone present as well — a graphic object-lesson in the tactics of conducting a political trial.

The outcome of the trial was, however, unexpected: all five of the death sentences — which Krylenko had demanded 'in the interests of political expediency' — were commuted. The Central Executive Committee (not without the Leader's participation, of course) pardoned the accused by commuting the death penalty to ten years of imprisonment. Even in prison, Professor Ramzin continued his academic work. At the very height of the mass terror, in the winter of 1936, he was granted a complete amnesty. Much later a terrible secret was let out: the eminent academic had agreed to play a sinister role in the OGPU's bloodthirsty show. Outstanding scholars had been arrested as a result of his denunciations; gazing calmly into their eyes, he had told them: 'I was in charge of a counter-revolutionary party, and you were a member of it.' This laudable work did not prevent him from designing a continuously operating industrial boiler, which Stalin allowed to be named after him and for which he was awarded the Stalin Prize in 1943. Ramzin died five years later, surrounded by all the honours and regalia due to a top academic. All except one: in a secret ballot this highly talented denouncer was rejected by his colleagues who were electing correspondent (non-voting) members to the Academy of Sciences.

Ramzin's astonishing fate provides confirmation that the purpose of the trial had not been to disgrace or indeed annihilate some of the accused, but to create a precedent and pave the way for a psychological attack on the population. This aim had been achieved: Vyshinsky had passed his crucial test with flying colours.

The result was not slow in coming. The trial ended in December

1930. For a few months afterwards the newspapers at home and abroad mulled over the reaction to it, and an increasingly powerful wave of propaganda began, the main aim of which was to search for new enemies and new wreckers and saboteurs. And then, just as it had subsided, and before a new one could begin, some joyful news spread across the country: on 11 May 1931 Andrei Yanuarievich Vyshinsky was appointed Procurator of the RSFSR. Ten days later he was also given the post of Deputy People's Commissar of Justice of the RSFSR. It was a tremendous promotion, but his joy at returning to the legal system, and to such high-ranking posts, was dampened by one factor: Krylenko had been appointed People's Commissar of Justice. After all, he too had ensured the success of the 'Industrial Party' trial. The intellectual, eloquent orator and aristocrat became subordinate to a peasant's son who was noted for his crude manner of expression and ingenuous appraisals and conclusions. The recent Menshevik had been put in his place, leaving the leading role to the old Bolshevik. Now Vyshinsky had once again to prove which of them was the true Bolshevik and the best pupil of Comrade Stalin.

It was at about this time that the only, or at least one of the very few attempts were made to put up resistance to Stalin's dictatorship inside the Party – in the only way left now that all forms of opposition had been broken up and destroyed, and all manner of different thinking suppressed. (It was then that the very word 'opposition', meaning simply 'an objection', came to be synonymous with treason and betrayal.) The reprisals meted out by Stalin had a tremendous impact on the formation not so much of political as of legal thinking, by providing new and fundamental criteria according to which an action was defined as lawful or unlawful.

On 21 August 1932, in the village of Golovino near Moscow, fifteen people met in the apartment of Party member Piotr Afanasievich Silchenko, an electrical engineer at a local construction enterprise. Silchenko himself was not there. All those present were ordinary rank-and-file Party members – none held an important state or public post. They included Mikhail Ivanov, the head of the People's Control Group of the Workers' and Peasants' Inspectorate of the RSFSR; Vasily Kayurov, a Central Archives worker, a close friend of Gorky and a Bolshevik since 1900, who in the summer of 1917 had concealed Lenin in his apartment from the police of the Provisional Government, and in 1919, on Lenin's personal orders, had delivered Lenin's famous letter 'To the Workers of Peter'; Pavel Galkin, a printing-house director;

54

and Pavel Fedorov, a professor at a peat research centre. They had gathered to discuss, edit and approve the text of a document written by a like-minded comrade.

Although this man had already been dismissed from all active work, he had refused to give up and sink into oblivion, and his name was known throughout the country. It was Martemyan Nikitich Ryutin.[1]

Here is an excerpt from what he wrote in the document which his friends had gathered to discuss[2] (only a few months later this meeting would be referred to as a 'secret assembly of conspirators', and would determine his fate):

> The Party and the proletarian dictatorship, having been led into an unprecedented impasse by Stalin and his retinue, is going through a mortally dangerous crisis. By means of deception and slander, by means of incredible violence and terror, ostensibly fighting for the purity of the principles of Bolshevism and Party unity, relying on a powerful, centralized Party apparatus, over the past five years Stalin has cut off and dismissed from the leadership all the very best, genuinely Bolshevik cadres of the Party; he has established his own personal dictatorship in the All-Union Communist Party (Bolsheviks) and all over the country he has broken with Leninism, and chosen the course of the most unbridled adventurism and wildest personal arbitrary rule.

Today, made wiser by bitter and compelling historical experience, knowing for a fact rather than hypothetically how Stalin's course turned out, and drawing conclusions rather than predicting the future, we can accurately calculate the price the country had to pay for the lust for power and cruelty of one man, obligingly aided and abetted by a handful of political gamblers who had placed their stakes on him. Ryutin did not, and could not, know everything that lay in store, but the accuracy of his analysis is astounding: other parts of the 'document' could have been written today, so that all one has to do is replace the present and future tenses in the text with the past tense:

> The adventuristic pace of industrialization, entailing a colossal cut in workers' and office workers' real wages, excessive open and concealed taxes, inflation, a rise in prices and a fall in the value of money; adventuristic collectivization aided by the dispossession of the *kulaks*, which is in fact mainly directed against the village masses of average and below-average means and, finally, the expropriation of villages by all manner of requisitions and extortions, all this has

55

plunged the country into the deepest economic crisis, bringing mass impoverishment and famine.... In the future the proletariat faces further impoverishment.... All individual interest in farming has been stamped out, labour is maintained by sheer coercion and repressions.

Although theoretically right, and committing no crimes, the others present at the meeting – after the tragedy that befell them we shall not allow ourselves to be unfaithful to the truth through compassion – were nonetheless struggling for power, for a place at the Party and state helm. Ryutin, who had never risen higher up the cadre ladder than the middle rungs, was acting only for a principle, for the truth and the good of the Motherland. Only for this and nothing else.

'The whole country has been muzzled,' we read later in his manifesto 'To All Members of the All-Union Communist Party (Bolsheviks)', an appeal which over half a century later has still to reach the Party:

lawlessness, arbitrary rule and violence, constant threats are hanging over the head of every worker and peasant.... Science, literature, art have been reduced to the status of lowly maidservants and props of Stalin's leadership. The struggle against opportunism has been debased, caricatured, and used as a weapon of slander and terror against independent-minded Party members. The rights of the Party laid down by the Statutes have been usurped by a tiny bunch of unprincipled intriguers.... The Party apparatus has grown into a self-sufficient force standing over the Party and dominating it, constraining its consciousness and will. The people who are appointed for Party work are more often than not ... dishonest, cunning, unprincipled people, ready on their superiors' orders to change their convictions a dozen times, careerists, flatterers and lickspittles.

He had most probably said as much to the Leader's face two years before, albeit in less scathing and emphatic terms, and in a less sharp tone of voice. The result had not been slow in coming forth. On Stalin's demand the Presidium of the Central Control Commission of the All-Union Communisty Party (Bolsheviks) had expelled Ryutin from the Party for 'double dealing' and 'discrediting the Party leadership'. A month later – on the same high-level instructions – he had been arrested. However, the Yagoda-Yezhov-Vyshinsky terror had not yet begun. This was still a different age. By a resolution of the OGPU board of 17 January 1931 Ryutin was acquitted 'on account of insufficient proof of the charge brought against him' (organizing a counter-revolutionary group, and anti-Soviet agitation).

Did this teach Ryutin a lesson? Yes, it most certainly did, but not the usual one in such cases. An entirely different one, in fact. If a graphic illustration of two political exact opposites were needed, I should suggest Vyshinsky and Ryutin. On the one hand, we have a chameleon, cynic and sycophant, and on the other, a man of inflexible will and staunch views, for which he was even prepared to die.

On 14 September 1932 two Party members, N. K. Kuzmin and N. A. Storozhenko (both shot in 1937), sent a denunciation to the Central Committee in which they let it be known that Vasily Kayurov's son had given them Ryutin's manifesto so that they could familiarize themselves with it. The denunciation was immediately dispatched from the Central Committee to the OGPU, and the arrests began the very next day. A visit was paid to Silchenko's apartment near Moscow; the cache was immediately uncovered and found to contain both the manifesto and an earlier work of Ryutin's – 'Stalin and the Crisis of the Proletarian Dictatorship', which has still not been found in the cluttered archives.

The Presidium of the Central Control Commission assembled for an extraordinary sitting. There were twenty-four present, including Rudzutak, Yenukidze, Shkiryatov, Solts (the 'Party's conscience'), Yaroslavsky, and Lenin's sister, Maria Ilyinichna Ulyanova; no fewer than fifteen of them were soon to be shot. The resolution was unanimously passed 'to expel them from the Party membership as degenerates who had become the enemies of Communism and Soviet power, traitors of the Party and the working class.' The issue was transferred to the Politburo and then to a Central Committee plenum. Stalin demanded the death penalty for Ryutin. The first to argue against this was Kirov, who declared that it would be disastrous if the Bolsheviks started executing Communists with different views. He was seconded by Kosior, Kalinin, Kuibyshev, Rudzutak and Ordzhonikidze. Many refrained from making their position clear. Stalin was firmly backed only by Kaganovich. Ryutin's and his comrades' lives were put in the hands of the OGPU.

At that time the OGPU possessed legal powers not only to imprison but also to pass judgement. Back in April 1927 it had been given the right to examine cases 'extra-judicially, including the application of the death penalty'; and what's more – what a superb amplification – for actions committed 'both with and without malicious intent'. In

Ryutin's case there was undoubtedly malicious intent. He was sentenced to ten years imprisonment.

'It is disgraceful and ignominious for proletarian revolutionaries,' Ryutin had written in his manifesto,

> to tolerate Stalin's yoke, arbitrary rule and the mockery of the Party and the working masses any longer. Whoever does not see this yoke, does not feel this arbitrary rule and oppression, whoever is not exasperated by it, is a slave, not a Leninist, a serf, not a proletarian revolutionary....
>
> Lenin's fears regarding Stalin, regarding his disloyalty, dishonesty and unscrupulousness, regarding his inability to use power, have completely come true. Stalin and his clique are destroying the cause of Communism, and an end must be put to Stalin's leadership as soon as possible.

An end was certainly put to this matter, but not to Stalin: the author had clearly underestimated his real power. Four years later Stalin was to remember Ryutin, who was then languishing in the 'specially appointed Suzdal Prison'.

The 'totally confidential' order given by Lyushkov[3] – the second-in-command of one of the departments of the Main Directorate of State Security of the NKVD – about the conveyance of 'political prisoner Ryutin' to Moscow has remained intact, and so too has the report of the Suzdal Prison commandant, Alliluyev: from which it appears that Ryutin refused to go, and that 'it was necessary to use physical coercion.'

After being delivered 'in a separate compartment of a prisoners' carriage under reinforced escort' – according to the report – Ryutin was confronted by Boris Berman, who presented him with a charge of terrorism. As Ryutin had spent all these years in prison, this charge of 'terrorism' referred not to some new crime he had committed but to the same manifesto for which he had already been convicted, and in particular to the phrase 'an end must be put to Stalin's leadership as soon as possible'.[4]

Most probably during this case a clinging stereotype began to emerge, which was to exert its influence on legal and political thinking. This stereotype made it impossible to separate a notion from an action, a position from a criminally punishable act, or the 'Leader' from the country as a whole. By an extraordinary sleight of hand, Stalin changed various concepts around, so that disagreeing with him, Stalin, became tantamount to disagreeing with the Soviet social system, and any criticism of him was equivalent to betraying one's country.

Lawyers were needed who would accept these legal notions whole-heartedly and put them into practice – if, that is, they could be called either legal or notions.

Vyshinsky wholeheartedly approved the idea behind the gigantic political game, on the conditions stipulated by it, and for many decades to come subjected the entire theory of law and the administration of Soviet justice to the influence of his outstanding personality.

In those days not a single famous trial was held without his taking part in it, especially if it was political: he was quite obviously contending for the country's highest legal post. Not one? No, there was one exception. When a trial was organized against some ex-Mensheviks in 1931, no role was found for Vyshinsky. The Leader's guile was undoubtedly sophisticated enough to suggest a stunning *mise-en-scène* to him: just imagine an ex-Menshevik at the prosecutor's stand (for he was already a prosecutor) holding other ex-Mensheviks up to shame. The accused were 'ex-Mensheviks' because they had all moved away from politics a long time ago and were all working as modest economists in various state establishements. But evidently in those days Stalin did not yet have the exclusive right to stage farces of such a kind: his loyal comrades might have objected, and he could not yet cast such objections aside.

However, another farce was actually staged five years later. At one of the 'Moscow Trials' Vyshinsky was to exclaim pompously:

> 'It is well known that the Mensheviks and SRs, those most malicious enemies of Socialism, have always lurked behind the name of Socialism. But, you know, this did not prevent them from falling down at the feet of the bourgeoisie, landowners and White generals.
>
> 'We remember how the Mensheviks in Petliura's Council[5] summoned the troops of Wilhelm II to the Ukraine, how they traded in the Ukrainian people's freedom and honour ... how the Menshevik government [of Georgia] of Noi Zhordania faithfully and truly served the foreign interventionists! ... Everyone knows that there were, and still are, no more consistent and more cruel, brutal enemies of Socialism than the Mensheviks and SRs.'

Who was he attacking so viciously? Surely not himself? Or was he feverishly trying to prove that he had never been among those cruel brutes, and that if he had, then he had completely changed, had been completely transformed, was devoted through and through, in body and soul?

But all this was to happen only five years later. For the time being, the task of attacking the Mensheviks fell to Krylenko and his assistant, Grigory Roginsky, who was soon to become Vyshinsky's assistant, take part in the 'Great Terror', receive an Order of Lenin for doing so, get sent to a labour camp and make appeals from there for even harsher punishments to be meted out to the 'sworn enemies of the working people'. Vyshinsky's usual place at the table of the Chairman of the Special Judicial Presence was taken by Nikolai Shvernik, then head of the Soviet trade unions. He was assisted by two other old Bolsheviks, reputedly decent people, both members of the USSR Supreme Court – Vladimir Antonov-Saratovsky (who would live until 1965) and Matvei Muranov, a former deputy of the State *duma* (who would live until 1959).

Among the accused were several ex-Mensheviks, once well-known figures in the Party and, naturally, absolute authorities for Vyshinsky – Vladimir Groman, Vasily Sher, Mikhail Yakubovich, and particularly Nikolai Sukhanov, whose works on revolutionary history had been enthusiastically read by Lenin (they are still periodically reprinted in the West), and who had published the newspaper *Novaya Zhizn* with Gorky, in which the latter had printed his *Untimely Thoughts*. It was in the apartment of Sukhanov and his wife, Bolshevik Galina Flakserman, that Lenin's staff had gathered in October 1917 to decide upon the armed uprising. As Bukharin's widow, Anna Mikhailovna Larina, then a young girl in her teens, has testified, Sukhanov admitted to her, 'I went out of the flat while they settled this matter.'

Now his comrades and he were answering the derisive questions of the prosecutors and judges, who were attempting to convince the world that these ex-Mensheviks, who had left politics long ago, had formed the counter-revolutionary 'Union Bureau', established contact with internal and foreign enemies (including the 'Industrial Party' and the 'Labouring Peasants Party'), had been involved in wrecking and espionage, and had been preparing an intervention. Sukhanov was interrogated and the charges brought against him investigated by the investigator responsible for the most important cases at the Pro-curator's office of the RSFSR, Mikhail Solomonovich Strogovich, shortly to become Vyshinsky's closest associate and, some time later, his opponent and antipode. We shall come across him again later.

An astonishing feature of the trial was that the accused did not conceal their own views even while confessing to actions they not only had not committed but could not have done (the alibis of their 'accessories' were proved by documentary evidence, though some had managed to pass away long before they were made 'accessories'). For instance, in response to a question from the defence, Sukhanov declared:

'I considered that the tremendous, completely unforeseen and unexpected pace of the collective farm movement had been caused by nothing other than the misfortunes of the peasant commodity producers induced by the unreal burdens of grain procurement. I considered that the grain procurement plan of 1929 was exaggerated and excessive ... that the collective farm movement and the entire grain procurement campaign of 1929–30 was bound to have a catastrophic effect on all our economy. And, consequently, this catastrophe brought about by the destruction of the countryside, the crisis in agriculture, the insufficient supplies to the towns, this catastrophe, it seemed to me, was bound to come to pass in the near future.'

He also asserted that the renunciation of the New Economic Policy 'is damaging for socialism and the people's well-being'.

At previous trials, when Vyshinsky had been the presiding judge, the accused had not dared make such bold statements. Nor would they when he became state prosecutor. For in either role he would be in supreme charge at the trial, and, what's more, perfectly mindful of his prime objective.

According to the French writer Victor Serge, the accused had been persuaded to slander themselves during the investigation in return for secret freedom and even rewards, and it was Sukhanov who had uncovered this corrupt operation. More likely than not, this story is true, for Krylenko dealt with him in a particularly ruthless manner. 'I can find no social usefulness,' he declared in his speech for the prosecution,

'in Citizen Sukhanov ... while his social harmfulness has been sufficiently proven.... I shall not hesitate even for an instant to affirm that our revolution, world revolution, and especially world history will lose nothing if one of the personages whom Citizen Sukhanov represents were to disappear off the face of the earth.'

'I would ask you,' he concluded his speech with an appeal to the judges, 'to display maximum severity with regard to the accused.'

And so, it goes without saying, they did, although for the time being they did not wipe them off 'the face of the earth': Sukhanov and the other main accused were sentenced to ten years imprisonment.[6]

It does not take much imagination to see how easily, if fate had taken a different turn, Vyshinsky could have landed up in the dock at this trial. But he did not. And this inspired him to accomplish new feats to the glory of the Communist Party and its great leader, Comrade Stalin.

Never again was Krylenko to sit at the prosecutor's table, or get a chance to display his remarkable eloquence in his speeches for the prosecution. His 'bosom' friend, on the other hand, was to display himself to his utmost, of which Krylenko was deferentially to say, in the last edition of his speeches for the prosecution to be published in his lifetime, 'These gentlemen ["the Trotskyite–Zinovievite gang, Bukharinites and Rykovites who have operated within our ranks in the base guise of doubledealers" is how he would later describe them] have already been dealt with by Comrade Vyshinsky, and his speeches are, for their part, most valuable historical material for future historians, not to mention their political topicality for our day and age.'

Before 'Comrade Vyshinsky' started dealing with 'these gentlemen', he made another advancement in his brilliant career. A Procurator's office of the USSR was finally established, and Ivan Akulov, until recently first Vice-Chairman of the OGPU, was put in charge of it. This 'romantic of the Revolution' and 'convinced humanist', as he was described by colleagues, was clearly not cut out to be a security officer of the new mould, but as he was an old Bolshevik with a fighting record, and staunchly loyal to the Party line, a high post was still found for him. And an even more loyal supporter of the Party line was appointed as his commissar – A. Ya. Vyshinsky: from June 1933 the latter became the Deputy Procurator-General of the USSR. Simultaneously – a seemingly inexplicable paradox these days, but perfectly normal in the Theatre of the Absurd functioning then – he remained Deputy People's Commissar of Justice of the RSFSR; in other words, Krylenko's deputy. The ludicrous situation had all the danger of a fire about to burst into flames. And sure enough, the fire went on smouldering and then, finally, flared up.

Two special anniversaries followed in close succession, one after the other, and congratulatory articles appeared in the press in general, and in specialized legal publications in particular: the first was Krylenko's thirtieth anniversary as a Party member, and the second, shortly afterwards, his fiftieth birthday. By now he was very well-known across the country, so it was only natural for both these very special dates to be celebrated publicly. For instance, the journal *Soviet Justice*, an organ of the people's commissariat which was run by Krylenko, devoted several pages to the first anniversary, including cordial congratulatory greetings from the country's top lawyers. Vyshinsky's name topped the list. After stressing a fact dear to Vyshinsky's own heart, namely that Krylenko had fought selflessly against the Mensheviks and SRs, the well-wishers concluded: 'With all our hearts we hope he will continue the struggle for the cause of the working class and Socialism with the same energy and the same talent and the same Bolshevik fervour as he always has.'

Three months later the second special date was celebrated, but even if we search through the reams of congratulatory messages for Vyshinsky's name, we shall not find it. Did he already know what post he was going to get? Or had he worked out what was going to happen to Krylenko? Or had he decided to stop being hypocritical? This last variant may be discarded immediately, but the first two, along with others not listed here, cannot be ruled out. This, however, was only the beginning. Krylenko was the first person on whom Vyshinsky tested his strength. He chose his victim in order to remove his mask of a respectable colleague, of just another loyal associate who modestly knew his place, and to move into the attack – in keeping with the well-known Russian adage 'Beat your own people if you want to strike fear into others.'

A chance soon presented itself: Stalin made one of his regular historic speeches on cadres (in which he made his famous revelation that 'cadres decide everything'), and in reply Vyshinsky immediately wrote an article entitled 'Comrade Stalin's Speech and the Tasks Facing the Bodies of Justice'. In the article Stalin's name is mentioned no less than sixty-nine times and printed everywhere in thick letters. Along with this eulogy, which was still most rare for those days, the author also methodically subjected the draft of the new Criminal Code, which had been compiled under Krylenko's authority, to sharp criticism. Enraged, the People's Commissar reacted immediately: 'We cannot leave Comrade Vyshinsky's article unanswered, although we see neither any particular need nor logic to link the issues at hand with Comrade Stalin's speech.'

This was the reply Vyshinsky had been hoping for, as he lay in wait like a hunter tracking game. So it seems that there are issues with which Comrade Stalin's speech has nothing to do? 'Comrade Krylenko clearly wrote this in a polemical rage, and I am sure, if he thinks about it, he will admit that his views are erroneous.' From his 'reply to the reply' it followed that he had had a good think about it himself and come to the conclusion that there were no issues to which any words issuing from Comrade Stalin's lips or pen did not apply.

The bitter irony here was that as a theorist and professional lawyer Vyshinsky was right while Krylenko, defending the position he took, seemed like a layman, dilettante and demagogue. The latter was disputing and trying to substantiate the most dangerous of 'principles', according to which the judge should have his hands untied, and be freed from the constraining provisions laid down by the law on the precise and specific composition of crimes. It took no effort on Vyshinsky's part to prove that this paved the way to the arbitrary rule of judges and deprived the defendant of all legal guarantees. So it looked as though Krylenko was advocating lawlessness and reprisals, and Vyshinsky the strictest protection of human rights.

The real crux of the dispute, however, lay elsewhere. Totally incapable of thinking on more than one level at once, Krylenko was seriously attempting to substantiate the practical application of 'revolutionary justice' and to make laws accordingly. Vyshinsky had a penetrating grasp of Stalin's tactics: to introduce and publicize democratic institutions of law while doing completely the opposite under their cover, pulling the wool over gullible people's eyes, both in the West and at home. And he did so wonderfully well. Let us recall, running ahead, that Stalin's Constitution contained an article which had been developed in detail by the Leader in his, it goes without saying, historic address on the right of any constituent republic to freely secede from the USSR. Even in his worst nightmares Comrade Stalin could never have dreamed of anyone taking this seriously as a practical guideline. Equally, he would have pulverized anyone who tried to deprive the republics of this 'sacred right' on paper. Stalin's Constitution (on paper) had to be the most democratic in the world.

The same was true of everything else. Intelligent and cunning, Vyshinsky understood the Leader's insidiousness, and took it as a key directive. And Stalin knew that he knew – and this is what sealed their union. For the time being and, what's more, for some time to come, they needed each other.

Taking the bit between his teeth, Krylenko stubbornly went on with the polemic:

I have no desire to dispute further with Comrade Vyshinsky. There are different kinds of disputes. There is the dispute of which, as the Ancients used to say, truth is born, and there is the dispute which only obscures it. This occurs when, instead of a dispute to the point, matters of principle are evaded. . . . I am leaving the methods of the dispute . . . to Comrade Vyshinsky's conscience.

Both contestants expressed the same hope: 'We shall leave it up to the future to decide' (Krylenko); 'The course things take in the future will show which of us is right' (Vyshinsky). And it did.

By now Vyshinsky had at least two widely publicized speeches for the prosecution to his credit. One was intended 'for the domestic market' although, compared to the grand-scale productions Procurator Krylenko had taken part in, it seemed very unimpressive. The case had to do with the 'dispatch of incomplete combine harvesters', and the trial of eleven extremely minor financial managers charged with negligence contained neither exciting subject matter nor the sensational element always present at celebrities' trials. So, a combine harvester had been sent off to some collective farm without a carburettor in it – what was so astonishing about that? Was such a small case really suitable for a giant like Vyshinsky? Today it is of interest only because it deals with the origins of some of our constant blights – exaggerated results, slovenliness and ubiquitous theft. However, it was not without reason that, of all the many available cases, Vyshinsky chose this one: the famine which had affected a vast area of the country, and the high mortality rate which had claimed millions of lives, demanded convincing explanations. Scapegoats were needed. Along with the 'wreckers' and 'saboteurs' (who were not yet counted in millions) there were also, apparently, idlers and rogues. They had no intention of tolerating their behaviour, but they could, of course, tell them apart from the traitors and spies. The sentence was really impressive: a warning and a reprimand for six of the defendants, and a small percentage taken off their wages (for three, six or twelve months) for the remaining five. The difference was impressive – look what happened after Krylenko's speech at the trial and what happened after Vyshinsky's!

The other trial was intended for the foreign public. Minutely detailed reports appeared about it abroad. It formed the subject of an entire book – *The Moscow Trial* – written immediately afterwards by A. J. Cummings, and published in London. Not much importance was attached to it inside the Soviet Union, and compared to the nightmarish mass trials which were soon to come, this small affair seemed totally insignificant.

This trial, in which six of the accused – exactly one third of the total – were British citizens, was known as the 'Metro–Vickers Trial', but it went down in Soviet official history as the 'wrecking at electric power stations trial'. According to the charges levelled against a group of engineers and technicians, the accidents that had taken place in the boilers, engines, turbines and generators of the electric power stations in Zlatoust, Chelyabinsk, Ivanovo, Baku and other towns, had been caused by 'counter-revolutionary wrecking' rather than by obsolete machinery, shoddy workmanship and other objective factors. State Prosecutors Vyshinsky and Roginsky, who was now his deputy, demanded the traditional 'confessions' of all the accused, but by no means always succeeded in obtaining them. Some of the counsels for the defence, such as Aron Dolmatovsky and Isaak Pines, who genuinely attempted to fulfill their professional duty and help their clients, were never to defend at political trials again and themselves became victims of the terror later on. A. G. Dolmatovsky and several of his colleagues were shot.

The fact that the scenario of the murderous show trials of the future was worked out and rehearsed here was not, however, the most important feature of this trial, which ended with fairly mild sentences being pronounced (some of the accused were even acquitted). It was here that the friendly team who were destined to act out this scenario on stage came together for the very first time. Vyshinsky was the chief producer from the very start, but the rest were by no means simply extras: each had been allotted a role of his own, and any slip-up could have ruined the whole show.

One of the team was always to remain off-stage: the investigator of important cases at the Procurator's office of the RSFSR (and then USSR), Lev Sheinin. He was only twenty-seven, but he had already succeeded in making a name for himself by skilfully uncovering criminal murders and publishing very lively and readable short accounts of how he had managed to solve them.[7]

This time the presiding judge was Vasily Ulrikh. It is hard to say how many victims he had notched up by this time, for he had controlled people's destinies at tribunals of the Military Board of the Supreme Court since 1920. However, what can be said with absolute certainty is that during the 1930s and 1940s he dispatched many thousands of people to their deaths, including the most illustrious figures in the arts and sciences, major politicians and military commanders.[8]

Finally, among the counsels for the defence were three outstanding lawyers whom Vyshinsky would select to take part in future large-scale shows: Ilya Braude, Nikolai Kommodov and Sergei Kaznacheyev. All three were well known from the important criminal trials which were still being quite widely reported by the press, particularly Braude, who, like Sheinin in his *Notes of an Investigator*, had gained great popularity by highlighting his experiences in the legal profession in his *Notes of a Lawyer*.[9] The presence of these revered lawyers gave the trials an air of respectability and legality. At ordinary criminal trials they had been true professionals, using all their skills and doing everything possible to fulfill their duties as defence lawyers, but at the shows produced by Vyshinsky they turned into timid bleating sheep, submissively fulfilling the 'social contract' they had been given.

This valiant team would go through all the 'Moscow Trials', demonstrating artistic virtuosity and a keen sense of comradeship.

Over half a century has passed since then, but for the present generation 1 December is still a well-known date, in the Soviet Union, at least. This is how deeply it is engraved on people's memories, dividing the century into two unequal halves: before and after 1 December 1934. It was on this day in Leningrad that Kirov was killed.

The events surrounding Kirov's assassination and its consequences, which are quite unique in the history of the Great Terror, have been described so copiously in just about every language of the world that it makes sense to be as succinct as possible here so as not to repeat well-known facts. From the vast wealth of facts we shall therefore only single out those which have a direct bearing upon Vyshinsky and his extraordinary career.

After being informed of Kirov's assassination (Leonid Nikolayev's shot was fired, according to the official communiqué, at 4.30 p.m.), Stalin immediately set off for Leningrad. In many accounts it is claimed that he arrived at Leningrad's Moscow Railway Station that same evening, which is, of course, impossible: even the special government trains, which were never subject to delays, took at least ten, and sometimes all of twelve, hours to reach Leningrad from Moscow.

It is necessary to amplify this point in order to dismiss the claim that Stalin dictated the tragic and infamous Decree of 1 December 1934 over the telephone from Leningrad, having personally 'convinced himself' of the fact that Kirov's assassination was the work of 'enemies of the people'. The fact is that until at least the dawn of 2 December Stalin was still on his way, and without telephone links with Moscow.

This means that Stalin dictated the Decree – there is not the slightest doubt that he was its author – while still apparently not knowing who had murdered Kirov and why. But what if (hypothetically) the murder was the work of a madman? Or if it was simply a question of settling personal accounts – jealousy or who knows what else? Could this really be ruled out? (Incidentally, the motive of jealousy, caused by Kirov's liking for Nikolayev's wife, a Latvian woman by the name of Milda Draula who worked in the Smolny Institute canteen, was considered when choosing an assassin to assist Yagoda in carrying out Stalin's orders.) None the less, the scenario had already been written and its implementation went according to plan. The communiqué on Kirov's death stated plainly that the assassin had been 'sent by enemies of the working class'. The Decree ordered that 'for terrorist cases the investigation was to be finished in ten days', 'the indictment was to be delivered within twenty-four hours', 'the case was to be heard without the participation of sides', 'appeals and petitions for pardon were not to be allowed' (not 'declined' but actually not allowed – that is, the convicted person was to be deprived even of paper and ink), and, finally, 'the death sentences were to be executed directly after the pronouncement of sentence'. This Decree of Stalin's was signed by Kalinin and Yenukidze. The latter was to be executed in keeping with this Decree just over two years later.[10]

Stalin was accompanied to Leningrad by Molotov, Voroshilov, Zhdanov and Yezhov (still in charge of the Central Committee's personnel department). There is nothing particularly surprising about the members of this retinue. But Vyshinsky and Sheinin also arrived by the same train. This, too, would seem quite normal: the prosecutor and investigator. However, if the General Secretary and half the members of the Politburo were speeding to Leningrad, the most logical thing (in such a unique case) would have been to send the Procurator-General of the USSR, Akulov, to the scene of the murder. But his deputy was going instead. And the most logical thing would have been to send the head of the investigative department of the Procurator's office of the USSR. But no, one of the investigators of the Procurator's office of the RSFSR was being taken along. And the trials, the first of which were to begin only two weeks later, were to be presided over, it goes without saying, by Ulrikh; and the whole team listed above, who had been prepared and tried out in advance, and well matched up, would set to work.

During December 1934 Ulrikh and another invariable member of the court, Ivan Matulevich, jointly and individually conducted several trials of 'White Guards', 'terrorists', and 'wreckers' which ended with death sentences being immediately executed, in keeping with the Decree of 1 December. At last, on 28 December they once again both met Vyshinsky at a trial behind closed doors to pass judgement on fourteen accused known as the 'Nikolayev-Kotolynov Group' (the latter being a recent member of the Komsomol Central Committee). The investigation led by Sheinin was completed in the record time of less than three weeks. To be absolutely precise, Sheinin had only led the interrogations, and the case had been 'set up', and the 'culprits' exposed, arrested and handed over to the investigator by the new Leningrad chief of the NKVD, Yakov Saulovich Agranov, a truly vile sadist who posed as an intellectual and lover of the arts, and was a close friend of the poet Mayakovsky and of Lily Brik. Even today there are still writers trying to romanticize, elevate and mourn him – for he, too, of course, was subsequently annihilated.

Vyshinsky's role in this closed trial looks most odd. His place was definitely not in secret courts of law but on a floodlit stage, in front of distinguished guests, some of whom would be from abroad. He knew how to create an illusion of lawfulness, and this was precisely the bait these guests willingly swallowed. Behind closed doors there was simply nothing for him to do, for they could manage perfectly well without him. Especially as the Decree of 1 December prevented the prosecution and defence from participating in cases involving terrorism. Evidently, they had been preparing an open show trial, but must have had doubts at the last moment as to whether the accused were really ready to play the parts that had been prepared for them without a hitch: unlike the other public trials, this one had been put together with lightning speed, and there was a chance that the accused had not been properly worked on.

The two-day trial ended, naturally, with all the accused receiving death sentences. By then Zinoviev, Kamenev, and well-known leading Party officials such as Grigory Evdokimov and Bakayev had already been arrested. On 15 January 1935 they were brought to trial in Leningrad, again behind closed doors, and again with Ulrikh presiding: no shorthand report of the proceedings was issued. The newspaper published only a brief general summary of what had gone on in the court-room, after which a slim volume was brought out in a minute edition, which became a rarity overnight, containing the minutes but not the shorthand report of the trial. Vyshinsky appeared very insipid in it – not because he could not look otherwise, but because his brilliant talent for prosecuting had not been needed: let me repeat that Andrei

Yanuarievich only made sparks fly and dazzled onlookers when he was in the limelight and had hundreds and thousands of eyes fixed on him. There had not been thousands, hundreds, or even dozens present at this trial, only the escorts and the NKVD operatives.

And once again let us note a most curious detail: the indictment bears two signatures – those of Procurator-General of the USSR Akulov and his deputy Vyshinsky. Why two? This is not stipulated by any law, rule or tradition. Either one of the two signatures would have sufficed. But Akulov's was there for appearances' sake and Vyshinsky's for a specific purpose. His name was needed because it was being systematically popularized. He had already been selected by the Leader for a historic mission. And he would definitely not let him down, come what may – Stalin's choice, as is well known, proved correct.

It was he, Vyshinsky, who prosecuted at the closed Leningrad trial, and he rather than Akulov who gave the following important directive: 'Cases in which there is insufficient documentary evidence for them to be examined in a court of law are to be transferred for examination by the Special Board of the NKVD of the USSR.' The 'Special Board' – that sinister extra-judicial body which dealt out justice to millions of people – had been created a few months before Kirov's assassination. It, too, I believe, is a clear indication of how the Great Terror was prepared in good time.

Vyshinsky's name began to appear constantly, almost daily, in newspaper reports. It was on everyone's lips and became a part of everyday life. It also figures in a great many secret decrees and instructions. In particular, on 13 May 1935 several secret Central Committee decrees were passed, most of which have yet to be published. As a result of one of these a Special Security Commission of Politburo members was formed to direct the liquidation of 'enemies of the people'. Vyshinsky became a commission member along with Stalin, Yezhov, Zhdanov, Malenkov and Shkiryatov. This very significant and telltale fact indicates the position which he held by then in Stalin's most intimate circle.

Sapienti sat: 'For a wise man it is sufficient.' Yagoda, still the all-powerful head of the NKVD, realized perfectly well what role Vyshinsky was already performing, and what role he himself would soon be relegated to. It was now that they became unusually friendly: the obsequious, obliging and sugary-sweet manner in which the professional executioner addressed the impartial guardian of lawfulness was noticed by everyone who happened to see them together in those days.

On 24 May 1935 the première of Nikolai Pogodin's play *The Aristo-crats*, a hymn in praise of the NKVD and its valiant work in trans-forming ex-convicts into decent Soviet citizens, was staged by the Realist Theatre, then in the hands of Nikolai Okhlopkov. It was a celebration of Semion Firin, the deputy head of the GULAG and the man in charge of the excavation – by prisoners – of the White Sea-Baltic Canal, where the play's action was set. Firin invited a great many high-ranking officials, headed by Kaganovich, to watch this special tribute to him. One of his guests was Yagoda, who arrived arm-in-arm with his own special guest, Vyshinsky. Yagoda had never been on friendly terms with Vyshinsky, tending to look down on him: he was, after all, an ex-Menshevik and, as far as his social origin was concerned, from an alien class – and, besides, who was he compared to Yagoda? But on this occasion he not only invited him along as his guest but as a sign of courtesy and magnanimity sat him down in a seat intended for someone higher-ranking – alongside Kaganovich.

Higher-ranking? Yagoda always heard the news before anyone else. And Kaganovich, of course, had heard it as well.

And the news was that the decision had been taken to appoint Vyshinsky to the post of Procurator-General of the USSR. The official announcement would be published in June.

Vyshinsky's calculations had proved correct. He had backed the obvious favourite, and had not been mistaken. Two years earlier, when official eulogies to the 'Dear Father' were not yet a normal part of everyday life – at least, they were not yet obligatory: the 17th Party Congress with its ritual adulation of Stalin had yet to take place – Vyshinsky had already dotted his 'i's by calling Stalin 'our great leader and teacher' in the foreword to his book *From Prisons to Educational Institutions* (which was published in 1934 but sent to press in 1933). And now, in response to his new appointment, he wrote a letter which is worth citing in full (it is printed here for the first time from the typed copy in Vyshinsky's personal archive):

Dear Iosif Vissarionovich,

Embarking upon my new appointment as Procurator-General of the USSR, I feel an insuperable desire to express to you my most profound gratitude, touching me to the very depths of my soul, to the Party, to the Government and to yourself, our leader and beloved teacher, for the trust you have bestowed upon me.

For fifteen years I have served our Communist Party and the

cause of the working class, which has been working miracles under your great leadership.

Sparing neither my strength nor my life, I am ready to serve the great cause of Lenin–Stalin to the end of my days.

Please accept, deeply respected teacher and beloved leader, dear Iosif Vissarionovich, once again this expression of my sincere gratitude.

A. Vyshinsky

It had been worth giving up that piece of meat way back in the Bailovka Prison cell! I do, of course, realize that there is no firm or binding link between that trifling incident and this appointment to the post of Procurator-General, and that there cannot possibly be one either. It is neither firm nor binding, but it is still a link. The reasons why Vyshinsky was considered fit for the floodlit stage of history are numerous. The main one was his unique personality. When it came to fulfilling Stalin's grandiose designs, there was nobody to match him.

4

As far as Stalin was concerned, the sentences pronounced at the January trial in Leningrad on Zinoviev (ten years in prison) and Kamenev (five years in prison) were only the start of the final act of his spectacular mystery play. Only later would it become apparent that there was going to be no finale, since the tyrant could never get his fill of blood.

No sooner had they been convicted than they were being prepared for another trial. This time the intention was not only to brand Lenin's comrades-in-arms as foreign spies, terrorists and criminals (in a letter shortly before Lenin's death, Krupskaya had called Kamenev and Zinoviev Vladimir Ilyich's closest comrades), but do so at a public trial rather than behind closed doors. To mete out punishment in some isolated dungeon required only executioners, but to achieve the same objective in public, while outwardly observing the law and making the murder seem a triumph of justice, required not only executioners but first-class actors capable of bringing the idea to life and getting the spectators to believe in the authenticity of the proceedings.

The men who until only recently had been the country's leaders (with their assistance, Stalin had got rid of his main rival, Trotsky) now topped the list of the accused who could be brought to a public trial. Essentially, the main (if not the only) question was whether they would let the side down or not. If the prosecution had no evidence, and it was known that it could have none, the only way out for a public court of law was to hope that the victim would confess his guilt. All the accused had to do was refuse to confess and the show would be a complete fiasco: the prosecution would have nothing left to offer. Of course, the victim could still be eliminated, but in that case it would be better not to produce him in an open court.

This is the production Stalin entrusted to Vyshinsky. He had been watching him closely for a very long time, and now made a perfect choice. True, he did not have much of a choice. Krylenko, with his embarrassingly direct approach, sharpness and inflexibility, would have been no good here. He would have willingly done anything he was told to, but he would have done it crudely, and without the Jesuit charm which made Vyshinsky unique among his colleagues at the time.

The person who put Stalin's idea into practice was to be not only the main producer and leading actor in this show but also the director. He was to run the trial. All Ulrikh could do was to close a session and announce a recess whenever necessary, and then pronounce the sentence, which he had neither written nor edited. But he could not, of course, conduct the trial in the true sense of the word. He totally lacked ingenuity and flexibility and could not react instantly to the slightest change in the behaviour of the accused, the atmosphere of the court-room or, indeed, the mood of the public. He had had no legal training, he was repulsive to look at, and there could be no question of his entering into single combat with these seasoned politicians and expert speakers. Vyshinsky was his complete opposite, and seemed to have been created for this role. What's more, he had brilliantly conducted the rehearsals by proving at the trials that preceded those which were to go down in history as the 'Great Moscow Trials' that he was up to any mission.

We are not going to repeat what has already been written about in great detail – the demonic ploy Stalin devised and used successfully, persuading Zinoviev and Kamenev to slander themselves in exchange for a promise to keep them alive. The political game proceeded at Politburo level, and the 'physical preparations' and 'legal arrangements' were all conducted by a vast army of Lubyanka experts assisted by Vyshinsky's favourite, Sheinin, then an investigator at the Procurator's office. His purely decorative participation gave the investigation and trial an aura of respectability and legality, but the high decorations 'for carrying out a special mission' (they were not even ashamed of publishing this) went to nineteen members of the probe team, headed by Yagoda's personal secretary, Pavel Bulanov. Two years later Bulanov would be sitting in the dock next to Bukharin and Yagoda in the same hall, acting out in exactly the same manner the very scenario he had taken such an active part in writing (and been awarded an Order of Lenin in the process) but then his role would be that of a spy and wrecker.

While the victims who had agreed to be sent to the slaughterhouse were being 'worked over' in the dungeons, Vyshinsky prepared for his moment of glory.

He was destined, however, to gain nationwide fame three months before the start, in 1936, of the first of the three 'trials of the century'. It is astonishing what a windfall the case presented to Vyshinsky (and, consequently, to Stalin). One can safely say that had such a case not actually occurred, it should have been concocted.

This case was not political, which is precisely why it was so timely. Of course, with the way things were in those days any trial could be given a political colouring. Class roots, the influence of bourgeois ideology and social hostility were looked for and, of course, detected in any crime. The same applied here, too, but on a very small and unusually modest scale for that insane time.

This tragic episode could be told in detail – it certainly deserves to be as one of the many bloody stains on the macabre canvas of that era. The head of a remote polar station on Wrangel Island, Konstantin Semenchuk, and Stepan Startsev, a dog-driver, were charged with the murder of Doctor Nikolai Vulfson.

Monstrous though the crime might be, from a lawyer's point of view it could not be considered out of the ordinary: every year, unfortunately, a great many murders were, and still are, committed for the most varied motives. Not once had Vyshinsky appeared at a murder trial throughout his career as a prosecutor in the twenties and thirties. What's more, this trial was being examined by the Supreme Court of the RSFSR. In keeping with a long-established and hitherto unbroken practice, an official of the Procurator's office of the RSFSR, even the Republic's Procurator himself, was called upon to prosecute. This time, however, the Procurator-General came to support the state prosecution.

It was, in my opinion, a very accurately and brilliantly calculated ploy. The sinister and exotic nature of the crime, which had allegedly been committed on the edge of the world under cover of the polar night, was bound to attract considerable publicity. Its enigmatic nature made the trial particularly piquant – there was no direct evidence of Semenchuk's and Startsev's guilt, and the investigation only managed to collect some scraps of circumstantial evidence, again with the help of the ubiquitous Sheinin. Vyshinsky's presence, and his impassioned speech for the prosecution, gave the case a dimension it would hardly have had with any other prosecutor.

Even today this trial is still debated, but the case against Semenchuk and Startsev was halted by the Supreme Court of the RSFSR. A verdict based only on circumstantial evidence always leaves a feeling of dissatisfaction, and may be disputed. If an inquiry had shown that there was insufficient material for a charge of murder, then we should accept that its decision was well-grounded. It is clear, however, that neither the prosecutor nor the investigator nor the overseer and director of this trial had any grounds on which intentionally to falsify this particular trial. On the contrary, its main purpose was to demonstrate a genuine triumph of justice just before the most monstrous miscarriage of justice was perpetrated.

Of what use were these unknown and politically uninteresting figures? Why discredit the prosecutor who in three months' time was to present the world with a superb piece of deception which really did have all-embracing and far-reaching political objectives? On the contrary, it would have been beneficial to give a convincing public demonstration of an honest, impartial lawyer inexorably defending the truth, and nothing but the truth.

The accused pleaded 'not guilty', and nobody forced them to slander themselves, although it would hardly have been difficult for our crack team of experts to have extracted any confession they liked from them. The defence was conducted by the top lawyers Nikolai Kommodov and Sergei Kaznacheyev, who did not agree with the prosecution's line but disputed it in a resolute and uncompromising manner. There was nothing here – not a single detail – which remotely resembled the previously formulated and repeatedly rehearsed plan of the faked trials.

And three months later, when the mysterious curtain rose and the former statesmen and leaders of the Revolution who had been branded as 'fascist spies' were facing Ulrikh and his comrades, sitting at the prosecutor's table was a man who had just won recognition and popularity, a man of learning, an analyst, a defender of the law, the epitome of truth and justice. To execute his plan the mastermind of this mystery play needed someone cunning, forceful, and popular – not a faceless, mechanical 'tool'.[1]

The Semenchuk-Startsev trial was concluded at the end of May. The Zinoviev-Kamenev trial began in mid-August. However, it is unlikely that anyone in May knew for sure when the latter would take place. Or, indeed, whether it would do so at all. Stalin, calling upon the help of one 'loyal comrade' after another, conducted negotiations (in the Kremlin? at the Lubyanka?) with the cornered leaders of the concocted 'Associated Trotskyite-Zinovievite Terrorist Centre'. He convincingly proved to them that their only chance of survival was to accept his conditions. As these people had no principles for which they were prepared to die, and as they themselves had been denigrated long ago by lies, deceits, intrigues and repeated changes of position, the struggle for survival was the only motive force they had left – so it did not take much to break them yet again. The only problem might arise if for some unforeseen and unpredictable reasons they 'rebelled' during the trial itself, or played some kind of obnoxious trick with all the foreign diplomats and journalists watching. Stalin could no longer influence this stage of the proceedings himself: the conducting of the operation, and responsibility for its outcome, was now shouldered entirely by Vyshinsky. The Leader withdrew not only figuratively but also literally by going off to Sochi for a holiday.

In the meantime the population was subjected to a powerful and subtle campaign of brainwashing. What mattered most was to create the general atmosphere of a happy life bubbling over with optimism, a festival of triumphant youth, regardless of age, 'because everyone here is young now in our youthful and beautiful country', as a popular song of the time went. So this was what those despicable hirelings of capitalism, these spies and wreckers were encroaching upon – the eternally youthful country's eternal and happy youth!

A sports parade, the non-stop flight by the pilots Chkalov, Baidukov and Belyakov from Moscow to the tiny Far Eastern island of Udd, their return, their meeting with Stalin at Shchelkovo Airport near Moscow – such were the events which took place in the days leading up to the trial. 'If you want to be Chkalov,' declared the country's top current affairs writer Karl Radek, addressing the eternal youth in his usual pompous style, 'then carry out the appeal of our Leader and Teacher Stalin: study, study and study – to catch up and overtake the capitalist world.' Mikhail Kaganovich, the head of the main directorate of the aircraft industry, was awarded an Order of Lenin for organizing this flight. The laureate's smile and strong handshake with Stalin were captured by photographers and printed in all the newspapers, inviting the whole country to take part in this joyful occasion. Another special family occasion also looked as though it was going to be celebrated throughout the country: just before the trial a theatre in Birobidzhan[2] was named after Mikhail's brother, Lazar Kaganovich.[3]

Political life was also in full swing: it was announced that a commission was being set up to work on the draft of the Constitution of the RSFSR, and it was called upon to develop Stalin's All-Union ideas of democracy and humanism on a constituent republican level. The commission consisted of Yezhov, Bukharin, Stetsky, Yakovlev, Pashukanis, Krylenko, Vyshinsky and Y. Yevdokimov. Only Vyshinsky survived: all the rest were annihilated. But this was to happen later. For the time being, setting up such an imposing commission for such a noble cause was a source of inspiration and reassurance. According to the memoirs of Bukharin's widow, Anna Mikhailovna Larina, it was hardly a coincidence that Bukharin had been in excellent spirits in Paris – from where he had only just returned – and most hopeful about the country's democratization: soon they were going to have Stalin's Constitution, the greatest ever. After waiting for the birth of his son, he blithely set off to rest in the Pamirs: he did not care what happened to those 'scoundrels' and 'rogues', as he went on calling Kamenev and Zinoviev, who were doomed to be executed.

A few days before the trial Franco's rebellion took place in Spain, and the reports on it attracted wide attention and suitably influenced public opinion. Even this truly international tragedy proved quite timely in terms of putting Stalin's scenario into action: the accused were 'aligned' with the latest news – as a fifth column they had been preparing a similar rebellion in their own country, but the valiant NKVD, and, above all, Stalin's genius had disarmed them in time.

For many years it was claimed that Vyshinsky had nothing to do with the procedures before the trial – in other words, with the 'investigation', the torture, the decisions arrived at in advance regarding the fate of the doomed victims – and that all he did was to dextrously carry out decisions that had been made without his knowledge, giving them publicity and the necessary judicial form.

According to 'General Alexander Orlov' (Lev Feldbin), the author of *The Secret History of Stalin's Crimes*, 'the main secrets of the investigation were not accessible' to Vyshinsky, who 'used to rack his brains trying to guess what extreme means the NKVD had used to break and paralyse the outstanding Leninists' wills and make them slander themselves'. Most probably he did not know all the cutthroats' secrets or, to be more precise, the methods used to bring pressure to bear on the doomed victims, but as a high-class lawyer he could clearly see that the accused were innocent, and that the charges were unsubstantiated. However, the idea that he played no part in the investigation itself has been destroyed by documents to which limited access has only recently been granted.

In a report prepared for the Politburo Commission after a further examination of materials relating to Stalin's repressions, the Party Control Committee, the Institute of Marxism-Leninism, the Procurator's Office of the USSR and the Committee for State Security (KGB) of the USSR confirm that:

A.Ya. Vyshinsky played a provocative role in the judicial inquiries. At conferences, displaying an extremely harsh attitude towards the investigators, he enjoined them to obtain direct evidence on the terror from the prisoners. When the evidence was analysed, he demanded sharper political conclusions and generalizations and, essentially, the falsification of cases.

Strictly speaking, Vyshinsky was himself the principal falsifier. In the most important cases the indictments were compiled by him personally before the 'investigation' was even over, and the drafts were then presented to Stalin so that he could edit them, ascribing to the accused other 'crimes' as he saw fit. Vyshinsky then made the necessary corrections to the indictments, and the investigators adjusted the records of the examinations accordingly, beating out of the victims all the evidence required by Comrade Stalin and Comrade Vyshinsky. This is what happened, for instance, in the Zinoviev-Kamenev case: it was Stalin's personal wish that Zinoviev should be considered the mastermind behind Kirov's assassination. Vyshinsky fulfilled his wish by making an appropriate entry in the indictment, after which the investigators had no difficulty in obtaining the necessary confession from the 'assassin'. Stalin personally included Vagarshak Ter-Varanyan on the list of the accused nine days before the start of the trial although the 'investigation' had neither the intention nor the evidence (even falsified) to include him. Vyshinsky not only considered him guilty, following Stalin's instructions, but also 'substantiated' his guilt, so that all the investigators could do was to obtain the necessary 'confession' from the accused at lightning speed.

Vyshinsky played an even more sinister part in the Pyatakov-Radek trial in January 1937. He paid several visits to Stalin, deftly picking up not only everything the Leader said but also the tone of voice in which he said it. Instead of simply relying on his memory, he jotted these conversations down, and his notes may now be studied in his personal archive. He received instructions on the confessions to be obtained from the accused and the way he was to conduct himself during the trial. So how was he to conduct himself? 'Don't let [the accused] speak too much ... Shut them up ... Don't let them babble.'

Stalin personally edited Vyshinsky's speech for the prosecution while the latter, for his part, did the same with the final words of the accused and even the experts' reports. Karl Radek helped the Procurator with particular zeal.[4] Vyshinsky often dropped by to see him in his prison cell, and the two of them wrote up the trial's 'scenario' and the text of the roles. Ulrikh and Vyshinsky also worked together well in advance on the text of the sentence in which Vyshinsky's faithful assistant,

79

Radek, and all the other accused were to be given the death penalty. However, as Radek might still come in handy, Stalin decided to defer his murder, and so it was that Vyshinsky saved Radek's life for the services he had rendered.

Recent archival research has convincingly shown that on their own initiative Vyshinsky and Ulrikh asked Stalin for instructions on how to proceed with various prisoners: 'We deem it necessary to give the death penalty ... to the main accused, and varying prison sentences to the remaining accused. We ask for your instructions. A. Vyshinsky, V. Ulrikh.' A great many inquiries of this sort were made, and the answers they received, though detailed at times and short at others, were always specific. Ulrikh also asked Stalin what to do about the death penalties, and whether to execute them or not. 'Comrade Vyshinsky considers it possible to execute the sentence,' he informed Stalin. Let us note that Vyshinsky expressed his opinion *before* receiving instructions from Stalin. That surely means that he had the authority to do so, otherwise he would have never risked airing his views. 'Don't stick your neck out!' was a wise formula which had to be followed in those days.

The archive materials dismiss another 'mitigating' claim – that Vyshinsky knew what the NKVD investigators were up to (the torture, taunts, blackmail, threats, etc.) and even covered up for them, but was still not 'personally' involved in these heinous crimes. Alas, this is not so. It is unlikely that Vyshinsky, a member of a noble Polish family, 'personally' took part in the physical coercion – at any rate, there has been no evidence so far to support this. However, according to the trustworthy testimonies of victims and eye-witnesses, he 'personally' took part in extorting the necessary statements by threatening to implement the death penalty, to annihilate the victim's family, and to hand the person over to even more brutal sadists. This was how he supervised investigations in his capacity as Procurator-General.

Of course, in Zinoviev's fateful case everything was somewhat different. Completely different, in fact. Everything was decided by Stalin himself. But the trial's procedure and tactics, and all its details, were worked out in conjunction with Vyshinsky and Ulrikh. And even the final version of the Procurator-General's speech for the prosecution – a model of impassioned eloquence by a great orator – was edited and approved by the Leader and Teacher before he set off on holiday to the shores of the Black Sea.

The Hall of Columns of Trade Union House had long since been the traditional setting for such bloodthirsty shows. The political *agent provocateur* Ivan Okladsky who had betrayed his comrades in the Narodnaya Volya Party, the famous Social Revolutionary Boris Savinkov, the Shakhty engineers, the Mensheviks, the members of the mythical 'Industrial Party' and the English 'wreckers' had all been tried here. But for this insane drama Stalin chose the October Hall, a much smaller hall in Trade Union House, barely seating three hundred spectators, two-thirds of whom were to be NKVD operatives. The remaining places were given over to foreign diplomats, Soviet (with special passes) and foreign correspondents, and distinguished and carefully checked guests of honour. They were greeted by a slogan on the wall which began with the words 'Workers of Moscow!' followed in huge letters by 'To the mad dogs – a dog's death'.

The small number of prominent Party figures seated in the dock between Lubyanka *agents provocateurs* and international rogues honourably and conscientiously carried out their promise to Stalin. So much has already been written about this trial and the two others which followed it that there is not the slightest point in repeating widely known facts.

We shall only note one specific feature of this trial which eye-witnesses have firmly remembered. Whenever the Prosecutor posed a point-blank question which was impossible not to answer, Kamenev, and sometimes Zinoviev, would ask Vyshinsky to formulate it himself. Vyshinsky would then meet them half-way by suggesting an answer using the interrogative form: 'Is it true that? ...', 'Do you confirm that? ...', 'Do you agree with that? ..'. And the accused would reply succinctly and clearly: 'Yes, you are correct', 'Yes, that is how it was.'

'What has particularly stuck in my memory,' recalls one spectator at the trial,

> is the part which went wrong when the defendants were 'cooperating' with the Prosecutor. Several times Vyshinsky demanded the one-word answer 'yes' to the question: 'Did your Associated Trotskyite-Zinovievite Counter-Revolutionary Centre establish contact with that of Bukharin, Rykov, Tomsky, Uglanov?' Neither Zinoviev nor Kamenev replied 'yes' or 'no'. Then Vyshinsky cited their affirmative statements during the preliminary investigation and demanded confirmation of them. ... In the end their answers tallied.

Another detail worth noting is that this was the first occasion on which the Prosecutor had used abusive language – not the sharp expressions he had used before, but abusive language of a kind that had undoubtedly been approved if not dictated by the dramatist. All those delightful touches to his oratorical style, such as 'bandits', 'scoundrels', 'despicable adventurers trying to trample down the fragrant flowers in our socialist garden with their filthy feet', no longer satisfied the Prosecutor. In the rich and powerful Russian language he found other evocative expressions, such as 'liars and buffoons, despicable pygmies, pug dogs and puppies raging like elephants', 'arch-scoundrels', 'disgusting creatures'. These were the kinds of terms constantly used by this top legal authority and scion of a cultured family as substitutes for the only true weapon a lawyer can ever have – indisputable evidence. There was no evidence, but the abusive language created a psychological illusion of there being some.

The apotheosis of the bellicose speech came at the end:

> The enemy is guileful! The guileful enemy must not be spared. [A paraphrase of a cannibalistic formula by Gorky, who had died under mysterious circumstances two months before the beginning of this trial: 'If the enemy does not give in, he is destroyed'.] The entire people rose to their feet at the first announcement of this villainy. The entire people is trembling with rage. And I, too, as a representative of the State Prosecutor's office, add my indignant and outraged voice of a State Prosecutor to the roar of the millions!
>
> I demand that the mad dogs be shot – every single one of them!

Taken up and given legal standing, the Prosecutor's expressions instantly found their way into everyday conversation and journalese. Hearing that his name had been mentioned at the trial, Bukharin sent a telegram to Stalin from Central Asia, demanding a confrontation with Zinoviev and Kamenev.[5] After hurriedly flying back to Moscow, he immediately dispatched letters to Stalin, the Politburo and Vyshinsky, protesting against the 'monstrously vile accusations'. In a letter to Voroshilov he wrote: 'I am terribly glad ... that the dogs have been shot.' It is not his 'joy' I am drawing attention to here, but the fact that until then the prominent theorist and Party's favourite had been noted for his original style and had not needed to imitate that of an ex-Menshevik and provincial rhetorician. He did now, though.

Now everyone started speaking in the same way as the Prosecutor, including leading current affairs writers. Karl Radek demanded that the 'Trotskyite-Zinovievite Fascist gang ... paid with their heads,' and foretold that they would 'not escape the curses of the world proletariat'. 'Mercilessly destroy the despicable murderers and traitors!' urged Pyatakov: 'They must be annihilated, annihilated like carrion. It is a good thing that the NKVD organs have uncovered this. It is a good thing that it can be destroyed. Honour and glory to the NKVD operatives.' 'There should be no quarter,' asserted Khristian Rakovsky, demanding that the 'mad dogs be shot'. None of these people had long to live: their entreaties would be heard and turned against them.

The then totally unknown young Boris Ponomariev, who was one day to become a Central Committee secretary, Politburo candidate member and leading expert on the international workers' movement, hastily put out in several languages his first scholarly work, *The Trotskyite-Zinovievite Gang – Direct Agents of Fascism*. Leaving aside his scholarship, we shall simply note that in his choice of words he clearly developed and enhanced the Procurator's style in his own creative manner. 'Dogs of the Fascist bourgeoisie', 'mad dogs of Trotskyism', 'dregs of society', 'decayed people', 'terrorist thugs and degenerates' – these are some of the literary gems picked at random from this deservedly forgotten work.

After the politicians, scholars and journalists, it was the writers' turn to display their mastery of the written word. 'We have a request to make to the court ... to apply the highest degree of social defence to the enemies of the people' – this modest request bears the signatures of many foremost writers including Konstantin Fedin, Leonid Leonov and Boris Pasternak. There also appeared some highly metaphorical and high-flown poems on the subject. The poet Alexei Surkov transformed Vyshinsky's speech into poetry:

> The spite of jackals and hatred of hyenas
> Led the traitors along the path of murder.
> Poisoned are their black deeds
> With the pungent stench of putrid corpses ...
> So that the viper does not strike anew
> With the deadly poison of her secret sting
> May Kirov's fiery blood
> Reduce the coward's reptilian heart to ashes.
> May the people's court bring to light
> All the abomination of the treacherous scoundrels' deeds.
> For those who raise their hand
> Against the people's leaders
> There is no justification, no quarter.

Before beginning his speech for the prosecution Vyshinsky publicly announced that, on the basis of the testimony given by Zinoviev,

Kamenev and the others, proceedings had been instituted and an investigation begun against Bukharin, Rykov, Tomsky, Uglanov, Radek and Pyatakov.

Tomsky immediately committed suicide, leaving behind a letter for Stalin: 'I appeal to you not only as the Party's leader but also as an old comrade-in-arms, and this is my last request – do not believe Zinoviev's insolent slander – I have never been part of any blocs, or been involved in any conspiracies against the Party.'[6] He was an intelligent person, but he had not realized that the accusation was not 'insolent slander' on the part of Zinoviev but a play written personally by his 'old comrade-in-arms' in which, quite simply, Zinoviev was obediently performing his part. The others, who had not yet been arrested, were taken into custody, the only exceptions being Rykov and Bukharin, who were given some respite. What was the point in hurrying, after all? Stalin enjoyed playing cat-and-mouse.

Zinoviev, Kamenev and the other convicted prisoners were executed almost immediately after the sentence had been read out, on 25 August: the People's Leader had kept his Bolshevik's word of honour. Alexander Smirnov's comment (according to well-informed sources) as the condemned men were being led out to be executed – 'We deserved this' – is possibly the most accurate appraisal of these events.

After reporting to Stalin in Sochi on the successful execution of his orders, Vyshinsky was not given a chance to rest: he had to roll his sleeves back and get straight on with preparing a new trial. On 8 September he was invited to the Kremlin, to the confrontation which Bukharin and Rykov had requested between them and the prisoner Grigory Sokolnikov.[7] The meeting was supervised by Kaganovich and Yezhov. Already a broken man, Sokolnikov repeated the confessions he had made to his investigators on Bukharin's and Rykov's participation in a 'general conspiracy' uniting both the 'Rightists' and the 'Leftists'. By this stage, however, Stalin's plan had evidently changed somewhat: he had decided to transfer the execution of Bukharin and Rykov to the third scene of his gigantic play's final act, focusing his attention for the time being on the second scene, in which the leading roles had been reserved for Pyatakov, Radek, Sokolnikov, Serebryakov and several lower-ranking officials. First of all, though, Ordzhonikidze, who had openly and defiantly opposed the new executions, and had unambiguously shown that he would be against the arrest and annihilation of Bukharin and Rykov, had to be removed from the action. That is why at the confrontation – the only one Bukharin was able to obtain at the time – Sokolnikov did not give any damning testimony but alluded to some conversations with Kamenev so as not to make it look as though he was renouncing his previous testimony. The way things stood, apart from the statements of Kamenev, who had already been executed, the prosecution had nothing specific to pin on Bukharin and Rykov.

It is quite obvious that this temporary retreat was planned by Stalin, who knew how to react quickly and flexibly to any turn of events, and was not in the habit of clinging to past decisions with fanatical obstinacy. He efficiently made the necessary alterations, and next day, 9 September, Vyshinsky hastily announced in the press that the investigations into the Bukharin and Rykov case had been halted due to lack of evidence of their having taken part in a conspiracy. It goes without saying that he could not possibly have made such a bold statement without Stalin's direct instructions. And I mean instructions, not agreement! Agreement would have meant that it had been on someone else's initiative. But nobody could have taken such an initiative.

Yezhov, who had taken over Yagoda's post as People's Commissar for Internal Affairs, went on gathering (extracting) statements from his prisoners against Bukharin, Rykov and the other doomed victims. In the meantime, Vyshinsky demonstrated the triumph of lawfulness, objectivity, and law and order. Each had his own role to play.

Nearly all those accused at the second trial were already in Yezhov's iron clutches and had virtually been won round. Some went on resisting for a while, but not for long. One of the last, if not the very last, to be arrested was Radek, a veteran of the Polish and German socialist movements and one of the organizers of the German Communist Party, who was on very close terms with the Politburo and with Stalin himself. His name was world famous – it was perfectly obvious that this would make the trial a sensation abroad. His testimony would carry particular weight. And Stalin also knew that he would almost certainly capitulate, for he would do anything to save his skin. In this way Vyshinsky gained a powerful ally.

All this coincided with the arrival of the highly esteemed German writer, Lion Feuchtwanger, who had escaped abroad from Nazism and was almost better known in Russia than he was at home and in neighbouring Western countries. He was invited to the preparations for the trial as an authoritative and impartial observer. A few days before the trial began he went to see Stalin and spent over an hour with him. 'Stalin,' he wrote later, began speaking about Radek [of course – all his hopes were pinned on him], the writer and most popular person among all the defendants in the second Trotskyite trial; he spoke sadly, in an agitated manner, describing his friendly relationship with this man.... He spoke of the long letter Radek had written to him protesting his innocence and cited numerous false arguments in it; however, the very next day, under pressure from witnesses' testimony and evidence, Radek confessed.

Of course, there were no witnesses or evidence, but there certainly was pressure. Radek had carried out his master's wishes. He devoted nearly all his final words to Bukharin, just as the scenario required him to. Sounding just like Stalin, he began: 'He and I are close friends, but an intellectual friendship is stronger than any other ..., I was convinced he would give honest testimony to the Soviet authorities. That is why I did not want to bring him with his hands bound to the Commissariat of Internal Affairs.'

This time, it seems, Vyshinsky did not have to work as hard as he had at the Zinoviev trial. The accused willingly put their own heads on the chopping block, and even dragged their friends after them as well. And to make life easier for the Procurator they sometimes even took over his laborious functions. I wonder if any of them realized, as they shared the weight of the unwieldy and important trial with Vyshinsky, that just then he was partially, if not totally, absorbed by matters of an entirely different and purely personal nature?

Here we shall have to break off our story and digress for a while.

The documents I have in front of me take us back to the end of the twenties and beginning of the thirties, and concern issues which have, not surprisingly, been passed over by historians. The dramatic events of public life, the political struggle and murderous ends to human destinies were all a far cry from the crumbling old protocols, testimonials and financial reports relating to aspects of life which are usually bashfully skirted – in other words, to the mundane, everyday affairs of illustrious people.

In those days several dozen such celebrities, worthy people who had contributed considerably to Russia's culture, formed one of the first *dacha* cooperatives. It was set up in the village of Nikolina Gora, which is still flourishing today. Among its first members, representing the academic fraternity, we find the familiar name of the then Rector of Moscow University, Andrei Yanuarievich Vyshinsky, who was living at the time in a modest one-storey detached house which had several outbuildings attached to it.

In 1931 a much more spacious plot of land became vacant on the high bank of the Moscow River in Nikolina Gora. The writer Vikentii Veresayev and the statesman Leonid Serebryakov, Lenin's comrade-in-arms and a Central Committee secretary in Lenin's lifetime, who had recently become head of the Chief Directorate of Roadways, both had their eyes on it, but it went to Serebryakov.

Once in a while Vyshinsky used to visit his distinguished neighbour, especially as many of Serebryakov's writer, painter and artist friends also used to gather there. Serebryakov's first wife was Galina Serebryakova, a writer whose historical biography, *Women of the French Revolution*, had recently hit the literary headlines.

Vyshinsky used to enjoy walking along the well-trodden woodland paths in the Serebryakovs' grounds, taking in the view of the river. 'I simply cannot tear my eyes away from it,' he used to exclaim joyfully. An educated and gallant man, he would not forget to pay his host an innocent compliment: 'You are a lucky man, Leonid Petrovich. Everything you have is wonderful – your life and your *dacha*.' And his host would politely smile back and thank him.

Did Serebryakov see Procurator-General Vyshinsky's signature scrawled in red pencil on the warrant for his arrest? I doubt it: who bothered to present warrants in those days? He was 'taken', and that was it.

Leonid Petrovich Serebryakov was arrested on 17 August 1936, immediately after his return from a long trip to the Soviet Far East on particularly important state business – two days before the start of the Zinoviev-Kamenev trial. That same night a team of energetic thugs headed by the sadist Agranov (his deceased friend Vladimir Mayakovsky must have turned in his grave) started beating confessions of espionage, wrecking and terror out of him. The Procurator-General personally took part in the investigation of this vital case, for it was he who would soon have to appear on the stage to convince the world of the justice of all the indictments.

All his tireless concern for society's well-being did not prevent him from thinking about his own. On 23 August he demanded the death penalty for the 'mad dogs' Zinoviev and Kamenev, on 24 August Ulrikh carried out his demand, on 25 August they were liquidated, and on 29 August, in keeping with all the regulations in force and with a precise knowledge of the law, Professor Vyshinsky (not Procurator-General Vyshinsky, just Professor Vyshinsky) wrote to the *dacha* cooperative's board and 'most humbly requested' them to transfer 'the plot of land and all the outbuildings on it belonging to exposed enemy of the people L.P. Serebryakov' to cooperative member A.Ya.Vyshinsky.

Because many *dacha* owners tried to spend the late summer season in the south, the board could not meet as quickly as circumstances required. However, on 23 October, at one of its first meetings under the chairmanship of Nikolai Semashko, an old Bolshevik and statesman of impeccable repute, and attended by the illustrious opera singer Ivan Semionovich Kozlovsky, a cooperative (but not board) member, the cooperative's directors uncomplainingly satisfied their powerful 'comrade's' request and also handed over the plot of land and the *dacha* he used to live in to Mikhail Markovich Borodin, then editor-in-chief of *Moscow News* but better known for his previous work as political advisor to Sun Yat-sen. The new owner swiftly gave Vyshinsky back what he had originally paid for the *dacha*, its outbuildings and 'the expenses he had incurred during the cultivation of the land' – namely, the sum of 38,990 roubles.

So, on to November 1936. Serebryakov had had all the confessions beaten out of him that were needed by the Leader of All Peoples, and it was now perfectly clear that Lenin's recent comrade-in-arms had run an anti-Soviet Trotskyite centre, had been preparing terrorist acts against Stalin and Beria, and had been selling Trans-Caucasia to foreign powers for a considerable sum. In December the investigation was already on the finishing straight, and the Procurator-General could turn to the production of the second (after the Zinoviev-Kamenev trial) spectacular and bloodthirsty show.

In Nikolina Gora meanwhile, far from the public eye, the curtain went up on another show, which was much less impressive but, on a personal level, far more important for the chief producer. And, naturally, of no less concern to him. Especially as in this show he was not only the chief producer but also the leading protagonist, playing a key part in the action.

He had got the *dacha*. Now all he had to do was get the money for it.

Not only was he not going to pay the required amount for the new (cooperative) *dacha* which he had long since secretly coveted and had now actually acquired, but he was also going to be awarded its cost price. This is what the country's top lawyer had in mind. The rest was a piece of cake: he just had to carry his plan through.

The correspondence in his archive enables one to see through the red tape of incoming and outgoing papers to the full drama of this battle being waged off the public stage.

The administrative department of the Procurator's office of the USSR arranged for the top priority refurbishment of Serebryakov's *dacha*, their intention obviously being to eradicate all traces of the previous owner and to gratify the new one, their all-powerful chief. The law was observed: the cooperative transferred 20,000 roubles for this work to the Procurator's office, and cooperative member Vyshinsky reimbursed it.

January 1937. Any day now the trial was to begin of Lenin's close associates, the eminent Bolsheviks Yury Pyatakov, Karl Radek, Grigory Sokolnikov and Leonid Serebryakov. Vyshinsky wrote his impassioned speech for the prosecution and, in between times, several terse letters: to the Central Executive Committee of the USSR, requesting that the *dacha* be taken out of the cooperative and made state property; to the Procurator's office of the USSR (that is, to himself), requesting that Serebryakov's old (recently refurbished) *dacha* be demolished and a new one constructed on the same site under the administrative department's direction; to the directors of the cooperative, requesting that not only the 20,000 roubles (spent on the unnecessary refurnishment) be returned to him, but also 17,500 roubles (the amount initially paid by Serebryakov, whom Vyshinsky would be bringing to trial in a few days time).[8]

Dealing with his victim's life, however, proved a quicker and simpler matter than appropriating his money.

'Please tell me when it was that you renewed your anti-Soviet criminal activity?' the State Prosecutor politely began his examination of Serebryakov on 24 January 1937. 'Renewed' ... The fact that he had previously been engaged in it (and, most likely, always had been?) was not even discussed. Why should it be? The ex-Central Committee secretary, ex-head of the Red Army's Political Board, ex-People's Commissar for Communications willingly, eagerly, almost zealously accepted any blame the Procurator laid on him. Beria's murder? Yes, of course, and Stalin's, too. 'So you wanted to kill Stalin?' 'What a question, of course I did!' 'Thank you. Be seated.'

The decision to put the *dacha* 'being constructed by Comrade Vyshinsky in the charge of the Administrative Department of the Council of People's Commissars of the USSR' was dated the same day, 24 January. Thus, the champion of lawfulness created an unprecedented situation by building a piece of state property on a plot of land belonging to a cooperative, while its occupant-to-be continued to be a member of the cooperative but ceased to be one of its contributors and was thus released from all obligations to it. But who could contend the legitimacy of an unprecedented situation when it had been created not by someone used to breaking the law but by its chief guardian?

However, it was ordinary ledger clerks, not high-powered officials, who had to pay out the actual money, and they could not understand all the intricacies of the instructions with which they had been issued. Pedants and pettifoggers, they could not find the answer to the most important question in any legal document, namely how and on what grounds they were to give the disinterested cooperative member back not only his own initial payment for the *dacha* but also that of the man he had executed.

Yes, executed: on 30 January, immediately after the passing of sentence, Serebryakov and nearly all his co-defendants were shot ('I accuse ... the most serious criminals, worthy of only one penalty – execution, death!'). Serebryakov's final words were, 'It is hard to comprehend that I ... have ended up an enemy of the people and come to be here in the dock.'

He did not, of course, know that after a hard day's work destroying doomed victims, the State Prosecutor used to set off for Plot No. 14 in Nikolina Gora, and spend the long winter evenings relaxing in the comfort of *his* study, in *his* high-backed chair, under *his* Chinese standard lamp.... If he had, he might have found it even harder to understand everything that was going on.

'The property of all the convicted prisoners, belonging to them personally, is to be confiscated,' reads the sentence. I do not know what happened to the property of the other prisoners, but in the case of Serebryakov only part of the sentence was carried out: the state did not receive the 17,500 roubles which he had paid for 'the property personally belonging to him'. Instead, it went to Vyshinsky – after quite a tussle.

In so far as no financial expert could understand the grounds on which the confiscated sum of 17,500 roubles should fall into 'private hands' rather than go to the Treasury, the cooperative, through the Administrative Department of the Presidium of the Supreme Council of the USSR, the legal successor of the Central Executive Committee, applied to the Presidium's secretary, Alexander Fedorovich Gorkin, for an explanation. This was swiftly followed by a letter from the Secretariat of the Procurator's office of the USSR, Ref. No 1/632, signed by its head, Ivan Grigorievich Kharlamov. This loyal associate of Vyshinsky, who had followed his superior through all the various stages of his tumultuous career and was subsequently appointed by him to the lucrative post of head of the diplomatic corps' service management, where he succeeded in thoroughly disgracing himself, had a clever knack for finding flexible formulas containing threats and pleas at the same time.

> When construction work initially began on the new *dacha* Comrade Vyshinsky intended paying for it.... When the total cost of the newly-built *dacha* on Plot No. 14 became apparent, there was no longer any question of Comrade Vyshinsky acquiring it for his own possession. In view of the fact that the repayment of 37,500 roubles [20,000 plus Serebryakov's down payment of 17,500 roubles] has been delayed for too long, which places Comrade Vyshinsky in a difficult position, I would ask for your instructions to transfer to his name the above-cited sum which belongs to him.

M. Rydayev, a high-ranking official of the Council of People's Commissars, immediately gave instructions for the *dacha* owner, who had been put in a difficult position, to be given everything he was seeking. But – you cannot help marvelling when you read it – someone (nobody knows who) wrote the following resolution on this document: 'When A. F. Gorkin was reported to, he ordered the money not to be transferred, and for Comrade A.Ya. Vyshinsky to be consulted personally on this matter.' In those days that was to be truly bold.

Did such a conversation take place, I wonder? Very possibly. It was already 1938 and Comrade Vyshinsky was carrying out yet another Party and Government mission: preparing the most spectacular of all the murderous political shows: the Bukharin-Rykov trial. His influence was rapidly increasing, his power even more so. It is unlikely that anyone could risk standing in his way now.

A. F. Gorkin did not resist for long, but some very ordinary pedant, 'the manager of *dachas* in the Moscow Region [that is what it says in the text] Gatchenko', issued instructions that upon the transfer of the 'requested monies 2,574 roubles were to be withheld from Comrade Vyshinsky for making curtains for him for eight windows'. History has left us with no information on people's reactions to these costly instructions. To make up for it, two weeks later the long-awaited note finally appeared: 'Monies transferred in full'. The Procurator-General had won this time-consuming, complex case as well, convincingly confirming his right to be considered the country's top lawyer and chief defender of the law.

The state *dacha* was soon built on the cooperative plot, and, according to official estimates (the document has remained intact), the work cost the Treasury 600,000 roubles. Along with the curtains, which had been paid for by the Council of People's Commissars, and the state floor-coverings, the *dacha* was handed over rent-free to Vyshinsky, who grew so fond of it that during the war, just as the Germans were approaching Stalingrad, he added on – without asking anyone's permission – another plot of a similar size, comprising a hillside and a section of the river bank with its own private beach. Only after he had put a fence up did he inform the cooperative of what he had done. The plot around the house now covered 15,000 square metres. Later a swimming-pool, a tennis court, a volleyball court and other leisure facilities were added for his guests: Vyshinsky himself was not very keen on sport and preferred strolling by himself along the woodland paths behind his high fence.

According to the settlement's old residents, one day in 1943, or perhaps 1944, Stalin paid a visit to him, and was pleasantly impressed by the house, and the view over the river. Maybe he did not actually visit him, but it was rumoured that he had, and this was enough to increase the owner's prestige. But could it be increased any more? There was a limit to everything, even prestige.

Meanwhile Serebryakov's family was living in quite different conditions. Galina Iosifovna Serebryakova, who had left her husband for his friend, G.Ya. Sokolnikov, lost both husbands at the same trial and went through the hell of the labour camps, not to return for seventeen years. The same fate awaited the Serebryakovs' daughter, Zorya Leonidovna, who after being released had to wait over thirty years for her father's rehabilitation.

Mikhail Markovich Borodin went the same way as the other victims, but after the war. After spending only a year and a half in Vyshinsky's old *dacha*, he changed it for the more spacious house of Alexander Gavrilovich Shlyapnikov, the first Soviet People's Commissar of Labour, a Bolshevik from 1904, who had been arrested. But a few years later Borodin shared the same fate.

By the time Zorya Leonidovna Serebryakova returned from exile, Vyshinsky was already dead, but his family was still living in the *dacha* where she had spent her childhood and from which she had been evicted. His widow, Kapitolina Isidorovna, refused to see the ex-convict, for, after all, Zorya was still the daughter of an enemy of the people while she was the widow of an eminent statesman and Party official.

True, two years later Vyshinsky's family was obliged to vacate the *dacha* they had come to love so dearly. From a legal point of view the *dacha* was still 'state' property, and after the occupant's death his family was only entitled to reside in it for a limited length of time. This rule still exists. But there is no need to feel sorry for them: for several years they had had their own 'reserve' *dacha*, which nobody could take away from them. On the instructions of the Council of People's Commissars of the USSR No 2638 of 14 October 1945, which had been signed by Stalin himself, officials who had particularly distinguished themselves during the war were presented with fully-furnished *dachas*, curtains and all. They included Academician Vyshinsky, who was presented with a *dacha* in the village of Lutsino. This is where his widow and daughter were to enjoy the rest of their lives, as the family not of a prosecutor who had been responsible for sending people to their deaths but as the family of the academic who had pursued lofty and eternal ideals in the realm of pure science.

Since then another thirty years have gone by. During this time the *dacha* on Plot No 14 has been occupied by other high-ranking officials, but never for very long: mostly it has stood empty – according to old residents it has a curse hanging over it. As for Vyshinsky's old *dacha* – his first one – it has been occupied by all sorts of people, the most recent being the conductor Gennady Rozhdestvensky. He does not find it at all cramped but, as he recently admitted to me, the spirit of the Great Inquisitor returns sometimes, bringing with it a vague feeling of unease and a chilling sensation in the back.

More than half a century after being evicted, Zorya Serebryakova, a doctor of historical sciences, has been given back her right to the *dacha* which, in a highly hypothetical sense, she may call her own. The story of her life, which not even Shakespeare could have dreamed of, has ended in old age with a return to childhood. But how can one go inside it now, this *dacha*, this shrine built on blood?

We left Vyshinsky in the October Hall of Trade Union House as Radek was pronouncing his final word. The pact with the devil had taken place. Even he hinted at it in fairly transparent terms:

> When I was at the People's Commissariat of Internal Affairs, the head of the investigation said to me: 'You're not a small child. Here are the fifteen testimonies against you, you cannot get out of it and, as an intelligent person, you cannot set your sights on this.' For two and a half months I gave the investigator a rough time. If I was asked if we were given a rough time during the investigation, I should have to say that I was not *given* a rough time but I *gave* the investigators a rough time by making them do unnecessary work.

Even then it was not difficult – and it is even less so now – to guess exactly what 'unnecessary work' the investigators were given. Of course, it was worth confessing to being a spy, conspirator and terrorist straightaway without waiting for their questions, since there was then no need for this 'unnecessary work'. A conflict was now in progress, if one could so describe a fight in which the predator had already sunk his teeth into the victim. Radek was needed by Stalin and Vyshinsky in order to get even with their hardest opponent – Bukharin. Radek now started to demolish this 'intellectual friend' of his, after spending two months wearing down his long-suffering investigators with his denials. Having deceived Zinoviev and Kamenev in the most primitive and crude manner, reneging on his deal with them, Stalin now kept his word with Radek. Although Radek requested that no leniency be shown towards him, the merciful court spared his life and sentenced him instead to ten years imprisonment: he had yet to give a dazzling display of eloquence at the Bukharin trial, establishing the guilt of his 'friend' should the latter decide to play hard to get. Radek's international reputation would give his incriminating evidence much more weight than if someone else had provided it. However, his services were not called for after all, and they managed without him. After the trial he spent two years in prison, and then one day he was struck over the head with a brick and killed.

All the other defendants also heeded Vyshinsky, and painstakingly carried out his plans. A reading of the shorthand report of the proceedings reveals the producer's and performers' splendid mutual understanding, which is undoubtedly the result of careful preliminary planning. The mechanism worked in a precise and well-coordinated manner: the first performance had needed several rehearsals to be a success. The amazing thing, however, was that even in these unthinkable conditions other defendants tried to pass on valuable information to the outside world. I shall cite just one example: a short exchange between Vyshinsky and Nikolai Muralov, who at sixty was the oldest among the defendants, a Bolshevik with a heroic past and one of Trotsky's closest associates.

To make the show more authentic it was essential for Vyshinsky to stress that the defendants had put up a struggle and refused to confess their guilt, but that once faced with an indestructible wall of (non-existent) evidence, they had given in. That is why he dwelt so long on the fact that Radek had resisted for over two months and Muralov for no less than eight.

Vyshinsky: Why was it you finally decided to confess?

Muralov: I told myself that I had to submit to the interests of the state I had struggled for during twenty-three years, for which I had fought in three revolutions where dozens of times my life had hung on a thread ... And I said: all right, I'll go and reveal the whole truth. I do not know if my reply has satisfied you or not?

Vyshinsky: Everything is clear. I have no more questions.

What more questions could he have? The defendant had submitted and repeated a well-rehearsed lesson off pat. 'Everything is clear.' The answer had satisfied the Prosecutor.

In his final words Pyatakov also sent a fairly clear farewell message to humanity: 'I am standing before you, covered in filth, crushed, deprived of everything through my own fault, having lost my Party, without friends, having lost my family, having lost myself.' How much clearer could he be? What was it Pyatakov called 'his own fault'? Not the crimes he had never committed. No, it was not those, it was the readiness to submit which they had all demonstrated. But could one really expect someone to turn into an unfeeling lump of rock?

Alexei Shestov, a board member of the Vostokugol Combined Works Construction Trust, had been accused of preparing a terrorist act against Stalin's loyal comrade Robert Eikhe. A year later this same loyal comrade would turn out to be an accursed enemy and shortly afterwards share the same fate as his unsuccessful assassin. However, the Prosecutor would never admit that a slight mistake had occurred and that terrorists and wreckers were unlikely to plot the assassination of their own accomplices – and that if they had, then the whole affair would smack more of a scandal in an aristocratic family than of a conspiracy against a party and government. Incidentally, according to the prosecution's version, Pyatakov had intended killing Kosior and Postyshev, and Serebryakov had intended killing Nikolai Yezhov, Stalin's most loyal comrades, whom he succeeded in dispatching into the next world much more swiftly and simply than Pyatakov and Serebryakov had.

In his final speech the 'assassin' Shestov declared: 'I do not ask for mercy. I do not need leniency. The proletarian court should not and cannot spare my life.... I want one thing: to calmly mount the execution block and wash away the stain of a traitor of the Motherland with my blood.' This general plea for 'no mercy' echoed through all the penitential speeches and characterized the second trial.

And it made the role of the defence at the trial seem even more ludicrous (I cannot find another word for it). At the second trial, unlike the first, Prosecutor Vyshinsky had 'opponents' in the form of three lawyers who were defending the secondary, as opposed to the main, defendants – Knyazev, Pushin and Arnold. It would seem these counsels for the defence could not demand the court show 'no leniency'. But, in fact, it only seemed that this was the case.

I do not know whether these three unfortunate victims actually asked for counsels to defend them. It looks to me as though it was Vyshinsky's clever idea to insist on counsels for the defence to give the 'open' trial an even greater semblance of decorative lawfulness. He knew perfectly well that the defence would not spoil the show in the slightest. On the contrary, they would increase its prestige in the eyes of the West. And of the Soviet people ...

The 'defence' was entrusted to barristers whose political maturity had already been tested out at previous show trials, and who got on exceedingly well with Vyshinsky and enjoyed his high esteem. The situation acquired an even greater sense of drama because all three were very highly skilled lawyers, who had begun their legal careers before the Revolution and had gained nationwide fame. Unfortunately, I never heard Nikolai Kommodov, but I can truthfully say of Ilya Braude and Sergei Kaznacheyev that they were born lawyers, highly skilled at the most subtle legal and, in particular, psychological analysis. So this made the role that befell them even more horrific.

I shall now cite examples of their unprecedented 'defence' which have not appeared in print for over half a century:

Ilya Braude: Comrade Judges, I am not going to conceal from you the exceptionally difficult and immeasurably hard position a counsel for the defence finds himself in in this case. After all, a counsel for the defence, Comrade Judges, is first and foremost a son of his Motherland, he is also a citizen of the great Soviet Union, and the feelings of great indignation, wrath, horror which all our country, both young and old, are now seized with, the feeling which the Prosecutor expressed so clearly in his speech, these feelings are inevitably shared by the counsels for the defence as well....

I am defending Knyazev, the head of the railway, who in order to please the Japanese Intelligence Service derailed trains carrying workers and Red Army men. I shall not conceal that as I was reading over the materials of the case, as I was leafing through the documents,[9] as I was listening to Knyazev's testimony, I imagined the crash of the carriages as they were being derailed and the groans of the dying and injured Red Army men.... Driven into a corner, Knyazev agreed to join the counter-revolutionary Trotskyite organization. Thus began the first page of Knyazev's despicable actions which had been dictated to him by the Trotskyite terrorist organization.

Sergei Kaznacheyev: Comrade Judges, the picture of treachery and betrayal which has unfolded before you in the course of these few days is monstrous. The gravity of the defendants' guilt is immense. The wrath of the popular masses of our Union is understandable. Both the work itself of the Trotskyite organization and the methods it used to entice people into its midst have been revealed here in court with the utmost cogency and clarity.... The range of arguments which may be brought to your attention, the range of debates which may be produced as factors extenuating the guilt of one or other accused in this case is becoming extremely limited.

Nikolai Kommodov: Comrade Vyshinsky was profoundly right.... If we, the counsels for the defence at this trial, ask you, Comrade Judges, to deviate from the sentence of capital punishment proposed by the State Prosecutor, then it will not be for reasons connected with the nature of the crime or the personality of the defendant but for reasons arising from the sheer fact of the power, strength and might of the Soviet Union.

I do not know about the reader, but I for one cannot tell the prosecutor's and defence lawyers' speeches apart. The only difference is, perhaps, that they did not use the virulent invective Vyshinsky so enjoyed. In all other respects – in stance, train of thought, appraisals, and style – they are identical.

The unity, the well-coordinated way in which the entire machine worked without a hitch, the amicable assistance which the defendants rendered the Prosecutor to make it easier for him to establish their guilt, all had a powerful impact both on the spectators following the course of the trial in the October Hall, and on those who heard about it from the reportings of the small number of authoritative correspondents and commentators. 'Brilliant in form, remarkable in depth of analysis, in passion of feeling, in strength of indignation,' *Pravda*'s leader gushingly extolled Vyshinsky's speech for the prosecution. He was seconded by authoritative Western observers. 'The defendants' guilt has now to a considerable extent been proven,' the renowned democrat and humanist Lion Feuchtwanger was already asserting after the first day of the trial, without even waiting for the speech for the prosecution. 'A most convincing speech by the prosecutor, an absolutely just sentence', commented another humanist also present at the trial, the renowned Danish writer Martin Andersen Nexø.

Sitting alongside the foreign writers, their Soviet colleagues Alexei Tolstoy, Alexander Fadeyev, Nikolai Tikhonov, Bruno Yasensky, Lev Nikulin, and Piotr Pavlenko all confirmed the unshakeable lawfulness of the trial, the 'brilliant cogency of Comrade Vyshinsky's speech', and the correctness of the 'severe, purifying, inevitable sentence'. The sentiments of these humanist writers were echoed by humanist doctors: 'We demand that the vermin and all their progeny be mercilessly exterminated.' Among the latter were the well-known therapists Meer Vovsi and Boris Shimeliovich, who were themselves to join the list of vermin (or their progeny?) fifteen years later. Shimeliovich would be 'mercilessly exterminated', Vovsi would be saved, but not thanks to the prosecutors and henchmen: quite simply, Stalin died in time to save him.

'I am not the only one!' Vyshinsky bombastically declaimed at the end of his speech for the prosecution, raising his hands and eyes to heaven:

> The victims may be buried but they are standing here beside me, pointing at this dock, at you defendants, stretching out their terrible arms which have rotted in the graves you dispatched them to!
>
> I am not the only one to accuse you! I accuse you together with all our people, I accuse the most serious criminals, deserving one punishment only – execution, death!

After these words it says in the shorthand report: 'Protracted applause throughout the hall'. Throughout the hall. Does this mean that Feuchtwanger and Nexø, the British Ambassador and American journalists all applauded 'protractedly' along with the others? Whatever the case, of the seventeen, there proved to be thirteen 'deserving one punishment only'; two secondary defendants – Arnold and Stroilov – and, more importantly, Radek and Sokolnikov appeared only to deserve prison. It cannot be ruled out that Britain's reaction, strange though it may seem, influenced this sentence: the raging of Nazism in Germany at the time still seemed dangerous to Stalin, and he did not wish to strain relations with London.

The sentence was announced at dawn on 30 January. The information agencies broadcast the news worldwide. This sensation was, however, overshadowed by another: on the very same day, the fourth anniversary of the Nazi Party's coming to power, Hitler officially announced Germany's renunciation of the Treaty of Versailles. According to confidential information in the archives of the British Foreign Office, the German Government considered the trial which had just finished in Moscow a great success because the 'leaders and most serious Soviet statesmen were being removed from power'.

Governments and diplomats the world over closely followed the preparations and course of the trial, trying to understand what was happening off-stage while Andrei Vyshinsky worked with such virtuosity. The Zinoviev-Kamenev trial had not caused as much of a shock as the Pyatakov-Radek did, possibly because the names of Zinoviev and Kamenev had become too familiar after they had been expelled from the Party, sent into exile and brought to trial more than once. Neither, especially Zinoviev, was really regarded as an unfortunate victim: everyone recalled his role in punishing those who 'disagreed' when he was in charge in Petrograd, and his frenzied speeches on 'the world revolutionary conflagration' which had horrified Western politicians. And although Pyatakov's name was linked to the trial of the Social Revolutionaries which he had presided over, the death penalty had not been imposed then. It is unlikely this was due to his own personal efforts, but even so Radek and Sokolnikov were well-known in Europe and, despite any reservations one may have, still undoubtedly regarded with a certain amount of esteem. Sokolnikov was certainly respected, as is clear from various uncensored original documents. He was the first Soviet Ambassador to London, and that is why as soon as the information on his arrest leaked through to the West, there was a particularly lively reaction in Britain.

On the day of Zinoviev's and Kamenev's execution the British Government's Foreign Affairs Committee had held an urgent meeting under the chairmanship of Ramsay MacDonald. It was not, however, to discuss the outcome of the trial, which had finished the day before: a ciphered telegram had arrived from the British Ambassador to Moscow, Viscount Chilston, informing them of Sokolnikov's arrest. 'We cannot abandon Mr Sokolnikov in trouble,' declared Ashton-Gwatkin:

He worked superbly over here and did a considerable amount to promote Anglo-Soviet relations. Our ambassador must appeal to the Soviet Government not to exacerbate relations between our two countries. The death penalty for Sokolnikov may cast a shadow over these relations and it will have a horrifying impact on the British public.

The Chancellor of the Exchequer Neville Chamberlain, the Foreign Secretary Anthony Eden, the Minister of Commonwealth Affairs Malcolm MacDonald, and the First Lord of the Admiralty Samuel Hoare were just some of the many who took part in the discussion. The committee members agreed unanimously with Eden that there was no point in defending Sokolnikov: firstly, because the matter of executions and reprisals was an internal affair of the Soviet Union and, secondly, because it would not make any difference anyway, since Stalin would still do what he deemed necessary.

The British Ambassador's daily reports to his government testify to the fact that the foreign diplomats, and the British in particular, well understood the real alignment of forces and actual 'guilt' of the defendants in the crimes they were charged with but had absolutely no idea of the leadership's motive forces or of the intrigues inside the Kremlin, and this caused them to make political forecasts which can only bring a sad smile to our lips today. For instance, Lord Chilston stressed repeatedly that Vyshinsky was the key figure in the trials, that he and not the People's Commissar of Justice or the Chairman of the Supreme Court's Military Board held the reins of power, and that it was he who was Stalin's proxy and the executor of his designs and instructions. But what can one make of passages like these from his reports:

> The New Soviet Constitution restricts the role of the NKVD which, afraid of losing its influence, is attempting to make its force felt and frighten the Soviet leaders.

Or:

> The removal of Yagoda from the post of People's Commissar of Internal Affairs is an admission of the fact that the NKVD has overstepped the mark by trying to get even with Bukharin and Rykov. It is clear that they will now apologize to them and that Yagoda will be punished.

Or:

> Yezhov is a very strong figure and, what is very important, a Party official and not a Chekist. Most likely, he will be Stalin's successor, he has great prospects . . . Stalin gave the NKVD to Yezhov in order to reduce the power of this monstrous organization. That is why Yezhov's appointment should be welcomed.

I do not know whether one can blame diplomats working in a country in the grips of insanity and terror and with a blanket of total secrecy thrown over it for such naïve conclusions and prognoses. Of much greater significance are the perceptive appraisals in coded messages of the trials and the people taking part in them. In particular, the British Ambassador's January reports already contain information on Marshal Tukhachevsky's imminent arrest, which only occurred in May 1937, although in another report the same ambassador assured his government that it was impossible to see anything suspicious in Ordzhonikidze's demise.

Sergo Ordzhonikidze was forced to shoot himself, or was simply assassinated by Stalin's agents, on 18 February 1937, less than three weeks after the execution of his deputy, Pyatakov, and other of his closest colleagues, and on the eve of the opening of the Central Committee plenum where, according to Stalin's dramatic intent, the issue of Bukharin's and Rykov's fate was to be decided and their arrest implemented. Ordzhonikidze was categorically against this and had said as much to Stalin's face.

Together with the Leader and all the Politburo[10] Vyshinsky deeply mourned the death of the outstanding revolutionary and friend of great Stalin. At the same time he began preparing for Stalin materials against yet another close friend who had already been selected for sacrifice: now that Ordzhonikidze was out of the way, Stalin assumed he would not have much trouble dealing with the remaining opponents to Bukharin's murder. Vyshinsky had brilliantly carried out Stalin's main instructions by achieving the January trial's far-reaching ulterior objective to pave the way for accusing Bukharin and Rykov of being involved in a conspiracy. This is why Pyatakov's trial delighted the Leader so much, as was reflected in the decorations which were then showered on all who had been 'privy' to it. Vyshinsky was awarded an Order of Lenin by a separate decree. Orders of Lenin also went to the judges who had signed the death sentences of Zinoviev, Kamenev, and Pyatakov – Ulrikh, Matulevich, Nikitchenko, Rychkov, and Vyshinsky's closest associate from the Procurator's office, Grigory Roginsky; the 'civilians' Lev Sheinin and another investigator on especially important cases, Mark Raginsky, were awarded the 'Labour Red Banner', and the military judges Goryachev, Dmitriev, Zaryanov, Kozlovsky and Orlov, who day and night had indefatigably tried enemies of the people from the 'despicable Pyatakov band of traitors and double dealers', received the 'Red Star'. The Order of the 'Sign of Honour', recently introduced and the most modest of them all, but nevertheless an order (and in those days they were given out in a fairly sparing manner), was awarded to all three counsels for the defence – an unheard-of event, without predecent and never to be repeated. Thus, the lawyers were rewarded for their splendid show of support for the Prosecutor.[11]

The orders were awarded in the Kremlin by 'grandfather' Kalinin. The speech of thanks was made by Ulrikh, and not Vyshinsky, who stood by modestly: he could thank Comrade Stalin personally, not just Kalinin, whose wife would soon be sent to prison and a labour camp. Ulrikh gave his word 'to continue the merciless struggle against the enemies of the people: Trotskyite-Bukharinites [although there were still seven months to go to the Bukharin trial], Japanese-German spies, wreckers, saboteurs, terrorists'. All the country's top lawyers gathered at a meeting to mark this occasion in the Red Hall of the Supreme Court of the USSR. Indefatigable Ulrikh again promised to 'punish mercilessly the brutal enemies of the people ... Trotskyite-Bukharinite traitors'. Vyshinsky noted 'the great mission of Soviet justice', the head of which, it appeared, was not the Chairman of the Supreme Court but the Chairman of its Military Board. Ulrikh returned the compliment by hailing Vyshinsky as the 'people's punitive sword'. This solemn occasion took up these two busy people's valuable time which they could have spent dispatching several more enemies to their deaths.

There was by now a long queue of people waiting to be sentenced and executed. The conveyor worked non-stop. Of course, Vyshinsky could not have taken part in the investigations of all such cases as their numbers ran into hundreds of thousands. But let us put it like this: there is no doubt he had a hand in all the cases of state importance. Once again I repeat: the claim that Vyshinsky merely 'presented' other people's work in public, that it was actually anonymous NKVD operatives who took care of falsifying cases while all he did was make speeches, courageously taking on the henchmen's crimes without having anything really to do with them, that his role consisted merely of making speeches at the open trials – this claim has been totally disproved by documents. Perhaps the most graphic evidence of this is to be found in the documents showing exactly how the case of Marshal Tukhachevsky and the seven other top military commanders was organized and conducted.

The details of this case and the tragic fate of Tukhachevsky and his seven comrades are well known. It has often been described how Hitler and his circle conceived the idea of depriving the Red Army of its leaders, how a fake document concerning the treason of the Marshal and the army commanders was fabricated and leaked to Stalin through President Beneš of Czechoslovakia and how the suspicious Father of Peoples swallowed this bait. But only recently has it become known from archive documents that it was Vyshinsky who personally falsified the legal materials in this anything but public case, which the Procurator-General did not officially take part in.

No other trial had been got ready in such haste. For some reason or other Stalin was in an incredible hurry to liquidate the military commanders; it did not satisfy him that they were in the hands of the NKVD and no longer presented any danger. Was he really afraid of them even after they had been incarcerated in Lefortovo Prison?

Only two of the eight – Corps Commander Vitaly Primakov, the ex-Commander of the Red Cossacks, and Corps Commander Vitovt Putna, the ex-Military and Air Attaché in London – had been in prison for a few months; the remaining six were arrested in the middle and some even at the very end of May 1937 (including Iona Yakir, who three months before had vehemently demanded the death sentence for Bukharin and Rykov – they were to outlive him by nearly a year). The so-called court martial took place as early as 11 June and the convicted men were executed the very next day. It had been Stalin's arbitrary decision to link these unfortunate victims together in a common case, and the group of 'conspirators' could just as well have consisted of others. The 'investigation' took two or, at most, three weeks. During this time a whole gang of Lubyanka thugs succeeded in breaking down the resistance of these staunch military commanders who had looked death in the eyes numerous times before: in certain cases only a couple or perhaps four days were needed to make them lose control, fall into despair and agree to the investigation's fabrications.

On 7 June, before the investigation ended, Vyshinsky and Yezhov went to see Stalin, Molotov, Kaganovich and Voroshilov to acquaint them with the indictment that Vyshinsky had compiled himself (before the investigation had even been completed) and make the necessary corrections. The Leader's instructions were carried out the very same day, and the final text of the indictment was edited and printed. Only at this stage were the arrested military commanders formally charged, and the aim of the ensuing interrogations was to get their answers to fit the formulas Stalin had put in the indictment: they had been involved in a conspiracy of a military-Trotskyite organization operating on the instructions of the German High Command and Trotsky, and had been linked both with men who had already been executed and with others who were still to be convicted

(Bukharin, Rykov), as well as in wrecking, sabotage and terror.

Two days later, on 9 June, Vyshinsky himself conducted the interrogations of all the accused. He was accompanied by the Chief Military Procurator's assistant, Subotsky.[12] Vyshinsky immediately sent copies of the proceedings of the interrogations to Stalin and received his full approval. At 10.45 pm Stalin saw Vyshinsky again. Molotov and Yezhov were also present in his office. After Stalin had given his final approval to Vyshinsky's work, Vyshinsky signed it with much relief. The indictment now became official and less than twenty-four hours later the Leader was handing it over to *Pravda*'s editor-in-chief, Mekhlis, to be printed.

The next morning found Vyshinsky on the rostrum of a hastily convened Special Board of the Supreme Court of the USSR. The Procurator-General informed the judges of the investigation's completion, the contents of the indictment, and of Stalin's orders, namely, that the military commanders were to be tried by the Special Judicial Presence under the ever-willing Ulrikh's chairmanship and not by an ordinary court. Furthermore, the judicial board was to consist not of lawyers but of other military men, naturally, of the highest rank – two marshals and five army commanders. On this last day before the trial began the investigation was formally completed and the Lubyanka experts beat out of the accused evidence against their judges of the following day – Marshal Semion Budionny, Army Commanders Ivan Belov, Pavel Dybenko and Nikolai Kashirin. One can easily imagine the defendants' astonishment the next day when they saw these men, whom they had implicated in their 'conspiratorial group' on the judicial board and not in the dock. However, by that stage it is unlikely anything astonished them. Of the eight marshals and army commanders trying Tukhachevsky, five would soon be shot on the same indictment. Budionny refused to be taken under arrest, and managed to get through to Stalin by telephone, and the latter, chuckling, applauded his associate's bravery and magnanimously cancelled the arrest.

There are documents and eye-witness accounts (in particular, that of Military Board member Ivan Zaryanov, who acted as a secretary at the court hearing) which refute the fairly widespread claim that the trial of Tukhachevsky and his comrades never took place at all, that they were annihilated 'in the usual way', and that the reporting of the trial was then fabricated. No, when there was a need to, Stalin endeavoured to furnish the annihilation of his imaginary enemies with all the necessary procedures, involving (or, rather, incriminating) as many people as possible in the crime they had concocted. Here, too, Vyshinsky was irreplaceable – with his servile devotion, his ability to grasp instantly any of Stalin's designs and his phenomenal efficiency for carrying them out, immediately finding the ideal, legally sound and therefore even more impressive formulas for them.

On 11 June, not long before midnight, after a one-day hearing, the Special Presence pronounced judgement. During the recess Ulrikh visited Stalin, who, in the presence of Molotov, Kaganovich and Yezhov, ordered him to execute all the defendants. No doubt, on the Leader's behalf Vyshinsky had also given Ulrikh suitable instructions, but it was an exceptionally special case, and the Chairman of the Special Judicial Presence preferred to hear the instructions first-hand.

'One has to remember Comrade Stalin's instruction,' wrote Vyshinsky in the unforgettable year of 1937, 'that there are sometimes periods, moments in the life of a society and in our life in particular, when the laws prove obsolete and have to be set aside.'

These periods were long and drawn-out – the laws were 'set aside' virtually all the time. They were substituted by other laws, right at the time, but also soon to become obsolete and 'set aside', and so it went on. Vyshinsky's special talent was for making 'alterations' to the law seem like a triumph of lawfulness, and for justifying it not only on moral and political grounds (there were plenty of experts in this field besides him) but, first and foremost, on legal ones. In his usual laconic manner Stalin would toss out an idea in a few short sentences, which not everyone would grasp at once. But Vyshinsky would catch onto it instantly, and then develop, substantiate, and, finally, put it into effect. Apart from his 'closest comrades-in-arms' in the Politburo there were not many who associated with Stalin as often or as freely in those fateful days as Vyshinsky. These almost daily visits were a source of joy and delight to him: they made him feel omnipotent, and, quite frankly, he had every right to feel so.

The third, final and most sinister of all the 'Great Moscow Trials' drew nearer. There were not many who believed Stalin would dispatch Bukharin – Lenin's favourite, the 'Party's favourite', and his recent friend – to his death. It is unlikely it had dawned on anyone yet that Stalin had no friends and could not tolerate rivalry, that for this reason Bukharin had to be annihilated. One can quite safely say Stalin had no doubt that Bukharin and Rykov would be 'got ready' for the trial, that they would break down and give in, and Vyshinsky would conduct the show in a satisfactory manner. Otherwise there would have been no announcement of their 'treachery', 'service in the Gestapo', 'espionage' and 'participation in a conspiracy' directly after the February-March (1937) Central Committee Plenum at which they were both arrested. It is clear that such an announcement inevitably presupposed an open trial, especially as the other three named in Lenin's 'testament' – Zinoviev, Kamenev and Pyatakov – had already been tried publicly.

At the Plenum, Politburo candidate member Postyshev and Central Committee candidate-member Kaminsky spoke out against the arrest of Bukharin and Rykov. Stalin made a wise decision: to stop the discussion and form a special commission 'on the Bukharin and Rykov case' comprising thirty-six people under the chairmanship of Mikoyan. Twenty of the thirty-six spoke at its sitting. Yezhov, Budionny, Manuilsky, Kosarev and Yakir suggested that Bukharin and Rykov be 'tried and shot'; Postyshev, Shkiryatov, Antipov, Khrushchev, Nikolayeva, Kosior, Petrovsky and Litvinov were in favour of them being 'tried but not shot'. Stalin again displayed wisdom and succeeded in getting a consensus (to use a fashionable word). He suggested that they should neither be tried nor shot but that their case should be handed over to the NKVD. He was enthusiastically supported by Krupskaya, Ulyanova, Vareikis, Molotov and Voroshilov. This was their decision.

The resulting scenario is well known: once again the October Hall of Trade Union House; once again the team of Ulrikh and Matulevich, who, for a change, were given the assistance of Boris Ievlev; Vyshinsky; Braude and Kommodov (Kaznacheyev was not needed for the time being). The modest role of 'court commandant' was played by the head of the Internal (Lubyanka) Prison, Alexander Mironov (not to be confused with Lev Mironov, the head of the 'Economic Department' of the NKVD, a delegate to the 17th Party Congress, who had also taken part in the investigation of the Zinoviev case; by this time he was already buried in an unmarked grave with a bullet in his head). The commandant's main task was not so much to announce the start of the session as to check that the defendants were seated correctly and prevent any 'provocation' from them.

Everyone had his own role to play: Vyshinsky's main concern was to prevent the slightest suggestion of the defendants having any ideas and principles at all, of any of their actions being governed by their stand, their position on the country's present and future, or of the trial, albeit in a tragically mutilated and terrible form, reflecting an ongoing struggle in society. To brand them criminals and traitors: this was the Leader's key directive, and the Prosecutor was required to develop, substantiate, and drill it into the minds of millions of people.

Never before had the Prosecutor's vocabulary – not exactly noted for its propriety at the previous trials – been so vulgar or coarse. This foul language was not simply to compensate for the lack of evidence, its deafening drum beat was to prevent anyone from noticing that there was none, that the ends did not meet, that one piece of testimony contradicted another, that lies were being heaped upon lies, and that the 'confessions' were unbelievable, absurd, ridiculous. After all, it was only twenty years since the Revolution, and nobody had yet forgotten it. But now it appeared that the Revolution had been accomplished by Lenin and Stalin with a huge army of foreign spies and secret agents.

'Scum', 'stinking carrion', 'dung' – this is what Vyshinsky called the ex-Politburo members, Bolsheviks from the end of the last and beginning of this century, who had been through Tsarist labour camps, prisons, and exile, who had organized and led the October Revolution, and who had now been driven into the dock. Let us pick at random a few other examples of the Prosecutor's eloquent language to recreate the atmosphere of the so-called 'trial': 'a foul-smelling heap of human excrement', 'the most inveterate, the most arrant and decayed dishonest elements', 'the despicable bunch of adventurers', 'mad dogs', 'accursed vermin'. To describe Nikolai Bukharin he used Gorky's scathing description of one of his literary characters – 'a wretched cross between a fox and a pig'. Rumour has it that it was Stalin who advised Vyshinsky to use it of Bukharin. This is quite possible. But it blended perfectly with the Prosecutor's usual vocabulary; it sounded natural and quite unconstrained coming from his lips. And what an amazing choice of verbs: according to Vyshinsky, the defendants did not speak, they 'crowed', 'grunted' and 'barked'.

The defeated men were not only to be physically annihilated, they were to be insulted, humiliated and trampled. Vyshinsky created a hitherto unknown type of trial where there was not the slightest need for evidence: what evidence did you need when you were dealing with 'stinking carrion' and 'mad dogs'? Curiously, after cursing and bullying the defendants, who could not reply, and without presenting a scrap of evidence, Vyshinsky triumphantly concluded: 'the evidence is too strong and the proof too convincing.'

To be fair, one should say that abuse was first used instead of arguments in the pages of the press and not in the court-room. It was there – before the trial and in place of the trial – that the brainwashing of public opinion began in the tone suggested by the Chief Producer.

Skilled writers joined in the general chorus. What I wish to do least here is criticize from our distant perspective of today the people who were fated to be caught up in the raging elements of those days. There were many (even among the honest) who seconded the people who approved, stigmatized and criticized. The Moscow writers' letter ('We demand the spies' execution! We shall not allow the enemies of the Soviet Union to live!') was signed by Boris Pasternak, Mikhail Sholokhov and Alexei Tolstoy, and a similar letter from Leningrad was signed by Mikhail Zoshchenko, who in 1946, along with Anna Akhmatova, would become a victim of persecution. Among those demanding the death penalty on behalf of the editorial staff and authors of the journal *Znamya* were Vasily Grossman, Konstantin Paustovsky, Viktor Shklovsky and Konstantin Simonov. 'No mercy to the Trotskyite degenerates, the murderous accomplices of Fascism!' – such was the appeal signed by Andrei Platonov, Isaak Babel and Yuri Olesha. 'Something without a tail is squirming, and making one shudder in the darkness of this foul place. Now one of these creatures is turning its face round. The cold, cruel eyes look enviously out from behind the court-room barrier.' This elegant eye-witness account is by Leonid Leonov. Soon the author would become an Academician of literature. Lev Slavin, an honest and courageous writer, came up with the following definitions for the accused: 'lying blockhead', 'cynical traitor' and 'brutalized Philistine'. Among those who enthusiastically copied Vyshinsky's manner of speech, one can immediately single out the people who tried to mock and kick the accused as cruelly as possible when they were virtually dead already. 'Brutish abomination' is one of the expressions used by Lev Nikulin, a friend of Mayakovsky, a refined European, aesthete, frequenter of Parisian cafés, who wore a velvet jacket and a huge silk neckscarf and possessed a head of exceptionally fine grey hair. He also described Bukharin as a 'hypocrite', 'idiotic scoundrel', 'trembling goatee-beard', and 'squeaky tenor'. But all these are rather feeble and unimpressive. They may be humiliating, but they are not humiliating enough. Stronger words follow: 'grimaces', 'cracks open like a provincial tenor' (what a gift of language!), 'wags his tail' which 'the State Prosecutor has trapped'. In other articles on the same page of the newspaper as Nikulin's we find them referred to as 'typhus-ridden lice' and 'bloodthirsty monkeys'.

The Procurator's lexicon was thus approved and adopted by the writers' fraternity, in particular, by its most revered and authoritative representatives, who sanctioned it and made it part of everyday life. It now became customary to insult, humiliate, taunt and trample underfoot – for those in power that is, or at least those associated with it.

Fitzroy Maclean, a young British diplomat in Moscow, was among those who succeeded in getting into the trial as a foreign observer. At one point he thought he saw the flash of Stalin's profile (and even the pipe in his mouth) through the thick glass of the projector room 'above the stage'. It could not have been in this position as, fifty years ago, it was naturally at the far end of the hall, just as it is today. The then head of the Foreign Ministry's press department, Yevgeny Gnedin, also described this as something he himself had noticed; and, in charge of the foreign journalists' passes and seating arrangements, he remained in the hall almost the entire time.

This sounds hardly plausible, but then, could you call the trial and everything that went with it plausible? No, it was not plausible, but it was true: in those days everything proved possible. In one way or another Stalin not only followed the show in progress but evidently changed the *mise-en-scène* as it was being acted out. You see, at the very beginning of the trial an embarrassing incident (or, to be more precise, setback) occurred which, had it not been put right, might have cost Vyshinsky his job, and possibly even his life.

When asked if he pleaded guilty, the old Bolshevik and diplomat, Central Committee secretary under Lenin and ex-Deputy People's Commissar of Foreign Affairs, Nikolai Krestinsky, replied that he did not. According to the law, at this stage in the trial it was not customary to justify or elaborate one's plea of 'guilty' or 'not guilty'. All the explanations and commentaries came later. But in a hurry to get the most important part across, Krestinsky made a short statement: 'I do not plead guilty. I am not a Trotskyite. I have never been a member of the Rightist Trotskyite bloc, which I did not know existed. Nor have I committed any of the crimes I am being charged with, in particular, I do not plead guilty to having links with the German Intelligence Service.'

Vyshinsky could not interrupt; it was not customary for the Prosecutor to speak at this point. It was all up to Ulrikh. He clutched at a straw: 'Do you confirm your confession during the preliminary investigation?' A strange question after the statement he had just made. But Krestinsky was firm: 'Yes, during the preliminary investigation I confessed, but I was never a Trotskyite.' Ulrikh kept at it: 'I shall repeat my question: do you plead guilty?' Krestinsky, even firmer: 'Before my arrest I was a member of the All-Union Communist Party

(Bolsheviks) and I remain one now.' Everything was crashing down before the diplomats' and journalists' very eyes. According to eye-witnesses, Vyshinsky's ears went bright red, but he could not intervene. It was a disaster. Ulrikh was at his wits' end: 'Do you plead guilty to being involved in espionage and to taking part in terrorist activities?' It was no good, Krestinsky would not budge: 'I have never been a Trotskyite, and I have not participated in the "Rightist-Trotskyite bloc", and I have not committed a single crime.'

It was only at this point that Ulrikh gave up, realizing that every new question he asked simply made the knot tighter and tighter. It was now up to someone else to break it. Vyshinsky, the 'court commandant' and other 'comrades' who had been allotted five or six rows in the court-room, had at least one night at their disposal to get the 'non-conformist' into the right frame of mind. And it did the trick. The next day Krestinsky said everything he was meant to according to the scenario.

This unique incident (there had been nothing like it at any other public trial) is already widely known; it has been described at some length in practically every language in the world (although for some reason the dialogue between Ulrikh and Krestinsky is never quoted in full). It has also been widely claimed that Krestinsky was beaten so savagely that his place in the dock was taken the next morning by a double. I, for instance, received a letter from a geneticist, Professor V. P. Efroimson, who has since died, in which he cited the testimony of an old Bolshevik acquaintance of his, S. I. Berdichevskaya. Apparently, she had been in a labour camp with a woman doctor from the Lefortovo Prison who told her that 'on the evening of the trial [a doctor] was summoned to examine Krestinsky and report on whether he could be presented to the court the next day. But he was just a sack of bones who could no longer be helped in any way.'

Professor Efroimson did not reproduce the doctor's original story very accurately (which he could not, of course, be blamed for). This head doctor of Lefortovo Prison's medical unit (from December 1936 to January 1939) was Anna Anatolevna Rozenblum. When the case of henchman Boris Rodos, one of Beria's closest associates (whom Khrushchev in his speech at the 20th Party Congress called a 'person with the brains of a chicken'), was investigated and then heard in court in 1956, she was summoned as a witness. She testified that 'from the interrogation Krestinsky was brought to us in the medical unit in an unconscious state. He had been severely beaten, his entire back was one large wound, all battered and bruised. He was in the medical unit, if I remember correctly, for about three days in a very serious condition.'

From this testimony I think it is clear that she is referring to the torture which Krestinsky underwent during the investigation, when the confession was beaten out of him, and not during the trial. There were other means of forcing him to perform his role the way the dramatist had written it, by threatening him not only with death but with an agonizing one or by some other means. In those days there were great experts working in this area at the Lubyanka.[13]

As for the 'doubles theory', this story started circulating while the trial was still on, and, as we can see, lingered on. 'Many at the time considered,' recalls Anna Mikhailovna Larina, 'that substitutes were used at the trial, and that Bukharin also was not the real Bukharin. But substitutes would have been too crude and dangerous a forgery'. One is inclined to agree with her. It would have been impossible for such proceedings in a small hall where the stage was clearly visible, and where most of the spectators knew the accused very well by sight. In any case the point of the trial was to act on the safe side and not to risk failure.

How should a 'normal' prosecutor at a 'normal' trial have reacted upon hearing a defendant deny his previous testimony? There is only one answer; he should have thoroughly checked out this statement which was of such importance. But what did Vyshinsky do? He did not even wish to cross-examine Krestinsky. The shorthand report of 'defendant Krestinsky's cross-examination' is five pages long, but contains no such thing. Instead, it is the cross-examination of defendant Rakovsky, who was forced to play the role of second prosecutor, and so incriminate his close comrade. Whenever Krestinsky tried to get a word in, Vyshinsky and Ulrikh rudely interrupted him.

'Your turn is still to come, accused Krestinsky', the impartial judge menacingly promised him. And, sure enough, it was; Vyshinsky called Krestinsky's conduct at the beginning of the trial a 'Trotskyite provocation'. And after being worked over during the night, Krestinsky made his historic statement with which his 'cross-examination' begins and ends:

Yesterday, momentarily overcome by an acute feeling of false shame induced by the conditions in the dock and the oppressive impression made by the pronouncement of the indictment, and aggravated by my poor state of health, I could not bring myself to tell the truth, I could not bring myself to say I was guilty. And instead of saying, yes, I am guilty, I almost without thinking replied, no, I am not guilty.... I could not bring myself, in the face of world public opinion, to admit that I was conducting a Trotskyite struggle all the time. I ask the court to record my statement that I plead totally and utterly guilty to all the most serious charges brought against me personally, and I accept full responsibility for my high treason and treachery.

To avoid any misunderstanding Prosecutor Vyshinsky immediately summed up: 'I have no further questions to put to accused Krestinsky for the time being.'

As we can see, Vyshinsky did not have the slightest desire, even for appearances' sake, to verify anything in Krestinsky's statement. Curiously enough, two years later when his turn came too, Yezhov was to make the following accusation against Vyshinsky during the investigation into his case:

The Procurator's office of the USSR could not, of course, help noticing [the lawlessness and falsifications]. I consider that the conduct of the Procurator's office of the USSR and, in particular, of Procurator-General of the USSR Vyshinsky to be the result of his fear of antagonizing the NKVD and of showing them to be insufficiently 'revolutionary' in carrying out the repressions. Only thus can I explain the lack of supervision in these matters by the Procurator's office and the lack of protests about the NKVD's actions to the Government.

No, it was not the NKVD Vyshinsky was afraid of antagonizing, it was Stalin: Vyshinsky was in no doubt as to whose orders he was carrying out and for whom he was working. And – it is difficult not to arrive at this conclusion – Vyshinsky behaved in this way both because he was afraid and slavishly obsequious and because as an ex-Menshevik he delighted in legally and publicly annihilating Bolsheviks who had boasted so much about their principles and yet turned out to be just as weak and vulnerable as all the rest.

All the rest? Vyshinsky had one other difficult 'client' at this trial: Boris Kamkov, a leading Left SR activist, who was summoned to the trial from prison to confirm that in 1918 Bukharin and he had together organized a conspiracy to assassinate Lenin, oust the Soviet regime and set up their own government. Kamkov had previously had considerable experience of 'dealing' with the Tsarist police, and they had never managed to break him, nor did Vyshinsky. Kamkov courageously argued with him as though they were on equal terms, heedless of the consequences. Two very short replies give one an idea of the tone of their exchange.

Kamkov: Either I do not understand you, or we are speaking of different things.
Vyshinsky: I understand you very well.
Kamkov: But I do not understand you at all.[14]

Bukharin stood his ground just as boldly. He used the court's witness box to send a lightly coded but easily readable message to his contemporaries and descendants. This message was decoded long ago, and then examined with the greatest thoroughness by American historian Stephen F. Cohen. We shall merely note that Bukharin certainly did not react to Vyshinsky's rudeness by keeping humbly silent. With characteristic dignity and as an individual, not a dumb creature, he did not let a single of the high and mighty Prosecutor's taunts or brutal attacks pass unnoticed. Just look at this, for instance, during Kamkov's cross-examination:

Bukharin (to Kamkov): Now I wanted to ask....
Vyshinsky (to Kamkov): Who were then members of the Left Social Revolutionaries' Central Committee?
Bukharin: I have not finished my question, Citizen Prosecutor.
Vyshinsky: But I am asking a question of my own.
Bukharin: I stopped in mid-sentence.
Vyshinsky: You asked one question and received a reply.

Here are two other excerpts from exchanges between Vyshinsky and Bukharin during defendant Ivanov's[15] cross-examination: they, too, give one a fair idea of the atmosphere of the trial and the manner in which doomed Bukharin chose to conduct himself, as well as of how muddled the hastily compiled and poorly coordinated case materials were.

Vyshinsky: During the preliminary investigation you said that this [organization of mythical 'insurrectionary detachments'] dates back to 1926.
Bukharin: Yes, but not in the sense that this is understood here, Citizen State Prosecutor.
Vyshinsky (addressing the court): Allow me to turn to Volume 5, Page 113. Allow me to read it out.
Bukharin: Excuse me, which page?

Vyshinsky: Page 113, Volume 5, Bukharin's testimony. This is your testimony of 25 December 1937 ...

Bukharin: On Page 113 there's something different.

Vyshinsky: Is this your signature?

Bukharin: The signature is mine, but I have a volume of the case in which the numbering is quite different.

Ulrikh: Accused Bukharin, it is not the numbering that matters here.

This excerpt is also worth noting because it reveals the way one of the numerous falsifications worked. The copies of the 'case materials' handed out to the accused did not tally with the ones that lay in front of the judges and Prosecutor. Vyshinsky personally conducted the cross-examinations during the investigation and in court, but even with his phenomenal memory he was unable to remember all the manipulations. I shall cite just one excerpt to illustrate this:

> *Bukharin:* As far as foul play is concerned, I ask you to pass judgement on me, and I shall bear responsibility in both instances [for the strategy and the tactics of the 'insurrectionary orientation'].
>
> *Vyshinsky:* We shall pass judgement on you without you petitioning us to. ['We' is an interesting slip of the tongue: he had forgotten who were the judges and who was the Prosecutor.]
>
> *Bukharin:* Quite correct, without me petitioning to. I do not consider this a particularly suitable time or place for making jokes. I am good at making jokes too.
>
> *Vyshinsky:* I have no intention of joking or contending with you in this instance. I only wish to say that your petitioning is not of substantial significance for you are going to be tried regardless of your petitioning.
>
> *Bukharin:* This I realize even without competent explanations, Citizen Prosecutor.

All the defendants had very thick dossiers containing excerpts from the case materials. But was that really all they contained? There is every reason to suppose that they were also given written texts that each was meant to learn by heart and expound with maximum spontaneity. Bukharin, however, learned none of it and only said what he saw fit, while one of the Prosecutor's most conscientious pupils, Vasily Sharangovich, until only recently First Secretary of the Central Committee of Byelorussia (who even dared improvise once by rudely interrupting Bukharin with an insulting remark), simply dashed off his previously prepared and approved text, helped along by Vyshinsky and Ulrikh. The exchange between them has been examined more than once before, and we shall look at it here as well. It is a truly glaring example of 'play-reading round a table', to use a theatrical comparison.

Vyshinsky: Let us briefly sum up what you plead guilty to in the present case.
Sharangovich: Firstly, to being a traitor of the Motherland.
Vyshinsky: An old Polish spy.
Sharangovich: Secondly, to being a conspirator. Thirdly, to being directly involved in wrecking.
Vyshinsky: No, thirdly, to being one of the main leaders of the National Fascist Group in Byelorussia and one of the active participants in the 'Rightist Trotskyite Anti-Soviet Bloc'.
Sharangovich: Correct. Then to being personally involved in wrecking.
Vyshinsky: Acts of sabotage.
Sharangovich: Correct.
Ulrikh: To being the organizer of terrorist acts against the leaders of the Party and Government.
Sharangovich: That is right.
Ulrikh: And all this was done with a view to. . . .
Sharangovich: And all this was done with a view to overthrowing the Soviet regime, with a view to Fascism triumphing, with a view to defeating the Soviet Union in the event of war against the Fascist states.
Ulrikh: Directed at the division of the USSR, the separation of Byelorussia, its transformation . . .
Sharangovich: Its transformation into a capitalist state under the yoke of Polish landowners and capitalists.

The performer, as we can see, did not even wish to use normal everyday language which would not have given the game away so obviously. No, he read it out just as it had been written: 'under the yoke', 'with a view to Fascism triumphing'.

Fitzroy Maclean describes Vyshinsky thus:

Neatly dressed in a stiff white collar, checked tie and well-cut blue suit, his trim grey moustache and hair set off against his rubicund complexion, he looked for all the world like a prosperous stockbroker accustomed to lunch at Simpson's and play golf at Sunningdale every weekend. 'A rather decent chap'.

The trial was rough-going, and like a prosperous stockbroker, Vyshinsky had to work hard, and not just look good and make fine speeches. Only ex-diplomat Sergei Bessonov answered his questions exactly as he was supposed to; it was with this accused that Vyshinsky began his cross-examination in order to establish the guilt of the others with the help of his evidence. But these 'others', even Trotsky's old associate Rakovsky, whom the Prosecutor used against Krestinsky, tried to resist, either by denying the charge of espionage or terror or an organized conspiracy.

The name of Khristian Rakovsky, who was born in Kotel, Bulgaria, was to go down in the annals of the Russian, Ukrainian, Bulgarian and Rumanian revolutionary movements. In France he was known as one of the most ardent and indefatigable defenders of Alfred Dreyfus, the officer slanderously charged with treason. The son of a rich land-owner, he donated all his inheritance to Party funds, financing the Rumanian Social Democratic Party and its newspaper, whose editor he became. A significant part of his money went to help Russia's revolutionaries who were being persecuted by the Tsarist regime, including the sailors of the battleship *Potemkin*, whose rescue he organized in the Rumanian port of Constanta. He attempted to explain this at the trial, but Vyshinsky did not let him say a word. With his derisive questions he merely got Rakovsky to confess to having money, and, consequently, to having an 'enemy background' and 'noxious bourgeois ethics'.[16]

A new feature of this third trial was the presence in the dock of three famous doctors sitting alongside the well-known politicians and top-ranking NKVD operatives. This was the first appearance on the political scene of the 'assassins in white coats', and, evidently, not without some prompting by Stalin, who imagined swarms of poisoners everywhere: this was his greatest 'obsession'. Yezhov appeared at the trial claiming to be the victim of a poison attack. Vyshinsky put this on a broad historical footing. Making use of his erudition, he reminded the court that:

from the time of Tacitus such incidents have come to light as the murder of Sejanus with a poison which made it appear that he had died from an ordinary illness. Herein lies the criminal art. It is well known that for poisoning purposes Philip ii widely used a poison which even a careful examination could not detect, a poison which he called 'Requiescat in pace' ['May he rest in peace']. It is well known that Pope Clement ii was killed by the smoke of a poisoned candle.

Thus, in the absence of any living witnesses to testify against Professor Pletnev and doctors Kazakov and Levin, the evidence of the ancient Roman historian Tacitus, King Philip of Spain and Pope Clement II was used instead. In this company Vyshinsky felt both more at ease and more highly esteemed.

Unlike the other accused, all three of the doctors wished to be defended at the trial. Was it their own decision? Or was it in the scenario? The oldest of the accused, Doctor Lev Levin (then sixty-eight), was represented by Ilya Braude; Professor Dmitry Pletnev (then sixty-six) and the youngest, Doctor Ignatii Kazakov (then only forty-seven), by Nikolai Kommodov.

The only episode Braude ever related to me, and which I promised earlier to recount, has to do with this case. I remember the day Vyshinsky's death was announced. Gloomy, deep in thought, Braude muttered: 'The man who knew everything.' A few weeks later, as we were returning from a trial together, he suddenly glanced round and whispered: 'Seventeen years have passed since then but I still remember the whole rehearsal.' In short, abrupt and disjointed sentences he described to me how in Vyshinsky's office they had rehearsed the 'defence's' nonsensical questions to the medical experts who were supposed to confirm the prosecution's fabricated charge at the public trial.[17] After rehearsing a question and defining more precisely exactly when it was meant to be posed, Vyshinsky had warned sternly: 'At this moment look at me.' 'Why?' I asked Braude, puzzled. 'He had hypnotic powers. Looking into his eyes, I would start cringing like a rabbit before a snake.' Corpulent and breathing heavily, Braude then cringed in such a way that I felt, almost physically, the magic force of the all-powerful Prosecutor's stare.

Only Kommodov's client, Pletnev, was shown any pity and given twenty-five years; he would serve them with Bessonov and Rakovsky and perish with them on the same day. From prison he would write to Vyshinsky, supposing the latter still to be Procurator-General: 'When I did not concede, the investigator said: "If the leaders decide you are guilty, then even if you are a hundred per cent innocent, you will still ... be guilty".' He wrote to Marshal Voroshilov:

Appalling invectives, threats of execution were used against me; I was dragged about by the scruff of the neck, throttled, and tortured with lack of sleep – for five weeks I slept 2–3 hours a day; they threatened to rip my throat out along with my confession, to beat me with a rubber rod ... after all this I ended up with half my body paralysed. . . . I am becoming numb from the lies and severe cold I am surrounded by, among the pygmies and worms who are conducting their subversive work. Show me that it is just as possible to get at the truth here in the Soviet Union as it is in other civilized countries. The truth will out.

But Pletnev received no reply to either of these appeals or to his letters to Beria. Let us, however, thank the bureaucrats and pedants of Beria's and Vyshinsky's organizations for saving for us these genuine, poignant testimonies.

The rehearsal Braude told me about is indirect confirmation of a story quite widely circulated in recent years, claiming that the accused in this case, the hardest and most important for Stalin, were led out onto the stage of the overcrowded October Hall four times and each time they denied the evidence they had given during the preliminary investigation, thinking that the real trial was in progress. Each time the spectators then started laughing and the investigators got up from their seats and set about the beatings all over again: in this manner Yezhov and Vyshinsky decided to break the accused once and for all and deprive them of any hope of a favourable outcome.

Such events are not totally impossible. With Stalin's advice or, at least, agreement Vyshinsky could do whatever he pleased. And the authenticity of other seemingly implausible claims has been corroborated directly as well as indirectly. For instance, it was rumoured that not all the accused were executed directly after the trial and that some of those whose assistance Yezhov, Vyshinsky, and later Beria could count on were left alive to exert influence on new victims. By staying alive and in relatively good shape they proved that the investigators had actually kept their word when they had promised that, if they behaved well, their own lives would be saved. This claim is not repeated so often these days, but I have found at least one corroboration for it.

In 1956 the ex-head of Lefortovo Prison, Zimin, was questioned in connection with the Rodos case. Here is a brief excerpt from his blood-curdling testimonies:

Every night Beria used to drive over to the prison and beat the prisoners. I remember Marshal Blyukher being brought over for an interrogation. He was interrogated by Beria, Merkulov [his assistant] and Kobulov [the head of the Special Investigation Board of the NKVD]. I was near the office, as I was supposed to be. They hand-

118

cuffed Blyukher and started beating him. Blyukher shouted out: 'Stalin, can you hear what they are doing to me?' His eye was seriously injured. He was taken off to the Internal Prison [at the Lubyanka] and Doctor Rozenblum was summoned there.[18] I was aware that some of the prisoners were tortured by the investigators before their executions. Yagoda, though, was sentenced to death at an open trial, but for a year and a half afterwards he was held in cell 102 of Lefortovo Prison. What happened to him after my arrest, I have no idea.

This very important testimony needs checking out, if only because Zimin was arrested less than one and a half years after Yagoda was sentenced to be shot. Of course, he could have got the dates muddled, especially after nearly twenty years and all he had suffered in the camps. But whatever the case, the testimony is still interesting because it indicates how many mysteries still remain unsolved and what discoveries lie in store for us.

I am not very inclined to believe the claim regarding the trial's rehearsals in the October Hall. Hundreds of people would have had to take part in such rehearsals, and it is unlikely they could have carried it out without taking a considerable risk. There was not one hint of rehearsals until years afterwards. And, then, was there any need for them? If we read just the end of the final word of Arkady Rozengolts, the ex-People's Commissar of Foreign Trade, we shall understand what the accused were already prepared to do without any elaborate rehearsals. Here is what Rozengolts said the day after Vyshinsky had demanded the death sentence for him:

> I say: long live, prosper and grow stronger the great, mighty and splendid Union of Soviet Socialist Republics going from one victory to the next, over which the splendid sun of Socialism is shining!
> Long live the Bolshevik Party with the best traditions of enthusiasm, heroism, and self-sacrifice in the world, under the leadership of Stalin! In the inevitable clash between the two worlds Communism will vanquish. Long live Communism the world over!

Perhaps Rozengolts resorted to this macabre pathos, thinking he was taking part in a rehearsal?[19]

On the evening of 9 March the court sat behind closed doors in an empty hall. Yagoda is supposed to have confessed to plotting the murder of Gorky's son, Maxim – and to actually carrying it out – for personal as well as political motives. But why 'supposed to'? He confessed to whatever Vyshinsky demanded of him. Especially, as was common knowledge, in his young days Yagoda had been in love with the cultured and charming Nadezhda Alexeyevna, Maxim's wife (whose pet name was 'Timosha'), and had tried to win her love.[20] 'All Moscow' had known about this for quite some time. Rumour had it that he was 'prepared to do anything' out of love for this delightful woman. Vyshinsky made use of this universally known fact by giving it a sinister criminal twist. Insinuations in the newspaper reports on this subject supposedly gave authenticity to the other charges brought not only against Yagoda but all the rest as well.

Vyshinsky spent the entire next day getting ready for his speech. Strictly speaking, it had already been written and simply needed Stalin's approval. Tested and well-known, its outline remained the same. And it also ended with some familiar turns of phrase: 'All our country, both young and old, is waiting for and demanding that the traitors and spies who sold our country to the enemy be shot like mad dogs! Our people demand that the accursed vermin be stamped out!'

Stalin approved the text: the 'mad dogs' and 'accursed vermin' he enjoyed especially. This was the Stalin approach. But, even so, it sounded rather pessimistic. It did not end on an optimistic note. It was not forward-looking. And so after the 'dogs' and 'vermin' Vyshinsky added on another ending:

> Time will pass. The hateful traitors' graves will become overgrown with tall weeds and thistles, covered with the eternal scorn of Soviet people, of the entire Soviet nation. While over us, over our happy country, the bright rays of our sun will continue to shine just as radiantly and joyously as ever. We, our people, shall continue marching along the road, cleared of the last filth and abomination, with our beloved Leader and Teacher, Great Stalin, ahead of us, on and on towards Communism!

To be fair, Vyshinsky did not usually resort to such a rollicking flowery style. However, he declaimed the sacred text in a conscientious manner.

At dawn on 13 March Ulrikh read out the sentence: eighteen of the twenty-one accused were to be executed. The following day they were shot.

Stalin rewarded Vyshinsky most lavishly: he ordered him to identify the executed men's corpses and sign the necessary papers. Besides the sadistic pleasure he derived from giving his lackey this humiliating task and making him admire his own handiwork, he had another ulterior motive in mind, to bind all the people involved in the trial together as tightly as possible and, if needs be, use this against the traitor when the opportunity presented itself. However, there was no longer any way Vyshinsky could become an apostate, he could only plunge into the abyss along with Stalin himself.

He had tremendous difficulty identifying Bukharin. Tortured physically and mentally, Bukharin, the Party's favourite, an intelligent and vivacious man, had changed almost beyond recognition. Vyshinsky was extremely worried he might make a mistake. If he did, who knows what might happen and whether anyone would be able to identify him either? In the end, however, he was satisfied with his decision and signed the document which was then sent off to Stalin. 'The Soviet people approved the sentencing of these monsters and got on with the next tasks to hand,' Stalin was to write in his *Short Course* when informed of the carrying out of the executions.

The news of the latest executions in Moscow was broadcast worldwide. The names of Bukharin and Rykov were well-known everywhere. But just as after the Pyatakov-Radek trial, the news of the Moscow tragedy was eclipsed by sensations of a far greater scale to the West than another blood-letting in the Lubyanka's dungeons: the day before Hitler had devoured Austria, and the announcement of the Anschluss was splashed across all the newspapers' front pages. Only the Trotskyist press attached any serious significance to the news report from Moscow. For the rest it was nothing but passing news. No wonder, for the Communists' annihilation and discord in the Soviet leadership was to the West's advantage. Exactly what the destruction of 'alternative socialism' and the affirmation – through thousands of corpses – of Stalin's brand of 'socialism' would mean for humanity was something that not many thought about in those days.

Here is one more excerpt from Fitzroy Maclean's memoirs:

> On the day the trial opened 'the court-room' ... was full of noise and chattering, like a theatre before the curtain goes up. People were laughing and talking, looking for their seats and waving to friends.... For, like all true drama, the performance on which the curtain was about to go up had the power of affecting the audience personally and directly; the characters in it were familiar to them, were men in whose place they could, without any great stretch of imagination, imagine themselves. And so they had come not only

to be excited and edified, but to be horrified, and perhaps even terrified, by a spectacle which would partake at once both of the medieval morality play and of the modern gangster film.

These laughing people who had come to be entertained filled the court-room not only on the first day of the trial but on all the other days as well; passes were given out to the most trustworthy members of the Central Committee, city and regional committees of the Party. As always, there were numerous writers and other celebrities – Alexei Tolstoy again, Ilya Ehrenburg, Mikhail Koltsov, the illustrious actor Ivan Moskvin, and the celebrated pilot Valery Chkalov.[21] But it was not for them that the rubicund Prosecutor with the neatly trimmed grey moustache tried so hard. Nor was it only for the People's Leader. It was for the whole world! You see, the Prosecutor's main aim was to convince humanity of the justice of annihilating these recent Party leaders and statesmen – they could have been annihilated without a trial, in secret, without the erudition of the splendid orator in his impeccably cut blue suit.

Fitzroy Maclean was by no means the only foreign diplomat repre-senting Moscow's diplomatic community in the court-room. Sitting alongside him were the US Ambassador, Joseph Davies, and a US Embassy official by the name of Charles Bohlen, later destined to play a prominent role in American diplomacy. Fitzroy Maclean told me that Bohlen, like himself, understood full well the political and juridical purpose of the trial, and did not doubt the defendants' complete inno-cence, and both informed their own governments accordingly. Ambassador Davies was of an entirely different opinion. He tried his hardest to convince Roosevelt of the validity of the charges, of the justice and lawful nature of the trial and of Stalin's sacred right to get rid of 'traitors'.[22]

The opinions of the diplomats at the trial were divided. Some, like Baron de Uniac, a French diplomat, and Hans-Heinrich Herwarth von Bitterfeld, a German diplomat representing Hitler's government but a convinced anti-Nazi, saw through the sham mystery play that Vysh-insky had staged, while others, like the Czech Ambassador Zdenek Firlinger, informed their governments that it was all lawful and pro-ceeding as it should.

However, what mattered more to Stalin were not these foreign diplomats' ciphered reports but the foreign observers' public statements and correspondents' reports. These would have a greater effect on influential people in the West.

Regretfully, it has to be admitted that Vyshinsky carried out his mission quite superbly, accomplishing not only the task at hand but other objectives as well. The people he managed to outwit were not simpletons but seasoned politicians, lawyers, shrewd observers whose analytical and critical minds had earned them well-deserved acclaim.

On Moscow's invitation the most authoritative International Association of Lawyers sent a delegation to the Zinoviev-Kamenev trial. It comprised the highly distinguished British lawyers Denis Noel Pritt, Dudley Collard and Robert Lazarus, and the American lawyer Joseph Edelman.

This delegation's extraordinary statement, which was unanimously upheld by the International Association, deserves to be quoted, if only in part:

> We consider the claim that the proceedings were summary and unlawful to be totally unfounded. The accused were given the opportunity of taking counsels; every counsel in the Soviet Union is independent of the Government. The accused, however, preferred to be defended individually.
>
> Hardly a state exists in which people involved in terrorist acts are not given the death penalty. In many countries, including England, appeals cannot be lodged against such sentences, but as in the trial in question the accused pleaded guilty, there could be no question of an appeal.
>
> We hereby categorically declare that the accused were sentenced quite lawfully. It was fully proven that there were links between them and the Gestapo. They quite rightly deserved the death penalty.

That, it would seem, is as far as they could go. But no, they went even further; Denis Pritt saw fit to make a separate statement:

> What first struck me as a British lawyer was the defendants' completely free and unconstrained conduct. They all looked well; they all stood up and spoke when they wanted to.... I personally am convinced that there is not the slightest reason to suppose the presence of any unlawfulness in the trial's form or contents. I consider the entire trial and the manner of addressing the defendants to be an example for the whole world in a case where the defendants are charged with a conspiracy to assassinate leading statesmen and to overthrow the government, which the defendants confessed to. In my opinion, under such circumstances the court of any country would have pronounced the death sentence and carried it out. [23]

Let us say, by way of consolation, that he was not the only one: the highly renowned British historian Sir Bernard Pares, for instance, considered the 'fact of the treason' of Zinoviev, Kamenev, Pyatakov, Radek and the others to have been 'proven beyond doubt'. The Anglo-Soviet Parliamentary Committee issued its report on the trial, noting the 'charges' indisputable well-foundedness'. Its Chairman, Labour MP Neil Maklin, noted in particular that the sincerity of the defendants' confessions had impressed him. Later, in his memoirs, Churchill, when recalling the thirties, was to write about 'the ruthless but possibly not unuseful purge of the military and political apparatus in Soviet Russia' and about the trials 'at which Vyshinsky appeared with such brilliance in the role of State Prosecutor'.

The International Human Rights League also declared the trials lawful. Its representative, a lawyer by the name of Rozenmark, gave the simplest explanation for doing so: 'We all look for a mistake only when the accused denies his guilt, when he shouts out his innocence to all and sundry. If Captain Dreyfus had pleaded guilty, there would have been no Dreyfus Case.'

Shrewd Vyshinsky was not mistaken in staking everything on the confession. Notwithstanding all the disavowals, harsh criticisms, and statements to the effect that a confession was worthless without other incontrovertible, objective evidence, only a confession left an impression on the minds of 'ordinary citizens' and most highly qualified lawyers alike: if you had a confession, you had proof of guilt.

However, not even this is surprising; the sense of justice of a normal lawyer living in a normal country in the middle of the twentieth century cannot reconcile itself to the thought that a confession of guilt in a public court of law could be forced, and not voluntarily given. What is surprising, though, is the position of the humanists, the 'Left', the intellectuals and especially those who saw everything with their own eyes. 'There was no way the people on trial could be called distressed, desperate beings, appearing before their executioner,' Lion Feuchtwanger testified to the world:

The accused were sleek, well-dressed men with slow, unconstrained manners. They drank tea, newspapers stuck out of their pockets, and they frequently glanced at the public. It was more like a discussion than a criminal trial, the kind of discussion educated people, attempting to establish the truth, conduct in a conversational tone.... If a producer had been instructed to stage this trial, he probably would have needed quite a few rehearsals to secure such team work from the accused.... The judges, the prosecutor, the accused – and this was no illusion – were linked together by the bonds of a common goal.

Feuchtwanger's book, published in a very small edition by an unknown Dutch publisher, had no effect whatsoever in the West; the lawyers' and diplomats' statements were much more important. To make up for it, his book was immediately translated and published in the USSR with truly incredible speed; it was typeset on 23 November and sent to press the very next day. It was published in an edition of two hundred thousand copies, which was an unusually substantial print run in those days.

Ten years later, with the same almost incredible speed, a team of five translated, and then immediately published and circulated, as widely as possible, a book by two American authors, Michael Sayers and Albert E. Kahn – no match for the world-famous Feuchtwanger – entitled *The Great Conspiracy*, which reproduced the official version of Vyshinsky and his associates, down to the minutest detail. Its authors cited one of the reports Davies sent to Roosevelt: 'Prosecutor Vyshinsky is very like Homer Cummings [the US Attorney General 1933–39], just as calm, impartial, sober-minded and wise.' 'As a lawyer,' Davies added, 'I am deeply satisfied and delighted by the manner in which he conducted this case.'

Directly or indirectly all the Left supported Stalin: Romain Rolland, André Malraux, Bernard Shaw and Jean Genet. Even André Gide, who had written in his *Return from the USSR*: 'In my opinion, in no country today, not even in Hitler's Germany, is the spirit more suppressed, more timid, more servile than in the Soviet Union' – even he did not say a word about the 'judicial' terror, the mass arrests, and reprisals against the innocent. The other powerful members of the Left simply kept silent and agonized over how to explain the inexplicable.

'The confession of the accused is a medieval legal principle', declared Bukharin in his final word, addressing the Prosecutor. Vyshinsky looked away. According to Fitzroy Maclean, Vyshinsky blushed to the tips of his ears. In general, he blushed easily and quite often. But one thing is certain: he was not blushing with shame but with excitement. And because he was wondering whether this very transparent insinuation would be understood by anyone in the court-room.

It was by some, of course. But this was of no consequence. Once again he had triumphed.

5

Lust for power and fear for his own safety were combined in Vyshinsky with insatiable vanity. At every stage of his rise up the state ladder, both early on when he was desperately struggling for a modest position to earn his daily bread, and later when he had already begun to control people's lives and destinies, he longed for an academic career and the honours of a top theorist; to be introduced to the company of 'immortals' venerated for their intellectual rather than for their official position.

After the Revolution jurisprudence suffered a loss of face in academic circles. Its 'dogmas' or fundamental supporting structures, without which no legal theory can be built, were lying in ruins. Its continuity had been destroyed along with the former state machine and judicial system. New shoots started forcing their way through the ruins: not yet a complete system but the elements of 'revolutionary law', which disclaimed all previous postulates and asserted the primacy of the 'proletarian sense of justice' before the law. The laws themselves had lost all their basic principles and were transformed into a set of random instructions dependent on the topic of the day, itself in constant flux.

In these conditions a new legal theory developed, literally from nothing, called upon to substantiate academically the confused practice of the law and give it a well-formed appearance, to systematize and regulate the chaos, by showing it to have regular laws and an objective necessity of its own. The intention was to create a theory of socialist law which had never existed before.

The indisputable leader of these lawyers of the new mould was Yevgeny Bronislavovich Pashukanis. Born of a Polish family who had settled many years ago in the ancient region of Tver, he had received his law degree under the Tsar but had failed to get anywhere in his profession until he was swept up by a revolutionary wave. At the age of twenty-seven, a year after taking part in the October armed insurrection in Moscow, he joined the Bolshevik Party and was immediately appointed a member of the Court of Appeal attached to the All-Russian Central Executive Committee. He was then sent south where, as a member of the Executive Committee of the Don region, he propagated revolutionary legality. Upon his return to Moscow he was elected as a deputy to the Moscow Soviet, and it was then that his career took off as a theorist trying desperately to create an integral concept of the law within a state which was not under the rule of law.

Pashukanis's theoretical works were noted for their revolutionary phraseology and for their revolutionary fervour. To the scholastic arguments on whether the law would die away under socialism or, on the contrary, grow stronger, he succeeded in adding lustre and even a sort of academic soundess. The ultra-left deviations, typical of any branch of the social sciences in those days, seem primitive now, but they reflect, with a fair degree of accuracy, the level and direction of legal thought at the time.

Pashukanis was undoubtedly also an outstanding organizer: he had headed the Communist Academy's Scientific Research Institute of Soviet Construction and Law, the Institute of Law of the Academy of Sciences, and, more recently, had spared no effort in the post of Deputy People's Commissar of Justice, having undertaken to elaborate the laws destined to become Stalin's Constitution. On this Constitution, which immediately became known as 'Stalin's Constitution', he worked exceedingly hard alongside Bukharin, Radek and others, endeavouring to give the formulations legal precision, especially the tenth chapter on rights and liberties which was later to be eulogized in poems and songs. 'No other country do I know where man breathes so freely,' the country began singing just at the time when the draft of the Constitution was published.

Simultaneously, he was directing the work on the country's new criminal code which was never to be published: the codes remained a prerogative of the constituent Republics. He did, however, manage to implement one of his main ideas: on his insistence the death penalty was totally excluded (as a form of punishment) from the draft drawn up by the working committee. In his opinion socialist law, the most humane and most democratic in the entire history of mankind, was incompatible with 'legalized murder in the name of the state', regardless of its motivations.

When, in the autumn of 1936, the vacancies for new full members of the Academy of Sciences were announced, Pashukanis was instantly nominated for the only place offered to lawyers. Strictly speaking, it was for him this vacancy had been intended. Articles appeared in the press vigorously supporting his election. A particularly enthusiastic article was written by Nikolai Vasilievich Krylenko, the People's Commissar of Justice, his immediate superior. He was among those who officially nominated him as a candidate to join the 'immortals'.

The election was set for December 1936, immediately after the 8th All-Union Congress of Soviets, which was to approve the Constitution, whose anonymous authorship had been re-attributed to the People's Leader.

Pashukanis was a delegate to this congress, as was Krylenko, and so they both had every reason to feel quite self-assured. They both enthusiastically applauded delegate Vyshinsky, who proclaimed from the rostrum that Comrade Stalin's report was 'a song of victory', 'a joyous hymn to triumphant Socialism'. 'On all the Constitution,' exclaimed the speaker, 'on its every article, on its every word lies the stamp of Stalin's genius, the inspiration and creator of the New Socialist Constitution.' As the auditorium applauded wildly, he turned to matters particularly close to his heart:

> To all the enemy's vile attempts and sorties against the most dearly loved leaders of the Soviet State and Soviet people, the Soviet court has responded, and will continue to respond, by mercilessly crushing the gangs of bandits, applying to them, to these vile criminals, all the force and fullness of Soviet law, punishing by death the henchmen of the working masses' happiness and freedom.

Krylenko was also given a chance to speak from the rostrum. 'The greatest continuer of Lenin's cause,' he exclaimed in the same impassioned tone as the Procurator-General and the other speakers,

> our very own, dearly beloved Stalin enables us to really be aware of, feel well and truly savour ... the fruits of the victories and labours.... It is a joy and wonder to create, it is a joy and wonder to feel oneself a member of our multi-million socialist collective and under the leadership of our Stalin – the greatest organizer of happiness and victories, of the victories and happiness of all humanity the world over – to go further, ever onward and onward, along the path towards Communism.

There is no doubt it was also a joyful and wonderful time for Yevgeny Pashukanis; his works were crowned with success and he was later to attain even greater heights. Of course, he did not lay claim to any laurels as one of the dozens of co-authors of the Constitution (could the People's Leader have a co-author?), but its triumphal acceptance meant his contribution to the general cause had been approved, and this further strengthened his chances of being promoted to the Academy.

The meeting of the Academy of Sciences took place as planned. Both the nominee and his chief patron, Krylenko, received guest tickets. With natural excitement but without particular anxiety they awaited the outcome which seemed a foregone conclusion. However, at this meeting the Academy not only failed to acquire new members but, on the contrary, lost some old ones. Pronouncing an anathema on the world-famous chemists Vladimir Ipatiev and Alexei Chichibabin, who had refused to return from an official trip abroad, the Academy expelled them from its ranks. There were six abstentions, remarkable in December 1936; the names of those who had courageously abstained were never disclosed. The meeting was then supposed to move on to the election of new members, but the Academy's newly elected President, Vladimir Komarov, unexpectedly announced, without explanation, that the election was to be postponed indefinitely.

One may assume that Yevgeny Pashukanis's nomination was, if not the sole, then the main reason for this postponement. Pashukanis was 'taken' in his Deputy Commissar's office on 4 January 1937, the reward for his loyal and conscientious labour.

The vehicle taking him to the Lubyanka made a detour and specially drove down Gorky Street past house No 33 – the home of the Academician nominee and Deputy Commissar who in a matter of seconds had become an ordinary prisoner and enemy of the working people. Was it a joke? A psychological experiment? Did Pashukanis see his escorts' colleagues hurling his archive into the back of a lorry – manuscripts, books, correspondence with eminent statesmen, academics and writers – documents of great historical value which would later prove untraceable?

As Pashukanis had dealt in his work with nearly all the most prominent officials of the NKVD, the investigation into his case was entrusted to objective and unbiased outsiders – Borisov and Bruk, important NKVD officials from the fraternal republic of the Ukraine. Their work was quite up to that of their Russian colleagues; a few days later Pashukanis confessed to having worked as a terrorist from 1933 – this date was invented by the investigation – to having been recruited by Milyutin,[1] and to being a member of the Bukharin-Rykov-Tomsky-Uglanov group. The wording of his indictment was particularly striking: 'engaged in counter-revolutionary activity in the sphere of the theory of Soviet criminal law'.

Evidently, Pashukanis was not hard to break. The investigation went smoothly and without a hitch. Realizing full well it was pointless struggling, the doomed head of the Soviet judiciary gave in without a fight. Shortly afterwards Captain of State Security Kogan and Lieutenant of State Security Makarov drew up an indictment in which they did not bother to concoct a very far-fetched charge, as there was no need to. Prosecutors from Vyshinsky's closest circle – Roginsky and Gatov – approved this indictment and, exactly eight months after his arrest, on 4 September 1937, Pashukanis appeared before the Military Board of the Supreme Court. Ulrikh scrutinized him impassively, as if he had not the faintest idea who the accused was. He had actually sat dozens, if not hundreds, of times with him at the same table at meetings and sittings, in presidiums and conference halls, applauding along with the rest when this 'enemy of the people' was invited to speak.

He was invited to speak here, too, but he declined to do so and merely waved his hand limply.

Nikolai Vasilievich Krylenko was not present; it was forbidden for anyone, even the People's Commissar of Justice of the USSR, to take part in the Military Board's secret sessions. However, he was here in spirit for, while the accused was awaiting his fate, Krylenko was frantically trying to avoid his, by the annihilation of his recent idol: Pashukanis.

But here, too, he was forestalled. On 20 January in *Pravda* the philosopher Pavel Yudin, a great expert on the theory of Communism, endowed with the privilege of initiating the dutiful to Marxism as well as excommunicating the profane, exposed both the 'masked traitor and double-dealer' Pashukanis, who had 'caused harm on the theoretical front', and those of his colleagues who had also been targeted. One citation from Yudin's article is enough to give us an idea of the style of the exposé: 'The judicial cretinism [of the defendants] reaches ... Herculean proportions.'

Krylenko's only chance was to voice his support of Vyshinsky as swiftly as possible; Vyshinsky had called the country's top theorist not only an 'enemy' but also a 'blockhead'. Krylenko did this at an open Party *aktiv* of the People's Commissariat of Justice, making a speech of such repentance that his sense of doom was made clear to everyone present. He was compelled to act in this way through an understandable sense of self-preservation and in response to the bold appeal of one of the speakers. In his speech at the *aktiv* Fedor Nakhimson, the Vice-Chairman of the Board on Criminal Affairs of the Supreme Soviet of the USSR, had turned to Krylenko (editor of *Soviet Justice*, the journal on which Nakhimson was deputy-editor), courageously looked him straight in the eye, and said: 'Many had hoped that the fight against wrecking in the legal system would be headed by Comrade Krylenko, but in order to carry out this task he will have to reveal a number of his own mistakes and put an end to them.'

Possibly, Krylenko had not been expecting a blow from Nakhimson, who had worked hard with him as well as with Vyshinsky. Psychologically, though, it seems he was prepared.

After branding 'the wrecking of Pashukanis and his stooges', Krylenko turned to castigating himself. Everything for which a few months earlier he had praised Pashukanis, 'who had long ago proved his right to the title of Academician', was now termed 'my own inexcusable mistake'.

'My defective ideas,' he exclaimed, turning to his subordinate,

demand a decisive rebuff – claiming, as I did, that it was possible to pass judgement without proven guilt, that the principle 'punishment proportionate to guilt' was none other than an uncritical interpretation of the principles of bourgeois law. Such vulgar, primitive contradiction does not become a Soviet lawyer.

In deadly silence the overcrowded conference hall of the People's Commissariat of Justice listened to the indictment of the recent Procurator:

I permitted myself the blasphemy of applying Lenin's system of punishment – in which every tenth member of a regiment in whose ranks a theft has occurred is put to death – to capitalists' families for the 'guilt' of the head of the family. But in doing so, I forgot that Lenin permitted these special forms of repression only under certain conditions of time and place and they were not applied through the courts ... Finally, I am guilty of one other sin, and I must speak of it honestly and sincerely, as befits a Bolshevik. I am responsible for a nihilistic attitude to the role of the defence at a criminal trial. In view of the double-dealer Pashukanis, and regarding this spiteful critic and slanderer in an uncritical light, I supposed that the defence at a trial was also a bourgeois survival, a fragment of bourgeois law.

Here he should probably have stopped, for he had already said enough and done what he could. But the eloquent speaker got carried away – he was, after all, a People's Commissar, and not a defendant. He could allow himself some mild criticism, barely criticism, more a flattering wish: 'I am greatly looking forward to the publication of theoretical works on this subject,' he said and then suddenly changed his tone, 'particularly from Vyshinsky [he did not call him "Comrade Vyshinsky" nor by his name and patronymic], who promised long ago to produce work on this subject. Unfortunately, so far no such work has appeared, while the need for it remains extremely acute.'

Vyshinsky was not present at this extended Party *aktiv*, but the shorthand report of Krylenko's 'indictment' was already lying on his desk the next day. For two or three weeks Krylenko waited for the Procurator-General's telephone call – so I was told in the early seventies by Krylenko's daughter, Marina Nikolayevna Simonyan. But it never came. Silence, however, was as good as a reply. After all, telephoning was not his only way of replying.

Directly after the *aktiv* at which Krylenko had made what amounted to a confession, Vyshinsky delivered an introductory lecture on the criminal trial to students of the All-Union Academy of Law. Unlike his opponent, the learned Procurator's speeches were noted for their mettle, not for their repentant tone. He did not mention Krylenko by name, but resolutely criticized 'those who underestimate such paramount principles of legal proceedings as publicity and controversy'. 'Those who' definitely referred to Krylenko. Look at this most curious detail: while flouting both publicity and controversy in practice – the Prosecutor's and defending counsel's equal rights at the trial, and the guarantee of the defendant's right to a defence – Vyshinsky crushed those who refuted these principles in theory or, in other words, who attempted to underpin the practice with the theory. The Procurator had no need for such underpinning.

Krylenko spent the whole of 1937 frantically trying to explain his position by means of the press in order to prove himself a loyal and devoted citizen who belonged to the right side.

So prolific was his writing, especially in the latter half of the year, that it enables one to understand the turmoil he was in and his acute awareness of the approaching end. Nearly every issue of the bi-weekly journal *Soviet Justice* contained an article by him or a summary of one of his speeches. 'Pashukanis-like wrecking', 'the loathsome reasonings of a concealed enemy, the pseudo-academic Pashukanis' are not even among the strongest invectives used by the threatened People's Commissar in his emotive denunciations. In August he announced in the press that 'deserved retribution inevitably awaits "Pashukanis"' and that he himself, Nikolai Vasilievich Krylenko, had dreamed for so long 'of starting as soon as possible on the work "Stalin on the Trial and

Criminal Policy"' in order to 'collate and present his instructions in this field in a systematized form'.

The prediction of People's Commissar Krylenko was fulfilled at once. After a few minutes of 'legal proceedings' Ulrikh sentenced Pashukanis, the opponent of capital punishment, to be shot. The sentence was carried out half an hour later.

But Krylenko's dream of producing a book on Stalin as a lawyer, unfortunately, never came true.

On 12 December 1937 he failed to be elected a deputy to the Supreme Soviet. Three days later the 4th Department of the Chief Administration of State Security of the NKVD finished compiling 'the arrest warrant of enemy of the people Krylenko', where it was stated that he:

> had been shown up by the testimonies of the prisoners Trifonov, Berman, Burmistrov, Yakovleva, Pashukanis, Bubnov and by operational materials ... as having been a member of the organization of Rightists since 1930, having created in the bodies of the legal system a wrecking organization and having led it.... He personally recruited more than thirty people to it.

The warrant was signed by Matusov[2], a name which crops up many times in Lubyanka documents of the thirties. Bukharin's widow, Anna Mikhailovna Larina, recalls how he gave her 'the good advice' of leaving for Astrakhan to start her exile, how he lied, promising her a meeting with her husband, and how he again interrogated her, resorting to blackmail and threats.

Various departments worked concurrently and independently of each other. While one was compiling the arrest warrant, another was writing out the guest ticket to the Supreme Soviet session which was handed to Krylenko two days after Yezhov had sent Procurator Vyshinsky a copy of the warrant 'for his own reference'. The Procurator and his future victim both received credentials for the session – one a deputy's mandate, the other a pass into the Kremlin Palace of Congresses. Vyshinsky had nothing on which to congratulate his colleague; Krylenko not only congratulated Vyshinsky but also handed him a heavy present: a volume of his selected speeches for the prosecution fresh from the printers. The title-page had an inscription: 'To Andrei Yanuarievich Vyshinsky – a comrade in the common cause – with tremendous respect and Bolshevik greetings'.

As it turned out this was a tactless and imprudent act: the present itself – to a prosecutor from an ex-prosecutor – was a collection of

Krylenko's old speeches, when Vyshinsky's recent speeches, not yet made into a separate book, were on everyone's minds. The familiarity of his wording was also somewhat unfortunate: 'To a comrade in the common cause'. The recipient of the present knew there was a cause, but it was not to be a common one. As for the 'Bolshevik greetings', was this not a hint that it was addressed to a Menshevik?

Such was their psychological duel. Such was their dialogue without words, their unvoiced threats, their firm handshake as comrades, companions-in-arms, friends.

Formalities were observed.

On 12 January 1938 the first session of the first Supreme Soviet of the USSR opened. The Procurator-General and Chairman of the Military Board assumed their places as deputies, each a member of his own delegation; Vyshinsky as the deputy of the Saratov Region, Ulrikh as the deputy of the Komi Republic. Krylenko, however, was subjected to a humiliation; he was deprived of the honour of appearing as deputy, and had to be content with the modest role of a guest in the balcony. This was a clear sign of the tragedy ahead. However, Krylenko put all such disquieting thoughts aside; he was still a People's Commissar, after all.

Let us note in passing that lawyers, who enjoyed great trust, then made up an impressive contingent in the supreme, albeit decorative, bodies of power but were soon to suffer a severe decrease in numbers. In 1938 when elections to the first Supreme Soviet of the RSFSR were held, almost half the members of the Military Board of the Supreme Court, authors of hundreds and thousands of death sentences, were among the deputies: Nikolai Rychkov, Ivan Golyakov, Ivan Matulevich, Iona Nikitchenko, Yakov Dmitriev, Vassily Bukanov, to name but a few.

To thunderous applause the Presidium of the Supreme Soviet of the USSR headed by 'all-union elder' Mikhail Ivanovich Kalinin was successfully elected. A short while later many of these presidium members would be rotting in prisons: Marshal Blyukher, Army Commander Fedko, Komsomol leader Kosarev, First Secretary of the Moscow City Committee Alexander Ugarov; others, including Lazar Kaganovich's brother, Yuli, were fated to disappear and die. But this happened later, not now.

Next came the election of the Procurator-General of the USSR, whose mandate (the law had to be abided by, after all) had expired and who, in accordance with the new Constitution, had to be elected by the Supreme Soviet. A speech apropos this was made by Grigori Petrovksy, the Ukrainian Party veteran, the oldest Bolshevik, and a member of the last State Duma before the Revolution. One of his sons had already been killed as an enemy of the people, the other was to die not long afterwards, but at least not at the hands of a henchman. Released from prison as a result of one of Stalin's caprices, he was to perish in the war on active service. Grigori Petrovsky proposed 'electing the eminent lawyer Comrade Vyshinsky to this responsible post again': he was 'renowned for his speeches at the trials of the traitors who had been exposed by those excellent bodies under the leadership of great Stalin's best companion-in-arms, Comrade Yezhov.'

This motion, as one may easily guess, was carried unanimously. The speeches continued to tumultuous applause. Krylenko applauded with everyone else.

Nothing hinted at the thunderstorm yet to come, but it was still on its way, and not under cover of night, or behind firmly closed doors, but openly, in full view of the public, here from the rostrum of the Supreme Soviet.

On 17 January the floor was given to Deputy Dzhafar Bagirov, one of Beria's closest colleagues, proxy, and right-hand man. Without revealing all that he knew, he subjected to criticism – in true Stalinist, Bolshevik style, with total and utter directness – a member of the same government that had just submitted its resignation to the Supreme Soviet. 'Whereas Comrade Krylenko used to devote most of his time to tourism and mountaineering,' joked Deputy Bagirov,

he now spends it playing chess. We really ought to find out who we are dealing with in the person of Comrade Krylenko – with a mountaineer or the People's Commissar of Justice? [In the newspaper account these words were followed by "Laughter".] I do not know which one Comrade Krylenko considers himself to be, but he is undoubtedly a bad People's Commissar of Justice. I am sure that Comrade Molotov will bear this in mind in his presentation of the Soviet People's Commissariat's new membership.

'Undoubtedly bad' was not the kind of expression used by a rank-and-file deputy in those days. And the State's second-in-command could only have been given instructions by the State's first-in-command. He was never more than his mouthpiece. Krylenko understood this as well as we do now.

He was not, however, arrested until two weeks later. He spent several days handing over his affairs to the new People's Commissar of Justice, Nikolai Rychkov, a recent member of the Military Board; Comrade Molotov, as we guessed, took Comrade Bagirov's joke seriously and bore his suggestion in mind. To make up for it, he now appointed great Stalin's most loyal comrades-in-arms to the Soviet People's Commissariat, men who had suffered all manner of grim ordeals and passed the examination on total devotion with flying colours: Vlas Chubar, Stanislav Kosior, Nikolai Yezhov, Mikhail Kaganovich, Abram Gilinsky, Robert Eikhe, Matvei Berman and others. Their turn was to come very soon; not one was to escape execution.

About five days before the arrest, as Marina Nikolayevna Simonyan,[3] Krylenko's daughter, told me, he received a telephone call from Stalin out of the blue. 'Don't worry, we trust you. You'll get a new appointment, but in the meantime get the Code ready. Be quick about it, the people are waiting. Work at it like a *Stakhanovite* (crack worker)!' I wrote what she said in my notebook: 'Papa believed him and cheered him. . . . Hearing of this conversation, Vyshinsky telephoned him, as if everything were as normal, and asked how work on the Code was coming along. "Comrade Stalin asks you to hurry up. Prepare some proposals. In the next few days there is going to be a commission." Papa set to work at once.'

Perhaps there really was a commission, but it did not include Krylenko. Instead 'in the next few days' he was arrested. Vyshinsky's sanction on his arrest was dated 18 January 1938, but Yezhov only gave the order to 'take' the ex-People's Commissar on 31 January. The order was carried out the very same night.

Krylenko really was an outstanding and extraordinary individual who sought to express himself as fully as possible. His principal work as the Procurator quashing 'nests of the counter-revolution', and subsequently as head of Soviet Justice, largely carrying out the same duties as before, did not prevent him from devoting his leisure time to his two favourite hobbies, mountaineering and chess. In both fields he reached great heights of excellence.

At the end of the twenties and beginning of the thirties considerable publicity was given to several expeditions to the Pamir mountain range which the Procurator of the RSFSR organized, led and took a most active part in. His ardent speech at the Shakhty Trial, which had stunned the nation (the glittering effect of this political spectacle was later to dim in comparison with the bloody shows staged by Procurator Vyshinsky), added a particularly exotic dimension to the mountaineering expedition, which was conducted in the name of science and sport, and was led not by sportsmen but by statesmen – Operations Manager of the Soviet People's Commissariat Nikolai Gorbunov; Procurator of the RSFSR Krylenko; Vyshinsky's longtime colleague at the People's Commissariat of Food and the People's Commissariat of Education Professor Otto Yulievich Schmidt, the future head of the Directorate of Northern Waterways, expedition member on the *Serov* and *Cheliuskin* ice-breakers (used in the Arctic Ocean 1937–39 for scientific research) and one of the first Heroes of the Soviet Union.

Some very distinguished scientists also took part in the Krylenko-Gorbunov Pamir expeditions, including the meteorologist Tsimmerman, the geodesist Isakov, the astronomer Belyayev, the geologists Moskvin and Shcherbakov, the zoologist Reinhardt and the geographer Korzhenevsky. The expeditions produced extremely valuable results, becoming a most important landmark in the conquest of the Pamirs. Krylenko displayed great personal courage, climbing singlehanded to an altitude of 6,850 metres with practically no mountaineering equipment, thereby setting a new Soviet mountaineering record. He left reminiscences of these expeditions in several large books of essays which testify to his indisputable literary talent.

The most publicized and conspicuous result of the Pamir expeditions was, however, Krylenko's wilful 'christening' of both well-known and newly discovered peaks, causing the scientific world great consternation, for when it came to naming mountain peaks, they were used to abiding by time-hallowed traditions, established regulations and an unshakeable protocol.

Krylenko personally conferred the name of Lenin on a peak which had previously been named after its discoverer, Kaufman, and gave the names of Dzerzhinsky, Krasin, Sverdlov and Tsyurupa to the unnamed peaks which the expedition had discovered. Afterwards the most up-to-date equipment was used to measure the altitude of other peaks in the Pamirs. It then became known that a peak discovered as early as 1916 and named quite legally and in keeping with all the rules, 'Garmo', was 361 metres higher than the one named after Lenin. Who could be higher than Lenin? Why, Stalin, of course. And nobody else. So that settled it; a radiogram was sent to the 'great Continuer of the Cause' notifying him of the gift he was receiving 'with respect and love' from all the expedition members. And as a consolation another, more modest peak was named after Garmo.

However, there were innumerable magnificent peaks in the Pamirs and the expeditions kept on making new discoveries. With regal magnanimity Krylenko bestowed Nature's gifts upon his friends Abel Yenukidze, Varvara Yakovleva, and Daniil Sulimov. One of the most dazzling peaks he gave as a present to his second wife, Zinaida, and a somewhat higher and more grandiose peak 'situated', as he was subsequently to write in his travel essays, 'at a short distance from Stalin's peak, we named after Genrikh Yagoda'.

But confusion arose when the presents came to be distributed; it was one thing sitting in tents, admiring the mountain views, naming peaks and sending out telegrams and radiograms, and quite another officially registering these names and putting them on maps. This procedure was entirely in the hands of the Russian Geographical Society, of which Academician Vavilov had been president since 1931, and he flatly refused to become involved in the dubious affair, declaring Krylenko's venture to be 'in contravention of the Society's long-established rules'. It is hard to say how this story would have ended if the names of the peaks' 'owners' had not started disappearing one after another – and not just off maps but off the face of the earth.

No less remarkable was Krylenko's contribution to the history of chess. Generally speaking, all Russia's revolutionaries were passionately keen on this game. It is well known what an obsessive player Lenin was, against whom Krylenko had battled across a chessboard in their years abroad. After the Revolution the lawyer and tribune, who was by then a celebrity, became head of the mass chess movement, initiating millions to the game, and organizing the country's first international chess tournaments, including the renowned one in 1925 which broke the 'cultural blockade' and played host to the world's top chess-players.

This was the famous tournament which gave rise to 'chess fever'. It was here at a session of simultaneous play that the future world champion, fourteen-year-old Mikhail Botvinov, beat the world champion of the day, José Raoul Capablanca.

Krylenko was not a bad player himself, not at all bad. In those days there were still none of the rules of conduct for officials to follow, and so without having to worry about ruining his authority as a statesman, he used to take part in open trade-union and club tournaments, usually coming between sixth and eighth. This was by no means a humiliation but, on the contrary, added to his popularity and authority; and not just among chess-players.

Vyshinsky was also afflicted by the 'disease' – a passionate love of chess – and also played it quite well on an amateur, not tournament, level. He used to play against colleagues and subordinates, and tremendously enjoyed winning, preferring a fast game, as he did not have the energy, patience or time to think and work out different combinations. He regarded the game as nothing more than a worthwhile form of intellectual relaxation for a cultured person. He found Krylenko's excessively serious attitude to it irritating as, incidentally, he did everything about this short stocky man, the wide-cheekboned son of a peasant who possessed a lively intellect and versatile talents, a Bolshevik of the old ilk with whom he had so little in common.

The unexpected and more unusual charges Dzhafar Bagirov levelled against Krylenko gave rise to speculation as to what exactly the celebrated orator's crimes might be, for only a short while before he had been contending with the Procurator-General for the laurels of the country's top lawyer. The charges were broadly these: that having sold himself to British (it could as easily have been German, French, Polish or Japanese; there was plenty of choice) Intelligence, and using scientific exploration and his passionate love of mountaineering as a pretext, Krylenko had wandered around the Pamirs, drawing up topographical maps for foreign agents and selecting landing stages for spies, covers for parachutists and secret rendezvous for people illegally crossing the Soviet borders.

This perfectly acceptable material was inspired by the unusual nature of his life and various stereotyped situations in the films flooding the screens just then. However, the Lubyanka fabricators had stereotypes of their own, and were not impressed in the least by the exotic and original aspects of the material. Mountaineering and chess did not actually figure in the final indictment against Krylenko, which was made to sound like all the rest.

The investigation was started by Kogan, the same man who had cornered Professor Pashukanis so effortlessly. An expert in jurisprudence, he dextrously selected widely used material. Krylenko, this close associate of Lenin, one of the leaders of the October armed uprising in Petrograd, the first People's Commissar of Military and Naval Affairs, the first Soviet Commander-in-Chief, the first Procurator of the RSFSR, and the first People's Commissar of Justice of the USSR – according to the material fabricated by the investigation, this man was an agent of every single foreign intelligence service, had plotted the assassination of the 'Soviet leadership' and had come to an arrangement with the Fascists, inciting them to an intervention. Along with him – and this was Kogan's only additional fabrication – Bukharin, Antipov[4] and Sulimov[5] had attempted to achieve the same goal.

For various reasons, which have still to be unravelled, Krylenko's arrest was prepared over a considerable period and organized quite substantially although the arrests and executions had already been on a production line for quite some time. It was not because Krylenko held a prominent position in the state – in those days much more prominent figures than he were treated without the slightest consideration. Nor was it because he had been on very friendly terms with Stalin – Bukharin had been very friendly with Koba but this had not changed anything. If anything, it added to his certain fate.

The most likely explanation is that no direct instructions were given. Denunciatory materials were compiled on every Central Committee member, leading statesman, celebrated scientist and figure from the arts. Some denunciations came at once or slightly later, others bided their time like delayed-action bombs. Sometimes they did not go off at all, and that was the end of the matter. But not in this case.

Unlike many others, Nikolai Krylenko's 'arrest warrant' contained 'substantial evidence', and had obviously been prepared in a thorough and painstaking manner. In it were detailed excerpts from the testimonies given against him during the investigations of 'arrested-and-exposed Bubnov,[6] Yakovleva,[7] Trifonov,[8] Pashukanis and others who exposed Krylenko as a wrecker'. Even the exact dates of their testimonies were given. It was stated, for instance, that Bubnov exposed Krylenko at an interrogation on 19 November 1937.

When the 'Krylenko case' was examined at the Chief Military Procurator's office in the summer of 1955 – it ended with his posthumous rehabilitation on 10 August of the same year – it was established that not one quotation in the warrant corresponded with the truth; even the absurd, falsified quotations, which had been forcibly extracted, were not found in the 'exposers' statements. They were all – every single one of them – fabricated by the people who wrote the warrant.

It would seem as though there were no limits to what could be done to anyone or anything; stories were concocted to make tormented and tortured prisoners say whatever was needed to implicate new victims. There was, however, no need even to do this, as none of the evidence was actually checked by anyone, and any fabrication was taken as the truth, no matter how implausible.

What was done to the Soviet Commander-in-Chief once he was thrown into a Lubyanka cell? It is not hard to guess. On 3 February 1938, on the fourth day of torture, Krylenko wrote a 'statement to the General Commissar of State Security Citizen Yezhov' in which he 'confessed' to having joined the conspiracy against Lenin even before October 1917, and to having been enticed by Bukharin in 1922 into an organization preparing a coup.

He was interrogated twice – on 3 April and on 28 July – or maybe more often. By then it was customary to compile 'generalized' statements; after the 'conveyor' torture where the interrogators changed continually and the person under investigation remained without sleep or rest for many days, a 'summary statement' would then be produced into which the henchmen crammed everything they saw fit. They made Krylenko reveal the names of about thirty 'accessories' with whom he had engaged in wrecking; others with whom he had prepared a coup and plotted to assassinate the Leader were betrayed.

Half of these conspirators and assassins were not even arrested – they simply did not get round to them. The People's Commissar of Justice of Byelorussia, Kudelsky, whom Krylenko had named as his 'accessory', was acquitted by the Military Board of the Supreme Court – a rare exception for those days but, as is now becoming known, not unique. None of the people allegedly in the 'conspiracy' with Krylenko gave evidence against him – their names are unfamiliar to our ears: Vishnyak, Lipkin, Bulat, Burmistrov, Degot, Kuzmin, Nyurin.

What difference did it make who said what against whom? It all depended on the investigator's caprice, on how impoverished or fertile his imagination was, and sometimes on the order he had been given. 'Pumping' testimony, that is, getting a prisoner to say what you wanted, was one of the investigator's main professional skills: some did it very well, others not so well, and others very badly. By 1937 there was no longer any need to corroborate different people's testimonies – the production line was working at full speed, and everything was running splendidly without corroborations, especially as each person had different investigators who sometimes knew nothing about one another or the cases being conducted, not just in the next town, but sometimes even in the next room.

Recently I received a letter from the well-known geneticist Vladimir Pavlovich Efroimson. Quoting 'an old Party member called Yakobovich who died a couple of years ago somewhere in Central Asia', he wrote that in prison Krylenko had 'personally persuaded several wreckers to confess, as their duty to the Party and Party honour demanded this of them.'

It is hard to believe that a courageous and intelligent man like Krylenko could invent such nonsense and push his unfortunate fellow prisoners into confessing. But who can today fathom all the secrets inside the Lubyanka? In those days logic, commonsense, decency, moral rectitude, let alone courage and intelligence, all failed to withstand the refined torture, both physical and mental – torture, the like of which history had never known.

Unexpectedly transferred to other cases at hand, Investigator Kogan handed over the management of Krylenko's case to his colleague, Aronson. Their destinies were to be very different: Kogan was shot in 1939, while Aronson lived to see the thaw, and in 1955 gave evidence to a military prosecutor, displaying a good memory. He told how Krylenko, seeing the new investigator, had taken heart, evidently viewing the change as a good sign. It gave him a new lease of life and he decided to fight. He disavowed everything he had signed in February.

But his euphoria was shortlived. Reading through the interrogation record that Aronson had compiled, Krylenko saw that Aronson had not recorded his disavowal of his previous statements. On the contrary, he had again written that 'the person under investigation confessed to everything'. Krylenko, according to Aronson, did not attempt to argue and grew 'depressed and signed the record and added that his fate no longer interested him, that he was concerned only for the fate of his family'.

Only a few months before, at a meeting in the Red Hall of the Supreme Court, Krylenko had delivered an ecstatic speech in honour 'of the country's very best judge Ulrikh, whom the people believes in and from whom it always expects the firmness and resolution distinguishing him as a lawyer of the Stalinist school.' Now Comrade Ulrikh had to live up to his reputation and not let the side down.

The trial of the head of the Soviet judiciary, as usual, lasted only twenty minutes. So says the record of the proceedings with astounding pedantry. And the record itself consisted of nineteen typed pages – the standard length for such cases. As far as one can go by the record, Krylenko confirmed everything but declined to give detailed evidence, saying he was tired. Neither Ulrikh, nor his assistants Nikitchenko and Goryachev raised objections; their function was merely to pronounce judgement – with firmness and resolution.

This they did. A few minutes later Nikolai Krylenko was dead.

The testimony Aronson gave in 1955 contains the following sentence: 'After starting to read the statement I had prepared, Krylenko paused at the surname Antonov-Ovseyenko and asked, "Him as well?" After I had confirmed this, he went on reading and did not return to this question again.'

Vladimir Alexandrovich Antonov-Ovseyenko had 'worked' with

Nikolai Krylenko twice. In 1917 they led the October armed uprising together, and then both took up seats in the first Soviet Government, having formed, with Pavel Dybenko, a three-man committee on military and naval affairs. Professionally, their paths crossed once more just before the end. While Krylenko was the People's Commissar of Justice of the USSR, Antonov-Ovseyenko, already doomed and already recalled from his post as Consul-General in Barcelona, was, on one of Stalin's caprices, suddenly appointed People's Commissar of Justice of the RSFSR (from 1934–1935 he had worked as the Procurator of the RSFSR), and spent two or three weeks in this post until the night of 13 October 1937 when he was arrested and fell into the clutches of another henchman – Shneiderman, the vice-head of the 13th section of the 3rd department of the Chief Directorate of State Security of the NKVD.[9]

Whereas Yezhov had graced Krylenko's arrest warrant (and many others) with the Procurator-General's signature, thereby adding the latter's name to the general list of people 'responsible', this was evidently not needed for Antonov-Ovseyenko; the sanction for his arrest had come from the highest quarter, by word of mouth.

In Antonov-Ovseyenko's case there was only one record of an interrogation, on an unspecified day in November 1937. A month was required by the persecutors to get this prisoner's signature under the words 'I confess to everything'. This 'everything' amounted to being a German and Polish spy, leading an underground organization of spies in the struggle against the Spanish Republic, and carrying out Trotsky's special missions, which the latter set him through his son, Lev Sedov, Krestinsky, Rakovsky, and Radek. All this was laconically listed in the prosecution's conclusion.

He was not summoned again, or at least, there is no evidence in his dossier of his being summoned again. As he was awaiting the inevitable, did he recall the trial of Zinoviev and Kamenev the previous year at which he had been present as a guest? Did he recall writing in *Izvestia* that his comrades – with whom he had shared his life, ideals and struggles – were a

Brutal, base and cowardly counter-revolutionary Trotskyite band of assassins. . . . They are not only double-dealers, cowardly, treacherous vermin, they are a diversionist detachment of Fascism . . . I have written to Comrade Kaganovich that, with regard to [Zinoviev and Kamenev], 'I would carry out any Party instructions.' Certainly – even shoot them myself as obvious counter-revolutionaries

... This whole band has to be destroyed, and so it will be.

Did he recall these impassioned words and curses of his and his readiness for anything?

He was brought to the prison office now serving as the 'court-room' of the Military Board of the Supreme Court on 8 February 1938, five days after a tormented Krylenko had finally made the confession required of him, and been thrown into the cell next-door.

'Do you confirm the testimony you gave at the preliminary investigation?' asked Ulrikh in his habitual weary tone, seated between the military lawyers Zaryanov and Kandybin. 'No!' resolutely replied Antonov-Ovseyenko. 'All my confessions are false. As a result of torture I have slandered myself.'

Ulrikh, Zaryanov and Kandybin had all heard this numerous times before in the same 'court-room', and so this final heroic stand by the man who on that unimaginably distant October nigʰt had led the storming of the Winter Palace and arrested the Provisional Government on behalf of the Military Revolutionary Committee made not the slightest impression on them. Again, twenty minutes later they read out the sentence to him but, contrary to the usual procedure, his escort took him back to his cell and not to the basement. Something had obviously gone wrong – perhaps there was no executioner available.

Antonov-Ovseyenko was shot two days later on 10 February; the execution certificate kept in his dossier was indirectly but convincingly corroborated by the short story of Yuri Tomsky, Mikhail Petrovich Tomsky's son, published in the monthly literary journal *Novy Mir* a quarter of a century ago:

> The supervisor summoned Antonov-Ovseyenko. Vladimir Alexandrovich started saying goodbye to us, then got hold of his black woollen coat, took off his jacket, boots, gave away nearly all his clothes and stood half-naked in the middle of the cell: 'I ask those who survive until their release to tell people that Antonov-Ovseenko was a Bolshevik and remained a Bolshevik to his last day.'

The rehabilitation of Antonov-Ovseyenko, which took place on 25 February 1956, was preceded by the customary inquiry of the Chief Military Procurator's office. It appeared that during the investigation there were no materials whatsoever – not even false ones – which would have exposed Antonov-Ovseyenko in any 'dubious' activity of any kind. None at all.

However, a famous writer and public figure at the time and Chairman of the All-Union Society of International Cultural Ties (VOKS), Alexander Arosev (who had not long before visited Paris with Bukharin to buy Marx's archive from the German Social Democrats and fell straight into Yezhov's clutches on his return) gave evidence – also under force, naturally – concerning his membership of 'a counter-revolutionary Trotskyite organization of spies', to which the diplomats Vladimir Antonov-Ovseyenko and Alexandra Kollontai, and the writers Vera Inber and Valentin Katayev also belonged. Of this 'four-some' only Antonov-Ovseyenko was arrested and tortured, while the rest may never have even learnt what team of people they were said to have been attached to. At the trial Arosev denied all his evidence – this, however, can only be ascertained from Arosev's dossier, and not from Antonov-Ovseyenko's 'court' case.

The inquiry carried out in 1955–56 revealed one other substantial detail: neither the KGB nor the Special Archive of the Ministry of Internal Affairs had either then or at any later date 'testimony concerning Antonov-Ovseyenko's colloboration with foreign intelligence services'. So says the certificate in his file. In other words, the case's organizers knew full well from all the documents that the charge was totally fabricated. But this did not worry them in the least, and they saw no need even to 'rig' it.

No announcement of the arrests was made in the press, but every now and then one could still make out whose turn had already come and even whose was drawing near. If in the newspapers and journals, on the radio and at meetings and conferences someone was referred to by his surname prefixed by 'comrade' and criticized for his 'defective views', 'compromising spirit', 'scatter-brainedness' and other qualities helping the 'base hirelings', everyone understood that he did not have long to go. If he was referred to by his surname only, without the prefix 'comrade', and spoken of only in the past tense like some obsolete object, there was absolutely no doubt his turn had already come.

And this is precisely how the news of Krylenko's arrest reached those taking part in the First All-Union Conference of People's Commissars of Justice and Members of the Judiciary the following day. During his speech Vyshinsky asked in an off-hand manner: 'Who does not know the character of the double-dealer Krylenko who was engaged in wrecking?'

In such instances there was no question of discussing the matter: it was simply communicated as a piece of information, and that was it. But the people in the hall were sufficiently intelligent, and they not only understood but even saw with their own eyes that the shells were falling closer and closer. They were not mere witnesses: they were taking part in this battle personally. They could also recall another crucial instruction the Procurator-General had given them: 'It is essential to conduct a deep disinfection,' he had told the judges and prosecutors at one of the plenums of the Supreme Soviet. The disinfection was being carried out fast, and it was a question of who would manage to disinfect whom first. That is, who would be disinfecting and who would be disinfected. It was either one or the other. And so the work gathered momentum.

One of the first to be disinfected was the first Procurator of the USSR, Ivan Alexeyevich Akulov, who had taken up this post in 1933 immediately after the Procurator's office of the USSR was established. Direct, sharp, but good-natured, despite having worked for some time as Vice-Chairman of the OGPU, a man of 'inflexible will, great integrity and tremendous courage', who enjoyed 'the special respect and trust of his comrades' – this is how Anna Mikhailovna Larina describes Akulov. He was totally unsuitable for the role which the Procurator-General was going to have to play in the near future, as envisaged by the Leader's plan. Neither a gifted speaker, nor an intriguer, nor, most definitely, a stage-manager, there was no doubt about it – he had to go. To start with, it was only his work he left.

By this stage the post of secretary of the Central Executive Committee (under the chairmanship of Kalinin), more a symbolic post than a key one, had become vacant following the arrest of Abel Yenukidze, who had held this post for many years. This was the post to which Akulov was transferred, freeing his place for Andrei Vyshinsky. So the Pro-curator-General of the USSR set to preparing public trials, and the secretary of the Central Executive Committee began awarding decorations.

While out skating one day, Akulov fell and was concussed. Accidents will happen, and skating rinks are, of course, slippery. However, the rumour at once started circulating, and stubbornly persisted for some time, that the fall had not been an accident, that someone had tripped him up on purpose to get rid of Yagoda's former deputy and the ex-Procurator-General, for, apparently, he knew too much.

However, the death prepared for Akulov was not so original after all. In fact, it was quite normal for those days; the charge was ordinary, and so was the 'confession' – being a member of Pyatakov's 'band of saboteurs' and 'a military conspiracy of spies' to which he had been recruited by Yakir.

Tried by Ulrikh, Rutman and Preobrazhentsev and given three minutes to speak, Akulov managed to say that he was guilty of nothing and that during the investigation he had 'lost his will as a result of beatings', and this was why he had 'confessed'.

The outcome was obvious. Now Vyshinsky had one less rival whose very existence had been a humiliation to him and who could remember *what* had happened in the past, and *how* it had happened.

Then, one after the other, the judges and prosecutors directly involved in the disinfection started disappearing themselves, as did, incidentally, others not involved who had been peacefully working on civil suits – family matters, legacies and other work.

At the time there were many Poles and Lithuanians working among the judiciary, just as there had been ever since the Revolution. Some had joined after working in the Cheka (secret police) while others had managed to gain diplomas at the Universities of Warsaw and Riga, where the Tsarist secret police had probably not been so vigilant and brutal as in other parts of the Russian Empire.

For obvious reasons, Vyshinsky had a high regard for Poles and took a particular delight in purging them. Among them was Stanislav Stanislavovich Pilyavsky, the Chairman of the Special Board of the Supreme Court and father of the celebrated Moscow Art Theatre actress Sofia Stanislavovna Pilyavskaya, who had worked with Vyshinsky at the Procurator's office.[10] This old revolutionary and member of the Social Democratic Party of Poland and Latvia, a Bolshevik since October 1903, was known for his independent views and harsh temper. He had often argued with Vyshinsky, who, at the beginning of the thirties, was still not unassailable or above criticism, and used to return to the NKVD cases he considered had been badly and tendentiously investigated. This was evidently enough for him to be declared a member of the (non-existent, of course) diversionist 'Polish Military Organization' involved in espionage and terrorism.

He was interrogated only once, according to the examination record, and categorically denied all the charges, stood his ground under torture and signed no confession. He was valiantly defended by his wife, Yelena Gustavovna Smitten, who tried to get through to Vyshinsky, whom she knew quite well. She wrote to him, and even Stalin, demanding the release of 'the honest Bolshevik and Leninist'. She herself had a revolutionary past, at one time heading the Central Committee's statistics department, and she still believed in justice, principles and ideals. Shortly afterwards she was also arrested, and taken away to a place from which few ever returned. She never did.

Pilyavsky held out exceptionally firmly despite his 'guilt' being confirmed by other 'Polish terrorists' including Unshlikht[11], who, when denying his evidence in court, managed only to say: 'I couldn't stand the torture.'

Pilyavsky could and did. He was convicted by Nikitchenko, Goryachev and Rutman, without Ulrikh taking part. He was given the death sentence and executed the same day – on 25 November 1937. According to the rumours which reached his family, other dates were named but all of them were false; the execution certificate has remained intact.

Not only Polish spies had penetrated the Soviet legal system, Latvian ones had as well – former Red Army infantrymen, Cheka officers, and the most loyal and indestructible Kremlin Guards. An outstanding figure among them was Georgi Yakovlevich Meren, a Bolshevik since 1905, the Chairman of the Water Transport Board of the Supreme Court, who had become, according to the charge levelled against him, 'an active participant in an illegal Latvian National-Fascist organization', a spy of the Latvian intelligence service, where he had been recruited by Yan Berzin himself.[12]

Meren not only did not confess to anything even during the terrible torture he was subjected to but 'displayed aggression', shouting out oaths and cursing his tormentors – both present and absent. To protect Ulrikh and his colleagues from too much nervous strain, it was decided not to prosecute Meren or even 'put him through' a special inquiry. The treatment he was given was completely without precedent. On 11 February 1938, less than two weeks after Krylenko's arrest, Vyshinsky and Yezhov signed a 'joint ruling of the Procurator's office of the USSR and the NKVD of the USSR' on Meren's execution – without compiling an indictment or a sentence, and without going through any legal procedure at all.

Three days earlier they had shot a 'Latvian spy' and 'active participant in the Latvian nationalist diversionist terrorist organization': the head of the special trials section of the People's Commissariat of Justice of the USSR, Yan Yanovich Kronberg, one of Krylenko's closest colleagues. At various times the same fate was to befall other members of the same 'Latvian terrorist organization' fabricated by the Lubyanka operatives: the Chairman of the Transport Board of the Supreme Court, Yuri Yurievich Mezhin, the assistants of the Chief Transport Procurator, Eduard Karlovich Sinat and Arkady Markovich Lipkin, and the Chairman of the Military Tribunal of the Moscow Military

District, Leonard Yanovich Plavnek, accused of being not only a Latvian spy but a German one as well.

Leonard Plavnek was a well-known figure who had distinguished himself on various fronts of the Civil War. He was among the very few at that time to be awarded the Order of the Red Banner and, not long before his arrest, the very prestigious Order of the Red Star.

The latter order, however, he received not for military services but for his particularly zealous part in the 'legal' reprisals against the military, including some of his erstwhile frontline comrades. Under his chairmanship the assizes of the Supreme Court devastated the Siberian Military District by executing almost all its officers. It was for this exploit that he was highly decorated and then almost immediately arrested.

A sufficiently clear indication of what happened to him in the torture-chamber is to be found in a letter which turned up in a dossier. It was addressed to Voroshilov and written by another prisoner, the former head of the political directorate of the North Caucasian Military District, I. A. Kuzin: 'To frighten me and make me give false evidence, I was thrown into a solitary cell along with half-dead Plavnek (your friend and comrade-in-arms in the Civil War, a comrade People's Commissar), who had been beaten in an organized and systematic manner for four days.' No reply came from Voroshilov but, to make up for it, one came from Yezhov, Ulrikh and Vyshinsky in the form of a death sentence.

The ultimate fate of another 'Latvian spy', Yan Yanovich Rutman, was especially strange; his name has already been mentioned as one of the judges who condemned Ivan Akulov and Stanislav Pilyavsky to death. A staunch Bolshevik since 1911, who had run the Military Revolutionary Tribunal of the Kiev Military District in a highly productive manner back in 1920, he was virtually the most active and inflexible member of the Military Board; he signed many of the death sentences of his recent legal colleagues. On 9 December 1937 he successfully dispatched into the next world two other close colleagues (Lipkin and Freidson) and then set off home in a carefree manner. After supper he went to bed and was awoken by a knock on the door.

His case begins with a statement addressed to Yezhov and dated 3 February 1938: 'After long denials during the investigation I have decided to recount sincerely all my crimes.' There are no traces of his 'denials' from 10 December to 3 February. He was not interrogated, he was beaten, and you cannot make a record of beatings. Eventually he confessed to having begun spying for the Latvian Intelligence

Service several years before and to preparing to overturn the Soviet regime and shoot its leaders on the instructions of Alksnis,[13] Berzin and Eideman.[14]

On 28 August 1938 he appeared before his colleagues Ulrikh, Dmitriev and Romanychev, with whom he had only recently sentenced others, and in the very same prison office. He now heard his own sentence read out with the same speed and terseness, and thus satisfied himself that the conveyor was still working non-stop, despite his absence – a consolation, perhaps, but not much of one.

It is worth mentioning, incidentally, that two members of his 'group of spies' managed to escape the traps and were in high-ranking posts by the time he was posthumously rehabilitated: N. P. Krumin was the Deputy Chairman of the Supreme Court of Latvia, and F. F. Gaishpuit a member of the Supreme Court. They had not even been aware of the danger hanging over them.

However, the triumvirate of Yezhov, Ulrikh and Vyshinsky, who methodically scorched the earth around them, was, of course, surrounded not only by agents of the Polish and Latvian Intelligence services; they had enough imagination to spread their other victims over the intelligence services of other countries, and accuse them of 'terrorist intentions'. They systematically annihilated Chief Transport Procurator of the USSR Gherman Mikhailovich Segal, Chairman of the Transport Board of the Supreme Court of the USSR Boris Yakovlevich Freidson, Chairman of the Civil Board of the Supreme Court of the RSFSR Alexei Alexandrovich Lisitsyn, Vice-Chairman of the Criminal Board of the Supreme Court of the USSR Fedor Mikhailovich Nakhimson[15] – who survived Krylenko by less than a year and by a bitterly ironic twist of fate was accused of being a member of the same 'terrorist group' as Krylenko – Vice-Chairman of the Commission on Amnesties under the All-Russian Central Executive Committee Nikolai Mikhailovich Nemtsov, Transport Procurator Anisim Anisimovich Romanenko, and many, many others besides.

Yakov Borisovich Shumyatsky had been a member of the Supreme Court of the USSR and then, after falling into Krylenko's disfavour, ran the complaints' office of Commissariat of Trade of the RSFSR. Arrested at the very end of 1938, after Beria had assumed control of the NKVD, he was accused of 'having close ties with enemies of the people Ryutin, Teodorovich[16] and Mosina, who had given evidence against him'.

During the investigation Shumyatsky denied all the charges – of terror, diversion and espionage – but what difference did it make? This usually had no effect on the outcome. But here it did. Shumyatsky was sentenced to only five years of imprisonment, after which he was exiled to Nizhnye-Angarsk in the Krasnoyarsk Region, where he managed to survive until the thaw and return to Moscow. He then immediately set about petitioning for his rehabilitation and succeeded. The results of the inquiry by the Chief Military Procurator's office cast light on how well-founded his conviction was.

Ryutin's testimony of 24 September 1932 enables one to understand the extent to which he incriminated Shumyatsky:

> My views were shared by Yakov Shumyatsky, a present member of the Board of the People's Commissariat of Labour, and Gerasimovich ... Incidentally, my last meeting with Yakov Shumyatsky and Gerasimovich took place only a month and a half ago. They dropped by to see me as old comrades. Shumyatsky started describing how he was being criticized for the opportunist errors he had committed in an article, and in doing so, of course, made light of this criticism. I felt he entirely shared my views. But when I expressed the idea that a change in the leadership of the Party was essential, he disagreed. I began accusing him of not being consistent, of previously having an unfavourable view of Stalin's policies and of now maintaining such an ill-defined position. Towards the end our arguments got rather noisy and we parted quite coolly. As we said goodbye after tea, Shumyatsky did, however, say that we should still meet again but I replied that I was not one of those unprincipled people who talked simply for the sake of it and that if we did meet, there would be nothing for us to discuss.

That is the way he was, unyielding Ryutin. Thus, in a roundabout way we receive yet more confirmation of the integrity and strong principles of this outstanding and courageous individual who not only staunchly withstood all the torture but refused to surrender any of his positions. We also get a glimpse of lawyer Shumyatsky's character: of course, Ryutin's evidence is in his defence, but it is sad to learn of Ryutin's defence of him.

Shumyatsky convincingly denied some more testimony given against him by Mosina, a colleague who had been convicted and executed the same day:

> The falsity of her testimony is confirmed if only by the fact that in 1938 when I allegedly admitted to her that I belonged to a Trotskyite organization, I was giving information about her to the NKVD in

which I described her moods. I was well aware that she might be arrested any day. For these reasons alone I could surely not have spoken to her about anything to do with Trotskyism.

Legal documents are meant to be without emotion: it is in their cold impassive official language that their force and conviction lie. This is precisely what strikes one about the certificate attached to page 75 of the file, and consisting of only a few lines: 'it is confirmed that Citizen Shumyatsky Y. B. from 3 November 1937 and until December [the date is not given] 1938 collaborated with the organs of the NKVD.'

The certificate was issued and sent to the court – not years later when the rehabilitations were taking place but immediately after his arrest. It could signify only one thing: indirectly but unequivocally the department which had issued it was petitioning for its collaborator. And they got what they wanted.

We should note in passing that, while dealing ruthlessly and efficiently with its own henchmen, and annihilating echelon after echelon of people who had organized and carried through mass extermination, it was not so uncommon for the NKVD/MGB (Ministry of State Security) to come to the aid of its informers, popularly known as *stukachi*. Not always, of course, but often. They were then either spared 'the punitive sword' or its blow was softened by various technical means. We shall have other opportunities to confirm this.

It was commonly thought, and still is, that it was impossible to defend people who had fallen into Yezhov's 'iron clutches' because anyone who dared to was also likely to be severely punished. In any case it would do no good for, as they were repeatedly told, people were not imprisoned without reason.

This is what usually happened, but sometimes defenders were found; and sometimes their words, names, and personal connections did have an effect on the victim's sentence and subsequent destiny. I mention this now because Vyshinsky's protection saved the lives of three of his assistants. Although it did not prevent them from being tortured and imprisoned in labour camps, they lived to be rehabilitated, and returned home in the mid-fifties, spiritually broken, worn-out and seriously ill.

Boris Lazarievich Borisov, Ruben Pavlovich Katanyan and Yevsei Gustavovich Shirvindt were arrested at the end of 1938 and accused of being members of a 'Socialist Revolutionary Menshevik terrorist group working within the legal system and Procurator's office', although the investigation did not have time to invent what these 'SR

Mensheviks' had actually been doing. These 'members' were thus tried without it being known what they had done or what they intended doing. After being tortured this was corroborated by the subsequent inquiry – they all incriminated one another and a great many other colleagues. But then some mysterious influential force intervened and the case began to fall apart.

The Military Tribunal of the Moscow Military District acquitted Professor Georgi Nikitich Amfiteatrov[17], a 'member of the group', with whom both Borisov and Shirvindt had confessed to conspiring. But while he was acquitted, they served eight to ten years of imprisonment in labour camps, and were then deported a second time. After Stalin's death they were freed and received an official acknowledgement of their innocence.

The well-known lawyer Ilya Braude, under whom I did my apprenticeship during the last two years of his life, was petitioning at the time for the rehabilitation of his old friend Ruben Katanyan. I remember the letters he wrote to him in exile in Spask in the Karaganda Region. I remember him telling me that it had been Vyshinsky who had saved the lives of Katanyan and two of his other former assistants. The way he had done so had been original but actually most elementary: in his conversations with Ulrikh he had, in every way possible, underlined their 'unimportance', 'uselessness' and 'primitiveness', harmlessness, to put it plainly. Ulrikh had taken heed of his all-powerful and wise friend and done as he wished. Had there been a figure 'i' marked against their names on the list of cases submitted for consideration to the Military Board, he could have done nothing, as this meant that the death penalty had already been decided upon. The figure '2' meant ten years of labour camps. When there was no figure, the judges were free to do as they saw fit. Vyshinsky was bound to know if such a figure stood next to the surnames of his former colleagues for it was his responsibility to look these lists over. So, in this instance he, too, had a certain amount of free scope.

What prompted him to take pity on them? We are just left guessing. All three, I believe, really did serve him loyally and, as he was not required to take any real personal risk, it was not such a high price to pay for this useful piece of work. But maybe the reasons were all much more mundane and routine: his patronage and protection were the subject of rumours, and this action would not only raise him in his subordinates' eyes but also inspire others to serve him with as much devotion and zeal.

But devoted service, as we already know, did not save anyone from being punished. On the contrary, being too well informed and participating too actively in the dirty work was the surest and most direct way to an unmarked grave. Nearly all the executioners involved in the annihilation of the leading judiciary were shot or sent to camps shortly afterwards: Lulov, Volkov, Gorbunov, Kogan, Sokolov, Sagaidak, to name but a few. Armenia's NKVD investigator, Ruben Arutyunyan, who conducted the investigation in Katanyan's case, was also shot. (It is not known why an investigator was summoned from Armenia when Katanyan lived and committed his 'crimes' in Moscow. But the intention is clear: to hand the victim over to be tormented by someone of his own nationality and thus compel the latter to be particularly cruel and absolutely intransigent so as not to be accused later of leniency.) The others avoided punishment in so far as I have been able to discover.

Was there some concealed reason for the investigator's surname being printed on the records of the evidence and other procedural documents without his name and patronymic or even initials? Perhaps there was. At any rate, they are nowhere to be found, thus making it practically impossible to track any of them down. Makarov ... Borisov ... How many thousands of honest people have the same surname. How could you find the identities of the henchmen and torturers?

Only one, by sheer chance, revealed himself – Leonid Yefimovich Itkin – a State Security Sergeant who at the end of the thirties was in charge of operations of the 6th department of the Chief Directorate of State Security of the NKVD. He took part in the torture of prisoners. In 1952 he was dismissed – not for unlawful actions or brutality but for unfavourable 'personal credentials'. In the mid-fifties he lived in Moscow. His telephone number was B17139. That is all the information we have on him. Maybe he will show up?

Vyshinsky reading out the sentence at the
Shakhty trial, 1928.

Ilya Braude, one of the defending lawyers at
Stalin's show trials in the 1930s.

Vyshinsky (left), Air Vice-Marshal Arthur Tedder and Marshal Zhukov.

The banner reads: 'Wipe the Trotskyite-Zinovievite band of murderers off the face of the earth – such is the sentence of the working people'.

Vyshinsky signing the
declaration of the
defeat of Germany,
Berlin, 5 June, 1945.

Leonid Serebryakov, the
prominent Central
Committee member
purged in 1937, whose
dacha Vyshinsky
'acquired'.

The three-power
conference at Potsdam in
1945. The Soviet
delegation: Vyshinsky,
Molotov and Stalin.

Valentin Lifshits. A
promising young lawyer
and acquaintance of the
author – accused of trying
to assassinate Stalin and
executed only days before
Stalin's death in 1953.

Vyshinsky, 1937.

Vasily Ulrikh, one of Stalin's most infamous
judges, 1937.

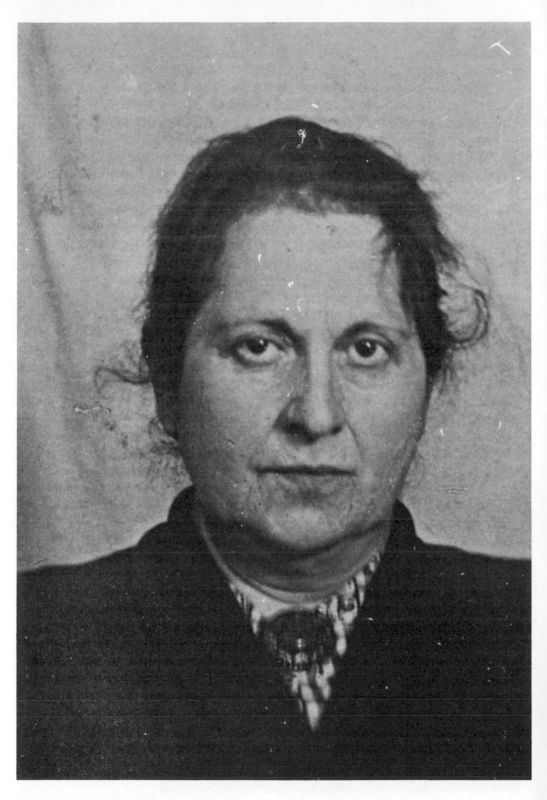

Professor Sofia Kopelyanskaya, a prominent lawyer and friend of the author's family.

Karl Radek, one of the accused at the Pyatakov trial, January 1937.

A studio portrait of Vyshinsky in the early 1950s when he was head of the Soviet delegation to the UN in New York.

The Gulag Boss, Boris Berman (first left), showing Molotov, Stalin, Yezhov, and Voroshilov the Volga-Moscow canal built by Gulag prisoners.

The Soviet Supreme Court in session. In the centre, Vyshinsky.

Opposite (top) Antipov (left), Shvernik, Yagoda and Kosarev, Moscow 1939.

Opposite (below) The Soviet journalist Koltsov, Malraux and Gorky.

Meeting of the military branch of the Supreme Court of the USSR. In the centre, Vasily Ulrikh.

Vyshinsky with his wife and daughter about to leave New York for his last holiday, summer 1954.

6

The country meanwhile was working at full speed. As the prison cells became increasingly packed and more and more blood flowed in the secret dungeons, the reports on the successive victories also grew more triumphant, and the heroes' smiles in the countless pictures in the press became all the more radiant. Polar explorers heroically conquered the Arctic, pilots made tremendously long flights, musicians won first prizes at the most prestigious international competitions. Nearly every day brought news of records being broken at factories, collective farms and sports arenas.

The Mint was also a hive of activity – printing the decorations which the Motherland awarded her glorious sons for mercilessly destroying the counter-revolutionaries' nests.

Grandfather Kalinin – whose wife was now imprisoned in a labour camp as a spy (although I could find no trace of her being under arrest in either the Procurator's or court archives) – smiled benevolently and shook his beard as he handed out the decorations to her tormentors, congratulated them on behalf of the Party and Government and wished them new success in their humane work.

Vyshinsky's name was constantly in the press. The endless meetings and rallies were permanent fixtures in the political calendar of those days. And as for speeches – Vyshinsky spoke a countless number of times, especially during the election campaign, which was conducted for the first time and therefore given special pomp.

The pre-election posters and brochures draw us a fine portrait of a staunch Bolshevik and indestructible humanist. The fact that until the age of thirty-seven the 'loyal son of the great Bolshevik Party' had struggled quite actively against the Bolsheviks is, of course, passed over. To make up for this, it is naturally stated that 'in the courts staunch, strong, uncompromising, ruthless with enemies Procurator-General Comrade Vyshinsky personifies the people's wrath. The entire Soviet people speaks through his lips.'

In pre-election posters and newspaper articles the Procurator-General's image as a 'brilliant professor', 'fine commentator on current affairs', and 'sensitive, responsive person' was drilled into the minds of millions of readers. Let us look at the latter set of virtues:

Last summer an elderly woman, Citizen X, a professor's widow, came to the Procurator-General's office in such an agitated state that she could hardly speak. She was grieving deeply: her husband had died only a few days before, her only son had been taken seriously ill, and now the heartless people she shared the apartment with had taken advantage of her completely helpless state and started a disgraceful lawsuit against her, intent on forcing her out of the apartment which was legally hers, and making her life a misery. These people had driven her to utter despair and she no longer had the strength to fight them. She was asking for Comrade Vyshinsky's personal intervention. Comrade Vyshinsky was not in his office at the time, and so she recorded her request in the complaints' book in a few desperately scribbled words and she left. Upon his return from a sitting of the Soviet People's Commissariat, Comrade Vyshinsky read through the message, telephoned one of his assistants and charged him to go to the woman's apartment immediately and invite her to return with him to the Procurator's office. Half an hour later this woman was sitting in the Procurator-General's office, telling him her story. Next day the Procurator visited the apartment in question, conducted a thorough investigation, and through the courts the Procurator's office subsequently obtained the full restoration of the woman's violated rights.

A worker by the name of Grigorieva once came to the Procurator-General to complain about not having received the alimony due to her for a year. Her ex-husband was stubbornly evading his paternal duties and the local authorities in the town of Gavrilov-Posad where her husband now resided were dealing with her complaint in a most callous manner by not replying or doing anything. Comrade Vyshinsky found time to hold a special meeting with his assistants about this complaint where he fully discussed the question and the measures to be taken by the Procurator's office to intensify the fight against inveterate defaulters of alimony. And to deal with Grigorieva's complaint at hand a representative of the Procurator-General's office was sent to Gavrilov-Posad to expose the red-tape mongers, take them and the alimony defaulter to court and see that everything he owed was recovered.

The recollections of contemporaries have left us with other striking illustrations of the Procurator-General's exemplary sensitivity.

Until about the end of 1935 the Procurator-General's office was open to everyone without passes, and once a week Vyshinsky used to receive visitors. He would speak calmly, never raising his voice, nodding sympathetically, and making indignant rejoinders when the visitor complained about the bureaucratic arbitrariness of local chiefs or their subordinates' callousness. Later, when vigilance was generally increased, the Procurator's office in Pushkinskaya Street was closed to the public, but every now and then Vyshinsky used to receive visitors by prior arrangement. After passing several military posts – at the outside gates, at the entrance to the building, on the fourth floor where his office was located and, finally, by his office door – and going through a filter of assistants and assessors, the visitor who had been permitted to see the legendary humanitarian would be greeted by the unsmiling but irreproachably correct Procurator. He conducted his conversations standing, surrounded by a large retinue, and never offered his visitor a seat. This was not because he was extremely polite but because he was in an extreme hurry – it is more difficult to remain standing for long. The procurators on duty – who were, naturally, not sitting either – hurriedly scribbled down his instructions and messages on means of assisting the petitioners. Sometimes, instead of relying on his assistants, he dialled a telephone number himself or asked to be connected immediately by direct government line to the important republican or regional officials on whom the visitor's fate depended. He never asked – he ordered, and issued instructions to be carried out very quickly, requesting to be informed as soon as they had been put into effect.

His responsiveness, business-like manner and determination were astonishing and impressive. It is easy to imagine how the visitor felt as he left the office: it had been worth it then – forcing your way up so incredibly high – if you got the result you wanted.

But usually there was no result. By the late thirties it was already impossible to get through to officials in their offices, let alone the Procurator-General. And, anyway, he received 'visitors' and issued instructions to his subordinates. So, what more could be expected of him? The anonymous assessors were also on the other side of the guard posts, and the receptionist used to send the 'visitor' back to the local-level officials who only slowed everything down and sabotaged it.

Thus, several aims were achieved at once: the Procurator-General bore out his reputation as a champion of ordinary people's rights, while ordinary people, as exemplified by those who unsuccessfully sought out the truth, convinced themselves that wrecking and sabotage really were going on everywhere.

Recently I received a letter from eighty-year-old Yevgeny Mikhailovich Kashendrovsky from the village of Saltykovka in the Moscow region. Half a century ago he worked in the Radio Committee's sound recording department and once helped Vyshinsky 'edit' the recording of his pre-election speech, cutting out the passages he did not like. The speech was broadcast the same evening. At the end the 'Internationale' began playing as usual but suddenly inexplicably broke off. 'A black car immediately came for the girl on duty,' recalled Yevgeny Kashendrovsky, 'and we never saw her again.' Wrecking and sabotage really were going on everywhere.

Engaged though he was in a ruthless struggle against enemies, the Procurator could not cancel his visits and meetings with the electorate. At one of these meetings a voter innocently asked where the honourable candidate-deputy had conducted his revolutionary work in 1910 and what it had been. It really was an innocent question: the voter thought he had met Vyshinsky then and this could elevate him in the eyes of his associates. But Vyshinsky went crimson and demanded: 'Who gave you the mission of organizing a provocation here?!' The *agent provocateur* was led away from the meeting and the candidate used this as an object-lesson: 'Now everyone can see what despicable methods a class enemy may resort to.'

However, Vyshinsky did not spend all his time punishing and saving people, and making speeches; he was also energetically engaged in academic work. His capacity for work was astonishing, his energy limitless. By this time few of his colleagues nor any of the co-authors of his academic works were still around. Professor Undrevich, with whom he had written his criminal trial textbook for students, had just disappeared. Vyshinsky had actually written it with Krylenko, but, when the latter had turned out to be an enemy, another co-author was instantly found who, with Vyshinsky's assistance, took over from his predecessor. Shortly afterwards his turn came too.

Now Vyshinsky reigned supreme in the realm of jurisprudence. To let everyone know of this and officially confirm his academic supremacy, leadership and superiority, the highest authority in the world of 'pure theory' – the Academy of Sciences of the USSR – intervened. Vyshinsky had addressed the Academicians, professors and doctors of science several times at the Academy, and the public had learnt of these 'historical addresses' from the extensive reportings in the press.

Vyshinsky had given one of these addresses, 'The dictatorship of the proletariat over twenty years and Stalin's Constitution', before the Bukharin–Rykov trial had actually started, but it was devised as an account of the already pronounced sentence. After calling Bukharin a 'Fascist agent', 'spies' hireling' and 'despicable offal, the filthiest of the filthy rabble of international reaction', Vyshinsky advanced the following hypothesis: 'now that Bukharin and Pashukanis have been exposed as members of the same Trotskyite-Fascist underground terrorist organization, is it not becoming clear why Bukharin's contribution was published in *The Revolution of the Law*, a collection edited by Pashukanis, and why Pashukanis was so well-disposed towards him?'

Another part of his paper was devoted to how Bukharin, Rykov and Tomsky had 'created the Ryutin platform'. He dumbfounded his erudite audience by unexpectedly announcing: 'It may be considered an established fact that one of the real authors of the Ryutin platform was none other than Bukharin.'

Incidentally it has now been authenticated that this false accusation was fabricated at the Lubyanka on Stalin's direct instructions in order to implicate Bukharin in 'illegal activities' when the latter had never taken part in any secret conspiracies and had openly argued with Stalin within the limits of the Party statutes.

Vyshinsky then suggested to his audience that they should 'destroy, root out Pashukanis' entire gang'and 'praise the great leader, teacher, creator, inspirer, maker of the immortal Constitution, the helmsman of the Revolution and great guardian of Lenin's behests.'

On the 120th anniversary of Karl Marx's birth, in 1938, Vyshinsky visited the Academy again with a paper on 'Questions of the Law and State in Karl Marx's Writings'. The speaker declared Stalin 'the great guardian of Marx's behests' and the 'great continuer of the Marx-Engels cause'. 'The present era,' he continued:

is the Stalinist era of flourishing Socialism, the era of the unprecedented triumph of Marxist ideas, developed and elevated by Stalin's works to an unprecedented height. ... All the so-called major philosophers and lawyers, celebrated theorists, primitive giants of thought are on closer inspection feeble and wretched.... These authors of an eclectic mash understand nothing of the classical structure of the law.

After settling accounts with all the Soviet lawyers who had already been arrested and annihilated or those who were still awaiting their turn, Vyshinsky turned to his favourite subject of slating Bukharin, who, only a month before, had been executed on his orders. He ended his thesis by defining Bukharin as a 'vile mongrel from a rabid Fascist pack'. The way to academic supremacy now lay open.

It was achieved on 28 January 1939 when a general meeting of the Academy of Sciences was finally held to conduct the election that had suddenly been postponed over two years before. This time everything was much more democratic: there was not one but two vacancies for members of the legal profession – with three candidates. Two got through – Andrei Vyshinsky with his specialist works *The Theory of Law* and *The Criminal Trial*, and Ilya Trainin, a taciturn old Bolshevik who made no impact on academic study before or after his election, or on anything else, for that matter. To make up for they, they rejected Professor Mikhail Gernet, who really was a leading theorist with a world name, the author of the multi-volume *History of the Tsarist Prison*, an achievement not only in academic but in human terms – he was completely blind. The results of the secret ballot were never disclosed, but by this time they were anything but secret. And so one may rest assured that Andrei Yanuarievich Vyshinsky was unanimously hailed 'immortal'. Three other lawyers were also elected to the Academy to fill the correspondent-members vacancies: Mikhail Alexandrovich Arzhanov, Sergei Alexandrovich Golunsky and Mikhail Solomonovich Strogovich.

The choice of Arzhanov was most odd: like a great many others, he was a very ordinary theorist who had made no impression whatsoever on jurisprudence. Like Ilya Trainin, he was a mediocre worker who had been promoted to an administrative post, and someone for whom family background and 'origin' were substitutes for academic potential. However, the two others held high posts in the academic hierarchy, as they were fully entitled to. Proof of this was to be found not only in their services before the election but also in what they did afterwards. They entered the Academy, of course, not without Vyshinsky's help: he alone had the absolute right to select a cell for everyone in the judicial honeycomb. As the official opponent when each of them defended his doctoral thesis, his appreciation of them had not simply been flattering, but positively rapturous!

All these good turns had to be paid back. In Academician Vyshinsky's book *The Theory of Legal Evidence in Soviet Law* – soon to appear in two editions, receive the Stalin Prize of the First Degree, and become a leading fundamental textbook for every lawyer in the country – the 'hallmarks' of these two undoubtedly high-level theorists are, for any observant reader, only too obvious. The moment their 'hallmarks' vanish and the Academician's appear, there is an abrupt and depressing change in stand, moral attitude and style; you can tell someone else has taken over.

It is in this work – where to begin with the democratic principles of justice are energetically and convincingly confirmed in a broad historical context – that not only passages, but whole pages suddenly appear demolishing these same principles. Here, too, after numerous complex Latin formuli demonstrating the author's erudition, and references to dozens of foreign sources; it is confirmed as an indisputable fact that 'the defendants' statements in state crimes are inevitably regarded as the main evidence, the most important, crucial evidence'; that the principle of controversy and that of the equality of the prosecution and defence at the trial are a bourgeois legacy; that the old formula 'The world may perish but justice will triumph' is nothing more than legal scholasticism; that another Latin formula 'The law is harsh but it is the law', demanding its rigorous and universal observation 'does not give room for flexibility in the matter of applying the law'.

Once again Vyshinsky did not take long to repay his debt: after taking the helm of Soviet diplomacy, he would recruit the loyal and highly-educated Golunsky to his office, and the latter would have a successful career as a top diplomat, sitting at major talks alongside Stalin and Molotov, acting as an interpreter as well as an adviser.

Strogovich would leave the Procurator's office to devote himself entirely to his academic work and would cautiously, but without reserve, contest the powerful Academician's stand when the latter conceived the idea of excluding the greatest achievement of legal theory and the main security against lawlessness – the presumption of innocence – not only from practice but even from 'pure' theory. Without troubling to reply, the leader of jurisprudence would sweep his opponent aside with the obscure remark that 'such assertions [with regard to the unshakeability of this principle] were groundless' and that 'discussions on this scholastic formula take us back to the times of Archpriest Avvakum.'[1]

But all this would happen later. In the meantime the academic world had cause to celebrate; the academic community enthusiastically applauded the Academy's powerful reinforcement of its ranks – that, at any rate, is how the newspapers reported it.

There was, however, every reason for elation. The one and only honorary member of the Academy left by that time was Nikolai Morozov, an outstanding revolutionary populist who had been incarcerated in the vaults of Schlusselburg Castle and written brilliant works on chemistry, physics, astronomy, mathematics and history. To make his name look less solitary, the Academy added two other great men to the list of honorary Academicians Stalin and, a few years later, Molotov.[2]

That day truly major figures not only in Soviet but also in international terms were elected Academicians: Piotr Kapitsa, Andrei Kolmogorov, Vladimir Obraztsov, Sergei Sobolev, Vladimir Fok, Nikolai Chizhevsky, Lina Shtern, and many other distinguished people. Also elected to the Academy were the writers Alexei Tolstoy and Mikhail Sholokhov; the semi-literate leader of 'scientific atheism' Emelian Yaroslavsky; the suppressor of genetics Trofim Lysenko; and the commentator on Stalin's 'works', philosopher Mark Mitin. Another philosopher, Pavel Yudin, who had been the first to call Pashukanis an imbecile, was awarded the more modest title of correspondent-member.

In the midst of the general jubilation literature was also given an occasion to celebrate: at one stroke of Stalin's pen one hundred and seventy-two writers were awarded government decorations. They included both celebrities and newcomers. Among the former were Mikhail Zoshchenko, soon to be called a 'vulgar individual' and 'scum', and Isaak Babel, who a few months later would become an enemy of the people, and the prominent Jewish writers David Markish, Lev Kvitko, David Gofshtein, Itsik Fefer, all of whom ultimately faced execution.

A day later it was the cinema's turn to celebrate: instead of being in alphabetical order, the huge list of decorated directors, actors and actresses, cameramen, and artists was headed by the name of Sergei Eisenstein, indicating his important role in the cinema.

'My hearty congratulations on the high decoration. I wish you further successes in the struggle to educate a new man born of the genius of great Stalin' – so read the telegram which was sent to the Writers' Union by the indestructible champion of lawfulness who for the very first time proudly signed himself 'Procurator-General of the USSR Academician Vyshinsky'.

So began the final stage of his career as Procurator-General, which was to be both exceedingly eventful and fruitful. At one and the same time he was in charge of the Academic Institute of Law and the journal *Soviet State and Law* and became the 'acknowledged head of Soviet lawyers'. Life never stopped for a second in the Procurator-General's fourth-floor office, where security and tranquillity were watched over by a host of bodyguards – in his eyes there were still terrorists swarming everywhere and it was not without reason that the legendary NKVD was struggling so fiercely against them.

Changes took place in the Yezhov-Vyshinsky-Ulrikh triumvirate. Yezhov, great Stalin's first favourite and most loyal comrade-in-arms, disappeared into the very same dungeons of the Lubyanka where he had herded and exterminated thousands of innocent victims. His place was taken by Lavrentii Pavlovich Beria.

7

In the late evening of Friday, 10 February 1939 the telephone linked to the Kremlin's top line rang on Prosecutor-General Vyshinsky's desk. Besides the ordinary telephone network, there was also the Kremlin network – known as the *vertushka*, a special line – linking a few dozen top Party, Government, and military officials, and a top line for Stalin and his closest associates. And it was into this latter category that Vyshinsky fell.

The telephone call was on behalf of Beria. Beria himself would never stoop to ring Vyshinsky even on the top line; he usually left this to one of his assistants. Possibly – most likely even – this was a humiliation for the Procurator-General. However, there was a positive side to it as well. Between the assistant's 'Comrade Beria wishes to speak to you', and Comrade Beria's 'Good evening, Comrade Vyshinsky', there was a gap of a few seconds during which, on Vyshinsky's signal, all visitors would vanish from his office in a flash, and he would rush through to his private office next door where there was another extension.

It was from here and here only that Vyshinsky used to speak to two of the people with top lines – Stalin and Beria. Only from here and only standing.

Once, Beria telephoned and Vyshinsky made the well-known sign to leave the room, but one person – a novice, no doubt – failed to understand and went on sitting at the table. Eye-witnesses say that Vyshinsky immediately chucked a paperweight at him and hit his mark.

This time there was no need for that; Vyshinsky was sitting alone, reading through recent correspondence.

'Comrade Beria wishes to speak to you.'

Vyshinsky dived into the next room and picked up the receiver.

'Yes, Comrade Beria . . .'

Beria did not come to the telephone for some time. At last, Vyshinsky heard his chillingly familiar voice, filling him at once with terror and adoration.

'Congratulations, Comrade Vyshinsky. Belatedly ... I apologize – the pressure of work ...'

The Procurator knew what the NKVD head was congratulating him on. He certainly knew, and it made him happy; in the flood of congratulations following his election to the Academy there had so far been no short approving note from the all-powerful Beria. The unexpected telephone call had filled this gap.

However, the congratulations were nothing more than part of a ritual observed even by the ruling élite. Beria had actually telephoned on quite a different matter. He announced: 'My special courier is on his way to you. Please give the matter your attention.'

'I will give it my special attention,' the Procurator-General replied firmly, standing to attention.

The courier appeared ten minutes later. He had come for the Procurator's signature on the arrest warrant of two top-ranking officials: Politburo member and Deputy Chairman of the Soviet People's Commissariat Vlas Yakovlevich Chubar, and Candidate-Member of the Politburo Pavel Petrovich Postyshev.

Both men, who were considered – not without reason – loyal comrades-in-arms of great Stalin, had been under arrest for some time; Postyshev had been picked up without any 'warrant' on 21 February, and Chubar, on 4 July 1938.[1] The disappearance of such officials could not, of course, pass unnoticed, as the Procurator-General knew better than anyone; he also knew that nobody had asked for his sanction on the arrest of these deputies of the Supreme Soviet – members of parliament who, according to the Constitution, enjoyed immunity. So why was Beria demanding his signature after such a long time?

Why? Simply to play, even belatedly, at lawfulness? Or by involving him in the annihilation of the 'leadership' was he simply keeping the Procurator-General in line with all the rest? But he had been involved in this, as it was, for many years. Actively. Conspicuously. One or two more or less people condemned to death by him could hardly make much of a difference to the list of his crimes.

It is difficult to work out exactly why Beria needed to secure the Procurator's sanction in this instance. It might well have had something to do with an incident – trifling by the standards of those days – which, however, had had a powerful impact on the NKVD heads of department. In an open 'revolt' an NKVD official had sacrificed himself in order to establish the truth. This not only seemed abnormal but served as a dangerous warning that even honest people could become involved in a gang of thugs.

One of the investigators who had been entrusted with this case was a certain Piotr Iustinovich Tserpento, the head of operations of the fourth department of the NKVD. On 29 April 1938, two months after Postyshev's arrest and the beginning of the inquiry, Tserpento had handed a report to Beria which I shall now quote in full:

As Postyshev has declared, the examination record, which is obviously already in the Central Committee by now, was written on the instructions of Lulov [one of the heads of the investigation bodies of the NKVD], by me and Vizel [an NKVD investigator] without Postyshev's participation; without his confession of guilt. Postyshev for the first time learnt of the contents of 'his' testimony when it was given to him to sign.

Something, of course, happened immediately after this 'report' in note form was handed in, and Tserpento's new report six days later is a reflection of these unknown but plainly obvious events. This is what he reported on 5 May, having sent a copy of his second appeal to Procurator Vyshinsky:

I wrote that Postyshev's statements and examination record were not the testimonies of Postyshev himself, that these documents were written as a summary of all the evidence on Postyshev, and that this summary was given the form of an examination record and Postyshev merely signed without making any effort to say anything at all about his guilt.

What strikes one most about this astonishing report – astonishing if only because it existed – is the last sentence: yes, of course, Postyshev did not have to make any effort himself – others were doing that for him. There are several eye-witness accounts of the condition Postyshev was in after these 'efforts' had been made – of his legs broken, missing teeth, his body covered all over with gashes and cuts. There are also eye-witness accounts of what Vlas Chubar looked like – the very same man who only recently had been the subject of articles in the press describing, for instance, his arrival at a polling station on election day, 12 December 1937: 'Comrade Chubar, accompanied by his wife, mother and child, dropped his voting-paper into the ballot-box in the large flower-decked hall of the Sverdlov Club in the Kremlin. "I am voting for our Bolshevik Party, for our very own great leader Comrade Stalin," he said with a happy smile.'
This happy smile soon turned into a grimace of horror: 'Tell Comrade

Stalin how I am being tortured,' he bellowed as he was being dragged along the prison corridor.

On 9 July 1938 Tserpento was arrested, charged with being a spy and a Trotskyite. Going by all the rules of primitive logic, a spy was supposed to disguise himself, make himself scarce, and be discreet. But who cared about logic? The 'spy' bore himself with stoicism and pride, declaring that no torture would make him deviate from the truth. At an interrogation on 28 January 1939 Tserpento confirmed that all Postyshev's examination records had been forged and that the main organizer of the forged documents was his immediate superior, Lulov. It is astonishing that Tserpento's evidence was actually recorded and not simply destroyed. It was not, however, included in Postyshev's case – it could have influenced such a champion of truth and justice as Vasily Vasilievich Ulrikh![2]

It was found in the mid-fifties, when the crimes of Beria and his associates started to be uncovered. Putting the dates together helps us understand the turmoil going on around the already-arranged murder of these top Party officials and statesmen. Along with Yan Ernestovich Rudzutak, they were the most important figures (after the ones in the show trials) to disappear from the 'board'.

On 11 February, the day after the Procurator had given his 'sanction', the report on Postyshev's and Chubar's cases was sent to the Central Committee, and, what's more, Beria's assistant, Bogdan Kobulov, personally included an important amendment in it: Postyshev had confessed to having worked for Japanese Intelligence from 1920, and Chubar had simply been the 'agent of intelligence services' (evidently, of absolutely all of them). They, of course, had both been in charge of 'anti-Soviet conspiratorial centres' and had prepared 'terrorist acts against Comrade Stalin'.

One may presume this report met with the highest approval, for on 14 February they were both informed of the end of the inquiry and the indictments were read out to them. These two documents were signed by investigators Kondratik and Goldman, and countersigned by their superior Rodos, and then by an even more superior official, Semion Milshtein. And, finally, Andrei Vyshinsky put his signature in the top right corner.

All the formalities were now over. On 26 February, one after the other, Chubar and Postyshev were led into Beria's office in Lefortovo Prison, where Ulrikh and his assistants had assembled. Actually, Postyshev was wheeled in in a wheelchair as he could no longer walk.

An hour later they were both dead.

Shall we ever find out why Vyshinsky signed some high-ranking officials' arrest warrants and not others? I doubt it. And, anyway, it is unlikely this conformed with any fixed pattern.

Alexander Kosarev, the Komsomol General Secretary, though not a Politburo member, enjoyed just as much popularity – if not more – and social clout. His name was constantly in the press, and he travelled extensively round the country, meeting young people. He was of that already almost extinct breed of revolutionaries noted for their simplicity and democratic mixing with the 'masses'.

The storm-clouds had been gathering over his head for some time now. At any rate, it was no coincidence that in March 1938, at a Kremlin reception to celebrate Papanin's successful Arctic expedition, Stalin came up to Kosarev with a glass in his hand, embraced him and whispered in his ear: 'If you betray me, I'll kill you!' Beria, insulted by the unflattering remarks Kosarev frequently made when his, Beria's, name was mentioned – informers, of course, immediately reported back to him – bore a deep grudge against him. So, the spectacular 'Komsomol Case' was set in motion, during which all the secretaries and numerous leading figures in the Komsomol were to be charged with sabotage and terrorism. However, the operation was foiled when they all refused to give evidence against each other. What's more, there was no evidence to substantiate the political denunciation of the Komsomol Central Committee instructress, Olga Mishakova. Of course, the evidence could always have been beaten out of them, but giving the young leaders a public trial would have been a risky affair; they might have wrecked the extremely important operation by denying their evidence in court.

Beria's hatred of Kosarev exceeded all bounds – this is already obvious from the fact that, after signing Kosarev's arrest warrant on 27 November 1939 and without receiving a 'sanction', Beria personally set out to arrest him the next evening. During cross-examinations in the fifties Beria's closest associates confirmed that Beria never again 'stooped' to taking part in arrests himself. Many other Komsomol secretaries were arrested the same night. Nearly all those previously arrested, who knew nothing of their comrades' fate, withstood the blackmail and torture without slandering anyone. Was this youthful romantic stoicism, or were they still hoping to be saved? But with very few exceptions, they all ended up the same way.

Beria ordered one of his closest henchmen, Lev Shvartsman, to torture Kosarev until he 'opened his mouth'.[3] It took even such a past master as Shvartsman a long time to crack this victim. In the end he must have succeeded. In one of the examination records Kosarev admitted to being an agent of German Intelligence and an 'old' Trotskyite. But is it his signature at the bottom of this record? And if so, who supported his limp arm? And did the person the arm belonged to still know what he was doing?

How many arrested Komsomol leaders were there? Thirty? Fifty? Seventy? Or more? Not one arrest warrant or indictment bears the Procurator-General's signature. Of course, Beria's organization had unlimited power and did not require anyone's authorization or sanction. What is curious is that it felt obliged to observe the law even formally, which stated that a person could only be arrested with a procurator's sanction. Vyshinsky would have signed any paper Beria needed. But Beria did not need him to. This was a blow to his self-esteem, or perhaps it hurt more than that? By going about his daily work the way he did, Beria kept this official in his place, this official who, according to the law, was most responsible for the supervision of legality. Vyshinsky, of course, knew about all the arrests of people of any standing. How, indeed, could it escape the notice of a man in the thick of politics and in the top echelon of power? But could anyone, even the Procurator-General, have disputed the arrests, trials and executions carried out by a body enjoying total impunity?

It would seem merciful not to be directly involved in the annihilation programme, not to be forced to turn the handle of the 'meatgrinder' crushing the top statesmen, military commanders and academics. But no, being involved in the orgy of destruction, taking a hand in it oneself and being admitted to the victim's execution meant that he, the Procurator, was needed and that his signature did, in fact, count for something. It did not happen often, but each time he was called upon meant a great deal. That is why Beria's 'request' for him to sanction Postyshev's and Chubar's arrests nearly a year later meant that Vyshinsky was still 'afloat'.

Still? Is this the right way to look at it? After all, we have already convinced ourselves of how important his role was and how successfully he had performed it all these years.

Yes, he had performed it, and done so very successfully, but where? On a stage watched by the whole world, where a superb spectacle had been put on, and he and he alone had been the dramatist – though not the inventor of the plot – the producer, and one of the leading actors. It was he who had written the complex scenario, had been responsible for its accurate interpretation. It was he who had supervized the *mise-en-scène*, worked out the interludes, prepared the

169

reprises, selected the soloists, and conducted the chorus. And here the truly exceptional aspects of his talent had come to the fore: his acumen, quick reaction to unexpected failures and changes of direction, skill for off-the-cuff improvisations, penchant for inflated mass-meeting rhetoric, and his inimitable way of combining cut-throat humour with rectitude. His natural gifts had improved with experience: as a rhetorician in juries, a polemicist in inter-party battles, an agitator and a propagandist.

The first trial had undoubtedly been a success for him. So had the second, more or less. The third, Bukharin's, had nearly been a fiasco. And it had become obvious that there could not be a fourth. New lists were still being drawn up at the Lubyanka, and the frameworks of superb future trials were being knocked together: the Komsomol case, the Diplomats' case, the Writers' case. But there were to be no more show trials intended to create a sensation and arouse mass hysteria. By the end of 1937 Stalin's main opponents were out of the way. The new 'enemies' who had been invented by the inexhaustible imaginations of the Lubyanka visionaries did not enjoy the world fame of Bukharin, Radek or Zinoviev. Neither the future victims' names nor the inevitable repetitions in subject-matter could capture the imagination any longer.

A page of history had come to an end, and another had begun, no less murderous or horrifying in its consequences. The action was now to take place not on a floodlit stage in front of millions of spectators but in the wings. And here another or, rather, other producers would be needed. The producer of grand-scale shows was no longer needed. Suddenly his oratorical tricks, exceptional gift for dragging idols into the gutter and rapturously finishing off defenceless victims to entertain the crowd, suddenly all this proved superfluous. As an art form it had worn itself out and was now set aside.

His blessing on the deaths of Postyshev and Chubar was one of Vyshinsky's last deeds as Procurator-General.

A new chapter was beginning in his life but not, unfortunately, in the country's.

March 1939 saw the 18th Party Congress. Only a small handful of the delegates from the 17th Congress had managed to escape execution. Of the seventy-one Central Committee members elected in 1934, only sixteen were now in the new Central Committee, and this number was soon to dwindle yet again after the next round of arrests. To make up for this, the Party's loyal son, Andrei Vyshinsky, was to become a

Central Committee member for the first time. So were not only Lavrentii Beria and Alexander Poskrebyshev but other prominent figures who had managed to pass through the snares of the NKVD, such as Maxim Litvinov, Dmitry Manuilsky, and Solomon Lozovsky. In one way or another all of them were to play a part in Vyshinsky's life, and each of them differently.

Beria's firmly-entrenched team was certainly impressive. Dzhafar Bagirov and Vsevolod Merkulov were now Central Committee members, and not only Bogdan Kobulov and Vladimir Dekanozov but all the rest of the king's men were candidate-members: Arutiunov, Bakradze, Gvishiani, Goglidze and Charkviani. They had managed to get Tsanava into the inspection commission. For the time being nobody knew them, except perhaps the people they had put in prison. However, they were soon to win popularity. A major place in the Central Committee membership was given over to the military, to the replacements of the annihilated marshals and commanders-in-chief. Nearly all of them had distinguished themselves in the Spanish Civil War, which had just drawn to a sorry close. Grigory Shtern became a Central Committee member, and Alexander Loktionov, Kyril Meretskov and Yakov Smushkievich became candidate-members.

They were all in a buoyant mood; after the violent storm life had seemingly returned to normal. After being shattered and destroyed, the feeling of a single family with its unquestioned and beloved head, Comrade Stalin, was once again restored. 'The Red Army,' promised Grigory Shtern from the Congress platform, 'is religiously carrying out, and will continue to carry out to the end, all the instructions of our great and beloved Leader, the great patriot of our country, our dear Stalin. The Red Army knows that Stalin leads only to victories.' The Leader joined in the stormy applause with which the auditorium responded to these words; at the mention of his name Stalin enjoyed applauding aloofly like an onlooker, along with all the rest.

'We know,' continued Shtern bombastically, 'that if we have to give up our own life, we must do so in such a way as to get ten enemies' lives first.' 'Ten's not enough, it must be twenty,' Voroshilov interrupted him. 'I accept the amendment,' Shtern readily agreed, 'May the record be amended accordingly.'

This is how they joked and kept count of their own lives and others'.

One evening in May Vyshinsky was summoned by Stalin. It was past midnight. Few top officials in Moscow left work earlier than just before daybreak. Stalin was a 'night owl' and could telephone or summon people at whatever time of the day or night he pleased. Some never got a summons or a telephone call but still stayed on late at their battle stations, waiting anxiously.

Things were simpler for Vyshinsky: he had quickly come to a friendly arrangement with Alexander Poskrebyshev, Stalin's permanent personal secretary, a stocky man with a shaven head and three folds of fat around the back of his neck. Poskrebyshev always informed him when the 'Boss' was finally going home to rest. One could say, I think, that Stalin and his Procurator – subsequently Minister – left work simultaneously but returned at different times: Stalin when he wanted to and Vyshinsky strictly by the rules. The recollections of the few remaining colleagues concur: always a model of discipline, the Procurator-General was never late for work, and thus had the moral right to chastise his subordinates who, working such insane hours, had no time to sleep.

Vyshinsky was not summoned to the very top often. But on the rare occasions that he was, he never knew whether to expect another urgent task or a reprimand.

This time Stalin greeted him with a benevolent smile. However, the Leader's smile was not always a sign of his approval. Vyshinsky knew this and so when he saw the smile, he grew even tenser – by pressing an invisible button Stalin could change instantly, turning his affectionate gaze into a savage scowl.

Molotov was also there, as taciturn as ever. He stretched out his hand, looked down and stared thoughtfully at the floor. Vyshinsky also expected to see Beria; the People's Commissar of Internal Affairs had been present at all Stalin's recent conversations with the Procurator-General. This time they made do without him.

We are unlikely to understand how Comrade Stalin's midnight guest was feeling unless we recall the important – most important, even – event preceding this summons, an event which had been concealed from millions of people but which the Procurator-General was well aware of: very recently Nikolai Ivanovich Yezhov had been arrested as an enemy of the people. Iosif Vissarionovich's favourite and most loyal comrade-in-arms, the illustrious People's Commissar, the terror of all Fascists, Trotskyites and Imperialists, the trustworthy guardian of the happy Soviet people's great achievements. The man whose iron clutches had inspired terror throughout the country.

On 21 August 1938, while still the People's Commissar of Internal Affairs, Yezhov had for some reason received a second ministerial portfolio as People's Commissar of Water Transport. Anywhere else in the world such a highly improbable combination of posts would have meant a considerable promotion, but Stalin's 'cabinet' was subject to a different scale of values and system of forecasts. Not many doubted that this was the beginning of the end.

The next act in this many-act drama, which had been finely devised and staged, took place three and a half months later on 8 December when the unassuming Deputy People's Commissar of Internal Affairs, Lavrentii Beria, took over as People's Commissar, allowing Yezhov, who was overloaded with work, to concentrate on the problems of water transport. A little over a month later Yezhov was seen in public for the last time at an evening gathering at the Bolshoi Theatre in memory of Lenin, where he was sitting to one side in the second row. It took great skill on the part of the photographer to single the 'bloodthirsty dwarf' out from the crowd of prominent figures and put him in the official photograph which was published in the press. He was never seen again.

Beria's rise, or rather, Yezhov's fall, marked a very brief and illusory period of 'respite' – the first wave of rehabilitations. The second half of 1938 already saw the release of several dozen people, acquitted on all charges, and rumours about this spread like wild fire across the 'mainland' and Gulag Archipelago, bringing hope, and giving rise to considerable confusion. Vyshinsky instantly joined in the new campaign, perfectly aware of its beguiling decorative function. With much commotion he not only fired but even instituted legal proceedings against the Procurator of the Omsk Region, Busorgin, and the head of the investigation department of the Regional Procurator's office, Nikiforovsky, for having dared sanction the arrests of two or three poor souls who had spent several months languishing in prison through no fault of their own. This triumph of justice (at a session of the Supreme Court of the RSFSR Busorgin was sentenced to two years of imprisonment, and Nikiforovsky was given a public reprimand) was immediately reported by the press in October 1938, and Vyshinsky received numerous telegrams thanking him for his staunch principles, integrity and loyalty to the law. At the same time the Komsomol was purged, its leadership sent to prison, and hundreds and thousands of new victims were already being deported under guard.

'I am bewildered and dismayed by your interpretation of Vyshinsky,' G. P. Sutotsky wrote to me from Leningrad after my first publication on Vyshinsky in the weekly newspaper *Literaturnaya Gazieta*:

I was an 'enemy of the people' and my life was saved by Vyshinsky! It happened like this: in October 1937, while a second-year student of a Sverdlovsk institute, I was given ten years of hard labour *in absentia*, by a NKVD 'Troika' [a 'special hearing' conducted by three NKVD operatives]. My father, an elderly intellectual, started writing letters to all the 'top brass' at the time (to all the Politburo members, procurators of all ranks, to Sholokhov and Ehrenburg, and so on) ... one hundred and five letters in all, to dozens of addresses. Then he decided to write to Vyshinsky, and he was the only one who did anything! My case was re-opened and I was acquitted of all charges!

It appears that it was by a stroke of good luck that this young man was among the fortunate few who were saved. Professors and military commanders were released, as were the poetess Olga Berggolts, after losing her baby and her health, and a number of other writers, actors, workers, collective farmers and students. The rumours spread and were exaggerated, giving rise to an illusion of releases on a mass scale, which, in turn, created a mood of elation and hope among the people. How strange that many years later such a clear-sighted and discerning man as Konstantin Simonov was still under its hypnotic power, as his posthumously published *Notes: Through the Eyes of a Man of my Generation* were to indicate: 'Beria's first work in Moscow was connected with the numerous rehabilitations, the closure of cases and return from labour camps and prisons of dozens, if not hundreds of thousands of people.' Alas, Beria's rise to power coincided not with hundreds of thousands of rehabilitations but with the rumour of hundreds of thousands of rehabilitations, substantiated by the actual release of a few hundred, or at most a few thousand people.

When the wave of mass arrests had reached its peak, there had to be a respite, a period of relative calm for both the executioners and the victims to get back their strength. And, more importantly, for society to as well, as it had been driven insane by the smell of blood. Once again several objectives were achieved at once: Stalin now appeared in the role of a peacemaker and humanitarian who had not known what Yezhov had been up to and had freed 'his' people from Yezhov's iron clutches; an individual who had known too much and had personally carried out the dictator's criminal designs had been removed; a murderer who had been hated by the whole country was replaced by someone who had proved his loyalty and was hailed by the people as the herald of humanity and justice. Meanwhile everything went on just as before, the arrests and the machinery of extermination, everything, that is, except the methods: instead of the bloody shows and the cursing and swearing at meetings, unpublicized massacres now took place out of the public eye. Flagrant gangsterism was replaced by concealed gangsterism. Only a short while before a person who had just been 'taken' was hastily denounced in public as an 'exposed enemy' with a kind of frenzied delight – cursed and decried in every possible manner. When, however, Academician Nikolai Vavilov was arrested slightly later, not only did nobody revile this 'enemy' and 'spy' aloud but, on the contrary, all inquiries from colleagues and friends abroad – by word of mouth, in writing, official and personal – invariably received the reply that he was alive and well, absolutely safe and sound, and working very hard in seclusion because he was tired of being in the limelight, of all the fuss and bother. This was true not only of Vavilov but of hundreds of other well-known figures.

The music went on playing but the key changed. And so did the style. A need was felt for new conductors. Yezhov and Vyshinsky were members of the same team; they were inseparable. While Yezhov's department had fabricated cases, Vyshinsky's department had 'legalized' them whenever necessary, giving them shape and cogency. Half the team had fallen by the wayside, why shouldn't the other half as well?

Stalin was businesslike and to the point. He quickly wiped away his smile, and began in a roundabout manner: 'What are you working on, Comrade Vyshinsky?'

So Vyshinsky gave a brief but thorough report on the present situation: the entire population was selflessly toiling in the radiant light of Stalin's Constitution, religiously observing the laws; there had been a steady decrease in crime; the procurators were being vigilant, but the enemy, unfortunately, was not giving in and still had to be well and truly rooted out; Beria and his fine security officers were exposing nests of spies as well as correcting falsifications – the handiwork of the spies and agents who had penetrated the NKVD along with the villain Yezhov. Hand-in-hand with Comrade Beria and under his wise leadership the Procurator's office was restoring flouted lawfulness, but they should not think, those despicable hirelings, saboteurs, diversionists, terrorists, spies, Trotskyites, Zinovievites, Bukharinites and other scum, they should not think that we are becoming less vigilant – on the contrary, we are becoming ever more so.

'That's good,' Stalin interrupted him. 'That's very good.' He went on pacing slowly up and down his office for a long time. 'What do you think of our cultural situation, Comrade Vyshinsky? In science, literature and art.'

Stalin never asked a question he did not already have his own answer to. All you had to do was guess what it was without making a fool of yourself.

Vyshinsky's phenomenal memory immediately exhumed from its secret recesses all the information there was on the 'conspirators' in the arts and sciences. Just like everywhere else, there was no shortage of them.

'On the whole,' he replied, vainly trying to follow Stalin's facial expression, 'the situation is normal, the successes in this field are evident.' He recalled the recent election to the Academy, the mass honouring of writers and film-makers. 'Party and government policies are being zealously supported. ... But there is also a lot of rubbish ... obvious enemies ...'

'That is well known,' Stalin interrupted him again. 'It is our opinion,' he nodded to Molotov, 'that people in the arts and sciences require your attention, Comrade Vyshinsky.'

Now, at long last everything became clear: a trial was being planned, not just of writers or scientists, but a large, all-embracing one to expose the Trotskyism which had affected a 'layer' of intellectuals who had got a false idea of their own importance. What a pity they had been in such a hurry with Pashukanis and shot him too early – he would have been the star of this trial.

But, unfortunately, Vyshinsky did not have time to say that he was always ready to set to work immediately because Stalin forestalled him with another question.

'Are you yourself, Comrade Vyshinsky, well acquainted with people working in our arts and sciences? Do you have good connections with them?'

That was all he needed! To be dragged down to the level of those upstarts and rogues!

'I would not say so, Comrade Stalin.'

'Really!' said Stalin in a surprised tone, casting Molotov a significant glance. 'So, Comrade Beria gives false information. That's a pity. We were of the opinion that it was no mere chance that the Academicians had accepted you into their close circle. Sheltered you, one could say.'

He enjoyed watching his torments, perfectly aware of what was going on in this procurator's soul which he had sold to the devil. However, Vyshinsky also understood what his Leader and Teacher had in mind: it was, of course, Vyshinsky's transfer to another post.

Yezhov had not been 'taken' straight away either: he, as we remember, had spent some time as People's Commissar of Water Transport, just as Yagoda had been the People's Commissar of Communications. The pattern was familiar, and the outcome a foregone conclusion. To which post was he to be appointed before being liquidated? The President of the Academy? But Komarov was there, and it was unlikely anyone would touch this harmless old man, wasn't it? The Chairman of the Arts Committee? Mikhail Khrapchenko had recently replaced Platon Kerzhentsev in this post – had his turn come as well?

Perhaps Stalin tired of playing cat-and-mouse because he again changed his tone.

'Comrade Molotov,' he said, 'is asking the Politburo to reinforce the leadership of the Soviet of People's Commissars. Efficient, discerning people who are devoted to Stalin are needed there. The motion is being put forward to make you Comrade Molotov's assistant in scientific and cultural matters. What does Academician Vyshinsky think of this?'

What did Academician Vyshinsky think of this? Most likely, that this post as Deputy Chairman of the Soviet People's Commissariat was too high to be offered if his arrest was being prepared. With such an end in sight Stalin would have chosen a less conspicuous post and not bothered to summon him.

'I am ready to carry out any task the Party and Comrade Stalin set me,' Vyshinsky replied.

This was a routine reply, the one and only formula for everyone no matter what place they occupied in the hierarchy.

'You are a cultured man, you're well-educated,' continued Stalin, 'are you respected? What do you think?' He gazed attentively at Vyshinsky as though expecting confirmation from him. The latter listened without so much as moving a muscle. 'you have ...' he was searching for the right word, 'You have a world-famous name. You'll find a common language with the writers, academics, painters, composers, artists, and architects ... With the fighters of our cultural front.'

'I am ready to carry out ...' Vyshinsky began again.

Stalin nodded. The audience was at an end.

On 1 June 1939 a regular session of the Supreme Soviet confirmed Vyshinsky's appointment to the office of Deputy Chairman of the Soviet People's Commissariat, having relieved him of his duties as Procurator-General of the USSR. The place in his office in Pushkinskaya Street was taken by the featureless and totally unknown Mikhail Pankratiev.

The country was told nothing at all about this man who had taken over from the world-famous lawyer and now held such a tremendously important position in the state. The post itself was not a key one at all, even in Vyshinsky's time. It was not the post that had given Vyshinsky power: it was he with his personal presence who had elevated this post, creating for it an illusion of power, which seemed to be naturally part of it. He remained in this post only while such an illusion was needed for state-level policies.

The offices where Vyshinsky had set up his new fighting headquarters immediately became a hive of activity. Preparations were well under-way for holding one of the numerous showy events which were then very popular – the First All-Union Conference of Theatre Producers. Conducted with great pomp and ceremony and invariably attended by top Party officials and statesmen, these all-union conferences and rallies on the most unusual pretexts, and sometimes without any pretext at all, were regular fixtures. Record-breaking collective-farm workers and *Stakhanovite* miners, the wives of Red Army commanders and exemplary Young Pioneers all gathered together at these rallies and congresses in the Kremlin or Hall of Columns of Trade Union House, and made speeches about how wonderful their lives were and how infinitely, boundlessly, totally and wholeheartedly they loved their very own Comrade Stalin.

The forthcoming producers' conference was like all the others but with its own special aim. After Moscow Art Theatre director Stan-islavsky's death and the total devastation of Meyerhold's theatre there was no acknowledged, indisputable leader left among the country's theatrical producers. It was essential to create the impression of a collective leadership, bring Meyerhold, who was then in disgrace, to his knees and compel producers to put on Soviet plays glorifying the concept of socialist realism.

The conference opened in the large hall of the Central House of Actors. Though it was called 'large', the hall seated no more than four hundred. On that day it was completely packed out, and its audience gave a rapturous welcome to the celebrities of the stage from all over the country. Despite having to contend with the most stringent restrictions in their choice of repertoire, there were still highly talented people working in the theatre in those days, and their names are still remembered in the history of the theatre. This conference was a genuine forum, not just for show: on the platform were top artists and producers such as Alexander Yablochkin, Prov Sadovsky, Yuri Yuriev,

Solomon Mikhoels, Alexander Tairov, Alexei Popov, Yuri Zavadsky, Samuil Samosud, Ruben Simonov, Maksim Shtraukh, Ivan Bersenev and the writers Alexei Tolstoy, Alexander Fadeyev and Konstantin Trenev. Meyerhold, however, was not up among the most honoured but modestly sitting in one of the last rows.

Everyone present had just finished applauding the election of an honorary presidium (comprising Comrade Stalin and his loyal comrades-in-arms; Lavrentii Beria, incidentally, was last on the list) when something made them start applauding again. It seemed as though the old walls and their bas-reliefs of the most celebrated figures of the Russian stage were going to come crumbling down under the weight of the thunderous ovation: a portly man with a narrow moustache and well-groomed, thinning hair had appeared: it was Andrei Yanuarievich Vyshinsky, and this was the first time he was appearing in public in his new post.

After the introductory speeches he was given the floor. He certainly had every right to participate in this forum and be its main speaker, and not just because of his new post. After all, what other producer had staged spectacular shows that had stunned the whole of the civilized world? Who else had succeeded in attracting such illustrious 'actors' to carry out his designs? Who else could have bent them so to his will and raised the standard of acting to such unprecedented heights?

Vyshinsky's appeal to them was 'to develop and augment great Soviet art which has been cultivated by the dearly loved hand of our great Teacher and Leader, Comrade Stalin.' And once again everyone present burst into ecstatic applause, old celebrities and young talents joining in with equal enthusiasm. The applause was hardly over when Vyshinsky began explaining to them that 'formalism signifies the condition of art when content lags behind form'. In his speeches for the prosecution he had been more eloquent but he obviously did not feel quite as much at home here. 'One must,' he continued, wagging his finger, 'know how to be critical of the work of various experimentalists who frequently try, under the guise of experimentation, to bring back the dead, concealing the crude survival of pernicious alien elements with all manner of "isms".'

Probably not wishing his entire speech to sound like a prosecutor's, he again appealed to his benefactor for help: 'Great Stalin has completed the Marxist-Leninist teaching on the intelligentsia and thus elevated it to a new historic stage of development.'

Eye-witnesses recall how the audience agonizingly followed not so much what the recent Procurator-General was saying as his intonation, trying to get even a vague idea of the ordeals that lay ahead – after all, Vyshinsky's name was associated with nothing but ordeals.

Finally, after conveying to his audience the greetings of the theatre workers' best friend, Comrade Stalin, the high-ranking guest returned to the platform to listen with accentuated concentration to the delegates themselves. They all said the same thing: even these most talented and brilliant people spoke of the unprecedented flourishing of society, and the great concern, the tremendous responsibility which 'our grandiose age' had laid upon them. And how encouraged they were by the attention being given to them. And how infinitely grateful they were. Wise and magical Solomon Mikhoels exclaimed: 'The only thing that can enlighten and enliven art, the only thing that can generate genuine enthusiasm ... is ... what the Party teaches, what Comrade Stalin teaches us.' All the others followed suit. Only Serafima Birman, an actress whose talent did not conflict with her sense of dignity and loyalty to the truth, dared recall the 'insulting narrowness given to realism'.

Vsevolod Meyerhold also spoke. Such was the applause – a show of deferential enthusiasm and demonstrative solidarity – that he could not start his speech for a long time. Vyshinsky sat still with his head lowered. One can easily imagine what was going through his mind and how he felt when the audience greeted this living genius who had been so reviled and insulted by the authorities he represented.

In his memoirs, which were published in the West, Yuri Yelagin, then a soloist of the Vakhtangov Theatre's orchestra, claims that he wrote up Meyerhold's speech from notes he took at the time. However, this account cannot be authenticated as no other notes of this speech exist. According to Yelagin, Meyerhold made a tragically inspired speech, which essentially resembled the farewell speech of someone about to commit suicide, and in which he contrasted the scene of devastation in the Soviet theatre with all the eulogies and idle talk about it.

However, according to the actress Y. Tyapkina, who met Meyerhold in Leningrad shortly before his arrest, Meyerhold was displeased with his speech, and considered it a failure. Not long before his premature death Meyerhold's biographer, the eminent theatre critic Konstantin Rudnitsky, told me that he had found the shorthand report of Meyerhold's speech which had been corrected by its author, and judging by it, the speech was delivered in the most loyal tones, and was in no way sharper than any of the others.

This is very possible. But Vyshinsky still did not like the speech. And I do not know when Meyerhold would have had the time to receive, read and correct the shorthand report of his speech. The fact is that as soon as he had made it, without waiting until the end of the conference, that very same evening he set off for the railway station and left for Leningrad: in disgrace and deprived of a means of earning his living, he was compelled to agree to the Leningrad Lesgaft Institute's proposal to prepare a theatrical show for a forthcoming physical training parade. He was arrested five days later when the conference's concluding session was still in progress. Thus, after taking up his new elevated post, Comrade Vyshinsky made an immediate impression on our culture.

According to the retired military procurator Boris Ryazhsky, who was in charge of Meyerhold's rehabilitation, 'what directly caused his arrest' was both the sharp letter his wife, Zinaida Raikh, had written to Stalin protesting about the theatre's closure, and what she had said: 'Tell Stalin that if he isn't a good judge of art, he can turn to Meyerhold', which had apparently reached Stalin's ears. However, I do not think anybody knows what the direct cause was, and, anyway, did any arrest in those days have an indisputable 'direct cause'?

The investigation took seven months. To begin with, Meyerhold confessed to having been a Trotskyite from 1923; to having 'led the "Left Front" anti-Soviet group in 1930 which had united all the anti-Soviet elements in the realm of art' (known as LEF, Vladimir Mayakovsky and Nikolai Aseyev participated in it and it only existed until 1929); to having 'made organizational contacts in 1933 with ... Rykov, Bukharin and Radek, on whose mission he had conducted subversive activity in the sphere of theatrical art', and to having organized, at his house, Rykov's conspiratorial meetings with British intelligence agents; to having been recruited three years later into a Trotskyite organization by Ilya Ehrenburg, and recruited as a British spy by Yurgis Baltrushaitis, a well-known poet who until only recently had been Lithuania's Ambassador to the Soviet Union; to having given secret information to British and Japanese Intelligence from 1934 until the time of his arrest. Exactly what the information was the record does not say.[4]

Meyerhold found the inner strength and courage to deny this nonsense while the investigation was still in progress. Several weeks before the trial he appealed in writing to Beria, Vyshinsky, and, finally, Molotov. He condemned Trotsky: 'along with the Party I cursed the

181

Judas Trotsky', and called him 'an inveterate rogue of the breed of political adventurers' capable 'only of base diversions and clandestine murders'. How can Meyerhold be blamed for saying this? His curses were no threat to Trotsky, and a drowning man will clutch at straws. After all, he had been accused of being a Trotskyite, which was something he most certainly never was.

More importantly, however, Meyerhold wrote to the Academician:

> I ... was placed face down on the floor and beaten across the heels and back with a rubber rod; then I was put on a chair and beaten across the legs with the same rubber rod. . . . And the following days, when there was considerable internal haemorrhaging in these parts of my legs, I was again beaten with this rod across these mauve and yellow bruises, and the pain was so intense it felt as though boiling water was being poured onto these agonizingly sensitive parts of my legs (I shouted out and wept with pain). I was beaten across the back with this rubber rod, and across the face.

And in another part of his letter he wrote:

> The investigator kept repeating in a menacing voice: 'If you don't write ... we'll beat you again, and leave your head and right arm alone, but turn the rest of you into a shapeless bloody lump.' And I went on signing until 16 November 1939. I deny my evidence which was beaten out of me in such a manner.

He received no reply from either Molotov or Vyshinsky.

Izvestia's correspondent Ilya Ehrenburg was working in Paris at the time and desperately wanted to get back to Moscow, totally unaware of having recruited anyone to any organization. Nor did the writers Yuri Olesha and Boris Pasternak have any idea that they had been recruited – into the same organization – by Ehrenburg. When the military procurator, Lieutenant of the Justice Ryazhsky, began his inquiry into the 'V. E. Meyerhold-Raikh case' in 1955,[5] he searched in vain for the dossiers of Ehrenburg's conspirators, Olesha and Pasternak, in the archives of the case. All three appeared, alive and well, before the Lieutenant but, fortunately, even from him they never found out about the plot against them.

It was, let us remember, only 1955, and several months were still to go before the 20th Party Congress, Stalin's portraits still adorned the streets and offices, and the words 'leader and teacher' were still appended to his name. The process of rehabilitating the victims of Stalinism had only just begun. That is why Ryazhsky decided to make his conclusion as sound as possible: his dossier contained over fifty testimonials on Meyerhold from the most prominent figures of the Soviet arts.

Nothing quite like it, I believe, had ever happened before. The fullest collection of testimonials on a producer's contribution to world art was to be found not in TGALI (the Central State Archive of Literature and Art) but in the Procurator's office. And what names there were: Dimitry Shostakovich, Boris Pasternak, Ilya Ehrenburg, Nazim Khikmet, Vsevolod Ivanov, Mikhail Romm, Nikolai Okhlopkov, Igor Ilinsky, Mikhail Tsarev, Ivan Pyriev, Erast Garin, Mikhail Zharov, Lev Sverdlin, Mikhail Shtraukh, Vladimir Sofronitsky, Lev Oborin, Sergei Obraztsov, Leonid Vivien, the Kukrinitsys, Yuri Zavadsky, Sergei Yutkievich, Yuri Olesha, Grigori Alexandrov, Yuri Gherman, Nikolai Ekk, Sofiya Giatsintova, Vasily Merkuriev, Dimitry Orlov.

Here are a few of these testimonials:

> I knew Vsevolod Emilievich Meyerhold from 1920 to 1938. In 1920 he was head of TEO [the Theatre Section] of the People's Commissariat of Education in which I worked. In those days he grouped around himself all the circles of the artistic intelligentsia who had actively supported the October Revolution. His productions of Verhaeren's *Daybreaks* and Mayakovsky's *Mystery Bouffe* were the first major happenings of revolutionary Soviet theatre. Subsequently he worked with Mayakovsky, they were bound by a great friendship, and Mayakovsky always held him in very high esteem. During the foreign tours of Meyerhold's theatre the performances of this theatre in Paris played a tremendous part in large circles of the French intelligentsia towards the Soviet Union.
>
> Vsevolod Emilievich Meyerhold's rehabilitation will not only be a means of enriching the history of the Soviet theatre but also play a positive role in the attitudes of artistic circles in the West.
>
> I. Ehrenburg

> To Military Procurator B. V. Ryazhsky
> Dear Boris Vsevolodovich,
> I have not kept my word and confirmed in writing our conversation about Meyerhold before now because I have been very occupied all the time.
>
> You remember our conversation. The main point of it was as follows. Just like Mayakovsky, I was closely connected to Meyerhold through my admiration for his talent, and the pleasure and honour

that a visit to his house or attendance at his performances used to afford me, but not through common work, which we never had; he and Mayakovsky were too leftist and revolutionary for me, and I was not radical enough for them.

I especially liked what were to be Meyerhold's last productions of *The Inspector General, Woe from Wit, The Lady with the Camellias.* Vsevolod Emilievich's house was a rallying point for all that was most advanced and artistically most outstanding among the writers, musicians, artists and painters who visited him. The person most similar to him in spiritual fire and convictions, the closest brotherly figure to him was, in my opinion, Mayakovsky. I do not know how crucial my opinion may be in this matter. In short, here is the most vital part of what I could say and recall of this.

With good wishes,
Yours, Boris Pasternak
24 August 1955

'The name of the genius Vsevolod Meyerhold,' Shostakovich wrote to the Procurator, 'his outstanding creative heritage must be returned to the Soviet people.' 'The charge of political sabotage in the sphere of theatrical art brought against V. E. Meyerhold is for all of us working in Soviet art monstrous and totally unfounded slander' – thus Yuri Zavadsky began his letter to the Procurator.

How did he come to be declared a spy? And why particularly a British or Japanese one? Sheer chance, a whim of fate? The young Japanese producer Yoshido Yoshima had come to Moscow with his actress wife, Okado Ioshko, to work under Meyerhold – was much imagination needed for the exposure mania to immediately draw a connection with Japanese Intelligence? Yoshido Yoshima and his wife were murdered in prison dungeons but later rehabilitated. One of Meyerhold's acquaintances was a man with the English surname of Grey – here was the longed-for pretext to associate the producer with British Intelligence. How about Baltrushaitis? He, too, was 'an agent of foreign intelligence services'. It seems laughable but our laughter today would be too bitter.

All alone in their prison cells with sadistic investigators, waiting for their trial and death, did the victims hope that someone somewhere would say just one word to support them? Or did they realize how futile it was even to think of this? After all, anyone who attempted such a reckless act was signing their own sentence.

Really anyone, without exception? Although great talents belong to the whole of humanity, they belong, first and foremost, to their own country – so in order to save them are people not impelled to achieve remarkable, even insane feats in their defence? The aged Academician Dimitry Pryanishnikov forced his way right through to Beria in order to drag Nikolai Vavilov out of his clutches. Academician Piotr Kapitsa intrepidly saved Lev Landau. Colleagues fought – and not without success – for Andrei Tupolev, Sergei Korolev and Leonid Ramzin. Who risked their necks to save Meyerhold? Then and not later?

Three weeks after Meyerhold's arrest his wife, Zinaida Raikh, was brutally murdered in their apartment. The rumour was instantly circulated that she had been in Meyerhold's 'band of spies' herself, and that she had been murdered by her accomplices for being too well-informed and loose-tongued. Nightmarish details of the crime were passed on by word of mouth, and we even know them today. Apparently, afraid of being recognized, the murderers put out their victim's eyes.

These conjectures must have made every decent and well-meaning person recoil in horror. Zinaida Raikh's children by her first husband, Sergei Yesenin, were warned to vacate the apartment the day after their mother's funeral. But they had nowhere to go. Their grandfather, Nikolai Andreyevich Raikh, managed to get through by telephone to the renowned artist and deputy of the Supreme Soviet Ivan Mikhailovich Moskvin. Here is how Tatyana Sergeyevna Yesenina described their conversation:

> After inquiring who he was talking to, Moskvin, without waiting for the murder victim's father to make his request, said: 'You're no doubt telephoning about the funeral. The community refuses to bury your daughter.' Grandfather then explained that he would bury his daughter himself but asked him to stop the illegal eviction of his grandchildren from the apartment. Moskvin's reply was short: 'In my opinion you are rightly being evicted'.

Who would cast aspersions on poor Moskvin now? After all, they were talking over the telephone, and by that time the whole country was terrified of bugging devices. There were not only swarms of spies everywhere but eavesdroppers as well.

After an 'inquiry' and 'investigation' lasting several years, the criminals were allegedly found: they turned out to be the well-known Bolshoi Theatre singer Dimitry Golovin and his son Vitaly. The son had apparently murdered Zinaida Raikh when she caught him burgling her apartment, and the father was an accessory because he had hidden the stolen goods and failed to report the murder.

However, this turned out to be nothing but a rumour which had been purposely and urgently spread by some invisible central source. And it lives on to this day. After I wrote a newspaper article about some documents from the archive of the Meyerhold case, I received a great many letters from people who wrote insistently, as though of an indisputable fact, of the 'Golovin murderers' who had 'boasted in Moscow cafés and artistic circles about the old watches and various jewellery that had vanished from the Meyerholds' apartment after Zinaida Raikh's murder.' Although no 'jewellery' did vanish after the murder, the rumour, as we can see, was invented in such an imaginative way that it still lives on. However, neither of the Golovins had anything to do with this tragedy.

Many people's attempts to cast light on this macabre affair have come to nought. It is known that during the war the Golovins, father and son, were convicted. It could not have been earlier than 1942, for at the end of 1941 the newspapers reported that Golovin was singing in front-line Moscow along with Obukhova, Lemeshev and other renowned artists. 'The well-known opera singer Alexander Baturin,' recounted Tatyana Yesenina in her unpublished memoirs,

> who was also a people's assessor of the Supreme Court, was present at the trial. Not long after the war I met Baturin in Tashkent while he was on tour there. In his opinion, the Golovins' case had been fabricated in an exceedingly obvious and crude manner but all attempts by the Bolshoi Theatre's troupe to intercede for their colleague failed.

In the mid-fifties, just after the thaw had set in, an actor by the name of Igor Ilyinsky, who had once worked in Meyerhold's theatre, tried to discover at least some of the pieces to this mystery, but he got nowhere. Much later Konstantin Rudnitsky, while researching his book on Meyerhold, made some official inquiries and received a reply from the Ministry of Internal Affairs that there were no relevant documents in the archive. There is no doubt whatsoever that this was one of the vilest and most skilful operations the NKVD had ever conducted.

I do not think Stalin made a mistake dispatching Vyshinsky into the arts: he was drawn to this world, he admired and respected talent. Many actors, producers and artists enjoyed his patronage, and some were even members of his family's social circle, including the founder and leader of the Chamber Theatre, Alexander Tairov, and his wife, Alisa Koonen, a leading actress in the same theatre. However, the connection did not prevent them either from being persecuted in the thirties or annihilated at the end of the forties.

When Kalinin presented the awards to the representatives of Soviet culture at the beginning of February, Vyshinsky – then still Procurator-General – came to St George's Hall for some spiritual rest from his bloody duties among the high priests of art. His appearance in the hall must have caused quite a stir, but it was no doubt particularly fascinating to see the wrathful denouncer close to with a meek and benevolent smile on his face. He went up to Sergei Eisenstein to congratulate him personally on his Order of Lenin and fine speech of thanks.

Later Eisenstein was to make use of this unexpected encounter and get through to him by telephone to ask about Meyerhold and find out all he could about his teacher and close friend. Vyshinsky coldly replied that he knew nothing about his fate as he no longer had anything to do with the work of the Procurator's office.

However, not only 'outsiders' who might be expected to get things wrong but even quite well-informed colleagues continued to bother Vyshinsky with matters he no longer had anything to do with. Ulrikh, in particular, sent a letter on to him from Aron Solts, a well-known Party official.[6] The fact that Ulrikh passed this letter on to Vyshinsky has been known for a long time, but the actual text of the letter was only published recently by the journalist Oleg Aksionov.

To the Chairman of the Supreme Military Court Comrade Ulrikh

Statement

At one time I worked with you in the amnesties' commission of the Central Executive Committee of the USSR, and the work went fairly smoothly, and we seemed to see eye to eye on matters and other people. This is why I now consider it possible to appeal to you.

On 21 April 1939 the Military Board of the Supreme Court passed judgement on my niece, Anna Grigorievna Zelenskaya, who had been living in my apartment ever since she divorced Zelensky[7] about ten years ago, and from there it was that she was taken in those evil days when cases were concocted and charges were trumped up under Vyshinsky's command. She was sentenced to nine years, with disenfranchisement for five; her belongings have been confiscated and she has already been deported to Norilsk in the Far North. But meanwhile she is not guilty of anything.

Pravda has recently begun carrying frequent reports on the trials of slanderers responsible for the convictions of many innocent people. I suggest that the slanderers' guilt is not so great if the court takes heed of slander so willingly and pronounces judgement by it. It is the unjust judges and procurators who passed such judgements who ought to be held much more responsible.

On 5 July 1939 an article by the Chairman of the Supreme Court of the USSR, Golyakov,[8] appeared in *Pravda* in which he stated that the judgement must be correct and the rights of the defendant must be protected. In actual fact, he admitted, in many cases this is not observed, and then he goes on to cite many examples. There are, unfortunately, many more – many thousands in all – and rather belatedly Golyakov is making appeals for the court's work to be improved.

More decisive measures are needed to bring influence to bear upon the gentlemen judges. It is the military procurators and military judges who take the greatest liberties with defendants ...

I ask you to request the case and give your opinion of it.

If you decline to do so, you will effectively also bear responsibility for this unjust case.

A. Solts
September 1939

Somehow Ulrikh was not particularly daunted by this prospect. Nor was Vyshinsky. They simply considered it unnecessary to reply to this madman.

Yuri Trifonov's documentary book *Camp-Fire Reflections* (1966) contains the following episode. Hearing that Valentin Trifonov had been arrested, Solts, then an assistant of the Procurator-General of the USSR, asked his chief for all the investigation's materials, saying that he had known Trifonov when he was in exile and was convinced that he could not be an enemy of the people. Vyshinsky refused, saying: 'If the NKVD has taken him in, he must be one.' Then Solts shouted out: 'You're lying! I've known Trifonov for thirty years as a true Bolshevik and I know you as a Menshevik!' And with that he threw down his briefcase and stormed out.

Trifonov's 'dossier' consisted of only seventy-five pages, none of which contained Vyshinsky's signature, nor, what's more, any signs of his 'interest' as a procurator. Solts's visit did not arouse the slightest curiosity in him. What had served as the grounds for this most eminent military official's and statesman's arrest was the testimonial written as early as 4 February 1936 by the head of the tenth section of the Main Directorate of State Security of the NKVD, Lieutenant of State Security Gorbunok, where it is stated that Trifonov was a 'secret Trotskyite' and that he was 'counter-revolutionarily inclined' and 'linked' with Kamenev and Zinoviev. Arrested on 21 June 1937, Trifonov was interrogated only once – on 13 December. Before that he was tortured, not interrogated. The result was a single statement in which Trifonov confessed to being a spy and named dozens of people as his accomplices: Pyatakov and Radek, Smilga and Mezhlauk, the Academicians Nikolai Vavilov and Nikolai Tulaikov,[9] Krylenko and Solts, even Aron Solts, whom the investigators made him denounce as 'a member of the Trotskyite Zinovievite bloc' – the same Solts who in desperation had placed his own head on the execution block for him.

On 15 March 1938 at a trial lasting fifteen minutes instead of the usual twenty (as was noted with fastidious precision in the records of the proceedings) Trifonov again confirmed everything about Vavilov, Solts, and all the others, and about having been recruited as a German spy by a certain Jacobson, a representative of the Swedish firm 'Gasoaccumulator'. He confessed to everything, regarding the procurators' supervision of justice as being a waste of time and bidding farewell to his life for good. He was executed the same day.

One winter, ten years later, in the town of Zvenigorod near Moscow, I became acquainted, quite by chance, with his son, who, at the time, was not yet a professional writer or the holder of the Stalin Prize, as he was to become three years later. It was then that we became friends for life. but only much later, in totally different times, was I to hear his story about how as a young boy, after his father's arrest, he had written letters to Vyshinsky asking him to intercede and help. He kept writing them and tearing them up. Over and over again. 'Why did you keep tearing them up?' I asked. 'You ought to have asked why I kept writing,' he replied after a long pause. 'Because I was a fool ...' He said this sharply, expressing in his voice all the hatred he felt for the supreme guardian of lawfulness of those dreadful years.

8

Vyshinsky's new appointment enabled him to devote more time to writing. He was, after all, an Academician now, and the position obliged him once in a while to confirm his commitment to academic study.

He realized that the pamphlets he had already published, 'The Subversive Work of the Capitalist Countries' Intelligence Services and their Trotskyite-Bukharinite Agents', and 'Some Methods of the Wrecking-diversionist Work of Trotskyite-Fascist Intelligence Officers', would hardly be regarded as academic papers by his contemporaries, let alone future generations. And, as we already know, it was academic glory that he longed for – no other would do. He considered himself an academic who had been summoned to a state post through force of circumstance, and certainly not an official who had also been 'released' into the academic world.

Behind the luxurious *dacha*'s high fence the light in the first-floor study window stayed on until the early hours of the morning. The entire *dacha* settlement of Nikolina Gora knew Vyshinsky was at work. This time it was to be a book entitled *The Theory of Legal Evidence in Soviet Law*, the Academician's principal work, which was to be published in numerous editions, awarded the Stalin Prize of the First Degree and declared a classic of jurisprudence. And indeed it really is a detailed, even thorough work. Its author, who has an excellent command of his material, has ploughed through huge piles of legal, historical and philosophical literature, exhibiting iron logic, astounding erudition and powerful conviction. The book is interspersed with Latin formuli, pithy sayings, a wealth of quotations, numerous references to dozens of Russian, Soviet, American, English, French and German publications, both old and new, including some of the very latest materials. The style is fairly light, and not ponderously learned as some law scholars' works were and still tend to be. Some chapters, where the author is a long way from politics and can allow himself to remain within the confines of pure theory, are, in my opinion, not out of date even today.

But it was not for these chapters that the book won fame or was awarded prizes. It had two basic merits which none of Vyshinsky's colleagues had successfully exploited before.

The first was particularly apt: in a forceful and coherent manner he asserted in theory what he had been fighting for in practice. 'A genuinely popular sense of justice,' he wrote,

> just like a judge's genuinely free inner conviction, is only possible in a genuinely popular and free country where justice itself is administered freely and independently, in the interests of the people and directly by the people itself.

Marx, Spinoza, Hegel – none of them would have been able to find fault with these truly classical assertions. How did the author illustrate their clarity and accuracy? By citing the sentences of the Military Board under the chairmanship of Ulrikh?

Or take a passage where he speaks for himself: 'Slander,' he asserts, 'is the most dangerous weapon against justice.' Fine, as long as one does not recall how much he 'armed' himself with it.

The second merit of the book has to do with theoretically substantiating the brazen flouting of the law, the sphere in which he had succeeded so well in practice, the defendants' confessions.

I have already mentioned the name of Strogovich, who joined the Academy as a correspondent-member at the same time as Vyshinsky. In the past he had been a close colleague of his and had worked with him in the Procurator's office, supporting some of his 'theoretical' dogmas. He had been against

> interpreting in our legal proceedings the 'presumption of innocence' as an abstract principle in the same way as in bourgeois legal procedural theory. In its abstract form this liberal principle would have a demobilizing, demagnetizing effect, and would result in a relaxation in the fight against crime.

At the height of the mass repressions Professor Strogovich, echoing Vyshinsky, was to assert that 'the intensification of the class struggle at any stage, in relation to any type of case at hand, may evoke a compression, a curtailment of the procedural form and of the procedural guarantees incorporated therein.' Putting it another way, he 'theoretically' substantiated the law of 1 December 1934, passed on the evening of Kirov's murder and laying the foundations for the pseudo-legal mass extermination of people.

This is the reason why Vyshinsky got his ally and comrade-in-arms into the Academy: his intellect and his pen might come in useful sometime. But his ally was not in fact as straightforward and obedient as the head of jurisprudence had thought. He allowed himself to have his own opinion. Timid perhaps, but nevertheless his own. Modest, but nevertheless an opinions. Swayed by the processes – social and legal – that he was personally witnessing, Professor Strogovich reviewed his attitude to such an 'abstract principle' as the 'presumption of innocence', and began insisting on its vital necessity for the very concept of justice – as a principle, at least, for one could not even dream of it being made part of legal practice. This was an open polemic with Vyshinsky himself; in those days nobody could dare commit such a blasphemy even in the most innocuous form.

'There is nothing to substantiate Professor Strogovich's emphatic assertion that "in the Soviet criminal trial the burden of proof ... is never transferred to the defendant and his counsel" ', the country's top lawyer nonchalantly swept his opponent aside. And that was it – if the Academician said there was nothing to substantiate it, then he was right, and there was nothing more to discuss.

'If it is a question of annihilating an enemy, we may annihilate him without trial.' On this extraordinary note we shall end our brief survey of the principal work of the top theorist of law. This formula is remarkable because it barely conceals the carnage that was taking place under the guise of justice, making it seem pre-determined, almost 'normal' even. The judicial and extrajudicial executions, which had been sanctified by such lofty theoretical authorship, fused together, becoming different forms of the same just, useful and necessary cause.

It is unlikely Vyshinsky knew what career was in store for him. He worked diligently in the arts, but did not forget his legal colleagues; every now and then one comes across reports on Vice-Chairman of the Council of People's Commissars Comrade Vyshinsky being present at various judges' and prosecutors' conferences. This inspired confidence – it meant one could rest assured that justice was being kept up to the mark.

The arts and sciences were also in an excellent condition now. Vyshinsky not only helped find money from the budget for their requirements but also thoroughly acquainted himself with purely creative processes, giving effective advice whenever he saw fit.

The annual Cannes International Film Festival was due to open on 1 September 1939, and Vyshinsky did much to ensure that the USSR took an active part in it. Selection was not as strict in those days as it is now, and every country taking part compiled its own programme. The Soviet film committee chose *Lenin in 1918*, *Tractor-Drivers*, and *On the Frontier*. When they reported back to Vyshinsky, he personally added Eisenstein's *Alexander Nevsky*. All this happened in the first ten days of August. Vyshinsky still knew nothing about Ribbentrop's impending visit and the sharp turning-point in history. On his initiative Sergei Eisenstein was also included in the Soviet delegation to the festival.

After 23 August it would no longer have been possible for 'great Germany's new friend' to present a film (*Alexander Nevsky*) condemning the Teutonic knights. However, the Soviet delegation did not attend the festival at all because by then 'reliable sources' already knew that the war was going to start on the same day as the festival: 1 September.

Meanwhile, the way was already being cleared for Vyshinsky, until so recently the celebrated and formidable Procurator, to reveal new sides to his talent as the Soviet diplomatic corps in the People's Commissariat of Foreign Affairs was being cut down almost to its roots.

In the late thirties the Soviet diplomatic corps had some outstanding professionals working in it who enjoyed considerable authority on the international circuit. It was they who had succeeded in establishing diplomatic relations between the Soviet Union and the USA and Spain in 1933, Albania, Bulgaria, Hungary, Rumania and Czechoslovakia in 1934, and Poland, Luxembourg and Colombia in 1935. The acknowledged leader of Soviet diplomacy was Maksim Litvinov, a man who exerted great personal influence in America and Europe and had important connections in political circles. He was trusted and his opinions were heeded. Many of the Soviet ambassadors who were diplomats of the Chicherin-Litvinov school also carried weight.

During the years of the Great Terror the People's Commissariat of Foreign Affairs suffered tremendous losses, which, of course, made it no different from any of the other people's commissariats and departments. All Litvinov's deputies except Vladimir Potemkin were annihilated – Lev Karakhan, Grigory Sokolnikov, Nikolai Krestinsky, Boris Stomonyakov – as were ambassadors Vladimir Antonov-Ovseenko, Yakov Davtyan, Marsel Rosenberg, Leonid Stark, Konstantin Yuryenev, to name but a few. The department heads of the People's Commissariat of Foreign Affairs, top experts on foreign countries and regions, were arrested and sometimes 'liquidated'. After taking part in the May Day celebrations as usual on 3 May 1939 Litvinov read in the newspapers that he had been dismissed from his post. Not only was this man who had been close to Lenin 'unsuitable' for Stalin's

193

team, he was also clearly unwanted when the idea of rapprochement with Hitler entered the Leader's head. A diplomat of clearly Anglo-American orientation, and a Jew, what's more, he did not fit in with the new policy. But Molotov did, and so the head of the government also became the head of foreign affairs. As his deputies Stalin appointed men who had no connections with diplomacy: one of Beria's closest associates, Vladimir Dekanozov, and an old Bolshevik and general secretary of the Trade Union International, Solomon Lozovsky. The former was a henchman, the latter a victim, but both ultimately shared the same fate: both would be shot, one towards the end of Stalin's rule, the other after his death, later in 1953.

Vyshinsky had a low opinion of diplomats; they hindered the conduct of the public trials by placing too much emphasis on what effect they would be having in the West. 'You can't please everyone!' Vyshinsky had retorted to Litvinov in an off-hand manner when the latter had once remarked upon the most glaring absurdities of an indictment being exposed in the foreign press. He liked platitudes and disliked rebukes, no matter how politely or discreetly put.

In his posthumous memoirs the following account is given by Yevgeny Gnedin, an ex-head of the press department of the People's Commissariat of Foreign Affairs, whose arrest warrant was one of the last signed by Vyshinsky in his capacity as Procurator-General. Gnedin once drew Vyshinsky's notice to the fact that Sergei Bessonov, a former counsellor of the Soviet Embassy in Germany, who had stood trial alongside Bukharin and Rykov, had in effect acted as a second prosecutor by diligently helping the Procurator to establish the other defendants' guilt (for which he was also rewarded by being sentenced to only fifteen years of prison officially, but unofficially he still got a bullet in the neck later on).

'S.A. Bessonov,' wrote Gnedin,

unfortunately stands out ... because of the particular significance of the role he is playing.... Attending the trial with the foreign correspondents in my charge in my capacity as head of the press department of the People's Commissariat of Foreign Affairs, I myself noticed the contradictions in the legend which S. A. Bessonov expounded in court; in their reports the foreign correspondents revelled in the absurdities they had uncovered. I noted this in my report on the telegrams that had passed through the censors which I sent out to Politburo members. Meeting Vyshinsky in the court's secretariat, I considered it necessary to tell him personally that the foreign correspondents had informed their editorial offices of the contradictory and unauthentic character of Bessonov's statement. The Procurator, who had officially stigmatized the 'enemies of the people' in court, replied in a purely business-like manner: 'All right, I'll talk it over with Sergei Alexeyevich' – this is the respectful way in which the Procurator spoke of the accused.[1]

Vyshinsky adopted this pragmatic and business-like manner at every critical turning-point, making his life considerably easier by not having to comply with any unshakeable principles, fixed views or established relations. He did not have to comply with any of these because he had none. What had been talented yesterday lacked ideological content today. Yesterday's comrade became today's enemy. This, indeed, was the principle of the age. And as an efficient and dependable Bolshevik, Vyshinsky followed it.

What else was making the news in the country just then? The crew of the legendary *Sedov* had just completed their ice drift in the Arctic Ocean, and Captain Badigin and assistant political instructor Trofimov telegraphed Stalin and Molotov from Murmansk to report the crew's landing on their native shore. Nothing of significance had happened on the Soviet-Finnish front. For the sixth week running the newspapers continued to carry a stream of congratulatory messages to Stalin on the occasion of his sixtieth birthday. Also published were extensive excerpts from Hitler's speech to mark the first anniversary of the National Socialists' assumption of power, and the decree of the Soviet People's Commissariat and Central Committee 'On the compulsory delivery of wool to the state'.

Each department got on with its own daily duties just the same as usual. And so did the legal profession, of course. On that particular day, 1 February 1940, the Military Board of the Supreme Court of the USSR was due to hear the usual number of cases. It had a rigid schedule: the same twenty minutes per case. The conveyor had to run at a steady pace and any hold-up would cause a halt in production. This was true everywhere.

The Military Board 'sat' in Beria's office in Lefortovo Prison. He had personal offices in all the prisons where there were 'politicals'. Nearly every night he would personally take part in what was referred to as an 'interrogation'. Towards morning he would go off to rest, putting his office at the judges' disposal.

Three military officers sat at the desk: the chairman, indefatigable

Vasily Ulrikh, flanked by two completely unknown judges, Kandybin and Bukanov. We shall find their names in hundreds of other documents all containing the same grim sentence, so they must have lived up to their reputations. They silently listened to the proceedings and just as impassively signed the previously prepared papers.

The man who was first led into the 'court-room' the judges knew exceptionally well. However, no unfamiliar faces appeared here as Ulrikh only tried celebrities. In this case, not only the judges but the whole country knew the accused by sight as well as name. His photograph had appeared in the press numerous times. The newsreels, which took the place of television in those days, and the journals were forever showing him on huge airliners, risking his life in Spain under the threat of Fascist bombs, in fields and mines, at military training sessions and first nights at the theatre.

He was also known in other countries a long way from home; Hemingway portrayed him as Karpov, a character in *For Whom The Bell Tolls*. He was a Russian journalist who had gone to Spain during the Civil War not only to report but also to serve as a political adviser to the Republican Government. Hemingway had called him 'one of the most important figures in Spain', and 'the most intelligent of all the people he had had occasion to meet . . . who had such a good head, so much inner dignity and outward daring and such wit'.

Vyshinsky agreed wholeheartedly with Hemingway. At a meeting with journalists on the political trials, he suggested they follow the example of this journalist 'who had such a good head' and whose 'reports were noted for their political maturity, excellent grasp of his task, knowledge of the law, and expertise befitting a Party propagandist'.

However, in his reports this journalist did not remain in debt to the 'brilliant prosecutor' and 'prosecutor whose very name makes the Trotskyite-Zinovievite scum' tremble; after deservedly rewarding the 'true spokesman of the Revolution', the 'loud and honest mouthpiece of the entire multi-million Soviet people', he went on to promise: 'All those who have conceived the insane idea of going against history, of halting its progress and barring the way of triumphant socialism, will be ground down into bloody powder.'

As the valiant pupil of Comrade Stalin and his favourite assistant, Comrade Yezhov, exposed more and more vile Fascist dogs, this journalist's tone grew increasingly incensed: 'When the rogues, officially referred to in legal terms as "accused", stand up,' he wrote 'from the courtroom' where Bukharin and his 'accomplices' were being destroyed, 'when they stand up and start describing their monstrous crimes in detail, sometimes with the crestfallen look of repentant sinners, sometimes with the cynical familiarity of inveterate rogues, you feel like jumping up and shouting, thumping your fist down on the table and seizing these filthy, blood-smeared blackguards by the throats, grabbing hold of them and finishing them off yourself.'

The author of these impassioned words was Mikhail Koltsov, a well-known writer on current affairs, an editorial board member of *Pravda*, a deputy of the Supreme Soviet of the RSFSR, and a correspondent-member of the Academy of Sciences. That, at least, is what he had been – now he was a common spy. And an agent of three intelligence services – German, French and American. And a member of the anti-Soviet underground since 1923 who 'had propagandized Trotskyite ideas and popularized the leaders of Trotskyism', a terrorist since 1932 who had intended to assassinate nobody knew quite who, how, when or why. And he had confessed to absolutely everything, as was stated in the indictment covering two and a half pages:

'Do you wish to add anything?' Ulrikh asked the accused.

'Not add but deny,' Koltsov replied, 'Everything that is written here is a lie. From start to finish.'

'Well, how is it a lie? Is this signature yours?'

'I put it there ... after torture ... terrible torture ...'

'I see, now you are going to slander the NKVD.... Your arrest was sanctioned by the Procurator-General, Comrade Vyshinsky, the charge has been proved.... Why increase your guilt? It's great enough as it is...'

'I categorically deny ...' began Koltsov, but Ulrikh interrupted him: 'Have you nothing else to add?'

He had been dealt with in twenty minutes, even slightly less.

I wonder what Vyshinsky checked out before sanctioning Koltsov's arrest? According to the sentence, Koltsov was recruited into the terrorist organization by Karl Radek, but for some reason Radek was not charged with doing so.

There, too, it was stated that Boris Shtein,[2] the Soviet Ambassador to Rome, was recruited at the same time as Koltsov. However, no case was raised against Shtein and he escaped punishment.

The writer and *Pravda* contributor Tamara Leontieva, who had been arrested several months earlier, 'confessed' under torture to investigator Makarov that she had been in some Trotskyite group with

Koltsov. However, a special NKVD meeting dropped the case against Leontieva – she was lucky.

Koltsov was not. 'Execution by shooting,' pronounced Ulrikh in his usual tone. The accused was not allowed to say another word; outside the door another victim was already waiting to be summoned.

This was none other than Meyerhold. They were both executed the next day while Ulrikh was passing judgement on Robert Eikhe, who until only recently had been a Politburo nominee, a first secretary of the Party's Western Siberian Regional Committee, and the People's Commissar of Agriculture of the USSR.[3] The conveyor continued to work non-stop. Vyshinsky had been in his new post for some time now, but his signature continued to decide people's destinies. That same evening, tired after his just labours, the military judge went out for a little relaxation. A reception was being held in the Kremlin for the *Sedov*'s crew, and Ulrikh was on the honoured guest list which was topped by Vyshinsky. After supper there was a concert starring the singers Barsova, Lemeshev, Reizen, and Kozlovsky, the ballet dancer Lepeshinskaya, the Alexandrov and Moiseyev dance ensembles, and the Pyatnitsky choir.

Who apart from Vyshinsky, Ulrikh and a few others knew that earlier in the day an executioner had shot a genius of the stage and a top-ranking journalist? The theatre programmes in the capital were running as billed. Gogol's *Dead Souls* was on at the Moscow Art Theatre, Ostrovsky's *Wood* at the Maly, and the illustrious magician Kio was entertaining a spellbound audience at the circus.

Six days earlier another world-famous figure who had been closely connected with both these victims – in real life and in sentence – had been executed: on 27 January Isaak Babel had been shot after being condemned to death the day before by the same Ulrikh (whose assistants that day had been Kandybin and Dmitriev). Fourteen years later the decision of Military Procurator Lieutenant-Colonel of the Justice Dolzhenko on Babel's rehabilitation was to state: 'From the materials of the case it is not clear what served as the grounds for Babel's arrest, as the authorization for his arrest was officially registered on 23 June 1939, that is thirty-five days after his arrest'. (He was arrested on 16 May 1939 at his *dacha* in Peredelkino, the writers' colony just outside Moscow.)

The world knew him as a great writer, the judges as a member of an anti-Soviet Trotskyite organization from 1927, and an agent of French and Austrian Intelligence from 1934. It is actually not hard to guess what served as the pretext rather than grounds for his arrest.

The grotesque Yezhov, who had held the country in a state of terror, had just been dispatched in the same manner as his victims, and Babel – as Ehrenburg also writes in his memoirs – was acquainted with Yezhov's wife and even used to visit her, knowing full well what he was risking. This was reflected in his sentence:

> Having organizational links in anti-Soviet activity with the wife of enemy of the people Yezhov Babel was drawn by her into anti-Soviet conspiratorial terrorist activity, shared the aims and tasks of this anti-Soviet organization, including terrorist acts ... against the leaders of the All-Union Communist Party (Bolsheviks) and the Soviet government.

The role of Yevgenia Solomonovna Yezhova has yet to be fully examined. Of course, she was a tiny pawn on the vast board the Grandmaster used for his insane combinations, but for just under three years, when her husband suddenly rose to power and started playing with millions of lives, she caused a sensation with her eerie beauty and dragged quite a few people down into the abyss with her. Her apartment was a salon where in a pleasant ambience, with music playing in the background, all sorts of people, the so-called élite of the day – artists, actors, writers, musicians, diplomats and academics – used to gather around tables laden with the most exquisite delicacies. There, too, were informers of various kinds – full-time, freelance, and volunteers. The ravishing hostess was the life and soul of all her gatherings, large and small: she greatly enjoyed singing, playing instruments and dancing, and could liven up even the dullest stick-in-the-mud. In his young days Professor Sugurd Ottovich Shmidt, the eminent archaeographer and son of the renowned academician O. Y. Shmidt, recalls Yevgenia Yezhova dancing energetically at Kremlin banquets, and never missing a single dance. (Incidentally the dances were mostly Western, not Russian.) Under the spell of her charm the regular visitors to her fashionable salon disappeared one after another into the Lubyanka's dungeons.

The illustrious writer and brilliant story-teller Babel was a welcome guest at this salon. It was sheer curiosity that drew him there: a desire to get inside the 'lions' den' and see something for himself and understand. Now we know how he ended up.

At the interrogation, which went on non-stop for nearly three days and nights on 29–31 May 1939, Babel at first denied all the charges and then suddenly, for some reason which was not explained in the records, sharply changed his 'line of conduct' and indicated that he was a member of a Trotskyite spy ring, to which he had been recruited by Ilya Ehrenburg (yet again), that their liaison was André Malraux, the well-known French writer, who was later to become a minister in de Gaulle's government.[4] What did Babel sell him? Puns and jokes? Good toasts to drink to? No, air force secrets, that's all.

Also worth mentioning here, I think, are the names of the other members of this group of Trotskyite terrorists: besides Ehrenburg there were the writers Leonid Leonov, Valentin Katayev, Vsevolod Ivanov, Yuri Olesha, Ludya Seifullina, Vladimir Lidin, the film directors Sergei Eisenstein and Grigory Alexandrov, the theatre artists Solomon Mikhoels and Leonid Utyosov, and Academician Otto Shmidt, to name only a few.

Nowadays it seems that nothing, not even the wildest fantasy of the madmen who concocted all the cases for Yagoda, Yezhov, Beria and Vyshinsky, could surprise us. And yet reading the list of 'underground workers', you feel as though you are going mad yourself. Leonov – a terrorist? Katayev – a diversionist? Olesha – a conspirator? You simply cannot believe your eyes.

However, the list is not as insane as it sounds. All of them were not only outstanding talents, not only independent-minded and critically inclined people, but nearly all of them had in one way or another aroused the Leader's wrath at one time or another: Leonov's *The Snowstorm*, Katayev's *The Small House* and Eisenstein's *Bezhin Meadow* – which he had begun work on with Babel[5] – were all criticised in the highest quarters. Seifullina and Vsevolod Ivanov had been hauled over the coals even earlier.

Only Academician Shmidt is perhaps the odd-man-out here. This is what the hero of Chelyuskin's expedition, recently welcomed home, praised to the skies and decorated by the Leader himself, said in his speech at the First Writers' Congress:

> There is no need for our work to be instigated, put under pressure, proclaimed; there is no need for the leader to be set off against the remaining masses. These are not our methods at all. I do not want to use the word, but these are the foreign methods of one of our neighbouring states.

It could not have been put any clearer. His audience understood Academician Shmidt perfectly well and it is not without reason that after these words 'applause' was written in the shorthand report.

At the same congress Babel had said to Shmidt: 'These fabricated, trite clichés . . . are playing into the hands of hostile forces. . . . We keep going on about our love in an unbearably loud fashion. . . . If it goes on like this, we shall soon have to declare our love through a megaphone like umpires at football matches.' It did not take much intelligence to work out whom he was referring to, and such audacity was bound to have repercussions.

His cycle of stories *Red Cavalry* was also held against him for, according to the indictment, 'he described all the cruelties and incongruities of the Civil War by highlighting only sharp and penetrating episodes'. The investigation declared these stories, now classics, to be sabotage and treason.

By 10 October 1939 Babel had denied all his confessions. 'I ask the investigation to take into consideration,' he said in his statement, 'that in making my previous statements, even though I was in prison at the time, I committed a crime – I slandered several people.' He wrote three times to Ulrikh about this, on 5 and 21 November 1939 and 2 January 1940. He asked to see Vyshinsky, to be sent witnesses, to be allowed to see his dossier and to be given a lawyer, but all in vain.

On 26 January Ulrikh had the case completely tied up in a matter of minutes and Babel was executed the very next morning.

The material on the other Trotskyite terrorists' criminal group, agents of all the various foreign intelligence services, lay biding its time in a secret safe. It was probably planned to stage a massive trial of well-known writers and artists, but, when Meyerhold, Koltsov and Babel refused, even after threats and torture, to confess to their 'evil deeds', this splendid plan had to be abandoned – for the time being at least. Obviously, like a time bomb, the material 'gathered' by the investigation could be exploded at any moment by simply pressing a button.

There were stacks of ready-made statements like these lying in safes which, if the Leader and Teacher so wished, could be instantly put in front of him. The case materials I obtained these facts from also contain information on how during investigations people had 'evidence' beaten out of them against Andrei Andreyev, Andrei Zhdanov and Lazar Kaganovich, Stalin's 'most loyal comrades-in-arms' – and against others no less loyal.

The 'evidence' might come in handy. But it was not heeded in the end.

The result was communicated to the victim's relatives. It was always the same for everyone: ten years of distant labour camps *without the right of correspondence*. Someone had invented and introduced this terrible euphemism for execution to prevent panic and hysteria from breaking out. In actual fact, though, everyone knew what it really meant, this mysterious sanction, which provision had not been made for, even for appearances' sake, by any law.

This is most likely why the device of purposeful rumours was set in motion and worked wonderfully well for many years. Every now and then news would filter through to the families and friends of prisoners who were not allowed to correspond, letting them know that he or she was alive and well, imprisoned in such and such a place and, on happy occasions, even passing on fondest greetings.

In his memoirs Koltsov's brother, the artist Boris Efimov, wrote about various people's mythical meetings with Koltsov. Babel's wife, Alexandra Pirozhkova, was officially informed several years running that he was alive, and in the summer of 1952 'on Babel's instructions' she was even contacted by a man 'who had been liberated from the Middle Kolyma' to pass on her husband's greetings. Meyerhold's biographer, Yuri Yelagin, quoted 'a man totally deserving trust' who said that he 'had held' a postcard 'in his hands' from Vsevolod Emilievich bearing the postmark 'of a small railway station in Eastern Siberia'.

Just about everyone whose execution had not been officially announced kept being 'met personally' by eye-witnesses all over the place. One Western woman journalist who had been imprisoned near Vorkuta from 1943 to 1953 described her meeting with Professor Pletnev, who had been dubbed 'a member of a special band of murderers' at the trial of Bukharin and Rykov.

According to the journalist, Pletnev 'was already past eighty', and he had told her how he had poisoned Gorky by treating him to some crystallized fruits which had been injected with poison. Pletnev died, according to this journalist, in the summer of 1953. This story continued to circulate until very recently and even appeared in the press. In actual fact, alas, Pletnev was shot on 11 September 1941 in Orlov prison, on the same day as many other completely innocent people – 154 in all – including Khristian Rakovsky, Varvara Yakovleva, Maria Spiridonova[6], Nikolai Antipov, Olga Kameneva (the wife of L.B. Kamenev and sister of Trotsky), and Bukharin's pupil, the economist Alexander Aikhenvald.

The repetitive character of the rumours and the way in which they were all devised along the same lines gives one grounds to believe that there was absolutely nothing fortuitous about their origin and circulation. Once Beria had been liquidated, they all simply vanished: the source dried up.

9

The whole world remembers 23 August 1939 as the day on which the Molotov-Ribbentrop non-aggression pact was signed, one of the most fateful days of the twentieth century. Another date no more than five weeks later – 28 September – is remembered perhaps only by modern historians. However, it was then that the same statesmen signed another treaty on their countries' behalf with the much more sinister and ignominious title of 'The German-Soviet Treaty on Friendship and the Frontier between the USSR and Germany'.[1]

Its conclusion was preceded by the Nazi invasion of Poland, which was obviously intended to destroy its people and state system. In the treaty's text the actual situation, which had arisen 'after the disintegration of the former Polish state', was stated in black and white, and then it went on to say that: 'the Government of the USSR and the German Government are examining ... reconstruction [on the territory of the 'former' Polish state] as a firm foundation for the subsequent development of friendly relations between their peoples.'

Exactly as had been previously arranged, the Western Polish lands went to Germany and the Eastern ones to the Soviet Union, leaving a narrow strip in the middle bombastically referred to as a 'region of Germany's state interests', signifying that the legal status of the territory then occupied by Nazi troops would be defined at a later date.

The treaty of 28 September gave legal force to a situation which had already arisen *de facto*: on 17 September the Red Army had crossed the state border and after encountering virtually no resistance had occupied Western Ukraine and Western Byelorussia. The territories' integration now had to be constituted and a legal base created for spreading central state power and Soviet legislation within them. An election to the People's Assembly of Western Ukraine was held, and this body urgently assembled and applied to become a member of the Soviet Union. Finally, an extraordinary session of the Supreme Soviet was convened to complete the fairly simple but multi-stage proceedings involved in legally registering this most important action.

On 1 November, less than six weeks after the troops' entry, envoys from Lvov, to all intents and purposes now the centre of the new Soviet territories, were standing on the platform of the Supreme Soviet and being enthusiastically welcomed by the conspicuously depleted rows of delegates who had been elected in December 1937 (a great many of them had already ended up in the Lubyanka or even in unmarked graves instead of the Great Kremlin Palace). And along with his comrades-in-arms who had survived, Comrade Stalin himself graced them with his paternal smile. The motion to include Western Ukraine in the membership of the USSR was debated. And who do you think was given the great honour of introducing this motion on the Government's behalf? Vice-Premier Andrei Vyshinsky.

Just as at the 'Great Moscow Trials', the decisions were of course made behind the scenes, and not in full view of the public. But in keeping with all the rules of art an experienced performer was still needed on stage, a top-class professional. And Vyshinsky, as it turned out, was a top-class professional in very many different fields. Everywhere he went he took with him his single-mindedness and erudition. An excellent speaker, he did not merely read out his 'text' but flared up before his audience's very eyes and masterfully set others alight as well, setting up around himself a particularly powerful 'magnetic field'. According to eye-witnesses at the Supreme Soviet session, when he bellowed something about the request 'of the freely elected People's Assembly of Western Ukraine', it sent shivers up their spines, although it was hard to say what was so special about what he had said or what made the people's deputies burst into such ecstatic applause.

This was the ex-Procurator's first public appearance in a completely new and unusual role for him, the first triumph of the Academician who had proved to be a specialist in international as well as criminal law. This speech was to mark a new and essentially final phase in his multifaceted career, which was to continue for another fifteen years.

However, for the time being he was still Deputy Chairman of the People's Commissariat, primarily responsible for culture and, of course, education as an integral part of it, a 'field' very dear to his own heart, for, after all, it was here only a short while ago that he himself had achieved such remarkable successes. History was repeating itself.

One of the important tasks he was entrusted with was to conclude the process of converting the written language of many of the peoples of the Soviet Union to the Russian alphabet, that is, by changing over from Latin script to the Cyrillic. By the beginning of 1940 in the RSFSR alone, this process, which, 'on the initiative of the toiling masses', was suddenly started and rapidly developed, had covered the languages of thirty-seven peoples. In the other republics the slow but gradual transfer to teaching in Russian was implemented with great difficulty. Although a ruling of the Central Committee of the All-Union Communist Party (Bolsheviks) and Council of People's Commissars had stated that 'the native language' was 'the teaching base in the schools of the republics and regions of the Soviet Union' and that 'the tendency to transform the Russian language from a subject for study into the language of instruction in the schools of the republics and thus encroach upon the native language' was 'harmful and wrong', in practice this tendency became quite widespread, accelerated in the provinces by zealous administrators wanting to dispatch a triumphant report on their own particular success 'to the top' as quickly as possible. Schools had also suffered considerably from the teachers' purges: among those arrested, deported and annihilated were many of the teaching profession's best representatives, the core of the intelligentsia, the traditional disseminators of eternal values.

At this dramatic and critical moment in the history of schools what did Vyshinsky speak about at the All-Russian Conference of the Teachers' *Aktiv*? Education had just lost its People's Commissar, Andrei Bubnov, Deputy People's Commissar Nadiezhda Krupskaya,[2] the most distinguished organizers of popular education, scholars and teachers. The totally unknown P. A. Tyurkin, about whom no information was available in any of the reference books, was now in charge of education. So what did the legendary Vyshinsky, who was given a stormy ovation, speak about after listening to the new People's Commissar's colourless report? Well, of course, first and foremost, about 'the great teachings of Comrade Stalin' who had raised everything under the sun 'to unprecedented heights', 'perfected' and 'illumined everything with the brilliance of his great intellect'. And what else?

He also spoke about the fact that 'in the indissoluble bond between instruction and upbringing' a very important link was provided by singing 'as a way of organizing, as a way of taming the recalcitrant characters sometimes in the class.' Singing, concluded Vyshinsky, was a 'fine instrument' with the help of which one could 'overcome a number of great obstacles'. And the audience readily agreed with him.

After the sixtieth birthday of the Genius of All Times and Peoples in December 1939 – which had been celebrated with great pomp and ceremony all round the country – a slightly more modest but no less important date for the nation drew near: 9 March 1940, the fiftieth birthday of Vyacheslav Mikhailovich Molotov. For all his ex-colleagues who had already been liquidated or deported to the Gulag Archipelago Molotov had always been the epitome of dullness and mediocrity, but here he was now at the summit of Stalin's Olympus. In the chorus glorifying the Leader, Vyshinsky's voice had been drowned by more powerful ones. But this time he was not going to be outdone.

His 'scholarly' article, 'The Head of the Soviet Government', which appeared on the first pages of the academic journal *Soviet State and Law*, of which he was also editor-in-chief, was even for those days remarkably sycophantic. All kinds of conceivable and inconceivable epithets and all sorts of striking word combinations were used to fill twenty-two typed pages. Was it a case of humility being the highest form of pride? Or did he reckon that the more fuss he made, the less likely he was to be noticed?

No other publication to mark the birthday of the 'head of the Soviet government' contained such unthinkable eulogies presented, what's more, in a quasi-scholarly form. There is no way of listing them all. Outstanding politician, irreconcilable fighter, profound thinker, major theorist, great scholar, tireless toiler, remarkable person. These are only a few of the qualities the rank-and-file Academician ascribed to the future honorary Academician. The latter, it goes without saying, was also a favourite comrade-in-arms of Lenin, 'an associate and friend of great Stalin', 'his first assistant in realizing all his designs'. There came, finally, a truly erudite ending:

> ... With new force V. M. Molotov comes to the conclusion that the working class and all the toiling masses are at present faced with the task of strengthening the Soviet state. Coming from V. M. Molotov this is not simply a theoretical proposition, a formula, an academic thesis, it is an idea of genius embodied in the creative practical application of state structuring.

The thesis on 'strengthening the state' is, indeed, a profound revelation which a simple mortal could not possibly arrive at himself – we understand this part of it. But the fact that some 'idea of genius' is concealed here is, I believe, completely beyond anyone. And in those days, incidentally, there was only one man who could be considered a genius. I do not believe there would have been room for two men of genius at the helm. In his ecstatic praise Vyshinsky had gone slightly over the top. What's more, he had taken an obvious risk by placing his stake too openly on Molotov and by regarding the Leader and his 'right-hand man' as a single unit. However, this is possibly the way things still were in those days, and, besides, Vyshinsky was directly under Molotov, and so entitled to feel particularly strongly where his superior was concerned. And yet, I repeat, by expressing his feelings too strongly, he could have lost.

But he did not lose.

Before his high stake was to pay off, however, he would have to suffer a new ordeal, the like of which neither he nor the country had ever experienced before.

Filling in the infamous personnel registration form at the end of 1939, Vyshinsky had quite truthfully written that he had never been abroad.

At the age of nearly sixty he was about to cross his country's border for the first time. However, far from bringing him either diplomatic honours or enjoyable travel experiences, this journey was only to expose him to the most severe ordeals, and unforeseen dangers. On the stage of Trade Union House, defended by Yezhov's lackeys and face to face with the condemned, he had felt much safer and bolder.

By June 1940 the map of Europe had already been significantly redrawn. Apart from the Anschluss, Denmark, Norway, Belgium and Holland had also fallen under Nazi occupation. Just then the troops of the Wehrmacht were approaching Paris. On 14 June Paris fell.

After the collapse of the Finnish campaign, which had, however, brought some territorial gains, the Soviet Union embarked on the next stage of securing its western borders. In mid-June the Baltic States were presented with ultimatums ending with a demand for additional contingents of Soviet troops to enter their territories (the first 'contingents' had entered back in October 1939). Immediately afterwards Red Army formations supported by tanks and artillery began their advance deep into the territory of Lithuania, Latvia and Estonia. They met scarcely any resistance.

They were given an especially warm welcome in Latvia. This is explained not only by Latvia's deep rooted revolutionary traditions, which had remained totally unshaken and unsullied, but also by its Russian, Jewish and Byelorussian inhabitants who were strongly drawn towards Russia. Various glorious recent events, such as the rescue of Cheliuskin's crew from the Arctic, the drift of Papanov's men on the ice flow and the victory at Hasan and Khalkin-Gol had had a profound impact on the Russian émigrés. In clubs where only a short while ago 'God Save the Tsar' had been sung in a whisper (Russia's pre-revolutionary national anthem had been banned when Latvia gained independence), the Soviet anthem 'Wide Is My Native Country' was now also sung surreptitiously.

Even the sad news filtering through from Soviet Russia, which few wanted to believe, did not affect many Letts' revolutionary sympathies. Of course, the Moscow trials – particularly Bukharin's trial – and Trotsky's denouncement as a Gestapo spy had shocked some Communists who were certainly not Trotskyites but loyal supporters of Stalin's regime. But they cast these anxious thoughts aside. In the tragic thirties many thousands of Latvian revolutionaries who had stayed on in Russia or fled there later shared the common fate of millions of victims of other nationalities. But the close relatives of these innocent victims were also among the Letts who enthusiastically welcomed the Soviet military units.

No such welcome was forthcoming in Estonia, or indeed in Lithuania, but on the whole the people were fairly well-disposed, especially as they had been solemnly guaranteed national and state independence and total security. In all three states the legal procedure involved in becoming a member of the USSR now had to be dealt with as quickly as possible, withstanding any attempts to foil this previously arranged 'protocol' or hinder it in any way. Stalin sent envoys with emergency powers to oversee the entire operation, and the Soviet ambassadors in the three states and commanders of the Soviet army divisions stationed there were all placed under their command.

Andrei Zhdanov was sent to Estonia.

Vladimir Dekanozov, a professional NKVD operative, and one of Beria's closest associates who had recently been appointed a Deputy People's Commissar of Foreign Affairs, went to Lithuania.

And Andrei Vyshinsky was given Latvia.

He arrived in Riga by train on 17 June, immediately after the Red Army units had entered the city. Although ostensibly official – the guest was called the 'special plenipotentiary of the Soviet Government for carrying through the Latvian-Soviet mutual assistance pact' – the visit was, however, strictly confidential, and nobody arranged an official reception for Vyshinsky. He was accompanied by three functionaries who were together to comprise the main operative staff: Ambassador Derevyansky, Vetrov, a representative of VOKS, the All-Union Society for Cultural Ties with Foreign Countries, and Counsellor Chichayev. From the station a private car drove Vyshinsky straight to the Soviet Embassy. After freshening up, he was given a briefing and, once he had found his bearings, he paid an official visit to President Karl Ulmanis.

Of course, in those days, in the midst of general enthusiasm following the downfall of the previous regime, a broad democratic government of the Popular Front responding to the real interests of the population as a whole might well have come to power naturally. Indeed, it most certainly would have done. However, Vyshinsky and the functionaries accompanying him, two of whom had concealed their true identity behind the pseudonyms of 'Vadimov' and 'Sergeyev', had arrived precisely to prevent this from happening. His mission was probably to stop the local Communists from forming a government by assuming control of the whole operation and using his own discretion to enlist the services of proxies whose personal qualities and political views made them absolutely trustworthy.

On the advice of his staff, who had a thorough knowledge of the local situation, Vyshinsky chose the venerable Professor Avgust Kirkhenshtein, a microbiologist known throughout Europe and a non-Party participant in the revolutionary movements: this revered nominee fitted the bill perfectly for he gave the future government soundness and respectability. Two years previously Kirkhenshtein's brother, Rudolf, had been arrested in Moscow, but the Prime Minister-to-be was still unaware of this or, quite possibly, did not wish to know.[3]

Most probably, he was the only one in the country's new leadership to react to Stalin's envoy with outward calm. According to a former secretary of Kirkhenshtein, Vilis Stalash, who is still alive today, the news of Vyshinsky's arrival had scared them 'half to death' and filled them with 'mortal terror'. The associations which the name of this man conjured were too horrific for words. While the names of Zhdanov and Dekanozov still meant little at the time, especially outside the Soviet Union, Vyshinsky's was universally known in one context only. The fact that Latvia's fate seemingly lay in his hands was especially insulting for the country. 'Seemingly' because, of course, Vyshinsky decided nothing himself – he was merely the skilful and disciplined executor of the Supreme Will, and an exceptionally ambitious one as well. Come what may, he was determined to outstrip Zhdanov and Dekanozov and complete this mission as quickly and efficiently as possible and without losses, to prove that he was intransigent and irreplaceable, that he was peerless wherever he was sent to carry out a Party and government mission.

The Communist Party members who had emerged from hiding came to Vyshinsky with two proposals: of immediately releasing all the politicals and holding a demonstration in support of the Soviet Union. The first proposal the envoy with emergency powers, of course, accepted, but the second caused him considerable anxiety: the masses' uncontrolled euphoria might spontaneously swing in any direction and ruin the whole operation. It was not Latvia's fate that worried him but his own.

However, his advisers predicted the demonstration's success and succeeded in convincing him of its expediency. Its success was, in fact, even greater than expected. On 21 June columns of demonstrators filed past the Soviet Embassy all day long.

Despite the sceptics' predictions, a great many Letts also took part in it. Nearly half a century later one of the demonstrators, Martinish Skulme from Riga, wrote in the press: 'In 1940 a revolution took place in Latvia which was led by the leader of the greatest genius Comrade Stalin and his most talented assistant Vyshinsky.' Another demonstrator from Riga, Anatoly Dikmanis, wrote to Vyshinsky on 5 May 1950 (the letter has remained intact in Vyshinsky's personal archive):

> The memorable anniversary of Latvia's liberation is not far off. I am happy to congratulate you on the great event in your creative work. Ten years ago among the people who were inspired by great patriotic enthusiasm and your presence, I was given the opportunity of hoisting the first red flag. Your handshake and encouraging words have illumined the past decade for me.

Attached to the letter are some verses also by him, which are remarkable more for their author's political inspiration than their poetic content, and as a vivid illustration of the atmosphere pervading Riga's streets at the time:

> By the shores of the Latvian waters
> Stands a Soviet steamer,
> The pride of the toiling people.
> I hoisted the flag up the pole.
> The country joyfully rejoices
> Under Ilyich's proud banner.
> Vyshinsky called me over
> And warmly shook me by the hand.
> Our red flag flutters in front of the castle
> And a song to Stalin sounds forth.
> The Soviet spirit reigns all around.
> It all seems like a happy dream.

To very many people in Riga in those days it really did all seem 'like a happy dream'. Watching the happenings from the windows of his residence, the British Ambassador sent a report to London saying that he was 'astonished and surprised' by the incredible mass scale of the demonstration and 'the undoubted sincerity' of the people taking part in it. No less than seventy thousand, and more like around eighty thousand people filed past the Soviet Embassy (the total population of Riga was then three hundred and eighty thousand). Vyshinsky's proxies ensured that the main conditions laid down in collaboration with the Communist Party members were observed: there were no slogans about Latvia joining the Soviet Union, as they had decided that it was too early for them.

For nine hours Vyshinsky stood tirelessly on the Embassy's balcony, waving to the demonstrators and every so often shouting out the one and only phrase he had learnt in Latvian: 'Long live free Latvia!'

The Soviet newspapers covered the events in the Baltic States very sketchily. When Soviet troops had entered Western Ukraine and Western Byelorussia there had been a widescale propaganda campaign, with massive headlines in some newspapers and numerous photographs, while the fateful transformations in the Baltic States were reflected in short inconspicuous reports as fairly ordinary events. The same is true of the demonstrations in Riga on 21 June. There was not even a photograph accompanying the brief report. And nowhere in the Soviet press shall we find even a mention of Vyshinsky, who played such a major role in these events. Indeed, no mention was ever made of his visit to Latvia or of Zhdanov's and Dekanozov's missions either. The Baltic states and the rest of the world knew perfectly well about this mission, so who was it kept a secret from? The Soviet people? Why? What danger was there in such a hot 'military secret' leaking through to Moscow, Tashkent or Tomsk? We are still left guessing.

The government of the Popular Front was formed in the Soviet Embassy and Vyshinsky went to the President's residence with Professor Kirkhenshtein to present it to Ulmanis. There could be no objection, let alone resistance, as all the real power was in Vyshinsky's hands. Kirkhenshtein, however, tried a skilful manoeuvre in a desperate attempt to get rid of his trustee. This 'manoeuvre' was both comic and tragic.

When Latvia had gained independence from Russia after the October Revolution and Soviet power had been established there for a short while, Kirkhenshtein, one of its sympathizers, had associated with many members of the revolutionary government. Among the Latvian Communists he had kept in contact with was Robert Eikhe, who had made a very fine impression on him. Kirkhenshtein decided that by inviting Eikhe to join the Republic's leadership he would quite effortlessly replace Vyshinsky with this splendid organizer, who was a Lett and not a Pole and, moreover, a candidate-member of the Politburo, that is, higher-ranking in the Party and state structure than Stalin's envoy.

Vilis Stalash was working at the time in the Latvian Ministry of Foreign Affairs. At Kirkhenshtein's request he sent a telegram to the Soviet NKVD asking them to 'send' Eikhe to Riga. But there was no reply. A telegram was then sent to the Central Committee requesting them to 'send the eminent revolutionary'. Again no reply. The third telegram was addressed to the Presidium of the Supreme Soviet and, naturally, no reply came from there either. At first Kirkhenshtein took umbrage but then he swallowed his pride, and went to Vyshinsky to explain matters.

Just then Vyshinsky was suffering from an attack of eczema which had been aggravated by severe mental stress. He tried not to leave the Embassy and took medicinal baths to ease the itching. The marble bathroom was equipped with telephones, including a direct line, and a special government line with the Kremlin. Kirkhenshtein's unexpected visit forced him to interrupt his treatment. He went through to the reception room and after impatiently listening to the Professor's long explanation, replied in an icy tone, 'I cannot guarantee that your Eikhe is alive. You would be best advised not to make enquiries.'

Did he actually know that Eikhe had been killed five months before? I am not sure. Beria was hardly likely to have kept the former Pro-curator-General informed of the executions. However, 'in general' he, of course, knew the secrets of the torture-chambers. And there was nothing mysterious about Eikhe's fate – it was just like so many others.

Was he himself free in all his decisions and actions? I very much doubt it. He was in the public eye just then, as, indeed, he always had been and always would be, and that is why 'public opinion' also linked any decision-making with him. In actual fact, however, it was really the envoys of the NKVD and not the Politburo who were in control of the situation. Ivan Chichayev[4] and VOKS representative Mikhail Vetrov, who officially held the modest post of Counsellor at the Embassy, had many different connections in Riga and were thoroughly conversant with the situation, appointing, removing and transferring old and new personnel. They, for their part, did not have much of a say in the matter as they were controlled by secret agents. For instance, Vilis Latsis, the new Minister of Internal Affairs, was accompanied everywhere by 'plainclothes escorts' who were responsible for his safety.

As the new bodies of power were being set up, various conflicts kept arising, as was only to be expected. One cropped up between Vyshinsky and Atis Kadikis, a Communist recently released from prison who preferred gradual decisions to drastic ones. Losing his temper, Vyshinsky threatened Kadikis with 'sanctions', but the latter was supported by Janis Spure, a fellow Communist and a second secretary of the Central Committee. As far as Vyshinsky was concerned, Kadikis was a nobody: how many secretaries had he sent off to be executed! However, this time the omnipotent emissary smoothed things over. Spure was in direct contact with Beria, and Beria also looked upon Vyshinsky as a mere 'nobody', and terrified him, just as he did everyone else.

There was also the task of restoring the Communist Party, which had been destroyed more by the purges conducted by Comintern envoys than by the police. Among the Latvian members of the underground organization the envoys had sought out Trotskyites, Bukharinites, and agents of every possible intelligence service. Some had been successfully lured to Moscow and liquidated. Now a real political force had to be mustered from the survivors who had stood their ground.

One of the main purgers sent here with a special mission from the 'foreign department' of the Latvian Communist Party was Jan Kalnberzin. In June 1939 he was caught by the police and locked up. This, however, happened long after his wife had been seized in Moscow. The warrant for her arrest had been signed by Procurator Vyshinsky. Now it was he, the recent Procurator-General, who went to the prison cell to ask the 'brave Leninist' to become the Communist Party's leader and also explain why the first (only the first, of course) government of the Popular Front for the time being (only for the time being, of course) consisted of people whom Kalnberzin regarded as reactionaries.

Contrary to what is written in Alexei Adzhubei's memoirs (*Znamya*, July 1988), Kalnberzin had been sentenced to death by a Latvian court although he was actually put in an isolation cell. Did he, I wonder, ask his visitor what had happened to his wife? And to his three children who had been left in Moscow? Or about the intrigues of the Latvian police? Or about the poor postal service?

Events meanwhile were taking shape as planned. Meeting after meeting was held, and Vyshinsky attended two of them – on 5 and 18 July. He was also seen once in a box at the opera house during the performance of an amateur theatrical group. In general, though, he preferred not to leave the confines of the Embassy, especially after one absurd incident. One day as he was going out into the street with his retinue, a young woman came rushing up to him shrieking, 'Darling Papa!'. Vyshinsky recoiled in horror and the 'daughter' was immediately dragged away.

The story of the 'foul provocation' spread across the city like wild fire but evidently it was no more than an ordinary case of mistaken identity: the young woman had genuinely mistaken Vyshinsky for her father, who had the same name and was also a lawyer and had remained on the other side of the border. Shortly afterwards Ambassador Derevyansky received a telephone call from Poskrebyshev in Moscow: 'What happened? Why aren't you keeping us informed?' A frightened Derevyansky mumbled something to the effect that he was writing a report at that very moment . . . The incident might have been amusing if it had not reflected who was really holding the reins of power: the envoy with emergency powers was himself under constant surveillance, and it was unlikely he knew for certain who had been specially attached to him in his retinue.

There are few descriptions of how Vyshinsky spent his time in Riga, but it is known, for instance, that the popular singer Irma Yaunzem, then on tour in Latvia, postponed her departure at Vyshinsky's request and went on giving concerts, thus reflecting the peaceful nature of events. She sang gypsy romances in the Soviet Embassy's reception hall, and Vyshinsky thoroughly enjoyed her performance and applauded enthusiastically.

In the autumn of 1988 I tried to see Elmar Briedis, Vilis Latsis's cousin, who was still alive in Riga. In the 1930s he had been a secretary of the underground Latvian Komsomol and during the war was in charge of a special department and 'Smersh'[5] of the 130th Latvian corps. He had often met Vyshinsky in June and July 1940. Briedis, however, flatly refused to meet me, saying over the telephone that Vyshinsky was a wonderful, noble and understanding man but 'through stupidity nobody believes that now' and so there would be no point in us talking.

Evidently, it was not Vyshinsky who played the main role in the Baltic states but Zhdanov. It was not Zhdanov who came to Vyshinsky for a briefing but Vyshinsky who went to see Zhdanov in Tallinn. He also went to Moscow to report personally to Stalin and then returned to complete the operation.

Much later, when studying these most dramatic days, some historians were to accuse Vyshinsky of organizing mass arrests, almost of arranging executions. This, however, is based on an 'illusion' created by the envoy's reputation. He was sent to Latvia with a totally different mission in mind. During his visit there were to be few arrests. It was only after 8 July, at the height of the Seim (Latvian parliament) election campaign, which lasted only ten days, that the members of the 'Thunderous Cross' pro-Fascist organization were arrested. The mass repressions, shootings and deportations were to begin later, once he had left.[6]

The people of Riga were, on the contrary, impressed by his mild manners, courteousness and civility. He guaranteed the defeated Ulmanis his total safety and unhindered passage to the West. Some kind of hitch, however, then occurred with his Swiss visa and at Vyshinsky's request Vetrov got the ex-president, by then an ordinary citizen, to give him his passport. A short while later Vetrov returned with another passport and another visa – to the Soviet Union. Ulmanis was forced to go East and not West. The same fate befell a number of Latvia's ex-leaders: Muntars, Beidneks, Ballodis, to name but a few. They all ended up in exile. Two years later Ulmanis died in a labour camp near Krasnovodsk in Turkmenia.

Vyshinsky spent about five weeks in Latvia. He returned home after having fully completed his outlined plan. On 21 July the hastily elected deputies proclaimed Latvia a Soviet Republic and asked Moscow to allow her to join the USSR. This request was granted. Yet again Vyshinsky had successfully carried out the mission he had been set by the Party, government and Comrade Stalin personally.

He was not, however, awarded a decoration for this. Only a few people at home knew what journey and mission he had been on while his ministerial office had stood empty.

So, not just in theory but in practice as well, Vyshinsky the lawyer had proved that he was also a diplomat, a politician and a masterful statesman. Stalin valued efficiency and loyalty – Molotov also. Vyshinsky's first and, what's more, most complex mission on the international scene had been a complete triumph.

This merely increased his workload, which he never minded. On the contrary, he always looked for more. He now became the right hand of the 'head of the Soviet government' in two capacities. While continuing as Vice-Chairman of the Council of People's Commissars, he was also appointed a Deputy People's Commissar of Foreign Affairs. In both appointments he was directly under Vyacheslav Mikhailovich Molotov. This was truly the 'honeymoon' period of their relationship.

10

Once again the telephone rang. This time it was early morning and not late evening. Dawn, to be exact. The telephone on the special government line was ringing shrilly and waking up the whole household.

It was a sunny Sunday morning. The settlement of Nikolina Gora was still peacefully asleep, and looking forward to a hot, carefree day. Only an early riser who had already been for a swim was drying himself off on the riverbank, setting up his rod and savouring the prospect of a good day's fishing.

A radio, which had been on since the early morning in a neighbouring house, was broadcasting the latest TASS news bulletin – a victorious report from Berlin: 'Yesterday and during the night German bombers made a successful raid on a fleet of British freighters, many of which were sunk.'

In this house, just as in millions of others throughout the country, nobody knew anything yet. But at that very moment the telephones started ringing in hundreds of houses. And the order was the same everywhere: 'You are requested to come immediately.'

The car was already rolling up to the gates. A driver on duty was at the wheel. The personnel who had dispatched the car had obviously not had time to wait for Vyshinsky's regular driver.

Molotov was sitting at his desk in his office with his head between his hands. In front of him lay a heap of telegrams and coded messages. The officials present, including the other deputies of the Chairman of the Council of People's Commissars – who had spent the night in town and arrived earlier – nodded silently to Vyshinsky.

He had already heard the news: they were at war.

It was past six o'clock. Far away to the West the fighting was already fierce and the first hundreds and thousands of lives had already been sacrificed for the victory which lay so unthinkably far ahead.

At midday the radio broadcast the latest news as usual: victorious reports from Berlin on the bombing of English towns, the sinking of passenger, rescue and transport vessels, and the 'routing of gangs of bandits' (partisans) in Yugoslavia and Greece. But not one word about what was happening just then on Soviet territory from Murmansk to Odessa and from Brest to Sebastopol.

Next came the call signals, and Molotov's faltering voice: 'Citizens of the Soviet Union! The Soviet Government and its head Comrade Stalin have charged me to make the following announcement.'

Like millions of my fellow citizens, I, too, a child at the time, listened to him, at my uncle's *dacha* near Leningrad. It was a calm and dazzlingly sunny Sunday morning; how strange and absurd it was to think that a few dozen kilometres away a real war was being waged.

It was quite impossible to imagine nearly half a century later that I was holding in my hands the draft (the original – not a copy) of that historic speech. Hurried, slanting, pencilled lines on pages torn out of a notepad with the author's corrections.

The end of this speech remains in the memory: 'Our cause is just. The enemy will be destroyed. Victory will be with us.' The second sentence does not appear in the first rough draft of the speech. It was inserted when the text was corrected.

Why am I describing this now? Because the original draft of this historic speech is in Vyshinsky's personal archive. It is kept as something of special value in a separate file. And besides those who sorted the archive out, nobody has ever touched this document. Why should the original be kept in Vyshinsky's archive and not Molotov's? A coincidence? I think not.

It has not been possible to have the handwriting analysed, but one day, I think, it will be. Vyshinsky's handwriting is instantly recognizable; his archive contains a great many other pencilled manuscripts – he was obviously not fond of ink! – undoubtedly in his hand.

Did Vyshinsky write the speech down at his chief's dictation? Or does it have several authors? Or perhaps Molotov, like Stalin, was overwhelmed by despair and confusion, leaving him stunned and powerless to act? Perhaps, at this critical moment when every minute counted and acumen was required, only Vyshinsky was able to muster the simple, succinct and profound words to address the people with? Perhaps.

One way or another, he was personally involved in the speech announcing the beginning of a new age. The material evidence of this remained in his personal archive as a much-treasured relic. And now it has enabled us to glimpse yet another of the many secrets of recent Soviet history.

Information on Hitler's planned aggression against the Soviet Union, and on the real possibility of war in the spring or summer of 1941, as is well known, had been flooding into Moscow through various channels. Soviet intelligence officers abroad, and, first and foremost, Richard Sorge, had even given the exact date. But Stalin refused to listen to their reports; at best, he was inclined to regard them as 'panicky light-mindedness' and, at worst, the intrigues of British and US Intelligence intent on spoiling his friendly relations with Germany.

Dispatches of this kind were sent not only through military and intelligence channels but also by Soviet diplomats. All of them passed through Vyshinsky's hands. He was conversant with the reports – categorized as top secret – which the NKVD were sent by their agents, including officials inside the Western embassies in Moscow. From these reports he then wrote up summaries for Stalin and Molotov. Some have recently become public with the advent of *glasnost*.

The following excerpts give one a fair idea of the atmosphere prevailing in the months and weeks before the war, the extent to which Stalin was actually informed, and how much Vyshinsky himself, on that sunny Sunday morning of 22 June, was prepared for the news of war:

In January of this year [1941] Soviet Ambassador to the United States K. Umansky reported at the request of Deputy Secretary of State Sumner Welles that the United States Government was in possession of information on Germany's intention to attack the USSR in the spring of this year....

On 19 April Churchill informed me [Vyshinsky] through his Ambassador in Moscow, Stafford Cripps, that the Germans were re-grouping their troops in order to attack the USSR and asked for this to be conveyed to Comrade Stalin....

On 10 April it became known through diplomatic channels that Hitler had met Prince Paul of Yugoslavia and informed him that Germany was going to start a war against Russia at the end of June.

On 11 April at a reception in the Bulgarian Embassy [in Berlin] the heavily drunk Western press chief from the Ministry of Propaganda, Karl Bemer, loudly declared: 'In less than two months' time our dear Rozenberg will become the master of all Russia, and Stalin will be dead.' It is said that Bemer has been arrested by the Gestapo....

On 25 April the Soviet military attaché to the Vichy Government, Lieutenant-General I. A. Susloparov, relying on information received from the Americans, Yugoslavs, Chinese, Turks and Bulgarians, reported that the Germans, having planned the start of the war against the USSR for the end of May, had now postponed the assault for about a month on account of the bad weather.

30 April. According to a report from Berlin of First Secretary of the Soviet Embassy V. Berezhkov,[1] First Secretary of the US Embassy in Berlin Jefferson Patterson acquainted him at home with a major of the Luftwaffe who confidentially informed him that his squadrons and many other air divisions of the German air force were being transferred to the East – to the aerodrome of Lodz (Litzmannstadt).

These are excerpts from the report Vyshinsky wrote at the beginning of May. It also includes the information of 'Ramsey' (Richard Sorge), and an NKVD agent with the code name of 'Georgi', who, judging by the contents of the information, most likely worked at the British Embassy in Moscow. So, on this score neither Stalin nor Beria kept anything secret from Vyshinsky: the information of such agents as Sorge was, after all, categorized as top secret. What is worth noting is not even the fact that he received it but that it was he who was responsible for making summaries of it for the Leader and his most loyal comrades-in-arms.

Here are a few more excerpts from another report by Vyshinsky at the end of May:

19 May. The Soviet Naval Attaché in Berlin, Admiral M. A. Vorontsov, has received a report from 'Walter', an officer in Hitler's headquarters, that Germany is preparing to attack the USSR through Finland and the Baltic Republics. Air raids will be made on Moscow and Leningrad. . . .

20 May. The Soviet Ambassador in Stockholm, Kollontai, reports that German troops have never been so powerfully massed on the Soviet borders before. . . .

22 May. The Vice Military Attaché in Berlin, Khlopov, reports that the German attack on the USSR is set for 15 June but it may take place at the beginning of June.

23 May. Our Military Attaché in Berlin, General Tupikov, has begun to send daily reports on Germany's military preparations. However, Dekanozov[2] has warned that the military are greatly exaggerating the threat.

Let us finish off these excerpts of reports and briefings with two more documents dated 21 June. They would be significant even undated, but this date makes them particularly tragic. Beria wrote to Stalin:

> I again insist on recalling and punishing our Ambassador to Berlin, Dekanozov, who keeps on bombarding me [the People's Commissar of Internal Affairs] with 'reports' on Hitler's alleged preparations to attack the USSR. He has reported that this 'attack' will start tomorrow....
>
> The same was radioed by Major-General V. I. Tupikov, the Military Attaché in Berlin. Relying on his Berlin agents, this thick-skulled general claims that three groups of the Wehrmacht army will be attacking Moscow, Leningrad and Kiev. He is insolently demanding that we supply these liars with a ration....
>
> But I and my people, Iosif Vissarionovich, firmly remember your wise plan: Hitler is not going to attack us in 1941.

Here are Beria's instructions on a report summarizing the information of Soviet intelligence officers – also dated 21 June 1941:

> For systematic disinformation grind the secret operatives 'Hawk', 'Carmen', 'Diamond', 'Loyal' into the labour camp dust as the abettors of international provocateurs wishing to make us argue with Germany. Strongly warn the others.

The identities of these code-named secret operatives have not yet been released, and so we do not know if the order of the People's Commissar was carried out or not. Going by the contents of their reports, 'Carmen' and 'Loyal' were obviously connected with the US Embassy, and 'Diamond' with the British. 'Why has nobody reacted at all to my signals?' exclaimed 'Carmen' – whoever he was – in an unusual tone for an intelligence officer. 'What's going on? I ask for my reports to be passed on to the highest authorities. [He, too, was naïve enough to think that wise Stalin knew nothing about this, that it was being concealed from him.] I ask and demand this as a Chekist, as a Soviet man who values the destiny of his Motherland.'

This dialogue is reminiscient of the nightmarish Theatre of the Absurd. 'As a Soviet man', 'the destiny of the Motherland' – these words meant nothing as far as the highest authorities were concerned. 'Grind them into the labour camp dust' – this was the language, the style, the *modus vivendi* of Stalin, Beria and Vyshinsky. They were together just as before. And they understood one another well.

Unprepared for the aggression and disorientated by the 'reassuring' directives and TASS reportings, the Red Army, while heroically resisting the advances of the Nazi troops on separate sections of the front, was rapidly forced back to the East. After the appalling massacre of senior military cadres – conducted not by the enemy but by their fellow countrymen – every talented general, officer and specialist was now of vital importance to the army and people.

But the carnage continued. Beria's department kept planting more and more 'conspiracies'. The fruits of Procurator Vyshinsky's work lived on and flourished: the most important part was to extract a confession, the rest could be arranged.

The following quotation is from a set of memoirs entitled *At The People's Service*, which appeared in three editions. Its author was Marshal of the Soviet Union Kyril Afanasievich Meretskov:

> It was the morning of the second day of the war. I received an urgent summons to Moscow. [Still an army general and a Deputy People's Commissar of Defence, Meretskov was in the Baltic Republics, commanding the resistance to the advancing Nazis.] That same day, 23 June, I was made a permanent adviser at the Chief Command Headquarters . . .
>
> In September 1941 I received a new appointment. I recall that for this reason I was summoned to the Supreme Commander's office. I. V. Stalin . . . took several steps towards me and said: 'Hello, Comrade Meretskov! How are you feeling?'

The Supreme Commander had every reason to ask the General that question for he knew where and how the General had spent the months between the first and second excerpts quoted. The author himself, of course, remembered them no less well than he did the first sentence he was greeted with at Headquarters.

On 24 June 1941 (26 June in other documents) the Deputy People's Commissar was arrested. What happened to him next, we shall find out from another excerpt. It is to be found in books containing the material of criminal cases. The author of this excerpt is one of Beria's most bloodthirsty executioners – Lev Shvartsman.

'Brutal continuous torture,' declared Shvartsman, already an accused in 1955,

> was applied to Meretskov first by high-ranking officials [he means Beria's closest associates, Merkulov and Vlodzimirsky], and then by myself and the investigators, Zimenkov and Sorokin. He was beaten with rubber rods. Before his arrest over forty witnesses had given evidence against Meretskov with regard to his participation in a military conspiracy. In particular, there was evidence of him having arranged with Kork and Uborievich[3] to fight against Stalin'.

Colonel of the Justice Likhachev, a member of the court, asked Shvartsman: 'Were you aware of the fact that you were beating a most senior army commander and a man of great esteem?' He replied: 'I had been given the kind of high-level order that was not discussed.'

In keeping with this high-level order the survivors of the nearly total annihilation of the highest-ranking Red Army commanders at the end of the 1930s were arrested just before or immediately after the outbreak of the war. A spectacular new 'Trial of the Military' was in the making.

Besides Meretskov, the 'conspirators' also included People's Commissar of Arms Boris Vannikov; Deputy Chief of General Staff, Twice Hero of the Soviet Union, Air Lieutenant-General Yakov Smushkievich; Chief of the Air Defence Directorate, Hero of the Soviet Union, Colonel-General Grigory Shtern – the same man who, at the 18th Party Congress, had jokingly promised to give his life for no less than twenty enemies' lives; Deputy People's Commissar of Defence, Hero of the Soviet Union, Air Lieutenant-General Pavel Rychagov; Deputy People's Commissar of Defence, Army Commander of the Baltic Military District, Colonel-General Alexander Loktionov; Deputy People's Commissar of Defence, Air Lieutenant-General Ivan Proskurov; Assistant Chief of the Main Artillery Directorate of the People's Commissariat of Defence Georgii Savchenko; the Department Chief of this same directorate, Stepan Sklizkov; the Head of the Air Force Academy, Lieutenant-General Arzhenukhin; an assistant to the Deputy People's Commissar of Defence, Major-General Matvei Kayukov; Deputy Head of the Armaments Board of the Chief Directorate of the Air Force, Ivan Sakrier; the eminent artillery constructor Yakov Taubin, and many, many others.

One could write a book about practically any of them. The 'conspirators' included people who had fought in the Civil War, in the battles in Spain, at Khasan and Khalkin-gol, outstanding experts in warfare. Three of them were members of the Central Committee, and five deputies of the Supreme Soviet. This was the 'second echelon' now that the top one had been liquidated. Rychagov, for instance, was only just thirty.

On 24 June 1941 his wife, the renowned air force pilot Maria Nesterenko, the assistant commander of a specially appointed air regiment, was 'taken' straight from an aerodrome. The indictment read as follows: 'as the beloved wife of Rychagov she could not fail to know about her husband's treacherous activity.'

According to one version of events, the reprisal against Shtern and the other generals was a reaction to the failure of the Stalin-Voroshilov *'Blitzkrieg'* in Finland. In Stalin's time all failures, it went without saying, could only be the result of someone's treason – but it is, I think, futile to try and find one particular reason for such insane action. Slipped into top gear, the destruction machinery was now working to laws of its own. It could no longer stop. There simply had to be conspiracies, diversions, assassination attempts, underhand plotting, and swarms of enemies everywhere. Otherwise the terror would begin to ease. Otherwise the well-oiled machine of coercion might start rusting and prove obsolete. Otherwise Stalin might turn his incinerating gaze upon those who were not meting out sufficient punishment.

It is pointless asking whether Stalin knew what sort of trial was brewing. Could he have not known about the people's commissars' and their assistants' sudden disappearance? Could he have not known – when the war had only just started – about the military district, army, corps and division commanders' sudden disappearance? Could he have not known that the post of adviser to the Headquarters, where he was Commander-in-Chief, had been especially devised to lure General Meretskov to Moscow from the front under a totally plausible pretext? Could Stalin have not known that – as Vannikov, who miraculously escaped annihilation, writes in his memoirs – his instructions, brought to Vannikov in his isolation cell, were 'to write down his ideas on ways of developing arms production now that military action had commenced'? Could he have not known that, at the height of the investigation when, as Shvartsman was to boast fourteen years later, they already had 'plentiful evidence on their enemy activity' (evidence forcibly extracted by the zealous investigators); that on his, Stalin's, supreme command Meretskov, Vannikov and another dozen and a half major figures in the defence industry were released? From their cells these fortunate ones either went straight back to their offices or to the Kremlin to report to Stalin. But not all of them, by no means all of them.

The brutally beaten victims eventually 'confessed' to what was demanded of them (except Loktionov, who heroically withstood all the torture). It is horrifying to read in the investigators' testimony later on how Vannikov screamed, clutching onto his heart, how Meretskov was beaten until he was covered in blood, how Smushkievich rolled across the floor, groaning, how tortured Shtern lost consciousness. 'Kirill Afanasievich, this just didn't happen, you know, it didn't, it didn't!' Writhing in pain, Loktionov stretched his arms out imploringly to Meretskov and then, catching his exhausted, lifeless gaze, fell silent.

Let us bow our heads before those who did not withstand the torture with just as much compassion and understanding as before those who did. And let us trust the most knowledgeable expert in these matters, Lavrentii Beria, who was to report to the inquiry twelve years later: 'In my opinion it is true beyond all doubt that, in the cases of Meretskov, Vannikov and the others, merciless beatings were applied; it was a veritable meatgrinder. In such a manner slanderous evidence was extracted.'

By naming the ones he needed, who were consequently to be released, and by keeping silent about the rest, Stalin made his choice. Beria understood the Teacher well: he could now act 'as he saw fit'. After being spies and wreckers, those whose loyalty the Supreme Commander believed in immediately became top military commanders. Before his release Meretskov was summoned by Merkulov, Beria's right-hand man. Investigator Vladimir Tikhonov, who was present during their conversation, recalls: 'Meretskov said to him [Merkulov]: "Vsevolod Nikolayevich, we used to meet on informal terms but I'm afraid of you now". Merkulov just smirked in reply.'

He had good reason to smirk: the power and force were still in the same hands. Even today, half a century later, the truth of what happened then is still horrifying.

While fighting was going on at the front, another round of enemies of the people were being interrogated at the Lubyanka although Moscow's prisons had been empty for a long time. They had begun to empty even before the start of the war. Paradoxically, on Stalin's orders, the military did nothing to ward off the aggression, whereas Beria's department displayed prudent foresight. The evacuation of the Sukhanov and Lefortovo prisons, where 'enemies of the people' were concentrated, had begun as early as May. But the internal prison of the NKVD at the Lubyanka continued to suffer from overcrowding as increasing numbers of new prisoners kept being sent there. There, too, waiting for his fate to be sealed, was the great geneticist Academician Vavilov, who had been condemned to death. All the investigators of especially important cases were made exempt from active service: their feats of arms were needed here in the rear, and not on the battlefield.

The front was rapidly approaching Moscow, but what concerned the NKVD now was not defending the capital but deciding their prisoners' fates: the population of the Gulag Archipelago continued to consist of over one million, and some of the camps were getting very close to the front-line. Orel Prison – which had been the Orel Central Prison under the Tsars – contained some of Vyshinsky's most recent victims who had been convicted at the last Moscow trial – Khristian Rakovsky, Sergei Bessonov and Professor Dmitry Pletnev – and who had been taken there before the war from either Solovki or Vladimir.

The names of the celebrities still to be liquidated were quickly looked through at the Lubyanka. All in all there were one hundred and fifty-four – all in the Orel Prison. The list was handed to Ulrikh, and with noteworthy speed the military judge, who was by then a colonel-general, passed judgement on them all *in absentia*. Each was charged with counter-revolutionary agitation and inciting a prison riot, and for this reason, in view of 'wartime conditions', they were all to be executed. On 11 September the prisoners who had been sentenced to death were led out of their cells and shot either in the dungeons or the yard. The next day all the rest were loaded onto trains and moved eastward to escape from the Germans. Orel fell only a month later, on 8 October.

Despite even these extreme measures the Lubyanka was obviously not expecting any sudden changes, and ordinary everyday life went on just the same as usual there. On 15 October Academician Vavilov – or rather condemned prisoner Vavilov – reported to Beria on the benefit his vast and comprehensive work could bring the country in wartime conditions. But within a few hours the situation had changed.

The German army's advance divisions broke through the front-line in several places and headed for Moscow. The city was seized by panic. In some incomprehensible way the news, grossly exaggerated at times, spread through the population like wild fire. Thousands of people started streaming towards the stations or roads heading East. Some of the particularly resourceful ones started robbing savings banks and looting shops: the radio and newspapers carried reports on the robbers and looters being executed to keep the rest in line.

The Soviet Information Bureau's official summary of operations was, as always, laconic but quite telling: it reported that there were battles 'on all the fronts' and that they were 'especially fierce on the Western sector'. 'Both sides,' it concluded, 'are suffering heavy casualties.' The editorial leader in *Pravda* defined the situation more precisely: 'Now that the situation is growing more complex, now that the Motherland is being threatened by grave danger, we shall be fearless in battle, steadfast and firm like Lenin and Stalin.' A state of siege was declared in the capital, and barricades were set up in the streets, but the cinemas stayed open, showing popular films like *The Determined Girl*, *Darling*

Girl, *The Lad from the Taiga* and *The Great Waltz*. Strauss's music kept being interrupted by blaring sirens.

On the night of 16 October the NKVD began hastily evacuating its internal prison. The prisoners were sent off with their 'assessors' – investigators from the special department. As the people being held there were important, they were dispatched to the town which had been previously selected as the temporary capital, and not simply into the interior. By a quirk of fate this town was Samara (renamed Kuibyshev after the Revolution), where many members – mostly Social Revolutionaries – of the dispersed Constituent Assembly had fled in 1918 and set up their powerless government for a short while.

On 16 October the diplomatic corps and part of the apparatus of the People's Commissariat of Foreign Affairs, headed by Vyshinsky, also set out for Kuibyshev. They reached their destination two days later. Even for special government trains this was remarkably fast. Molotov was already there but, after seeing to the accommodation of the apparatus and diplomats, he soon returned to Moscow. From then until the end of 1942 Vyshinsky was to be the 'reserve' minister in the 'reserve' capital, associating closely with all the ambassadors and virtually in charge of all Soviet diplomacy. Molotov would remain in Moscow with the Leader.

The prisoners had only just been incarcerated in the not overly spacious Kuibyshev Prison, and their 'assessors' had only just unpacked the belongings hurriedly thrown together in Moscow, when Beria – who had remained at his fighting post – came to a decision. He sent a letter by air to Kuibyshev with his specially trusted courier, Lieutenant of State Security Semenikhin, informing his men that the investigation was to stop, and the prisoners were to be shot immediately without trial. There then followed a list of twenty-five names.

It took another week to round them all up; even the 'especially important' prisoners had got lost in the crowds of others who had been driven here. The rank-and-file investigators were not informed of the order and went on working. On 27 October Iosif Rodovansky was still interrogating Arzhenukhin, and on the morning of 28 October Yakov Raitses[4] interrogated Maria Nesterenko. Suddenly Rodos appeared and said, 'Let's go!' without any explanation. A few minutes later five closed vehicles drove out of the prison gates.

Fourteen years later one of the people who took a major part in the execution, the then head of the first special department of the NKVD, Leonid Fokeyevich Bashtakov, said at the inquiry that he had been well aware of the fact that no sentence had been passed on the victims who had been put on the 'special list' but that he had assumed 'in wartime conditions a ruling could be passed by some kind of extra-judicial instance.' He still reported the matter to Merkulov and asked him what they should do. 'Carry out the sentence immediately!' came the reply. Especially as Beria and Kobulov kept ringing from Moscow. Why waste time? When? Right now! Report back when it had been carried out!

The 'group of commandants' found a 'special sector' near the town where the local NKVD operatives had their *dachas*. They were deserted now in the dreary autumn slush. And so twenty unfortunate victims from the marked list of twenty-five were brought here: 'to the village of Barbysh' – it says in the document. The rest were still being rounded up in Saratov. As soon as they were found, they were also shot outside the town. These five included Mikhail Sergeyevich Kedrov, a Party member since 1901 and Dzerzhinsky's closest comrade-in-arms, who had only recently been acquitted by the Military Board of the Supreme Soviet. However, the sentence of 'not guilty' in the archive of his case was replaced by a document compiled later and testifying to the execution of the death 'sentence'.

The generals – the very best of them – were shot on the outskirts of a rearline town. That day, 28 September, the troops 'fought battles on the Mozhaisk, Maloyaroslavsk and Volokalamsk sectors', but the fighter pilots failed to contain the Nazi planes, and they bombed Moscow. 'Casualties have been sustained,' said the Information Bureau's brief report. There were many casualties, an incredible number, but the people who lost their lives on the outskirts of Kuibyshev were, unfortunately, not among them. They too were the victims of Fascism, but, unfortunately, their own country's.

That evening the Bolshoi Theatre, which had also been evacuated here, began giving concerts in the local opera house; it was only natural it should be in the same place as the Government and diplomatic corps. And its greatest stars were here: opera singers Barsova, Mikhailov, Pirogov, Reizen; ballet dancers Lepeshinskaya and Messerer; and conductors Samosud, Fayer, and Melik-Pashayev. The diplomats were invited to this sad first night to listen to Verdi and relax from the stresses of provincial wartime life. There, too, among them was Vyshinsky, carrying out his official duty and enjoying himself as well. The inseparable duo of Shvartsman and Rodos was also in the audience. One can imagine how many people wanted to get to the first night, but did they all have the chance and such powerful connections? It had been a hard, stressful day, and they had fully earned the right to unwind and enjoy themselves.

The next day Merkulov and Dekanozov arrived from Moscow, and the executioners certainly had something to report. The newcomers paid their first official visit to Vyshinsky. There were two other Vice-Premiers besides him here – Nikolai Voznesensky and Mikhail Pervukhin – but Vyshinsky was closer, and more like 'one of them'. He had acumen. He immediately instructed the local authorities to vacate two more houses for the special department's needs. However, it is unlikely his visitors told him about the execution of the renowned generals, the pride and glory of the army, which had taken place nearby only the day before. Yes, he might be 'one of them' but not to that extent.

In the late afternoon of 6 November they all gathered together again in the local opera house. The seats in the presidium were taken by Voroshilov, Kalinin, Andreyev, Shvernik, Voznesensky, Shkiryatov, Yaroslavsky and Pervukhin. Vyshinsky made a speech to mark the anniversary of the October Revolution. For the first time in twenty-four years, he said, there was to be no ceremonial gathering and parade in Moscow, and it was he who had been given the great and sad honour of delivering the address – not in the capital but in the splendid town on the Volga. His audience, a significant part of whom were diplomats, applauded sympathetically. In keeping with tradition, the address was followed by a concert, and, in those days, there was no shortage of first-class artists in Kuibyshev. But Vyshinsky was the only one to stay behind in the Government box: the rest of the presidium disappeared somewhere. The war, the work . . . they had no time for concerts – who would not understand that?

In fact the rest of the presidium – except Vyshinsky, whose official position obliged him to stay with the diplomatic corps – moved across to the Palace of Culture next door, where they listened to a direct broadcast from Moscow of the main address which was supposed not to take place. Stalin delivered his speech underground, from the platform of the Mayakovskaya Metro Station – very few knew that this was the location. There with him were all the top officials who had remained behind in the capital: Molotov, Beria, Malenkov, Kaganovich, Mikoyan, Shcherbakov, Budionny and Shchadenko.

The next morning on the anniversary of the Revolution Vyshinsky stood on the tribune alongside the Politburo members Merkulov and his colleague Lozovsky, watching the parade file past. Here, in Kuibyshev, the parade was received by Voroshilov while at the same time in Red Square Stalin watched the Alexander Nevsky, Dmitry Donskoi, Alexander Suvorov and Mikhail Kutuzov columns march past and go straight off to the front.

In the evening Vyshinsky gave the first of the many receptions he would cordially host. Being the first, it was an historic occasion. The entire diplomatic corps was there, including the military missions of Great Britain, Poland, Czechoslovakia, and the special mission of the United States. The communiqué reported that 'a number of Soviet writers' were also present. Among them was Ilya Ehrenburg, who was given his first opportunity of speaking to the hospitable host. Already in disgrace, Litvinov was also graciously invited. Vyshinsky's intuition told him that Litvinov would not be without a post for long. Sure enough, on 9 November Litvinov was hastily summoned to Moscow to see Stalin and two days later returned to pack his bags quickly and receive Andrei Yanuarievich's farewell wishes. On 12 November he flew off to Washington to take up the post of Ambassador. Vyshinsky's first reception was a great success. The guests were entertained by various top artists; Vyshinsky remained a patron of the arts even in these hard times.

One should not imagine, however, that all they did in Kuibyshev was enjoy themselves. After celebrating the anniversary as well as they could, they got straight back to their daily work. The town became a hive of intense diplomatic activity. One of the first to arrive was the President of the exiled Polish Government and Commander-in-Chief of the Polish Army – now scattered all over the world – General Vladislav Sikorski. In July he had signed an agreement renewing diplomatic relations with Moscow. He now had to go further and agree to the Polish army fighting against what was now the common enemy. However, in order to do so the army, the officers and men first had to be assembled. The Polish Ambassador Professor Stanislav Kot had already approached Vyshinsky several times in Moscow at the end of September and the beginning of October, asking for lists of the Polish officers captured by the Russians. He had also presented his own list, wanting to receive information on what had become of the men on it. Their talks had yielded no results as Vyshinsky kept insisting that all the Polish prisoners-of-war had been released. And so General Sikorski flew in from London in search of a solution to this problem.

The day before Ambassador Kot had said to Vyshinsky by way of a warning: 'I hope General Sikorski will find all his officers.' Displaying his first-class qualities as a diplomat, Vyshinsky had replied with a phrase that could be interpreted in any way one liked: 'We shall give you back all the officers we have, but we cannot give back the ones we don't.'

Did he know about the massacre at Katyn? Or, to put it another way, could he have not known?

At the aerodrome Sikorski was welcomed by Vyshinsky and all the Allies' diplomatic representatives: the British Ambassador Stafford Cripps, the head of the British Military Mission MacFarlane, the Czech Ambassador Zdenek Fierlinger, the US Chargé d'Affaires Thornton and many others as well. They were pleasantly surprised when Vyshinsky, greeting the distinguished guest, suddenly broke into Polish[5].

There was nothing special about this and it did not affect the talks as such; interpreters from any language could be found even here in evacuation, and, what's more, Sikorski spoke Russian. Though a sign of specially stressed politeness, a reminder of their blood ties, the gesture was interpreted quite differently as an outstretched hand of friendship. In actual fact it was nothing more than a gesture, and had been suggested in the form of a guideline from Moscow. But the gesture was noted: in diplomacy such gestures win high praise, and the Academician started scoring points in his new post.

He no longer had anything to do with the arrests and executions, anything directly to do with them, that is. However, the seeds he had sown began to sprout. The adjacent departments were running smoothly – imprisoning and sentencing people without bothering with evidence. Nothing but the confessions mattered, just as Vyshinsky the theorist had ordered. Extracting confessions was as simple as ever: here in Kuibyshev, in Moscow and everywhere else in the country justice was run on this principle, and it worked splendidly.

He had given one other valuable lesson which nobody forgot either: the prosecutors were strictly forbidden to penetrate the sanctum where the NKVD did their plotting. The latter were subject to no control whatsoever. What had previously held true under Procurator-General Vyshinsky continued to hold true under his heirs and successors.

The situation around Moscow grew less tense. First Merkulov and Dekanozov, then Shvartsman and Rodos set off for home with their official thugs. A few months after the generals' executions, trained experts in Kuibyshev fabricated some pitiful 'documents' to serve as a basis for the unlawful shootings. This was definitely Vyshinsky's school: the aim justifies the means; whatever is useful is lawful. The villainous, brutal annihilation of innocent people – military commanders, heroes and patriots – was considered useful and therefore lawful.

Vyshinsky was still a household name, just as he had been in the thirties. He was talked about on the radio. He was constantly in the press, but in a different context these days: now it was all to do with meetings, talks, receptions and official farewells. And then more meetings and receptions. The outward, visible side of diplomacy which conceals (let it be said without irony) considerable hard work. Somewhere incredibly far away, but no matter how far still on home territory, a bloody war was being waged. But here in Kuibyshev there was not even a blackout. A short sketch of their everyday life will enable us to understand what it was really like here for this small group of people.

This is what the British Ambassador Archibald Clark Kerr, who succeeded Cripps, wrote in his letter to the Deputy People's Commissar of Foreign Affairs on 11 May, 1942:

Dear Mr Vyshinsky,
Your parcel was delivered to me this afternoon. The delicious contents have soothed my tension, my thirst and hopes.... I hasten to express my sincere gratitude to you. What you have done for me has fortified me in body and spirit but, first and foremost, it has warmed my heart, and for this a person cannot be too grateful.

The other wine you have sent ... delighted me. I hope that in the near future I shall be able to offer you something from my own country where our customs, I am pleased to say, are in many ways similar to those of your own people.

Poor man, he reckoned drinking fine wines was a popular Soviet custom. Just imagine, in those days – May 1942....

The superlative courtesy and concern shown by the Deputy People's Commissar of Foreign Affairs were evidently reflected in a highly favourable light in the Ambassador's dispatches, and no less than Winston Churchill himself expressed a great desire to meet the legendary Procurator, who had turned out to be a most delightful and hospitable host. On his way to Moscow Churchill decided to make a detour to Kuibyshev. However, in the end, he could not stop there; 'I should like to express my tremendous gratitude to you for all you have done [in preparation for the meeting] and convey to you how much I regret having missed this opportunity to meet you' – Churchill wrote

231

to Vyshinsky on 15 August 1942. He made up for his loss only two and a half weeks later when he met Vyshinsky at Yalta.

How strange it was. Here was this lawyer, this powerful orator, accustomed to taking snap decisions and certainly not mincing his words, quickly, smoothly and naturally gliding into his new conditions and tasks. And as soon as he embarked upon this entirely new career, he immediately found his feet and revealed hitherto unknown sides to his talents. There is no doubt Stalin had spotted them and given them an outlet. And, it seems, he had not been mistaken.

Of course, it was not in Kuibyshev that the major policy decisions were made but in Moscow, where Stalin and Molotov had remained. Vyshinsky, however, not only conscientiously carried out instructions and gave consultations but also, if needs be, actively helped. And in doing so, he frequently relied on loyal colleagues who had stood the test on numerous occasions.

On 24 February 1942 an explosion took place in Ankara, not far from the German Embassy, in Ataturk Boulevard. There was little doubt at the time that the bomb had been thrown as a provocation by people connected with the Embassy. The style of the people who had once set fire to the Reichstag gave them away. To the lawyers' question, 'Cui bono?' ('To whose advantage is it?') there could be only one answer. To the Nazis', of course. Turkey had still not decided whether to join the war or retain her neutrality, and Doctor Goebbels' exaggerated reaction to the 'Russian attempt upon the life of the German Ambassador von Papen' was to provide influential Turkish circles with the 'arguments' to push the country into making a fateful decision as quickly as possible.

On the instructions of these 'influential circles' the Turkish police supported Goebbels' version and arrested, as the TASS report read, 'two Soviet citizens, Pavlov and Kornilov', charged with an attempt on the life of von Papen. Who were these Soviet citizens, how did they come to be in Turkey and what exactly were they doing there? Not a word about this appeared in the Soviet press.

Most likely, they were people we usually refer to as 'intelligence officers'. It is unlikely their real names were 'Kornilov' and 'Pavlov'. There is no doubt also, however, that they had not attempted to assassinate von Papen: not only was there no plan to do so but there could not have been one. However, with unusual speed for the Turkish authorities a 'comprehensive inquiry' was carried out and five weeks later these suspects were brought to trial.

The situation was aggravated by the fact that the vacillations of the

Turkish leadership could end in a victory for the pro-German forces; Hitler's successes on the Eastern Front just then were playing into these forces' hands. The trial became a touchstone, as it were, in a large political game. It was not the first time, nor indeed the last, that legal and political issues were inextricably interwoven. Attention, naturally, focused on Vyshinsky, who just happened to be both a politician and a lawyer.

Among the deputies of the People's Commissar for Foreign Affairs it was Dekanozov who was 'responsible' for Turkey, and so he was put in charge of the whole operation to extricate the imprisoned officials who worked in the department he virtually belonged to, and also to safeguard Turkish neutrality. In his capacity as consultant, Vyshinsky advised that Pavlov and Kornilov should be provided with a qualified defence, that is, with first-rate Ankara barristers, and a Soviet specialist should be sent to supervise them and ensure the 'formation of a stand' (the defendants' personal fate was, of course, subordinate to global matters). One of Vyshinsky's closest colleagues and pupils, Lev Sheinin, who had proved himself numerous times at the Moscow Trials in the thirties, was nominated for the assignment.

The nomination was accepted. As Vyshinsky was in Kuibyshev, it was Dekanozov who briefed Sheinin. Rather than get embroiled in major politics, the Soviet emissary decided to adhere strictly to the case in hand. He suggested to Dekanozov they concentrate on proving the defendants' alibis. This won everyone's support; even if it were to fail, this plan of the defence would at least not do much harm.

While the trial was in progress – from the beginning of April to the middle of June – Sheinin flew several times to Ankara. According to Turkish law, he was not entitled to appear as a lawyer in court but, by presenting himself as such and producing the necessary documents as confirmation, he was allowed to see the accused. He thus gave them instructions and co-ordinated the plan of the defence.

Although, as usual, politics proved to be above the law – the accused were pronounced guilty and each sentenced to twenty years of prison – Sheinin had done all he possibly could, and earned the People's Commissar's thanks. Directly or indirectly this gratitude was intended for Vyshinsky, his guarantor and protector.

Two years later the Turkish authorities reviewed their assessment of the trial connected with the explosion in Ataturk Boulevard; in August 1944 Pavlov and Kornilov were released from Ankara prison and returned to the Soviet Union. All trace of them was lost as they acquired other surnames or were given back their real ones.

Meanwhile the situation at the front changed. It was no longer Moscow that was under threat but Kuibyshev. The Nazis were rushing towards the Volga.

The arrival of the Republican leader and possible candidate for the US Presidency, Wendell Willkie, was one of the last events in foreign politics to take place in the Volga town which had, so briefly, gained world fame. Vyshinsky apparently made a pleasant impression on Willkie – he was cordial, charming, and witty. This set the tone for the talks, especially for the meeting with Stalin which occurred several days later in Moscow.

A few weeks later Vyshinsky returned to Moscow with the Commissariat of Foreign Affairs and the diplomatic corps. The first thing he did, naturally, was report to Molotov, listen and note down instructions. One of them was quite extraordinary and might have come as a surprise (by those days' standards, not today's). Vyshinsky was capable of many things but surprise was not one of them; an order was an order – that was the principle he lived by all his life.

After many years of persecution Stalin suddenly decided to enlist the services and support of the Church, as its patriotic stand and influence on a significant part of the population could now come in useful in conditions of war. First of all, an agreement was reached to publish a limited edition of the Bible. Stalin entrusted Molotov with the organization and supervision, and Molotov handed it all over to Vyshinsky; his excellent qualities as both an organizer and supervisor were just right for the job.

This matter had to be carefully monitored, but not even Molotov or Vyshinsky could bring themselves to send it to the censors. It is hard to say which of them came up with the idea of finding a special censor for this assignment – and this assignment only. Someone they could completely trust. Someone who would have the honourable task of studying the Bible, pinpointing texts detrimental to the Soviet authorities and editing them out. In this sense at least there was nothing unusual about the work.

One way or another this idea dawned on them, and a censor with special powers was sent along to see the Academician in his office on Kuznetsy Most.

The honour fell to the well-known writer Nikolai Virta, not so long ago persecuted for being an 'Antonovite'[6] and the son of an executed White Guard priest, and then suddenly showered with praise, awarded the Stalin Prize and deemed worthy of enthusiastic reviews. Stalin, who, unlike his comrades-in-arms and successors, read a fair amount, had liked his novel *Loneliness*, just as he had Bulgakov's *The Days of the Turbins* and Pasternak's translations of Georgian poets.

Virta was later to describe how the proposal to become the Bible's censor and editor had thrown him into utter confusion. However, it would have been suicide to refuse. What's more, Vyshinsky – cunning as ever – had referred to the proposal as 'the task of Comrade Stalin and personal request of Metropolitan Sergii', the then *locum tenens* of the Patriarch. Vyshinsky added: 'The Church in our country is rich [in those days?] and pays well, so they can pay for it.' 'How much?' asked the realist Virta, no stranger to worldly matters. 'You can negotiate that yourself, the State does not interfere in the affairs of the Church', replied the lawyer Vyshinsky.

Virta set to work. At last he had the chance to read the Great Book in a calm and leisurely manner. Unfortunately, he was unable to enjoy its thoughts, poetry and spirit because he was not reading it for his own pleasure but to root out 'sedition' and undesirable 'allusions', insinuations, and associations. He made a special effort to detect any dubious features. Supposing a man with a moustache was to appear – would the reader, our simple Soviet reader, not interpret this 'moustache' somehow in the wrong way? In a modern context?

The Metropolitan at whose 'request' Virta had taken on this work, hearing that the latter intended editing the Bible, was completely astounded, but there was nothing he could do but wait. Fortunately, the censor-cum-editor failed to find any sedition, passed the edition and went to Vyshinsky to report on his task's completion. Vyshinsky was pleased enough but could not resist asking how much he had been paid. Not daring to deceive the ex-Procurator, Virta admitted quite openly: 'Half a million'. Even for those days when thousands were not worth so much, it was still an impressive amount. 'That's overdoing it a bit, isn't it?' replied Vyshinsky, taken aback, but after a moment's thought asked: 'Didn't they negotiate?' 'No, they didn't.' Then he grinned: 'In that case you did not ask enough, you could have got even more.'

A few years later Virta was again awarded the Stalin Prize, then again several times in succession. And each time Vyshinsky would congratulate him 'on his well-deserved high award'. And so would Molotov.

So, would it be an exaggeration to say that Vyshinsky was directly involved in the first Soviet edition of the Bible? I do not think so. He deserves credit for this.

This is not all he deserves credit for. The post he occupied involved all kinds of different work. In the course of his official duties the Deputy People's Commissar of Foreign Affairs – who, until 1944, also continued as Vice-Premier – came into contact with a great many people on a vast range of issues of both a general and specific nature. He was turned to for help, advice and permission and, first and foremost, for decisions.

It became a characteristic feature of a great many officials, starting from at least the mid-thirties, to try and avoid taking decisions or responsibility of any kind, and on the contrary, to withdraw and sink into the shadows, leaving it up to their direct superior or, as they used to put it, letting things take their natural course. And then it was that a new verb came into usage, which was to prove very tenacious: 'to kick aside', meaning to avoid decision-making by passing the burden on to someone else.

The infection struck all areas of our life, but in some departments particularly in the public eye, departments whose every decision could have far-reaching and not always predictable repercussions, the fear of taking responsibility reached epidemic proportions. One of the very first to be afflicted was the Department of Foreign Affairs, which had been brutally and devastatingly purged. How could this not taint the memories and mental state of those who had survived? New people came to the fore with an in-built sense of caution, bordering at times on cowardice.

Never in a hurry to take any serious decision until the position of his superiors had become completely and utterly clear, Vyshinsky was naturally cautious, not only in matters of principle but in petty issues too. So, what was it like, this legendary caution in the People's Commissariat of Foreign Affairs? And how did it affect the official's daily life if those working alongside him regarded him as a decision-maker and not someone who passed the buck?

There was one other deputy of the People's Commissariat of Foreign Affairs who not only dared but even strove to take decisions: Vladimir Dekanozov. But this was not surprising: he was Beria's right-hand man who had been transferred to the People's Commissariat of Foreign Affairs and could afford to do what was strictly forbidden for others. Was Vyshinsky anyone's right-hand man? Notwithstanding all the support Stalin gave him, he never felt in a firm or stable position. But there was no alternative: he had to take decisions by juggling all the various possible consequences, and try not to slip up.

For a very long time the Russian émigré poet and singer Alexander

Vertinsky[7] had been trying to get back into the country. He was waiting in China for his fate to be decided but so far had received no reply from the Soviet authorities. Whoever his pleas were either sent to in Moscow or forwarded on to by the Soviet Embassy always brushed them aside: who had time for that sort of thing in those days? Nobody wanted to accept responsibility; they still were not used to the idea of émigrés returning. They might be arrested for spying for an enemy intelligence service or for failing to remain sufficiently vigilant. Was it worth taking that risk over someone like Vertinsky?

It is still said that Vertinsky 'bought' his way home by sending the Red Army a train carriage full of medicines. There is nothing to prove this, and it is unlikely the émigré artist had such a lot of money in those days. Everything was far simpler. Someone put one of the artist's many letters recounting the long history of his undecided case into the file containing all Vyshinsky's routine business – requests, letters, memoranda and draft documents. Instead of pushing it to one side, Vyshinsky appended the instructions as requested. A few days later Vertinsky arrived in Chita.

He began giving concerts on his way to the capital. The rumour that he was coming spread across the city in no time. Thousands of his admirers from the days before the Revolution were still alive. The sweet magic of 'forbidden fruit' surrounded his gramophone records, which had been listened to behind closed windows and lowered blinds. And now here he was, a living legend, no longer prohibited but legal.

To begin with, the concerts were put on without any publicity or posters, and even so the halls were still completely packed out. Vyshinsky came to one of them and sat modestly in a side box hidden from inquisitive eyes behind velvet drapes. However, his presence was no secret to the artist on the stage. He knew perfectly well whom Destiny had appointed as his patron. When he started singing, as a token of respect he turned very slightly towards the box. Only very slightly but it was still noticeable. And he also bowed separately and with particular dignity towards the box.

Vertinsky was accepted back by his Motherland, but was also deeply affronted by her. Not by her, of course, but by someone in particular. Someone invisible and anonymous, as was the way, acting on her behalf. The artist had to suffer a shroud of silence around his name. An absolute void of newspaper articles and reviews – even critical ones. And, finally, a blow which struck him really hard: he wrote two ecstatic poems about the great Leader, full of adoration, gratitude, and warmth, but nobody wanted to publish them. So who was he in his

237

newly-regained country – a full member of society or an outcast?

Vyshinsky could do nothing to help. He, too, realized – no less than Vertinsky – that people were not keeping quiet about the singer and poet just to be on the safe side; someone's guiding hand could clearly be seen. However, he gave him the good advice to write a plaintive letter – not to Stalin but to his secretary, Poskrebyshev. This was a subtle piece of diplomacy. Writing to Poskrebyshev was just the same as writing to Stalin. If the Leader wanted to, he would respond and choose the way to himself. If he did not, he would say nothing.

The advice was taken. Vertinsky sent Poskrebyshev not only a shrewd and convincing letter but a poem as well, appealing for justice and commonsense. He even played upon 'the happy coincidence of our names': Poskrebyshev and he were both called Alexander Niko-layevich – a sign of fate.

No reply followed. The poem has yet to be printed. No reviews appeared either. And so Vertinsky continued to be both a member of society and an outcast even after being awarded the Stalin Prize.

However, this was not Vyshinsky's fault. He had done everything he could.

Everything he could? Or everything he could risk doing?

11

Vyshinsky never felt safer than he did during the war, although, of course, under Stalin and Beria nobody ever felt totally safe. In his memoirs Ilya Ehrenburg has already remarked upon this paradoxical truth: it was during the war – when the country was suffering and had been through the nightmare of 1937 – that people felt the greatest freedom and independence. It was more of an atmosphere than a visible social change. The feeling of camaraderie and shared misfortune made everyone stronger. The machinery of destruction went on working but with muffled engines and without causing panic. Nazism was producing quite enough of that as it was.

As far as Vyshinsky's personal fortunes – career and his personal life – were concerned, these years were marked by a steady and gradual advancement. Never before had he been so close to Stalin nor, indeed, would he be again. He regularly attended Stalin's speeches, and frequently received instructions from him which bypassed the People's Commissar.

His participation at the Moscow conference of the three Great Powers' foreign ministers turned Vyshinsky into a major figure on the international scene. It was taken for granted that he would also be going to Tehran, where the conference of 'The Big Three' – Stalin, Roosevelt and Churchill – was to take place at the end of November 1943. However, only Molotov and Voroshilov went in the end, and Lavrentii Beria – incognito, in dark glasses, hat pulled over his eyes – to see to the Leader's security.

Vyshinsky stayed behind to 'keep shop': during the conference he was the People's Commissar's first deputy in charge of the Council of People's Commissars and all its departments. This was his first rehearsal in such a high post.

Vyshinsky's absence at the Tehran meeting was obviously a mistake, and it was not repeated either at Yalta or Potsdam. He, too, no worse than Beria, could have seen to a few things – applying his legal expertise, for instance, and brilliantly accurate formulations to the approved documents – an art in which he was peerless.

The few of his colleagues still alive recall Vyshinsky's amazing and rare ability for dictating the text of any document, no matter how important, straight off – be it a diplomatic note, communiqué, draft agreement, treaty, speech or order, it made no difference. What's more, with such precision of expression and grammatical correctness that it required no further editing and could be sent directly to press.

This rare quality – among others – made Vyshinsky irreplaceable as an adviser, aid and consultant.

Vyshinsky was probably disappointed that Stalin did not take him to Tehran – and what an extraordinary drama it might have been: the journey there and back took in Baku. For Stalin and Vyshinsky Baku was not just a name on a map, nor indeed a city shrouded in nostalgic memories: it was the place where their fantastic destinies had arisen and taken shape, and where, even after the devastating purges, there were still some who remembered them.

It seems only natural that they would have wanted to drive through the city of their youth and have a look, if only through the gap in the closed blinds of their limousines, at the familiar streets and houses. However, Stalin drove straight from the airport to the railway station, boarded and set off.

Vyshinsky did not even manage to meet Stalin and Molotov on their return to Moscow. The visit to Tehran had not been official but strictly business, and kept quite secret. Instead of being brought up to a station, the train stopped at a platform for suburban electric trains between Moscow's Byelorusskii and Savelovskii stations. Stalin's limousine drove straight onto the platform and stopped by the carriage door. There was no welcoming ceremony.

Vyshinsky was still frightened to death of Beria. And the higher he rose, the more frightened he became. As he rose higher, he grew more powerful, and in doing so, gained extremely dangerous potential as a rival. Beria absolutely detested anyone with any career prospects. He would do all he could to collect compromising material on the 'upstart' to arouse Stalin's suspicion and provoke an investigation. Ranks, regalia, positions, titles, nothing helped – quite the contrary was true. And in no time at all Stalin's warm attitude to his favourite would completely change.

Vyshinsky knew all this perfectly well. And this is why he was afraid not only of Beria but of all of his retinue as well. He had a very clear understanding of the different relationships between them all – where to expect a dirty trick, where to be on the look-out.

The following brief illustration is very telling. Every Deputy People's Commissar, as I have already mentioned, had his own spheres or regions, as we would say today. For instance, Vyshinsky was in charge of relations with Britain and the United States, and Dekanozov with the Near East. However, whenever an important inquiry was sent in, it was dispatched, regardless of the country it involved, to the People's Commissar and all his deputies for their perusal.

No matter how urgent the matter, Vyshinsky usually took his time. He did not like taking rash decisions and, furthermore, the Leader's directives kept changing, both in general outline and in detail, and so there was always a danger of making a fool of oneself.

But Dekanozov always reacted fast. His drive and thrust were well known to subordinates. The moment he received material on a 'region' he was not in charge of, and which was intended purely for his own information, he often used to give instructions and dictate telegrams to Litvinov and Maisky, that is, to ambassadors of countries outside the range of his official duties. This was not only tactless and disrespectful with regard to his colleagues, it also exceeded the bounds of protocol. However, Vyshinsky put up with this uncomplainingly. He never raised objections and deliberately turned a blind eye. To have expressed his disagreement with Dekanozov and shown even the slightest dissatisfaction would have meant one thing only: that he was not afraid of Beria, that he did not care what he thought, because he had a right to.

Where Beria was concerned, Vyshinsky preferred to keep a low profile. The less noise you made, the quieter your life was. Humility worked better than pride. Let him despise you, just as long as he left you alone.

But, to make up for it, whenever it concerned others outside Beria's circle, inferiors in less protected positions, Vyshinsky gave no quarter.

Tired of waiting one day for the reply to his telegram to Roosevelt, Stalin furiously demanded that 'order be established'. Molotov's staff immediately ascertained that the cipher clerks only monitored the telegram's passage as far as Greenland, and then its passage from Greenland to Washington was controlled by the Americans. That would seem to be the end of the matter, but Molotov, unmindful of his deputy's pride, instructed his subordinates to summon Vyshinsky to him. The latter instantly rushed to the Kremlin.

He had the situation sized up instantly: if Stalin had demanded that 'order be established', he would see that it was. 'But these little liberal intellectuals here,' said Molotov nodding towards his subordinates, 'claim nobody's to blame.' 'How can that be so?' Vyshinsky fumed, 'Someone is always to blame! You don't have to look far for them.' He immediately reeled off the names of two or three people who, in his opinion, were definitely to blame even without any verification.

This was reported to Stalin and measures were taken. Shortly afterwards Roosevelt's reply arrived and the matter was dropped for everyone except those Vyshinsky had declared guilty. The next day they were no longer working at the People's Commissariat of Foreign Affairs. One official more, one official less – what difference did it make?

Nearly half a century has passed since that minor incident, but eyewitnesses still recall it down to the minutest detail. They remember the terror caused by the insecurity of their positions, the fact that any of them through a caprice or ill luck could be found guilty. What they remember most, however, is Vyshinsky's fear as he came rushing to the summons, which he was unable to conceal behind his ruthless, harsh exterior. The harsher he looked, the more obvious his fear became.

The Allied troops' landing in Sicily, their rapid advance to the North, the inevitable changes in Italy, her break with Berlin and withdrawal from the war resulted in the setting up of an Allied control council on Italian affairs whose headquarters were in Algiers. Stalin appointed Vyshinsky as the Soviet Union's representative on this council. Britain sent Harold Macmillan, the future Prime Minister, and the United States sent the eminent diplomat Robert Murphy.

Less than four years before Vyshinsky had travelled abroad for the very first time. From now on until the end of his life he was to spend much more time abroad than at home. Here in Algiers, far away from his usual surroundings – but with his wife at his side – he was to celebrate his sixtieth birthday in the luxurious Aletti Hotel. Here, too, he was to receive news of yet another Order of Lenin. And all the congratulatory letters and telegrams – a huge wad of official ones and a small trickle of unofficial, personal ones 'from friends' – were also sent on to him here. 'With all our hearts we wish you health and strength for the benefit of our motherland cordial greetings' wired Alisa Koonen and Alexander Tairov. An enthusiastic telegram came from Lev Sheinin: 'Recalling the twelve years under your leadership in the Procurator's office for whose foundation and consolidation you did so much from the heart I wish you many years of health and happiness ... I warmly embrace and kiss you! Your deeply devoted Liova.'

Vyshinsky was now dealing with issues in which he had no previous experience. But how many times in his life had he had to deal with completely new problems, each time making an in-depth analysis of them with astonishing speed, and displaying exceptional tenacity and acumen?

The rounding up and repatriation of Soviet POWs scattered all over North Africa and Italy was one of the first problems he started tackling with characteristic energy. His envoys visited the POW camps, handing out collections of Commander-in-Chief Stalin's speeches and directives to their compatriots who were eager for home news. Each of these envoys then presented Vyshinsky with a written report, mentioning in passing that certain 'privates and sergeants' were refusing to return while others, having given their verbal consent, 'upon arrival at assembly points [in Naples and other cities] had fled'.

But Vyshinsky knew they simply had no right to run away, and if such a thing was, unfortunately, to happen, it was nothing but the machinations of enemies – who for the time being were still allies. And so one of his main tasks, which he conducted with vigour and singlemindedness, consisted of endless searches and repatriations, come what may and at any price. Here he witnessed the emergence of a new problem – that of the so-called 'displaced persons' – which he was soon to encounter on more than one occasion at the United Nations and argue his Leader's viewpoint with his usual fervour.

We shall find reverberations of his position in many of his later writings. One of them, which was actually delivered as a speech but still reflects his opinion, for some reason struck me in particular. On 2 February 1953, a month before Stalin's death, when certain dramas were about to be played out, the mere thought of which still turns one's heart to ice, Academician Vyshinsky arrived at a general meeting of the Academy of Sciences to discuss the tasks of academics 'in the light of Comrade Stalin's new work of genius *On the Economic Problems of Socialism in the USSR*'. After listening to the loyal reports of President of the Academy Nesmeyanov and the ubiquitous Yudin, Vyshinsky took the floor. First he destroyed Truman, Acheson, Jackson, Dulles, Eisenhower and other American politicians – what could be more topical for Academicians in those days, and what was connected more with the economic problems of Socialism? He then switched to the main theme of his paper and began attacking two leading scholars in the field of international law – Iosif Levin and Yevgeny Korovin. What were they accused of? Of failing to write in their books that no POWs had the right to refuse to be repatriated by claiming that they had the free will to choose. No one could, and that was the end of it. If they refused, they would be forcibly repatriated. This is what the authors should have said. And 'all those who do not understand this' Vyshinsky referred to in what were fairly mild terms for those days as 'apologies for scholars'. At least not enemies of the people.

The member of the Allied control council was also entrusted with the urgent task of giving the Italian Communists, who had come out of hiding, as many chances as possible of taking part in the country's political life. It was with this end particularly in mind that Vyshinsky paid a visit to Naples, which had already rid itself of Fascism by that time. Here, the local Communist leader, Eugenio Reale, gave him an enthusiastic welcome both in person and in writing:

Dear Comrade Vyshinsky

We are confident that through your work you will succeed in alleviating our people's hardships as much as possible, just as you will succeed in giving our people a chance to regain the dignity and freedom they deserve. Our Party and the working masses ... are acting under the great leadership of Comrade Stalin.... In your person, Comrade Vyshinsky, we also greet the Procurator-General who crushed the Trotskyites and other such brutes with such staunchness and justice.

[Letter dated 7 November 1943]

When Vyshinsky arrived in Naples, Comrade Reale had the opportunity of personally telling him how delighted he was about the annihilation of those 'other such brutes'. At the same time he asked for the émigrés (Communists who had left to escape Fascism) 'whom Italy now had particular need for' to be urgently sent back from the USSR and other countries. These included Palmiro Togliatti, Eduardo d'Onofrio, Ruggiero Greco, Giovanni Germanetto, and Luigi Bianco, to name but a few. This request was soon granted.

All along the Eastern Front – from the Barents to the Black Sea – bloody battles were still being fought, and thousands of lives lost on the roads of war: devastated towns, burnt-out villages, famine and cold. Here meanwhile Vesuvius peacefully puffed away, Capri's blue grotto looked as dazzlingly beautiful as ever, Sorrento's villas basked in exotic vegetation and Santa Lucia echoed and re-echoed with the never-ending chords of serenades. Nor could the strident sounds of political arguments detract from the eternal charm of the Eternal City, where this member of the Allied council also went on official business. Things were even more hectic in Algiers, which was buzzing with diplomatic activity. One lovely spring evening Vyshinsky went to dine with General de Gaulle.

Vyshinsky was in constant contact with Moscow and frequently telephoned Molotov and sometimes even Stalin. 'How are things going, Comrade Vyshinsky?' Stalin would enquire affectionately.

Things were going well: in Yalta (February, 1945) he was already sitting next to Stalin and Molotov at the negotiating table, enjoying the full rights of a participant – his authority grew daily. His name was now linked with all kinds of international actions – talks, agreements, meetings, farewells – his picture was forever in the press alongside foreign dignitaries, and he looked wonderful in the new steel-grey diplomatic uniform displayed in all its glory in cinema newsreels.

He felt wonderful too when he was threatening, exposing and lecturing on his Leader's instructions. In Yalta, recalls former US Secretary of State Edward Stettinius, Vyshinsky was instructed to talk to his old acquaintance Charles Bohlen and thus 'privately' inform Roosevelt of Stalin's viewpoint on the Great Powers' rights. Vyshinsky recalled Bohlen from the Bukharin trial: with his professional prosecutor's eye he had singled this American diplomat out from the two rows of foreign observers in the hall. And so it was to him Vyshinsky had to explain that the 'small nations' would never be allowed to discuss the Great Powers' affairs. Vyshinsky greatly enjoyed expounding this 'viewpoint'; as the Russified representative of a 'small nation', he found it particularly to his liking.

Vyshinsky's 'viewpoint' confounded Bohlen, who tried to explain that the US delegation was obliged to consider the opinion of its own people, who were reacting adversely to the infringements of the 'small nations' ' rights. 'Never mind,' retorted Vyshinsky disparagingly, 'your nation will come round. Nations have to obey their rulers.'

However, alongside all this public activity another kind of activity was taking place out of the public eye, or, to be more precise, unpublicized; not secret but unpublicized. The whole world knew about it, except the Soviet Union, where not a single word was said on the subject.

Immediately after Yalta and almost as soon as he arrived back in Moscow, Vyshinsky got on another plane and headed South again, or rather, South-West. In a note for the personnel department kept in his personal archive this episode is described thus: '1945. February–March. Visit to Rumania with special mission'. So what was this 'special mission' which had been coded so enigmatically even for the omniscient personnel department?

Essentially, it was an identical mission to the one he had carried out so brilliantly in Latvia five years ago. This time it was not a question of another state joining the Soviet Union or even preparations for this, but of carrying through a prior agreement with regard to spheres of influence. Rumania was entering the Soviet Union's 'sphere'.

The Government of General Nikolai Redescu, which was then in power in Bucharest, was not the one to meet these conditions. The 'special mission' consisted of forming a more acceptable cabinet and then securing a change of government – only an interim coalition but one which would ensure the government's gradual transfer to the Communists.

For the first time in his life Vyshinsky had occasion in Bucharest to associate with a monarch. On 26 February the young King Mihai, who was shortly to be awarded an Order of Victory and then sent into exile, gave an audience to Stalin's envoy.

In a polite and then unequivocal manner Vyshinsky demanded that the King make Petra Groza Prime Minister of the coalition government. The King refused. It was a futile argument as Groza's appointment had already been approved by the Kremlin. Vyshinsky had come with ready instructions and so, even if he had wanted to, he could not have acted differently.

The next day he appeared in the King's palace again. Seeing that the King was still raising objections, he banged his fist down on the table so hard that the china started vibrating, and King Mihai instinctively stepped back, afraid he was about to be punched in the face. 'Right then,' roared Vyshinsky, 'by eighteen hundred hours the decree appointing Doctor Groza is to be signed. At your disposal you therefore have . . .' he glanced at the clock, 'one hundred and twenty-five minutes. If this is not done, we cannot guarantee the free existence of the Rumanian people.' And off he stormed.

The decree was, of course, signed but this was not the end of Vyshinsky's mission. According to his instructions, the ex-Prime Minister, Georg Tatarescu, who had displayed a readiness to cooperate with the Communists, was to be included in the government from the National Liberal Party. It so happened that the Rumanian authorities had him down on their list of wanted war criminals for not just sympathizing with the Nazis but actually collaborating with them. Just then, however, it was more important to have Tatarescu in a ministerial post than in the dock: political pragmatism has always had the edge on political ethics. Here, too, of course, Vyshinsky got his way.

Two years later the people of the Rumanian town of Sibiu sent a most humble request to Vyshinsky, asking him to agree to become an honorary citizen of their town. Vyshinsky had his assistants write him a detailed report on this town of which he had never heard. After finding out all about its population, schools, factories, churches and theatre, he evidently felt quite satisfied and gave his consent.

'The local authorities and citizens of the town of Sibiu,' read the telegram which arrived swiftly in Moscow, 'who gathered at the ceremonial meeting in the civic hall, wish for their heartfelt gratitude and warmest wishes to be conveyed to His Excellency the Deputy Foreign Minister of the USSR Mr Vyshinsky upon his acceptance of the honorary citizenship of this town. Mayor of Sibiu Vasily Hada.'

Did the people of Sibiu later repeal this hasty resolution? Or did they hide it away in some obscure archive and quietly forget all about it?

I do not know.

His important social engagements at home and abroad did not permit Vyshinsky to forget that he was an Academician and the head of the Soviet school of law. His capacity for work was altogether astounding; now, years later, it seems even more so. He was a member of the presidium of the Academy of Sciences and the lecture bureau; he gave reports and papers; he wrote books, pamphlets and articles and extensive reviews on lawyers' theoretical works. These reviews in his personal archive, which are hundreds of pages long, enable us to see how meticulously and studiously he read the works themselves, most of which are, frankly, not of the slightest interest to us today. A great many very intelligent people in those days worked on totally useless projects, wasting their entire lives on pseudo-scientific ruminations and devoting serious scholarly thought to the decrees and resolutions which kept being churned out.

He continued writing folios glorifying Stalin in which his own text consisted merely of short linking phrases between quotations from 'His' works. One only has to read Vyshinsky's articles under the heading of 'Lenin – the great organizer of the Soviet State' in two issues of *Pravda* just before the end of the war to see how little there is about Lenin and how much about Stalin.

When it came to work, Vyshinsky never did anything in a formal, routine manner simply for appearances' sake. He became totally immersed in everything he did. Returning from journeys of any length, from the highest offices or international talks on global issues, he used to sit down immediately and start tackling comparatively minor matters with just as much fastidiousness, for to him they never seemed minor. He took all matters, great and small, very much to heart.

I shall now cite – without commentary, I think – an excerpt from the shorthand report of one of his speeches from his archive which is published here for the first time. It relates to a sitting of the lecture bureau of the Committee on University Affairs at the Council of People's Commissars on 24 August 1944. I think it will give us a fairly clear picture of Vyshinsky at this stage of his career:

> In his public speeches Ilya Ehrenburg praises France far too much, despite us warning him – don't spoil de Gaulle by flattery, and don't praise him to excess ... you are a francophile, but moderate your ardour a little, and bring it in line with general state tasks... If a lecture on France is announced, all the spi – sorry ... the entire diplomatic corps in all its guises will be there....
>
> The second instance concerns Italy. One of our lecturers, despite the fact that we rejected one of his lectures, and strongly criticized and corrected it, ignored a whole series of corrections in his lecture. When we compared the shorthand report, there were five or ten places where he said completely the contrary to what we had approved. This lecturer, Comrade Shtein ....
>
> In ten places you [Shtein] deviated from the text ... I had two specialists study the shorthand report of your lecture in the Hall of Columns, and the text ....
>
> *Shtein:* 'There was no shorthand report ...'
>
> Yes, there was. We make no secret of this, shorthand reports are made of all the lectures.... You deviated from the text but we shall have a special talk about this.

I promised not to comment, but I cannot resist doing so. Just listen to the Prosecutor's sharp falsetto. One can easily imagine what their talk with Professor Shtein was like. Perhaps they hinted that he was playing with fire. Remember, Shtein had already been mentioned in Koltsov's 'case'. They already had enough compromising material on him and here was more.

However, let us return to Vyshinsky's speech, which contains other things of interest to us. Professor Nikolai Nikolayevich Polyansky, the most venerable Russian law scholar, whose lectures at the beginning of the century had been attended by all Moscow's intelligentsia, had complained about the censor removing the words 'Heine's prophetic verses' from the text of his prepared lecture. Vyshinsky immediately reacted as follows:

> and I would have removed them, too! Not because I'm against Heine but because I consider it improper in our present conditions to propagandize these names. Perhaps Heine should also be examined by the censors.... We cannot sacrifice a state policy for the sake of a word's beauty.

Finally, here is one other revelation by Vyshinsky directly concerning foreign policy tactics. I have no objection to what he is saying; what interests me here is his *way* of thinking: his style and phraseology reflect very precisely the principles of inter-state relations as Stalin-Molotov-Vyshinsky saw them. The issue at hand is Bulgaria. At that moment Soviet troops were already standing on the left bank of the Danube and just over two weeks were left until 9 September, when the pro-Nazi regime in Sofia would be ousted:

> Our relations with Bulgaria are such that we are also engaged in a well-known game ... Bulgaria is saying many nice things about the Soviet Union like 'it is our liberator, our patron' and so on. In actual fact, they are coming to an agreement [with Germany] on how to swindle us. But Bulgaria thinks it wouldn't be a bad idea to swindle us both. However, one must not speak about this at a public lecture because it would mean scaring the sparrow before we've sprinkled salt on its tail, and we have no doubts at all that this is indeed what we shall be doing.

Talleyrand said that man was given a tongue in order to hide his thoughts. This immortal formula became a guideline in the lives of very many people who had the profound misfortune to live under Stalin, and especially diplomats for whom it became a rule of conduct. On this occasion, though, it seems Vyshinsky was speaking his mind. And again it is not the subject-matter that interests me here but the way of relating to other nations and states clearly reflected in his manner of speech. It was not a matter of holding talks, disputing one's points of view, displaying consistency and adherence to principles, clarity and integrity, but of sprinkling salt on a tail.

This is the style that flourished in the post-war years.

The end of the war made life on the foreign policy scene even more tumultuous by giving it greater dynamism. In the last days of April Vyshinsky was actively involved in constructing ill-fated Soviet–Polish relations. After General Sikorski's mysterious death, the final break with the London-based émigré government, the tragic Warsaw uprising and open clashes with the Polish Army, a new era at last seemed to be dawning in relations between the two states. Considerable effort and diplomacy of the Stalinist school were required on the part of Vyshinsky to create a base for them. It is not fortuitous that after signing a treaty of friendship, mutual aid and post-war cooperation, Prime Minister Eduard Osobka-Morawski sent a telegram to Comrade Vyshinsky from Brest, as he was about to leave the Soviet Union, expressing his 'profound gratitude for the cordial reception' and for his 'beneficial personal efforts' which had resulted in some constructive decisions being reached. The word 'personal' was not chosen by chance.

All this seems like ordinary diplomatic protocol, but only at first glance. Within less than five years Vyshinsky, now over sixty, had not only mastered a new and most complex profession but had also assumed a pre-eminent position in it, having been virtually in charge of a great power's diplomacy at a momentous point in its history. Of course, he was no more than an executor of the dictator's supreme will, but a creative executor rather than a mechanical one, an executor who combined obedience and independence, submissive humility and great fighting qualities. And he really did make a considerable personal contribution to the debates without which the diplomatic scene was inconceivable, frequently implementing his skills to solve intricate problems. However, this was only understandable for, after the extermination – with his zealous help – of the most prominent and highly-cultured politicians who had enjoyed tremendous authority in the international arena, after the removal from active foreign policy making of diplomats like Litvinov and Maisky, Vyshinsky ended up as the most, or more precisely, the only, educated person in the whole of Stalin's leadership. Even Zhdanov, whose role in international diplomacy was non-existent, hardly had a better education. Stalin really did know the true worth of each of them. But Vyshinsky, let us remember, had been made a professor even before the Revolution.

Who among the survivors in Stalin's circle knew even one foreign language? I am afraid few even knew Russian properly. But Vyshinsky not only spoke Russian but also his father's language, Polish, and very good French which he had learned at a first-class Tsarist gymnasium. What's more, he had quite adequate working knowledge of both English and German. And when it came to the accomplishments that were essential for a statesman of any stature, there was nobody to equal him in Stalin's leadership of the forties. There was no place at all for accomplished people in this leadership – with fatal inevitability the machine of destruction had ejected them all to be slaughtered. All except Vyshinsky. Because Stalin's faith in him – in this totally domesticated, loyal and devoted slave who had always had the threat of death hanging over him and had always been aware of it – was virtually boundless, certainly very great, to put it more cautiously. Without realizing how unique the situation was, we shall not understand Vyshinsky's true place at the apex of the political pyramid.

It certainly was a high place. Higher in actual fact than on paper. Particularly then, in 1945. There could hardly be a more graphic illustration of this than the mission he was given on that historic day of 9 May.

A specially assigned high-speed plane carried him to defeated Berlin as Stalin's special emissary at the formal celebration of Russia's victory.

Although he was Stalin's emissary, from an official point of view he was nobody at all, just Mr Vyshinsky. The Soviet Union was officially represented by Marshal Zhukov, Great Britain by Air Chief Marshal Tedder, the United States by General Spaatz and France by General de Tassigny, the representatives of the Allied armies – the victors. It was to these men that the representatives of the Reich's routed army – Keitel, Friedeburg and Stumpff – had capitulated.

But take a look at the photograph that was printed on the front pages of newspapers all over the world. It shows the historic table at Karlshorst where the instrument of the unconditional surrender was signed. Seated at the table are four commanders – one from each of the Allied armies. And next to Tedder is a fifth person – Vyshinsky. A private individual representing no one.

No one? Everyone knew whom he was representing here. And no mandates or authorities were required of him. His mission was, of course, manifold. He had to scrutinize every single letter and punctuation mark in the instrument of surrender, checking their soundness over and over again, and foreseeing all the consequences, both probable and improbable. And he had to keep an eye on Zhukov – you never could tell. And make sure that everything was perfectly in order.

But not even this was really his foremost task. His foremost task was to represent – tangibly, visibly, in the flesh – the person who had sent him; the Chief Victor, Ruler and Triumpher.

Seated at the victors' table in Karlshorst, in the person of Vyshinsky and under his name, was Stalin.

12

I did not of course know Andrei Vyshinsky in his capacity as a lawyer, but as HM Minister and for long periods British Chargé d'Affaires in Moscow from February 1945 to October 1947 I saw him frequently on official business and on social occasions in his capacity as Deputy Foreign Minister under Vyacheslav Molotov.

So begins the letter I received from the well-known British diplomat Sir Frank Roberts, and with his kind permission I shall cite it in full. It enables us to see one of the foremost figures of Soviet foreign policy in the war and post-war years through the eyes of a Western colleague, reconstruct out of the vivid details the environment Vyshinsky worked in and himself created and, finally, draw attention to certain traits of his character without which an appreciation of this outstanding personality would be inaccurate and incomplete.

'He spoke good French,' continues Sir Frank,

was quick, clever and efficient, and always knew his dossier well, but whereas I had a certain unwilling respect for Molotov, I had none at all for Vyshinsky. All Soviet officials at that time had no choice but to carry out Stalin's policies without asking too many questions, but Vyshinsky above all gave me the impression of a cringing toadie only too anxious to obey His Master's Voice even before it had expressed his wishes. I can hardly blame him in the then conditions for reluctance to take decisions or responsibility, but for this and other reasons I always preferred to do business either with Molotov himself or with his subordinates, Novikov and Yerefeev, in the Second European Department, which dealt with the UK and the British Commonwealth. Their No meant No and their occasional Yes meant Yes. With Vyshinsky arguments were drawn out longer.

I recall in particular a meeting with Vyshinsky to reverse a decision of the Soviet Naval authorities that neither the British Naval Attaché nor I myself could be allowed to go to Sebastopol to meet

252

the Commander-in-Chief of the British Mediterranean Fleet due there in HMS *Liverpool* on an official visit within 48 hours. Vyshinsky wriggled and wriggled to avoid a decision, pleading lack of seats in aircraft and lack of facilities in Sebastopol (which I did not need, as I should be staying on HMS *Liverpool*) but then suddenly gave way when I said I would have no alternative but to telegraph the C-in-C that he should turn back into the Mediterranean. Like all bullies, he knew how and when to climb down.

At diplomatic parties Vyshinsky often set himself out to be agreeable, to an extent which drew from the representative of a small neighbouring country the comment: 'He sucks up to us before swallowing us'.

I always had the feeling with Vyshinsky that his past as a Menshevik together with his Polish and bourgeois background made him particularly servile and obsequious in his dealings with Stalin and to a lesser extent with Molotov. I recall being present at the Bolshoi Theatre for a major gathering with Stalin, the Politburo, and two or three hundred other members of the Soviet 'Establishment' on the stage, during the course of which Stalin, in need of some information, turned to beckon Vyshinsky, seated several rows behind, to his side. Vyshinsky, blushing with mingled pleasure at having been singled out in public and apprehension lest he might not be able to satisfy Stalin, rushed forwards like a schoolboy summoned to the Headmaster's presence, he not knowing whether it was for a prize or a beating.

Another of my meetings with Vyshinsky, which revealed his interest in detail as well as his natural tendency to make difficulties, was for the exchange of letters of ratification of the Peace Treaty which the USSR and the UK had signed with Bulgaria. In those days of post-war austerity, the UK document was in a simple papier-maché folder instead of one in gilded Morocco leather and I, having taken up my post in Moscow in war-time, was wearing my pre-war diplomatic uniform without the additional gold braid appropriate for a Minister. Vyshinsky, with even more gold braid on his uniform and with the Soviet document enshrined in richly gilded red leather, rebuked me for these derogations from peace-time diplomatic tradition, regardless of the far greater degree of austerity then prevalent in Moscow.

One last revealing episode came at a reception at Buckingham Palace during the Four-Power Foreign Ministers' Conference in the autumn of 1947. I had just returned to London as Principal Private

253

Secretary to the Foreign Secretary Ernest Bevin. As one recently returned from Moscow I was put by the side of the then very young Princess Margaret to help her in meeting the Soviet guests. When I asked Her Royal Highness who she would particularly like to meet, expecting the answer, Mr Molotov, she said Mr Vyshinsky. He had no doubt excited her curiosity because of his role in the pre-war Moscow trials. He was surprised and delighted to be singled out in this way, but clever enough to guess why. When I correctly introduced him to HRH as the Deputy Minister for Foreign Affairs, he commented at once in his excellent French 'but please add my former title as Procurator in the famous Moscow trials'.

Perhaps it was partly because I could never forget the way in which he had hounded his victims in those trials and twisted the law and the evidence to ensure their condemnation that I always felt uneasy in my dealings with him, in a way I did not in negotiating with Molotov or even Stalin, who had even more blood on their hands. And even today my first reaction to Vyshinsky is contempt.

I hope the reader will not mind me citing such a long piece, but it is too forceful and telling to abridge. Later on we shall hear – in a more condensed form – the views of other top diplomats on their famous Moscow colleague. These impressions and opinions, at times quite inexplicable, are based on facts and a long, close association.

Forty years ago, when still very young, Klára Mácsay worked at the Hungarian Embassy in Moscow and frequently attended diplomatic receptions with her ambassador. At the beginning of the fifties Moscow's high life was in full swing, and top officials enjoyed appearing at the receptions where the vodka and champagne flowed in streams and black caviar was devoured by the tablespoonful. One evening attractive Klára was courted by old Marshal Semion Budionny, the semi-literate 'Red Cossack' who had gone down in all the Soviet school text-books as a 'hero of the Civil War'. Wishing to impress Klára, he painstakingly tried to learn a Hungarian folk dance known as the *csardas*. But when the orchestra suddenly struck up a waltz, he found himself completely out of his element.

Seizing his chance, Vyshinsky took over: when it came to waltzing, neither then nor at any time later was there anyone in the top echelon of power to match him. Returning his young partner to the elderly marshal, the minister gave him a triumphant look, but the cavalryman, who did not like him, snapped: 'Still the bourgeois you always were.' And quite forgetting he was at a diplomatic function and not in the saddle, he added, 'While you were mincing about in school, we were making the Revolution.'

Vyshinsky said nothing. His face went puce. Bowing to Klára, he quickly left the hall.

Now all Vyshinsky's life was spent in the public eye, and abroad more than at home. He rushed about the world, carrying out special and 'ordinary' missions – ordinary in the sense that they consisted of everyday diplomatic business – congresses, conferences, meetings, sittings, multilateral and bilateral talks. With Vyshinsky's participation, however, any ordinary event turned into an extraordinary one; such was the manner in which almost every word was delivered and the tone in which he spoke, he always made himself the centre of public interest.

On 16 December 1945 the Three-Power foreign ministers' conference opened in Moscow: the US Secretary of State James F. Byrnes and the British Foreign Secretary Ernest Bevin arrived to confer with Molotov. Central to the talks were the preparations for concluding peace treaties with Italy, Rumania, Bulgaria, Hungary and Finland. *Pravda* published enormous photographs of the guests on its front pages – an honour, it seems, that had never been conferred on anyone of their rank before, and a sign of the significance Stalin attached to the talks.

At the conference table Vyshinsky sat on Molotov's right, and sitting next to Byrnes was Charles Bohlen, who, back in 1938, had formed a clear opinion of Vyshinsky which he had no reason to change. The American and British delegations were ready to sign the peace treaties with all the German satellites of World War II, but the internal situation in some of these countries, especially Rumania and Bulgaria, was causing them concern.

One outcome of the stormy debates was to be seen in the following lines of the joint communiqué on Rumania, which speak for themselves: 'The three governments are ready to give King Mihai advice concerning the expansion of the Rumanian government's membership. ... To include one member of the National Tsaranist Party and one member of the Liberal Party in the government ...' Further on it spoke of the need to give the Rumanian people a guarantee of 'free and unimpeded elections ... on the basis of a universal and secret vote'. The reorganized government was to give assurances on the granting of freedom of the press, speech, religion and meetings. 'As soon as these tasks have been carried out and the required assurances received, the government of Rumania ... will be recognized by the governments of the United States and the United Kingdom.'

To carry out these tasks – it was decided at the conference – Vyshinsky, US Ambassador to the USSR Harriman and British Ambassador Kerr were to leave immediately (that is what the joint declaration said – 'immediately') for Bucharest.

After watching a performance of Prokofiev's ballet *Cinderella* at the Bolshoi Theatre and dining with the Soviet leaders, the Western foreign ministers left Moscow, extremely satisfied with the way things had gone. And Vyshinsky, after seeing them off, immediately boarded a train. His carriage, which also accommodated his bodyguards, was fitted out in the most sumptuous European style. Harriman and Kerr travelled in another two – no expense was spared by the 'management'.

The Soviet Ambassador to Rumania, Sergei Ivanovich Kavtaradze, also travelled in the same train. Until only recently he had, like Vyshinsky, been a Deputy People's Commissar for Foreign Affairs and so had plenty to discuss with his 'colleague' while the train slowly crossed the war-ravaged lands of Russia and the Ukraine. Did he recall his years of exile – a punishment for his solidarity with Ryutin? The prison dungeons, interrogation and torture? The hell of the labour camps? Or the early days very long ago when he and Vyshinsky had worked together, when the renowned Trotskyist 'Comrade Sergo' was Deputy Procurator of the Supreme Soviet of the USSR? Or was it not 'the done thing' to revive such memories?

They had lunch together and dinner together in a convivial and informal atmosphere. At evening coffee Harriman suddenly asked Vyshinsky how many votes he reckoned the coalition 'government front' would get if elections in Rumania were totally free. 'Totally free?' repeated Vyshinsky and, spreading his fingers in the air as though he was playing a chord on an invisible piano, said, 'If they were totally free, around forty-five per cent.' He stretched his fingers even wider as if to play an octave. 'But with a certain amount of pressure – all of ninety.'

In the late evening of 31 December they arrived in Bucharest. Only a short time was left until midnight and so they hurriedly arranged a party and saw in the New Year all together. Without any protocol it ended up being a much friendlier occasion. Vyshinsky joked a great deal – when he wanted to, he could turn on the charm and be most entertaining and congenial.

On New Year's Day all three were received by the King. This time Vyshinsky had no need to shout at anyone. His instructions were to

256

smooth things over, not aggravate them. Friction arose over certain nominations but the disagreements were quickly removed. If only it were always like this.

Meanwhile a Bulgarian delegation had arrived in Moscow consisting of Prime Minister Kimon Georgiev, Foreign Minister Petro Stoinov and Interior Minister Anton Yugov. Their visit was in response to part of the three foreign ministers' agreement on Bulgaria:

> The Soviet government undertakes the mission of giving friendly advice to the Bulgarian government on the desirability of including two additional representatives of other democratic groups in the Bulgarian government of the Patriotic Front presently being formed. As soon as the United States and United Kingdom are convinced that this advice has been taken, they will recognize the government of Bulgaria.

On the second day of their visit the Bulgarians dined with Stalin at the Kremlin. The Leader's spirits rose not so much because he was drinking his favourite Georgian wine as because things were going exceptionally well. He had only just been informed that everything had been sorted out in Rumania and Vyshinsky was flying back to Moscow. Stalin demanded to be put through to Bucharest: 'Comrade Vyshinsky, do you have any really urgent matters to attend to in the Soviet capital?' One can imagine Vyshinsky's dismayed face as he tried to fathom his unpredictable Leader's complex sense of humour. 'If not, then perhaps you will agree to carry out a little request for Comrade Stalin?' Vyshinsky started mumbling about being ready at all times and in all places, but Stalin cut him short, 'Our Bulgarian friends will be pleased to meet you in Sofia ... To help sort out certain issues ... In a favourable spirit.'

Harriman and Kerr were setting off for Moscow. 'Dear Mr Vyshinsky,' wrote Harriman before boarding his train:

> Now that the commission's work is complete, I want to thank you for your cooperation in carrying out the commission's tasks. It is my belief that the Rumanian Government in the form it has now been restructured will carry through the resolutions of the Moscow Conference.

He believed so but, as is well known, you do not always need facts or proof to believe.

Vyshinsky did not believe in anything; he carried out instructions. On the evening of 9 January Acting Prime Minister Dobri Terpeshev,

Georgi Dimitrov (still only a 'private individual' with no official post but a hero's reputation after the Leipzig trial), Vasil Kolarov and other Bulgarian officials met Vyshinsky at Sofia Railway Station.

Here, in Bulgaria, just like everywhere else, his name was swathed in legend. And now here he was, informal and approachable – in person, in the flesh – to disentangle all the knots and solve all the problems. Not a man but a Messiah. And, sure enough, what had taken nine days in Bucharest took a day and a half here. On the afternoon of 11 January a cabinet was formed which met with universal approval, and in the evening Kimon Georgiev, having urgently flown back from Moscow, held a sumptuous banquet in Vyshinsky's honour in the military club, and from there they all went straight to the railway station in a merry cavalcade. Andrei Yanuarievich was in a hurry to get to London, with a brief stopover in defeated Germany on the way, in the city of Nuremberg.

He felt particularly at ease when his two professions – law and diplomacy – crossed and linked together. Life presented him with just such an opportunity when the Great Powers decided to try the chief war criminals and set up the International Military Tribunal in Nuremberg. Vyshinsky visited Nuremberg several times after the Tribunal started work in the autumn of 1945. Why did he go? After all, he apparently had nothing to do with the work of the Tribunal: neither the judges nor the prosecutors at this tribunal were subordinate to any government – it was an independent body – and a deputy minister of one of the countries which had set up the Tribunal could not, of course, inspect or instruct anyone here. Officially.

But in actual fact Vyshinsky could do everything – he was Vyshinsky, after all. Just as at Karlshorst, where he had been carrying out goodness alone knows what function and yet had been unquestioningly accepted by everyone present, here, too, in Nuremberg, officially he was nobody but in fact he was everybody rolled into one – even for the foreigners, not to mention the Soviet lawyers. There were some very close associates of his working at Nuremberg: among the judges there was Iona Nikitchenko, who had taken part in the 'Great Moscow Trials', and among the prosecutors, investigators, experts and so on there were Mark Roginsky, Solomon Rozenblit, and Lev Sheinin.

In the greatest of secrecy, totally unbeknown to foreigners and, for that matter, his compatriots too, Stalin had appointed Vyshinsky to another post of particular state importance. Directly after the end of the war a body had been set up which in different documents was referred to variously as 'the government commission on the Nuremberg Trial', 'the government commission on the organization of the Trial at Nuremberg', 'the commission on the direction of the Nuremberg Trial'. Stalin put Vyshinsky in charge of this top secret commission with specially designated functions. The commission consisted of the Procurator-General of the USSR Gorshenin; the President of the Supreme Soviet of the USSR Golyakov: the People's Commissar for Justice of the USSR Rychkov; and three of Beria's closest associates, his deputies Abakumov, Kobulov and Merkulov. The commission's main aim was to prevent at all costs public discussion of any aspects of Nazi-Soviet relations in 1939–41, and, first and foremost, of the actual existence, let alone contents, of the so-called secret protocols to the non-aggression pact of 23 August 1939 and to the friendship treaty of 28 September 1939. To ensure the secret commission's instructions were effective during the investigation, a specially appointed team of investigators led by Colonel Likhachev, one of Beria's most brutal henchmen, was sent to Nuremberg.

On 26 November 1945 on Vyshinsky's suggestion the commission passed a resolution 'to approve . . . a list of issues which are inadmissible for discussion at the Trial'. Upon his arrival in Nuremberg Vyshinsky was to use all his exceptional skills to drill his resolution into the minds of the members of the Tribunal from other countries. However, all his worries proved unfounded; the foreign members were quite kindly disposed towards their Allies and certainly had no desire to strain relations. One of the counsels for the defence, Doctor Alfred Seidl, had dug up some documentary evidence proving that such protocols did in fact exist, and wanted to use them in court (although in no circumstances could they have served as a justification for the Nazi crimes) but the British, American and French prosecutors, not knowing, of course, about either 'Vyshinsky's commission' or its resolution, spoke out against 'any attempts to draw the court into political arguments'. Vyshinsky had won yet another victory, for, you see, in Stalin's eyes, it was only he who had succeeded in influencing his foreign colleagues.

However, one still had to keep an eye on them – who knew what these unruly people might get up to? By mutual agreement the texts of the prosecutors' speeches were checked over beforehand by their foreign colleagues. And so it was that Vyshinsky's censors discovered something 'wrong' in the speech which the chief British prosecutor Shawcross was going to make. Following Vyshinsky's instructions, on 3 December 1945, the official Soviet delegation immediately demanded that the parts which were 'objectionable' to them be removed from his speech. They were. The Soviet prosecutors received the following instructions from Vyshinsky: 'The prosecutor must, whenever necessary, interrupt the accused, and not allow him to make anti-Soviet attacks.'

Those taking part in the trial from the three other Allied powers were to remember their rare but impressive meetings with Vyshinsky at Nuremberg. This is what the lawyer and diplomat Lord Shawcross, twice a colleague of Vyshinsky's, told me in London in 1988. After Nuremberg he became the Attorney General and then the United Kingdom's permanent delegate to the United Nations, where he 'crossed swords' with Vyshinsky on more than one occasion. Lord Shawcross has kindly allowed me to use the recording of his story in print.

I met Vyshinsky in Nuremberg on many occasions, and later in New York. After our first meeting he had already impressed me as being an intelligent, resourceful, well-read man equipped with an erudition which enabled him to feel completely at home both in a public debate and a private conversation. At any rate, in all respects he was a cut above the other Soviet lawyers I happened to meet – compared to him they all seemed very insipid. His other advantage over them was that he – you could tell this at once – was authorized to take decisions himself whereas the others (both the lawyers and the diplomats) had to receive instructions from Moscow on any issue and made no secret of this either.

We – I mean the British, French and Americans – simply could not figure out why he kept coming to Nuremberg. In the end, not understanding much about the special features of the Soviet state structure, we decided that he was still the Procurator-General and this most likely explained why he was giving instructions during the trial to the prosecutors representing the Soviet side. Strictly speaking, there was nothing for him to do here in this capacity, instructions from Moscow could have been delivered another way, but, strangely enough, his visits somehow did not surprise us.

But once – this I remember clearly – we were completely taken aback. This is what I was told by the British members of the tribunal. The judges of the four countries arranged to dine together one evening, and all of a sudden Vyshinsky walked in, moved up a chair and, totally uninvited, sat down at the table. In so far as he was considered a prosecutor and, I repeat, only in this capacity could his presence at Nuremberg be somehow justified, Vyshinsky's appearance at the judges' table was improper. The judges could not dine with the prosecutors and barristers – they did not have a right to, this was a violation of legal ethics. But, of course, nobody could bring himself to ask Vyshinsky to leave.

Everyone at the table suddenly became rather glum, and, sensing this, Vyshinsky tried to liven things up by raising a toast: 'I propose we drink to the health of the defendants who are about to be hanged.' This was not just dreadfully black humour, it went completely against the ethics of civilized people, no matter how great the defendants' guilt. It was also quite unacceptable as far as a British lawyer's sense of justice was concerned. You see, the sentence had not been passed yet, and the presumption of innocence was in effect at the international tribunal just as at any ordinary national trial. However, for Vyshinsky with his experience of conducting the Moscow trials, our tribunal was nothing more than a show whose outcome had been decided beforehand, and so there was nothing to make a fuss about. And no reason either to restrain one's black humour.

Generally speaking, everyone was wary of him. Both here at Nuremberg and later on at the United Nations. They knew he was Stalin's foremost proxy, and this perhaps said it all. In my observations of him I noticed that in conversation he was usually calm, patient, self-confident – at least in his dealings with foreigners. But as soon as he mounted the rostrum, for some reason or other he became a thug and a boor. It was as though some invisible tight spring had been released.

Like anyone who has renounced his own ideas and done a hundred and eighty degree about-turn, he was more orthodox than the Pope but did not give the impression of someone with ideas of his own. He seemed to fear for his life and for this reason thought a great deal more about what they would say about him in Moscow than in London and New York. In a quite astonishing manner his self-confidence was blended with fear and an expectation of trouble. Reprisals, to be more precise . . .

This expectation was quite well founded: the executioners were going the same way as their victims, so why should he be the only one to escape this fate? A wave of arrests, which had abated during the war, once again loomed on the horizon. The arrests had of course continued in the war, and the safes were packed full of new dossiers, but there had been no 'waves' of arrests – they simply had not got round to them.

The first to suffer were the heroes of the recent battles: Stalin decided to find scapegoats for the unprecedented disasters during the first months and years of the war, and mindful of his contemporaries and future generations, deflect the reproach, albeit silent but still foremost in people's memories. The other reason was to stop anyone from stealing the limelight from the Great Commander or pulling a single leaf from his laurels.

Why were some selected to go to prison and others to become heroes and marshals? It is unlikely we shall ever find this out. It is also unlikely there was any logic to it. As the renowned pilot General Mikhail Mikhailovich Gromov once said to me: 'You were summoned to the Leader and, when you went, you did not know whether you were going to get a cross on your chest or a cross in the ground.' He was lucky and always came out with 'crosses' on his chest; others were not.

Among the very many now imprisoned were Air Chief Marshal Alexander Novikov who, during the war, was the Commander-in-Chief of all the armed forces; Artillery Marshal Nikolai Yakovlev (Deputy Military Minister); Air Marshal Vorozheikin (First Deputy of the Commander of the Armed Forces); Air Marshal Sergei Khudyakov (during the war he was Commander-in-Chief of the Air Force); Admiral Lev Galler (the ex-head of the Chief Naval Staff) and General Vladimir Kryukov (the commander of a mechanized corps in the war). Some of them were to be executed.

Preparations were simultaneously underway for a case on a spectacular scale which was to go down in history as the 'Leningrad Case'. Intent on becoming Stalin's heir and afraid of rivals, Malenkov also keenly sensed who was drawing close to Stalin. In collusion with Beria – this twosome worked hand-in-hand for many years – he succeeded in playing on Stalin's pathological suspicion and in creating the conditions for it to produce the desired effect.

Shortly after the war Stalin suffered a minor stroke from which he only managed to recover with the help of those of his skilled doctors not yet denounced as 'assassins'. He spent the entire autumn of 1945 slowly recuperating near Sochi on the Black Sea. It was then that a rumour was spread around the small Kremlin circle that Stalin had apparently said that his 'deputy in the Party' was not Malenkov but Andrei Zhdanov. And as his 'deputy in state affairs' he had apparently nominated Nikolai Voznesensky – one of his most loyal men, who had created the key administrative economic system and supported a totally centralized economy. It is not clear whether Malenkov and Beria concocted and spread this rumour themselves or whether it originated elsewhere and somehow reached Stalin's ears, but either way the consequences were three years in coming.

In August 1948, under circumstances still to be fully unravelled, the ringleader of the punitive actions against all the Soviet arts and sciences, Andrei Zhdanov, died while holidaying in the Valdai Hills. On Poskrebyshev's orders, his mortal remains were accompanied to Moscow by Voznesensky and Andrei Kuznetsov, the First Secretary of the Leningrad Regional Committee, one of the organizers of Leningrad's defence during the German blockade of the city, and already by this time a Central Committee secretary. Soon their turn was also to come.

On Beria's instructions, his deputy, Abakumov, who headed the 'team of investigators' (the infamous Shvartsman and Rodos played first fiddles in this orchestra), invented a marvellous piece of fiction in the form of yet another 'Leningrad Opposition' who had sold themselves to foreign intelligence services and were set on opposing the Central Committee. Their most heinous crime was their intention to establish a Communist Party of Russia on the same footing as those of all the union republics, and transfer the capital of the RSFSR to Leningrad, leaving Moscow its status as capital of the USSR. Possibly, such ideas really had occurred to someone at some time or other, but Beria's department depicted them in the usual counter-revolutionary hues, and prepared a suitable report for Stalin.

The arrests began in July 1949. First to be arrested was Yakov Fedorovich Kapustin, First Secretary of the Leningrad City Committee. Abakumov informed Stalin that he was a British agent, and two days later Stalin sanctioned his arrest. Then the heads started rolling. Nikolai Vasilievich Soloviev, First Secretary of the Crimean Regional Committee, was summoned to Moscow from Simferopol by Malenkov and seized. A short while before he had been the Chairman of the Leningrad Regional Executive Committee (during the war in charge of all the blockaded city's supplies). Then the same trick was played on Kuznetsov, who had already been relieved of his Party posts, only this time it was Shkiryatov[1] who summoned him. A similar fate befell the Vice-Chairman of the Council of Ministers and the Chairman of the State Planning Commission, Politburo member Academician Nikolai Alexeyevich Voznesensky, the Chairman of the Council of Ministers of the RSFSR Mikhail Ivanovich Rodionov, and the Chairman of the Leningrad Executive Committee Piotr Grigorievich Lazutin. After brutal torture and an 'open' trial in the Leningrad House of Officers they were all shot.[2] The trial was not mentioned in the press and was attended only by Ministry of State Security officials and specially selected Party workers who had written pledges to keep it secret. The other accused and a great many other people under arrest – including the main 'conspirators" close, distant, and very distant relatives – were given long prison, labour camp and deportation sentences. Among those executed was Nikolai Voznesensky's brother, Professor Alexander Alexeyevich Voznesensky, Rector of Leningrad University and Minister of Education of the RSFSR, and his sister, Maria Alexeyevna Voznesenskaya, First Secretary of the Kuibyshev District Committee.

The country knew nothing about the secret happenings in Beria's dungeons or the 'open' trial; only very observant people noticed that the names of eminent Party officials and statesmen previously in the press every day had suddenly disappeared. The country did not know, but the likes of Vyshinsky knew all about it. Reports containing the horrendous demaskings and self-confessions were sent out to all the highest-ranking officials. In the whole leadership there were few who knew the technique of these 'confessions' as thoroughly as Vyshinsky. He must have understood that a 'second 1937' had begun, that this wave might sweep over anyone and that there was no guaranteed way of escaping it. One simply had to put one's trust in destiny.

At the end of 1948, just after Vyshinsky's return from Paris, where he had been attending the Third Session of the UN General Assembly, Beria, meeting him in the Kremlin, came up and shook hands in a very meaningful manner. Glancing theatrically round in all directions, the lenses of his pince-nez glinting, he whispered: 'Splendid snake you've been looking after in your foreign ministry, Comrade Vyshinsky!'

One can imagine the range of feelings Comrade Vyshinsky must have experienced at that moment. Beria did not need to imagine anything; he understood everything as it was. And, more importantly, he could see everything for himself. After gloating over his companion's confusion, he started explaining to him that he had meant the 'exposed spy, arrant Zionist, Lozovsky and his gang'.

Quickly recovering his composure, Vyshinsky parried: 'We dismissed him from the ministry nearly three years ago.' Beria retorted: 'Let us suppose it was not you who dismissed him but the Party ...' 'That's quite correct, Comrade Beria!'

Comrade Beria, who knew without Vyshinsky telling him that everything he had said was quite correct, considered it necessary to add, 'But the diplomats have been thoughtless, to put it mildly'. 'To put it very mildly ...' echoed Vyshinsky. 'Very mildly ...' repeated Beria, raising a finger. 'Now that's what I call correct!' And off he went, pleased with himself.

It really was over two years since Solomon Abramovich Lozovsky[3] had left the Foreign Ministry after working there from 1939 to 1946, like Vyshinsky, as a Deputy People's Commissar. A Bolshevik since the beginning of the century, for many years he had headed the Trade Union International (Profintern – a precursor of today's World Federation of Democratic Trade Unions). In 1937 he had fallen from grace and been demoted to the post of director of the State Literary Publishing House, and in 1939, after the diplomatic service had been totally purged, he was called to the colours by Molotov. In 1941 he received the additional post of head of the Soviet Information Bureau, and it was in this capacity that he became a national celebrity: the whole country waited for the Soviet Information Bureau's daily news bulletins on the position at the front. As part of his official duties he also sat on various anti-Fascist committees that had been set up at the beginning of the war, including the European Anti-Fascist Committee, which was run by the producer and artist Solomon Mikhoels.

Lozovsky was one of the first victims of the anti-Semitic campaign launched on Stalin's instructions: in 1946 he was dismissed from his post at the Foreign Ministry without any explanation. He was still, however, a Central Committee member and deputy of the Supreme Soviet of the USSR, and continued his work as an ambassador and consultant, and his academic studies (he was a doctor of historical sciences). So absorbed had Vyshinsky been by his constant top-level affairs that he had managed to forget all about his recent colleague. Beria's derisive whisper jolted his memory.

He understood perfectly well what Beria's 'information' meant, and its implications: Lozovsky had already been arrested. One can easily imagine Vyshinsky's surprise when a few days into the New Year the following note was put on his table on the headed paper of a deputy of the Supreme Soviet of the USSR:

Dear Andrei Yanuarovich [sic]
    I am writing to you about the following: I have been left high and

dry as far as transport goes – I shall not be getting a car from the Central Committee any more.

Could the Foreign Ministry assist me in this matter for my service of over seven years, if only during 1949 or until I have been appointed to another post?

If this is at all possible, I shall be very grateful.

With comradely greetings,
A. Lozovsky
January 1949

We shall not try guessing what went through his head as he read this note and remembered Beria's ominous whisper. The instructions he issued were: 'Comrade Molotov must be consulted'. And he kept the note – as a relic. It lay in his writing desk until his death. In a separate envelope. Why? What for? History? His memoirs? As an excuse if Beria was to start 'cooking up' something. Who knows. . . .

There turned out to be no need to consult Comrade Molotov. Lozovsky was quicky provided with other transport – and other work: he was arrested on 26 January.

As for the note. What was it? Complete naïvety on the part of a man who, one would suppose, had been seasoned by his experience of life (Lozovsky had just turned seventy) or simply the inability of a normally functioning intellect to believe in the cataclysms that had already started? But surely Mikhoels's murder was a signal that they had? After 1937 it seemed possible to believe in anything. But things were to turn out differently.

The creation of the state of Israel, the active contacts which various people in the Soviet arts quickly established with the new state's diplomatic mission and, first and foremost, with Israel's first ambassador to Moscow, Golda Meir – the future Prime Minister – furnished the ever-vigilant Ministry of State Security operatives with the wherewithal for new espionage plots. The establishment of these new contacts coincided – or, to be more precise, was most closely connected – with Stalin's far-reaching plans to find yet another batch of scapegoats by manipulating 'popular wrath' in a way that had been used numerous times before for the same purpose.

A whole team of expert investigators from the Ministry of State Security was alerted to create a vast trial. The trial actually took place, and it was certainly a vast but far from noisy affair, held behind very firmly closed doors. Gone were the days of the show trials which had been staged with such unsurpassed mastery by Vyshinsky. The

Leader's pathological fear now found solace in secret trials. As for the people, there were other ways of consoling them: once the main control panel was running smoothly, a campaign started, gathered momentum, and then worked at full tilt to fight against the 'rootless cosmopolitans', signalling an epidemic of anti-Semitism on a state scale.

This is all well known. But we know nothing about exactly how this closed trial was organized or how it proceeded. Its doors really were firmly closed. The information mainly gleaned from the very aged Academician Lina Shtern[4], the only one of the fourteen accused to mysteriously escape execution, is scant and, in many instances, unreliable. And, of course, how could she know what was going on behind the scenes?

It is hardly possible or, indeed, necessary to go through all forty-eight volumes of the evidence and the trial itself. I shall, however, cite extensively from one sufficiently telling document. But, first, some brief background information on the accused. In the spring of 1952 fifteen people were brought to trial, one of whom died before it began. The remaining fourteen, in addition to Solomon Lozovsky, who was at the top of the list, and Lina Shtern, included the Soviet Union's most eminent Yiddish writers Perets Markish, Itsik Fefer, David Bergelson, Lev Kvitko, David Gofshtein, the great actor and People's Artist of the RSFSR Veniamin Zuskin, the ex-head doctor of the Botkin Hospital Boris Shimeliovich and a group of editors and translators working on the European Anti-Fascist Committee, which had been founded during the war to fight against Hitler and Nazism. They were all charged with being US spies during the war, anti-Soviet agitation and propaganda, the creation of a counter-revolutionary organization and being involved in its work.

The inquiry into the evidence of this sinister case, which ended with the shamefully secret rehabilitation of all the accused, began in 1954 and was completed in 1955. At the same time, all the people were exposed who had been actively involved in its fabrication in various ways and to varying degrees. It was then that Marshal G. K. Zhukov, a Presidium member of the Central Committee and the Minister of Defence, instructed Lieutenant General of the Justice Cheptsov, under whose chairmanship the Military Board of the Supreme Soviet had passed sentence on completely innocent people, to explain how it had all come about.

The text of this explanation of 15 August 1955 covers eleven closely-typed pages. Here are the most important parts of it:

At the end of March 1952 or beginning of April, I was summoned by ex-Minister of the Ministry of State Security of the USSR Comrade S.D. Ignatiev, and in the presence of his former deputy, Ryumin (convicted in 1954 of falsifying criminal cases), he informed me that he and Ryumin were reporting on the case of Lozovsky and his co-defendants to the Politburo of the Central Committee of the Communist Party [CPSU] who had been ... ordered to condemn [all] the accused ... to be shot, and the accused Lina Shtern to three years of exile in outlying regions of the USSR.

It is now well known that, from 1935 onwards, it became common practice for the heads of the NKVD and later Ministry of State Security, to report on the most important political crimes to Stalin or the Politburo, where the defendants' guilt and punishments were decided upon. What's more, prior to a decision being reached by the most senior bodies, the members of the judiciary who were to examine such cases were neither allowed to familiarize themselves with the materials of the case nor invited to the Central Committee for discussions.

This being so, the Military Board frequently passed sentences which did not comply with the materials procured in court. Either fear or trust in the infallible nature of Stalin's decisions prevented the judges from reporting to the Central Committee on their doubts regarding cases, although in a number of instances they could see that the cases were not being interpreted objectively by the most senior bodies....

When interrogated, all the accused, including Lozovsky, pleaded guilty to nationalistic activity and spying for the USA and admitted that the EAC [European Anti-Fascist Committee] was really an underground centre of nationalistic activity and espionage. By the end of the preliminary investigation four of the accused – Bregman [an ex-Deputy Minister of State Control of the RSFSR], Shimeliovich, Shtern and Markish – had denied their evidence and pleaded innocent....

Apart from Abakumov and Ryumin [deputies of the Minister of State Security], who completed the examination of the case and reported on it to the Central Committee, thirty-four investigators were involved (some of whom have since been convicted). The investigation was supervised by several military prosecutors who took part in the interrogations of the accused.

Before the trial we, the judges, Ryumin and the prosecutors were informed that for a long period of time (about six months) all the accused had been in the prison run by the ex-Chairman of the Communist Party Commission Shkiryatov. He also verified the charge brought against the prisoners by personally interrogating them (the file contains transcripts of the interrogations of Lozovsky and others). One should note that at the interrogations Lozovsky gave clear evidence of his and the others' anti-Soviet activity....

During the very first days of the trial doubts immediately arose among the judges about the completeness and objectivity of the case's investigation. Before the examination in court began, a number of the accused petitioned for certain documents, disproving their charge, to be introduced, which had been refused them during the investigation.

To the court's first question regarding whether they pleaded guilty, five of the fourteen accused began by denying their guilt, citing the fact that their evidence during the investigation had been incorrect and forcibly given under physical coercion by the investigators....

Over many days accused Fefer persistently exposed all the accused of anti-Soviet activity, including Lozovsky as the organizer and leader of this criminal organization. However, influenced by the cross-examination [the usual term for the examination in court by the prosecution and defence in turn, though neither a prosecutor nor counsels for the defence took part in this trial] ... Fefer began giving muddled, untrustworthy evidence....

I decided to hold separate private interrogations ... outside the walls of the Ministry of State Security of the USSR, in one of the Military Board's rooms [the case was being heard in the Ministry of State Security club-room]. This also had to be done because Ryumin was interested in the outcome of the case and was interfering with its objective examination. Judging by the behaviour of the individual accused, one could presuppose that the investigators were putting pressure on them during the recesses. Ryumin had the judges' conversations tapped in their conference room; to a number of our perplexed questions to him about the investigation, he and his assistants clearly told us untruths.

At a separate private interrogation, a month after the beginning of the trial, Fefer announced to the court that since 1944 he had been a secret operative of the Ministry of State Security of the USSR. [Fefer made this announcement when the other accused were not present, after stating that as an 'agent working under the code name of "Zorin", he had acted on the instructions of operatives of these organs'. A statement issued by the Military Board on 22 November 1955 reads as follows: 'After verification it has been established that Fefer did collaborate with the organs of the Ministry of State Security.'] After being arrested and threatened with a beating he signed all the interrogation reports prepared by the investigators, and ... before the trial was warned by an investigator that it was essential for him to confirm his evidence in court....

As for my requests to Ryumin and his assistant Grishayev to present us with evidence ... Ryumin and Grishayev[5] avoided doing so ... Clearly, it was impossible to pass sentence in this case with such unverified and dubious evidence.

During the long judicial inquiry I often visited the ex-Minister of the Ministry of State Security of the USSR Ignatiev in the recesses and informed him of what was going on at the trial....

I told him that facts were being falsified by Ryumin and his investigators and that Ryumin was deceiving him. Ryumin was infuriated by these actions of mine. Only after Comrade Stalin's death did I learn from the explanations Comrade Ignatiev gave to the Central Committee of the CPSU on the Doctors' Case that Ryumin had enjoyed the total trust of Comrade Stalin, who did not trust Comrade Ignatiev at that time....

After suspending the trial at the beginning of July 1952, I appealed to ex-Procurator-General Comrade Safonov to go with me to the Central Committee of the CPSU and report on the need to submit the case for a further inquiry. However he refused to do so, saying, 'You've been given an instruction by the Central Committee's Politburo, carry it out!' Nor was I supported by the ex-Chairman of the Supreme Court of the USSR Comrade Volin. I then telephoned the ex-Chairman of the Party Control Committee at the Central Committee of the CPSU Shkiryatov, who had himself conducted the investigation of the case of Lozovsky and the others, but hearing that I wanted to raise the question of submitting the case for a further inquiry, he told me that he was convinced of the guilt of the accused and refused to see me. I then, like many others, believed him to be the conscience of our Party. And I could not presuppose that he was a double-dealer.

I then informed Comrade N.M. Shvernik, the then Chairman of the Presidium of the Supreme Council of the USSR, and was advised by him to refer this matter to Central Committee Secretary Malenkov. I telephoned him, and asked him to receive me and hear me out ... A few days later I was summoned to Malenkov, who had also summoned Ryumin and Comrade Ignatiev.

I presumed that Malenkov would support me and agree with my conclusions ... However, after hearing my report, he let Ryumin speak, and the latter started accusing me of liberalism towards enemies of the people, and of deliberately dragging the judicial inquiry on for over two months, thereby encouraging the accused to deny the evidence they had given during the investigation, and he also accused me of slandering the organs of the Ministry of State Security of the USSR, and denied using physical coercion. I again declared that Ryumin was committing an unlawful act; however, Malenkov literally declared as follows: 'You want to bring us to our knees before these criminals; the sentence, you know, has been approved by the people; the Politburo of the Central Committee has gone into this case three times, carry out the Politburo's ruling'.

Supposing that before receiving me he had reported on this matter to Comrade Stalin, of which I have several confirmations, I then told Malenkov that I would convey his instructions to the judges, that we had done our duty by informing the Central Committee of our doubts. However, as Party members we would carry out the Politburo's directive with the conviction that the Politburo of the Central Committee had special considerations where this case was concerned.

After the talk with Malenkov Ryumin caught me up in the Central Committee building. He swore hard at me and threatened me with reprisals. As the inquiry into Ryumin's case has established, in August-September 1952, he began collecting evidence against me.

After carrying out Malenkov's directive and sentencing Lozovsky and the others to the punishments we had been instructed to, I, notwithstanding Ryumin's insistence on an immediate execution of the sentence, granted all the convicted prisoners the right of appeal so that apart from these appeals, in which all the accused categorically denied their guilt, being discussed in the Presidium of the Supreme Soviet of the USSR, this matter would once again be on the agenda of the Politburo, as was the procedure at that time: decisions ... regarding the pardon of prisoners who had been given the death penalty were confirmed by the Politburo. Furthermore, after the passing of sentence I sent Comrade Stalin Lozovsky's statement, in which he totally denied his guilt. However, no directives were forthcoming and the sentenced prisoners were executed.

I consider that I took all the measures in my power to ensure this case's lawful outcome, but at that moment I was supported by absolutely nobody, and we judges, as Party members, were forced to submit to the categorical directive of Central Committee secretary Malenkov.

Member of the CPSU since 1927,
Party Membership No 04521575
A. Cheptsov

By exposing the usual method of preparing such cases, the depressing details of this document, related by its author in such a restrained, ingenuous and clear manner, exceed the bounds of an 'individual case'. And yet, even more significant, it seems to me, is the fact revealed here that – despite the assertions of fatalists and sceptics – even in those dreadful conditions it was possible to oppose the hellish machine of destruction. Or, more precisely, a need was felt to oppose it, it could be opposed, and it actually was opposed. By no means always with the desired effect, but it still was opposed.

The examination carried out by the Chief Military Procurator's office in the mid-fifties corroborated Lieutenant General Cheptsov's explanation to Marshal Zhukov. Among the charges brought against Ryumin was the falsification of the EAC Case. He was also charged with trying to provoke a case against Judge Cheptsov, who had dared 'doubt the work of the organs of the Ministry of State Security'. Let us note in passing that Cheptsov's suicidal action, which would have ended tragically for him if it had not been for the tyrant's death, was not the only one on his service record. As I mentioned earlier, before he became its chairman, as a rank-and-file member of the Military Board of the Supreme Soviet of the USSR, he was among the judiciary who acquitted Beria's personal enemy, Mikhail Kedrov, in the summer of 1941. The result, however, was still the same: even though he had been acquitted, Kedrov was still shot on Beria's orders.

We should not, of course, make heroes of Cheptsov and the two other members of the Board, General Dmitriev and General Zaryanov, on whose behalf he appealed to Malenkov; they also passed many unlawful sentences, including the death sentence on hundreds of totally innocent people. Once in a while, however, their consciences and professional honour enjoined them to rebel and try to deflect the axe's blow, and dissociate themselves from complicity in evident crimes. To my mind, for those who had not completely lost their humanity and were still able to feel shame, even a single attempt at defending justice, especially if it was successful, would give them enough moral satisfaction to, if not to atone for, then at least to assuage their feeling of guilt for yielding at other times to violence, Pharisaism and falsehood.

From 1948 the arrests in connection with the EAC Case continued relentlessly. An avalanche of repressions enveloped hundreds of people – their close and distant relatives, colleagues and acquaintances and complete strangers. Some of those arrested in connection with the EAC case had only known about its existence from the newspapers.

Rumours about the destruction of Jewish culture and the arrest of its foremost representatives spread to the West. They were contradictory and full of implausible conjectures. The top politicians and public figures of various countries were continually asking Vyshinsky and other Soviet diplomats and infrequent official Soviet visitors abroad for information on the celebrities who had suddenly disappeared from view, for their names really were widely known. Vyshinsky was approached, in particular, by Einstein, who was deeply concerned about the fate of Nikolai Vavilov, Mikhoels's mysterious death, and the whereabouts of the Jewish novelists and poets who had suddenly vanished. His answer was always the same: the rumours were lies and the usual slander of bourgeois propaganda; all the people who were the object of concern in the West were alive and healthy and working well. As for Mikhoels's death – this had been incontrovertibly proved an accident; after all, it was his, Vyshinsky's, closest associate, Lev Sheinin, a brilliant lawyer and man of integrity, who had taken part in the inquiry; surely this was a guarantee that the inquiry's conclusions were correct? In Iron Curtain conditions these 'denials' could be accepted as the truth for a while.

During his visit to Moscow in the summer of 1950 the well-known American singer and public figure Paul Robeson asked Fadeyev[6] to arrange a meeting for him with Itsik Fefer. The two of them had met and become friends when Fefer and Mikhoels had visited America during the war. What a stroke of bad luck Robeson wanted to see Fefer and nobody else.

A few days later Fadeyev invited Robeson to dine with him in the restaurant of the Hotel Metropole, where Robeson was staying. There were just the two of them but the table was laid for four. Soon Fefer arrived accompanied by a complete stranger who did not utter a word all evening. Later Robeson was to remark that Fefer looked pale and drawn but otherwise in excellent spirits. The evening was spent in lively and unconstrained conversation. Fefer asked for his greetings to be sent to his numerous foreign friends. Close on midnight they said goodbye, and Robeson went up to his rooms while Fefer went a few hundred yards further up the road to his prison cell at the Lubyanka.

No news of the investigation's proceedings reached relatives – the secrecy in those days was remarkable – while those still at liberty tried every channel they could. Vyshinsky received many appeals for help. Of course, the authors of these letters knew he no longer had anything to do with the Ministry of State Security, the Procurator's office or the trial — officially, that is. They also knew, however, that in actual fact he remained in constant close contact with all three, and that he was Vyshinsky, and that this was not just a name but an official post, all of its own.

To give their appeals legal foundation they used to write to Vyshinsky as a deputy of the Supreme Soviet of the USSR. Incidentally, in those days people used to send hundreds and thousands of appeals for help of all kinds to well-known public figures instead of to their 'own' deputies. A simple and infallible method of sparing oneself hazardous work was to remind the petitioner that he was not *his* elector as he did not live in his electoral district. Many resorted to this method of self-defence, including Ehrenburg, for many years a deputy for Lithuania, to whom unfortunate people from all over the country used to turn for help. I have seen quite a few of his replies in such a vein.

Vyshinsky apparently did not resort to this method. Instead, he sent the petitions, which had been addressed to him as a deputy, on to the heads of the appropriate competent bodies. What's more, he nearly always enclosed his own cover note. He also used to request to be informed of the inquiry's outcome and the measures adopted. The formalities were observed. Nobody could accuse him of callousness, lack of consideration or formalism.

However, if an intercessor really wanted to intercede, he would let the addressee know in advance by telephone or in a short handwritten note accompanying his official letter. This then meant that he really wanted to offer assistance or at least draw attention to the matter. And then the reaction might be different. Even so, there was no guarantee of success.

To the Procurator-General of the USSR
Comrade G.N. Safonov

Dear Georgi Nikolayevich,

Anna Solomonovna Romendik, the sister of Lina Solomonovna

Shtern (a member of the USSR Academy of Sciences), who is presently under investigation, has lodged an appeal to the Deputy of the Volsk Electoral District, Comrade A. Ya. Vyshinsky. Her letter is attached. It is requested that a verification be made in keeping with the provisions of the law with regard to the lawfulness of the investigation being conducted and that Comrade A. Ya. Vyshinsky be informed of the decision that is reached.

V. Gorokhov
Head of Secretariat
of Deputy of the Volsk Electoral
District Comrade A. Ya. Vyshinsky

Unfortunately, I do not know what decision was reached by the then Procurator-General or what he informed the ex-Procurator-General. We do, however, know it all resulted in a trial and a sentence. Obviously, no telephone call was made before the letter was dispatched. Even if one had been made, however, everything here was decided on an entirely different level, in other offices – without the assistance of procurators, past or present.

Vyshinsky was continually bombarded with written and verbal appeals for help, and, just as before, his name worked magic. What a paradox: his name inspired hope, not fear, and was seemingly associated with the triumph of lawfulness, charity and justice, not curses, punishments and death sentences. Such was the aura created around him and nothing could destroy it.

He was particularly sympathetic to Foreign Ministry officials' appeals. Someone or other was always having trouble – brothers were being imprisoned, wives dismissed from work, nephews thrown out of apartments. They all went to Vyshinsky and he immediately did something about it: he gave instructions to his secretaries to send the complaint on to the appropriate bodies with his, Vyshinsky's, personal request to follow the matter up. Sometimes such an inquiry produced positive results. And this soon became common knowledge. Sometimes the most improbable details were added. His fame as an intercessor, benefactor and champion of the oppressed grew and grew.

His help was sought, and he gave his opinion on other matters as well. In a letter to the poet and secretary of the Writers' Union of the USSR, Konstantin Simonov, he wrote: 'As I was sorting through my archives, I came across Comrade Nikritin's verses, ... which I was too occupied to familiarize myself with at the time. In my opinion the author undoubtedly possesses talents, and his verses are on a topical subject. I would ask you to read them and decide on the possibility of publishing them.' Enclosed were Nikritin's letter and verses, the evidence of the author's 'certain talents':

To Comrade Vyshinsky

> To thee, tribune of your native land of Soviets
> Whose mind is sharp,
> Whose eye is keen,
> Whose heart's on fire,
> Whose word shines diamond-bright.
>> Over yonder ocean
>> To the country of another world
>> Does my line of greeting
>> Speed to thee....
> You told them that the world fears not
> All these guns,
> These atom bombs,
>> That they cannot break
>> The Soviet country
>> No matter what aplomb
>> Their threats possess.
> ... Thus, when you spoke,
> Both here in your land
> And over yonder ocean
>> A vast world of hearts
>> Caught your words,
>> And the radio rang out
>> In defiance of the mists.

As far as I have been able to ascertain, these verses were not published, which means one of two things: either Simonov found the courage not to agree with Vyshinsky's literary taste, or neither of them had enough real power to force someone to give the versified 'topical subject' a public airing. The radio did not ring out in defiance of the mists....

The aesthetic criteria, likes and dislikes of Stalin's circle are a fascinating and totally unexplored subject waiting to be researched. However, Vyshinsky stood out from this circle on account of his origin, education and basic culture. In this respect, his cultural level was certainly no lower than that of an average pre-revolutionary intellectual, which meant, compared to the level of other members of the ruling elite, it was very high indeed. In which case what possessed him to recommend the nonsense of his graphomaniac admirers to professional novelists and poets? Complete blindness and deafness? Or some special considerations? What made him, for instance, send Fadeyev the composition of a doctor by the name of Pavlushin at the Foreign Ministry's Health Centre, who had won 'The International Stalin Peace-Fighter's Scholarship' and, furthermore, comment on 'the important theme, so graphically and compactly expressed in the following verses':

> Joseph the Wise, not of the Bible,
> Soviet, among us, real, alive,
> Born in Gori the son of a plebeian,
> Glorified as the King of Kings,
> Stalin

What made him do it? To my mind, the same reasons that made him – whenever and wherever possible, without in the least fearing silent reproaches and ridicule – hail the King of Kings' banal 'ideas' as revelations, quote him endlessly, and find the most powerful expressions he could think of to extol him. I have looked through a great many different draft reports, speeches, lectures, and addresses of welcome which he personally corrected and edited. The idea behind all these 'editorial amplifications' is always, literally always, the same: to glorify the dearly beloved and great Leader as ecstatically as possible, and give assurances of such great devotion that even the most insane flattery would seem insufficiently fervent. Even at the meeting of Foreign Ministry officials to mark International Women's Day he congratulated his female colleagues in the following manner: 'Every time we gather for our meetings, be they festive occasions or work, our thoughts, our minds, our hearts are always turned towards great Stalin'. That is why he could throw a good lyrical poem into his wastepaper bin but never refuse to support scribble glorifying Joseph the Wise.

Fear is stronger than commonsense.

Then some events took place which are still a mystery. We have practically no reliable information on them, and from the little we do know, it is very hard to come to any firm conclusions. Probably, in the not too distant future light will also be shed upon this shadowy page of our history. In the meantime we shall examine what we have managed to find out.

277

Towards the end of the forties the luck of Stalin's favourite and most loyal comrade-in-arms suddenly began to run out. It is hard to pinpoint the reason for Molotov's fall from grace. Perhaps there was simply nobody else left, and Stalin could not live without enemies among his closest associates. In fact, there was not a single person in the world he completely trusted and whom he could totally rely on. Molotov, the most loyal of all, was no exception.

His wife, Polina Zhemchuzhina, the closest friend of Stalin's wife, Alliluyeva, was placed under arrest. This was not the first time she had been in disgrace. In February 1941 she had been publicly castigated by being removed, on Stalin's instructions, from the list of Central Committee nominations. In charge first of perfumery (as the director of an all-union trust), then of fisheries (as a People's Commissar), she had always held fairly prominent positions and had enjoyed authority for her talents as an organizer. It was her friendship with Israel's first ambassador to Moscow, Golda Meir, that cost her her liberty. However, this was hardly the real reason: Stalin remembered that Zhemchuzhina was the last person his wife had spoken to before shooting herself. . . .

Party etiquette in Stalin's time made it impossible to petition for someone 'on family grounds'. Molotov could not intercede for his wife, neither could Kaganovich for his brother, Mikhail Moiseyevich Kaganovich, the People's Commissar of the Aircraft Industry, who committed suicide rather than face inevitable arrest; and no more could Poskrebyshev, despite being closer to Stalin than anyone else; he silently resigned himself to the arrest of his wife and mother of his children – Bronislava Solomonovna – and put up with the humane sentence Stalin passed: 'We'll find you another wife'. Towards the end of his life Kalinin did, however, persuade Stalin to free his wife, a 'spy' and 'wrecker', and she was able to attend his funeral.

One can imagine how powerful and invulnerable Poskrebyshev must have felt if he dared make fun of Vyshinsky. Nobody dared do that, nobody, that is, except Poskrebyshev.

When diplomatic uniforms were introduced, Vyshinsky took a particular shine to them. He never took his off, except, perhaps, when he was travelling abroad, and then he wore civilian clothes. On his initiative a small dagger was added to the diplomatic full dress to give the new uniform special panache. At a parade once when everyone from the main rostrum had gathered in the private room behind Lenin's Mausoleum, Poskrebyshev deftly lifted Vyshinsky's dagger out and slipped a cucumber in its place. Without noticing anything was wrong, Vyshinsky set off to the guest rostrums to greet the foreign diplomats. Nobody dared say anything until one of the officials accompanying him drew his superior's attention to this not very becoming detail of his full dress. Vyshinsky did not so much as bat an eyelid although he guessed straightaway who the prankster was. Such was their idea of fun. . . .

He was mortally afraid of Poskrebyshev, but only, it goes without saying, because the latter was well in with Stalin and able to whisper things in his ear whenever he chose to. In Poskrebyshev's smirk he could see Stalin's menacing grin. His fear of Stalin was quite understandable although Stalin clearly favoured him.

As Vyshinsky's star ascended, Molotov's set. There is probably no direct, clear link between the movements of these stars, but, as Vyshinsky was, of course, Molotov's first deputy, they may be regarded as part of a single integral process. With this in mind we can better appreciate the increased hostility Molotov felt for Vyshinsky. Who knows, perhaps in his nightmares he had horrific visions of the Hall of Columns and the dock with him in it, and Vyshinsky in the prosecutor's seat. Everything was possible, everything, even what seemed impossible.

But for the time being they – Molotov and Vyshinsky – were joined together by a single chain, along with another of the minister's deputies, the then very young Andrei Gromyko – a 'Molotov man', unlike Vyshinsky, who was a 'Stalin man'; Vyshinsky, as everyone knew, could not stand Gromyko. But he had to put up with him. He used to call him 'the boy in short pants', publicly showing his scorn for him but unable to do anything about it. He was too hard a nut to crack – for the time being.

On Molotov's instructions Vyshinsky and Gromyko always used to take their reports to the Politburo together. Both had two completely different draft solutions to the same questions. Whatever stand Stalin might take, they always had a document at their fingertips in the same key. 'We thought this would be your opinion, Comrade Stalin,' Vyshinsky usually said to begin with, taking the paper out of his file or suggesting Gromyko do so, 'and so we have prepared this draft accordingly.' Both drafts were prepared by Vyshinsky – he never trusted anyone else to prepare them.

So, this pair of 'bosom friends' got on quite well together until something happened that has yet to be fully explained. The fragmentary information we have is contradictory. In the first days of March 1949 Molotov was dismissed from his post as Foreign Minister, keeping his Deputy Prime Minister's portfolio while Vyshinsky took over as Foreign Minister. This was preceded by lengthy talks between the two of them, Molotov and Vyshinsky, and between all three, Stalin, Molotov and Vyshinsky.

Vyshinsky's promotion to a higher position in the state apparatus was accompanied by a demotion in the public sector. To keep the balance? As a warning – so that he did not get a false idea of his own importance? Nobody knows what was going on in Stalin's feverish imagination as he kept shuffling the pack. Whatever the reason, the fact remains that in the regular elections of the Supreme Soviet of the USSR Vyshinsky failed to win a place in Stalin's parliament. He lost the mandate he had held since 1937. And, again, for some unknown reason the same happened to Gromyko. It was a way of keeping the high-ranking and seemingly all-powerful slaves on an even tighter rein.

However, they were not the Leader's main – most important – targets. Stalin's true wrath was directed against Molotov, who had been responsible for the collapse of the West Berlin blockade: the reckless action when Soviet occupying troops refused to let transit trains and vehicles through with provisions for the city's people. As is well known, an airlift was set up to supply the city, after which the blockade was removed.

According to one version, none other than Molotov was the mastermind of this utterly insane venture, while Vyshinsky, who had been present at the UN Security Council sitting called to discuss this explosive situation, had not taken part in the discussions at all, 'pointedly', as one American journalist put it, 'leafing through papers, playing with his earphones, glasses, sheets of papers and a penknife for cleaning his nails'.

This collapse may only have provided a pretext for slightly clipping the wings of the falcon in charge of Stalin's diplomacy and for giving even greater wing-span to the prosecutor in his upward flight. Typically, when answering the *Pravda* correspondent's questions on the position in Berlin, Stalin saw fit to make a special mention of 'Comrade Vyshinsky', who had 'held unofficial talks' with the 'interested parties'. Stalin never named anyone fortuitously. Mentioning Vyshinsky in a positive context was his way of expressing his support and patronage. The response to this paternal show of concern was yet another even more powerful and passionate torrent of declarations of love.

As an example, let us read something that has never been published before – an excerpt from Vyshinsky's speech to the Foreign Ministry's diplomatic staff to mark the Leader's seventieth birthday on 21 December 1949:

> Not only Stalin's military genius but also Stalin's genius as an economist and organizer was the source and guarantee ... of the Great Victory....
>
> It is impossible not to mention here that extraordinary trait of Stalin's character reflecting the Russian people's and Russian military history's old fighting traditions and spirit. I am referring to Stalin's humour, his pithy sayings and inspiring words which raised the troops' morale. Take, for instance, the Order of 1 May 1942, when Stalin, noting the Germans' defeat at Rostov, Kerch,[7] Moscow, Kalinin, Tikhvin and Leningrad, used popular sayings to describe the Germans' 'fighting' ability – 'you're a dashing young warrior as long as you're up against sheep but when you're up against a dashing young warrior you turn into a sheep yourself'. Or take the Order of 6 November 1944, when, explaining why Soviet people hated the German invaders, he recalled the popular saying 'a wolf isn't thrashed because he's grey but because he eats sheep'....
>
> The greatest scientist and thinker, the greatest organizer of state socialist construction in any role, be it economic, political, cultural or military; a genius at legislation and diplomacy, at law and warfare, at art and criticism!

It is not fortuitous that Vyshinsky devoted so much attention in his birthday speech to his Teacher's 'humour' and little weakness for popular sayings and proverbs. He also, either following in his Teacher's footsteps, or thinking, feeling and expounding theories in unison with him, used exactly the same device in his own speeches, and this is primarily what won him fame among his foreign colleagues. Every time he spoke at the UN General Assembly, committees or Security Council sittings, he was expected to come out with more witticisms and sayings, and his interpreters used to rack their brains trying, sometimes without success, to come up with suitable translations for them in other languages.

It is very doubtful that such trivial expressions could have strengthened his arguments, no more than the endless references to the greatest source of wisdom and quotations from the speeches 'of our very own Stalin', the mere mention of which, to his mind, was enough to make any opponent lose heart. However, these sayings and quotations absolutely delighted his Supreme Master, whom he was primarily addressing from the various international platforms as his Main Listener was puffing away at his pipe thousands of miles away from the New York skyscraper.

Evidently, Stalin, who had shorthand reports of Vyshinsky's speeches sent to him at the Kremlin by special courier, was impressed by the unusual language Vyshinsky used as he grew more and more incensed. Nothing quite like it had ever been heard in diplomatic circles anywhere in the world before: the matchless and unparalleled mixture of high-flown Latin and scurrilous abuse was his rhetorical style abroad as well as at home.

Here he is arguing with the Australian Foreign Minister, Herbert Evatt: 'Mr Evatt, you have unscrupulous or illiterate advisers who are palming off all sorts of invalid documents on you in order to heat up your temper, which is hot enough as it is, either that or you yourself are an unscrupulous person.'

Of US Secretary of State Byrnes, whose enormous picture had just been splashed across the front page of *Pravda*, Vyshinsky says that he only opens his mouth to speak 'a load of nonsense of all kinds', and is 'consumed with a completely uncontrolled thirst for fame', that he 'holds forth with farcical familiarity', 'prattles' and 'goes in for self-publicity'.

Of Warren Austin, the permanent US delegate to the UN, he remarks: 'A parrot can repeat words but it does not understand what it's repeating'. The Belgian delegate, according to him, 'talks absolute drivel', while the Canadian delegate's speech is a 'cascade of hysterical attacks'. The Austrian delegate 'spreads crude gossip and lies worthy of the famous Baron Münchhausen'. He refers to Western journalists as 'psychopathological cut-throats, paranoiacs and schizophrenics possessed with delirious ideas or simply gangsters whose mercenary pens are ready to write anything they're ordered to'. As for Western diplomats as a whole, they are 'psychopaths and insane liars', 'inveterate provocateurs' who have let loose 'an unbridled stream of slander', 'pouring forth filthy torrents of insinuations'.

In the end people got so used to Vyshinsky's invectives that they stopped paying attention even to such expressions as 'frenzied madman' or 'filthy slanderer', which he used to address the diplomats in his audience.

However, there was apparently someone who did not put up with it. According to the well-known Soviet diplomat and scientist Victor Israelyan, he was told by Yakov Malik, one of Vyshinsky's closest associates, that a Western diplomat once lost his temper and after a successive volley of insults challenged the offender to a duel. Vyshinsky, naturally, turned the challenge down and gave instructions for the 'duellist' to be told that he despised him.

How could anyone believe Vyshinsky at all when his name was so closely linked throughout the world with the notion of monstrous and murderous falsehood? No matter what brilliant speeches he had made as a prosecutor, the West, represented by its governments and special services, knew perfectly well who was an 'agent' of various intelligence services, and who was not. You could pull the wool over anyone's eyes, set in motion any manner of propaganda machine, but British Intelligence and the CIA knew perfectly well whether they had recruited Bukharin and received secret information from Radek or whether this was vile slander. No bombast on the part of Procurator Vyshinsky, no bullying 'logic', nothing could convince them of things that simply did not exist. In this most important key issue they did not have to rely on blind faith, for they, and only they, had access to the facts and therefore the real truth.

This man's diplomacy was thus doomed from the start. Realizing this himself, he substituted his feeble olive branch of peace for a prosecutor's clenched fist. There was no other option open to him for he knew no other language or method.

Ernest Bevin, a leading member of the Labour Party and one-time British Foreign Secretary, whom we have already mentioned, admitted after meeting his Soviet colleague: 'When I look him in the face, I feel as though any moment now the blood of thousands of his victims may start trickling out of his monster's orifice.'

In fact, it was generally lies that trickled from his 'orifice'. He lied unashamedly, and increasingly as time went on.

Numerous meetings were held on the refugee issue. After a fairly lively start the repatriation of Soviet POWs and civilians (displaced persons) who had been deported by the Nazis ground to a halt as information began to filter through about the fate of many who had returned to their native country. Only recently in the Soviet Union have we learnt exactly what happened to them. But the West knew then.

How did Vyshinsky respond to the concern voiced by certain speakers at the UN and to their suggestions not to allow compulsory repatriation? Thumping his fist down on the lectern, he declared that 'the stories about sending prisoners-of-war to labour camps of some kind' were 'a mendacious and swindling distortion of the facts', they were 'deception and blackmail intended for the credulity of often politically inexperienced and, what's more, simple-minded people'.

There was worse to come: the dissemination of 'such disinformation' –
on the POWs' fate – was 'a most serious crime against which all the
forces of our reason and our conscience must protest; all the feelings
inwardly nurtured by honest people.'

We know that for disseminating 'such disinformation' at home,
in the Soviet Union, people really were denounced as 'most serious
criminals' and severely punished. Vyshinsky (let us give him credit
for his consistency) was longing to dispatch to the Gulag those UN
colleagues who had not feared the Soviet prosecutor and had dared
voice these views.

The rest of the world was also thrown into confusion when, in the
late forties, the infamous persecution campaign began against the
'rootless cosmopolitans'. One had to be completely blind not to see its
true character and far-reaching consequences. Naturally, alarm was
also expressed at the international forum of the UN. Anyone in Vyshinsky's position was clearly forced to produce some kind of justification.
But not Vyshinsky – he did no such thing. Instead, he thundered: 'Is
it permissible to ask what international rules and principles there are
forbidding one to criticise the culture of the Western world, and where
they can be found? I can see the US representative giving me a very
surprised look. He is probably hearing this for the first time ... I can
only feel sincerely sorry for Austin and his secretaries who ... have
palmed this crib off on him obviously without understanding what's
what.'

As soon as anyone in the debates touched upon a subject he was
not very keen on, Vyshinsky would immediately seize upon a well-
tried argument, namely, that his opponent was violating the UN
Charter. At the time Hartley Shawcross was the United Kingdom's
delegate to the UN. Unable to contain himself, he reminded Vyshinsky
that this was not the prosecutor's stand in Moscow's Trade Union
House but the United Nations Organization, and proof was required
here, not unfounded indictments.

This is what Vyshinsky said in reply:

Shawcross has deemed it pertinent to recall – and not for the first
time – my past as prosecutor, and the trials which, as he put it
today, brought me world fame, and so on. I do not know why and
for what purpose this was said. Of course, I am proud the great
honour befell me to defend the interests of my country against
Hitler's secret service, which was being set up in our country but
was successfully wiped out, and, incidentally, I would wish Mr

Shawcross the same in relation to his own country. . . .

Shawcross put the issue like this: produce evidence that the Charter has been violated. After all, you are not at a trial, he said, where someone has simply alleged that the defendant is guilty, saying, 'I have proof of it but I am not going to produce it and you simply have to believe me when I say that I have such proof' . . . Shawcross, of course, is an experienced prosecutor, and I give him every advantage over myself in this profession but . . . everything he says is pure fabrication! Evidence was produced and there was absolutely no violation of legal procedural rules.

The logic remained the same: I am right because I am right.

His outrageousness knew no bounds. Once, however, he was publicly 'knocked for six' with such inimitable style that it was remembered for a long time afterwards by everyone present.

During a discussion he started making derisive remarks about the Argentine's permanent UN delegate, Arce, who had tried to dispute Vyshinsky's editing of a resolution: 'Mr Arce, as far as I am aware, is an obstetrician by profession whereas I am a lawyer and therefore evidently have a better understanding of matters pertaining to international law'. Whereupon Arce replied, 'Your informers are mistaken, I used to be a general practitioner, not an obstetrician, and so I had to do not so much with bringing people into this world as sending them into the next. So in this respect, Mr Minister, you and I are on an equal footing.'

This left Vyshinsky literally speechless and he raised no more objections.

However, it would be wrong to think he had absolutely none of the professional traits of a diplomat. Far from it. But for some reason he carried them to the point of absurdity and shameless cynicism. On one occasion Vyshinsky called the Philippines' delegate, General Carlos Romulo, 'an empty barrel'. Suddenly, however, the same Romulo was elected President of the General Assembly, and in one of his speeches Vyshinsky noted the General's 'exceptional honesty', as if nothing had gone before, and sent him roses, champagne and caviar.

Reading through the collections of Vyshinsky's 'diplomatic' speeches in chronological order is laborious but interesting work. It enables one to see how his manner of speech became increasingly aggressive as time went by. Gone are the rhetorical asides which softened the sharp edges, gone are the centuries-old rules of etiquette, the protocol, and even the forced irony. Even if there is some rationale and commonsense in them, the contents are drowned in invectives. He gradually ceases to even call his foreign colleagues 'gentlemen'. Why bother when there are perfectly good words like 'rogue', 'liar', 'intriguer' and 'hysterical subject'?

Gone, too, are the arguments of any form: our position is correct because 'our great Teacher' said so, because 'our Leader of Genius' ordered so. Here is a typical quotation from one of Vyshinsky's speeches:

> I am asked what our position is based on. I may recall here the words of great Stalin when he said that 'there are old ideas and theories which have gone out of fashion and served the interests of the dying forces of society. Their significance lies in the fact that they halt society's progress, its movement ahead. And there are new, advanced ideas and theories serving the interests of the foremost forces of society. Their significance lies in the fact that they facilitate society's progress, its movement ahead ...' I think this makes it clear for everyone.

One can imagine how the professional diplomats felt listening to this primitive logic: after all, they had been educated at the world's best universities and read plenty of other works in their time besides the great Leader's erudite revelations. However Vyshinsky could not have cared less how they felt or, indeed, how the West reacted.

All that interested him was what Stalin would think, say and do.

13

There is no evidence, direct or circumstantial, to suggest that Stalin in any way changed his attitude towards Vyshinsky to the very end. Had he lived longer, he probably would have done so. After gradually eliminating all the accessories to his crimes, he would have eventually got round to Vyshinsky with just such a convincing, logical and well-formulated indictment at the ready as this: the ex-Menshevik, having forced his way to the high post of Procurator-General, proceeded on the instructions of enemy intelligence services to annihilate honest Bolsheviks – Lenin's Guards. The murderous multi-act drama would have had a fascinating denouement.

But it was not all over. Yet. For the time being the Leader still needed him: the only one of his kind, the only one ready for anything and capable of substantiating absolutely anything. And he sensed his indispensability, the security of his position, and played on it.

Reading the abuse the Minister subjected his foreign colleagues to, some may think that in this albeit not very parliamentary form he was expressing his attitude to 'class enemies'.

But here is one – only one – document from Vyshinsky's personal archive which, I think, tells one a lot about this archive's owner and his nature.

It is a long letter, and I shall cite the main parts. It is undated but filed along with papers relating to the beginning of the fifties:

Dear Andrei Yanuarievich,
Yesterday at supper when I was greeting everyone at the table, you hailed me with the words, 'O, Von Baron Osten-Sacken!' Solicitous about your health, I struggled hard to contain myself and did not reply to this name of 'von baron' which I utterly deplore. This name, which for some unknown reason you have invariably greeted me with during the eleven years I have worked at the People's Commissariat of Foreign Affairs and Ministry of Foreign Affairs (during which time I have not heard a single kind word from you), is a

287

deadly insult to me. The entire Saksin family suffered terribly at the hands of the German invaders and, together with all the Soviet people, has waged a fierce fight against the Germans. ...

I cannot change my surname even if for some reason you do not like it. ... I have no grounds to be ashamed of my surname for the name of the Saksins has never been tarnished. ...

I hope that ... I shall not hear this name from you again, Andrei Yanuarievich.

Counsellor G. Saksin, formerly (1916–26) a Leningrad scaffold worker and sailor of the Baltic Fleet

One can imagine the systematic pleasure his all-powerful chief must have derived over eleven years from taunting him if the ex-sailor, downtrodden and ridiculed, remembered his self-respect and launched into the attack, laying himself open to official anger and unforeseen consequences. And one can also imagine how astonished the addressee must have been by this cry of despair if, unperturbed by the verdict of posterity, he kept this indictment against himself in his very own personal archive.

Trampling and humiliating others was evidently not so much an engrossing pursuit as part of Vyshinsky's nature. The memoirs of colleagues, Soviet and foreign, draw depressingly similar pictures of his exceptional rudeness – even to people who were officially of the same rank as him. No minister, for instance, could introduce a motion to the Politburo or Council of Ministers concerning international ties without his sanction. Vyshinsky's favourite word was 'impossible', accompanied by the rude comment, 'You don't understand anything about foreign policy'.

He remained, just as before, the indestructible supreme head of jurisprudence, and delivered public reprimands at meetings and in the pages of the press with remarkable consistency. In the post-war years nearly all the distinguished law scholars, regardless of the sphere of law they were working in, were dismissed from their posts, slandered or, at best, subjected to humiliating vilification by him personally or with his most active involvement. All of them proved to be 'stateless cosmopolitans' or stooges of capitalism or ideological wreckers or (if they were very lucky) ignoramuses, scholastics and dogmatists. Law theorists Ilya Trainin; Andrei Denisov; Mikhail Arzhanov; Alfred Stalgevich; Maria Kareva; law historian Sergei Kechekyan; crime detection specialists Aron Trainin; Andrei Piontkovsky; Boris Utevsky; Mikhail

Shargorovsky. Nikolai Durmanov; international law experts Yevgeny Korovin; Vsevolod Durdenevsky; Sergei Krylov; Ivan Peretersky; Vladimir Lisovsky; legal procedure specialists Mikhail Strogovich; Nikolai Polyansky; Moisei Shifman; Alexander Kleinman; Mark Gurvich; civil law specialists Vladimir Serebrovsky; Yekaterina Fleishits; Alexander Karass; Raisa Khalfina; state law specialists Georgi Gurvich; Ilya Levin; Semion Osherov; labour law experts Nikolai Alexandrov,[1] Aron Pasherstnik and dozens of other professors of law – all were blacklisted with the help of the indefatigable and uncompromising head of the Soviet school of law. Some were vilified and pulled to shreds in full view of the public, while others were deprived of work and of any possibility of printing their works.

Remembering well how my teachers whose books and scientific articles had enabled us to understand the rudiments of our profession, had been exterminated *en masse*, I decided to re-read Vyshinsky's virulent attacks to better understand the reasons for this insane campaign. At that time 'enemies' were being tracked down everywhere, and everyone was competing to expose the greatest number: the philosophers, for example, against the producers; the historians against the chemical scientists; the architects against the astronomers. But where and how did Vyshinsky look for incriminating evidence against our unfortunate professors?

Practically all the victims this time had committed the crime of not citing Comrade Stalin or of having inadequately cited him. Vyshinsky, with his great wisdom, expertise and natural gifts as a leader, never failed in this respect.

Even so, despite all Vyshinsky's sycophantic devotion, not once did Stalin and his entourage let him into their circle. Somehow this erudite orator, this last Menshevik who had hung on for too long in the top echelon of power, stuck out from their normal circle and did not fit in. The only reason he was ever invited to a table was to deal with protocol. He was never invited to dine or join in the fun and games (slipping a tomato under a drinking companion's backside when he was not looking was Stalin's and his bosom pals' favourite prank). He was a servant, very important and much needed, but still a servant. Never was he to become even a comrade-in-arms, let alone a friend.

It was at grand social receptions and functions, in the company of enemies and other opponents against whom he fulminated at Foreign Ministry meetings, that Vyshinsky felt an equal and not a mere servant. He represented a great power: Stalin. The paradox was that it was here, in the company of the targets of his invectives, that Vyshinsky could feel most at home. His foreign colleagues, not always perhaps fully comprehending this but perhaps sensing that such a farcical situation existed, did not, it seems to me, take the abuse he poured out at them in his official speeches seriously. They accepted the role he had been given in the drama and sometimes joined in the action themselves.

Western diplomats' descriptions of the impression Vyshinsky made on various highly esteemed people in London, Paris, and New York have remained intact. They are not all negative. Many fell under his charm without pondering too deeply over what was concealed behind it. Can one blame them? After all, even Roosevelt was charmed by Vyshinsky at Yalta. The details that drew people's attention are interesting: Vyshinsky 'likes laughing', he is 'witty and ingenious', 'never gets drunk although he is not averse to good alcoholic drinks', 'notwithstanding his age he is a fine dancer', he has 'impeccable manners', he is 'gallant and aristocratic'. After maintaining that 'his special talent would have won acclaim in any system', the well-known journalist Edgar Snow goes on to say:

> Handsome, intelligent, somewhat egocentric, he is not devoid of such a pardonable human quality as vanity which is hard to satisfy in Russia. . . . But abroad Vyshinsky is always the centre of attention. Equipped with a brilliant, wonderfully trained mind, he knows all the secrets of eloquence to captivate an audience with . . . His memory is phenomenal.[2]

There was one other 'pardonable human quality' which made Vyshinsky differ from the ascetics of Stalin's school. This man who traded in hundreds of thousands of lives had a life-long flair for enticing the fair sex and rarely missed a chance offered him to fondle a woman's knee.

He often received requests to find jobs for wives, daughters, sisters and female acquaintances, and he never refused to speak to the applicant, no matter how lowly the position that she was seeking. The conversation was brief. There were only two possible outcomes. Either: 'Unfortunately, I cannot help you in any way', or 'I'm busy just now, my dear child, go downstairs and wait for me in the car.'

He grew particularly fond of one of these 'dear children' – a buxom young lady who was remembered by all who met her as having the air of an innocent schoolgirl. She started off as a typist – working on broad-frame typewriters, her colleagues at the Foreign Ministry called her the 'typist with the broad frame' – but soon became an irreplaceable member of staff for her boss not only in affairs of the heart. After graduating from the Institute of Foreign Languages by correspondence course, she received the diplomatic rank of attaché and ended her career as a counsellor. So immense was her power over the Minister that she could select people for delegations to international conferences, dismiss or pardon, win them favour with the authorities or, on the contrary, ensure they had none. Her protection was sought, her hands were kissed and she used to receive 'souvenirs' from top-ranking diplomats. Intellectuals from cultured families, 'aristocrats of the spirit', and polyglots showered flattering compliments upon their master's lady-love. This lady is now retired and on a special state pension awarded to her for her great services to the country.

Let me stress that, of course, Vyshinsky was not a sex maniac like Beria. He was not always on the look-out for new conquests like Dekanozov. Vyshinsky was more discerning and decorous, and observed the proprieties. However, as the Russian saying goes, 'you can't throw words out of a song'.

Vyshinsky's uneasy conscience sometimes betrayed itself – he used to see allusions to his weakness for women in even the most innocent comments. At one time Edgar Snow worked as a correspondent in Moscow and took Russian lessons from the same teacher who taught English to Foreign Ministry officials. One of her pupils happened to be Vyshinsky.

At a reception Snow, while engaged in polite conversation with Vyshinsky, commented that their mutual teacher was not only a fine teacher but also a charming woman. He wished only to pay a polite compliment to the Ministry of Foreign Affairs for their choice of personnel. But 'as soon as I had said this,' recalls Snow, 'Vyshinsky's blue eyes flashed. "A competent teacher, you say? Yes, I agree. As for her being charming ... I haven't the time to notice such details."' But his uneasy conscience made him carry on talking instead of changing the subject. 'Slowly choosing and, what's more, deliberately stressing every word,' writes Snow, 'Vyshinsky loudly added, clearly for the benefit of everyone present: "No wine, women or song! Only work! And that's how it's been all my life." Why did he consider it necessary,' comments the author in his article in *The Saturday Evening Post*, 'to let me and the other people around us know that he had no interest in female charms? I still do not know why.'

We could tell him.

On the subject of human frailties, let me say that there was one at least which he certainly did not have: he disliked alcohol. He was attracted to it for aesthetic rather than physiological reasons. A glass of good wine at dinner was perfectly acceptable, but he could not stand strong spirits. This did not prevent him, however, from having a glass or two when diplomatic duties made it absolutely necessary. But no more.

This inability to consume large quantities of alcohol once played a mean trick on him. A top-ranking Chinese delegation led by Mao arrived in Moscow. A complex psychological war was being waged and for two days Stalin declared himself sick, and did not receive his important guest. The guests were meanwhile looked after in an appropriate fashion in the Foreign Ministry's mansion in Spiridonovka (now Alexey Tolstoy) Street. Vyshinsky held a reception for Chou En-lai and his colleagues – the two ministers were about to sign a treaty on friendship, union and mutual help. The alcohol flowed and the tables were overladen with delicacies of all kinds. An experienced and observant man, Chou quickly summed up the situation and in a friendly manner invited Vyshinsky to a drinking contest.

He could not refuse. However, everything had been foreseen, and after the second toast Vyshinsky's glass was filled with water instead of vodka. But Chou was not going to be caught out: 'In our country we always swap glasses with friends. And, after all, we are friends, aren't we?'

Eye-witnesses recall what a terrible ordeal this was for the host. He literally drank himself under the table and then good-natured Chou helped him get up again. 'It appears,' he said, 'that China has got the upper hand. But seeing we're friends, we'll call it a draw.'

One could laugh but somehow it does not seem right to. My sympathies are on the loser's side. After all, is not being able to hold one's drink really such a terrible crime?

In general, he enjoyed a healthy way of life. He preferred walking to work, especially in the mornings – trying not to look too conspicuous with two bodyguards at his side. And trailing behind him would be an enormous captured Mercedes, which had reputedly belonged to Ribbentrop himself and which Marshal Zhukov had presented to Vyshinsky to commemorate their 'common' triumph on 9 May 1945. Many passers-by used to recognize Vyshinsky in the streets and stop to stare, and he used to smile with a satisfied look on his face, and there was nothing special about this ordinary human vanity.

In the evenings he would work or walk along the paths in the huge grounds of his house. Once in a while he would wind up his gramophone: he enjoyed listening to old romantic or gypsy songs, the ones that used to be heard in aristocratic Russian salons.

There was little time for pleasure as he was always in a rush to get things done as quickly as possible. Work meant everything to him in life. Many thought that, now he was absorbed in international affairs, he would leave jurisprudence behind. But could he?

He had been expected in the morning but matters of extreme state importance had prevented the high-ranking guest from arriving on time. While they were waiting for him, the people taking part in the All-Union Conference of Lawyers summoned to discuss the outline of a new theory of law text-book patiently strolled along the corridors, resting from the heated disputes which had been raging for several days: 'He' would come and settle them all for he had the last say in the matter.

I had not actually been invited to the conference but I had not 'gate-crashed' it either – in those days law students were readily admitted to any academic forums.

'He's arrived', 'he's on his way', 'he's coming upstairs' – I can still hear these hissed whispers. And I remember my heart missing a beat in a flurry of excitement as my benefactor's distinguished greying head of hair appeared down below, almost blending in with his mousey-grey uniform and steel-coloured epaulettes: in those days this strange diplomatic attire seemed the height of good taste and elegance. All the leading representatives of the Soviet judiciary were standing along the staircase, forming a wide passageway. The guest was jauntily climbing up the steps, file under arm, and then suddenly stopped. 'I can't today either. Or tomorrow,' he said to someone standing right by me. 'Do please forgive me, I simply can't'. What couldn't he do? Who was he apologizing to? I do not know. I could not see. All I could see was him, standing a couple of feet away: short, stocky, sweet-smelling. His handsome head of greying hair. His finely trimmed moustache. His elegant spectacle frames. And his tenacious, sharp, penetrating gaze behind them. His slightly screwed-up eyes that appeared steel-grey although they were actually blue.

This moment I was to remember for the rest of my life.

I also remember the overcrowded hall which had been named in his honour – there was a plaque by the entrance inscribed in gold letters on a black background with the words 'The A.Ya. Vyshinsky Hall'; his stocky figure on the high rostrum; his fluent speech without a single sheet of paper, without hesitations, without any superfluous interjections, grammatically perfect and ready to be sent to press; his superb oratorical devices, the way he modulated his voice, raising and lowering it with perfect timing, the effective pauses, the strong school of logic and rhetoric, the fervour skilfully injected into every phrase; his memory and erudition – the extensive citations from old and the latest treatises that he knew by heart, his free-and-easy command of names, dates and facts. And, finally and most importantly, what was most striking – the unparalleled combination of academic manners, learning, almost posturing erudition and insulting abuse which flowed from his lips in such a natural and unconstrained manner that it seemed as though this bizarre combination of styles was now a normal part of everyday speech.

The abuse was by no means plain and simple: every word had a sinister, politicized slant. The person subjected to his criticism had not merely made some mistake (even if he really had) but he was definitely up to no good or working for foreign sharks.

I also remember the following episode. Touching upon problems of international law, Vyshinsky noted that the Soviet Union was the first power to officially recognize the state of Israel immediately after its formation. Just as he had said this, someone clapped – it sounded strange and out of place in this audience. Vyshinsky broke off his speech and stared into the hall. His sharp, tenacious stare sought out the culprit. More likely than not he failed to find him. But at least he had tried.[3]

Let us return, however, to jurisprudence. Vyshinsky at this time was not only concerned with theoretical questions, he was also directly involved with legal practice. After a break of ten years, discussion had once again begun on the issue of creating a single, all-union criminal code, the draft of which Pashukanis and his colleagues had managed to complete before being executed. It was this old draft that now became the core of the new one whose authorship the 'working group' was only too willing and pleased to cede to Vyshinsky. On its behalf the draft and all the clause-by-clause materials, proposals, corrections and comments were sent to Vyshinsky by Professor P. S. Romashkin, shortly to become a correspondent-member of the Academy of Sciences.

As we remember, execution by shooting as a punitive measure had been excluded from Pashukanis's draft code – a source of particular pride for the professor, and convincing proof of his association with spies, traitors and wreckers for his prosecutors. Looking through the draft of Romashkin's group (in other words 'his code'), Vyshinsky particularly noted the retention of such an 'exceedingly necessary measure of social defence' as the death penalty as one of its most important merits.

But a few months later everything drastically changed. The great humanitarian Stalin decided to abolish capital punishment. The decree was printed. Who was the first to respond? Why, Vyshinsky, of course: 'The Soviet people,' he wrote in ink in his own hand, setting his favourite pencil aside on this particularly unusual occasion, 'will greet this act of socialist humanism with great satisfaction.'

A short while later Stalin thought the better of it, stopped flirting with world public opinion and reintroduced capital punishment 'for spies, wreckers and terrorists'. Who immediately commended this act for its 'wisdom and justice' and the 'sacred right of the proletariat to punish their sworn enemies'? I think the answer is obvious.

However, in the draft of the Criminal Code of the USSR, which was never to be carried through, there is one proposition worth looking at. Article 17 of the draft stipulated a rule which did not exist in domestic legislation. It contained principles of international justice, which was very topical just then, forming the foundation of the work of the Nuremberg Tribunal and giving it, in essence, lawfulness. There is nothing fortuitous about the fact that this principle was disputed in Nuremberg both by the accused and the defence. Here is how it was formulated in Article 17 of the draft: 'The carrying out of an order or instruction whose criminality was manifest for the subordinate does not absolve him from criminal responsibility'.

Vyshinsky fervently supported the wording of this article, and rarely had he been so absolutely right, or so far-sighted. To this day there is still no such principle in Soviet law – it has only just been included in the draft of the new all-union criminal law which was published for discussion in 1988. If one follows this principle, all those who obeyed Stalin – Vyshinsky, Yezhov and Beria – do not have a right to allege that they were obedient executors of the supreme will, the disciplined 'rank and file of the Party'. And according to this principle, Vyshinsky, who enthusiastically rushed to carry out the Leader's plans, is also a criminal. Could the intelligent, perspicacious lawyer really not see in what context this legal principle, which he so fervently supported, would be viewed years or perhaps even decades later?

However, Vyshinsky's position on this issue cannot be detached from the fundamental statements contained in his printed works of the latter half of the forties and beginning of the fifties. If one did not know their author, or indeed what life was like in the Soviet Union at that time, one might think that a change of power had taken place in the country and that true justice had begun to triumph in the courts. What, for instance, are we to make of the following splendid idea which it is unlikely any lawyer today would refuse to endorse:

> It is necessary when passing sentence not only to have the highest degree of probability but to be absolutely sure of its correctness ... Some comrades consider such a requirement to be onerous for the investigative and judicial organs in so far as it is supposedly excessive and impracticable.

And in a spirited article in the journal *Soviet State and Law* (June 1948) Vyshinsky ridicules these fears and convincingly shows the lawlessness that could be caused when elementary principles of justice are forgotten.

In this work and others dating from this period it is easy to detect a grand design corresponding with Stalin's in other domestic and foreign policy issues. Namely that theory was being given the task not of 'substantiating' defective and inhumane practice but of confirming democratic ideals as though they were actually being carried through in real life. In fact, there was a flagrant discrepancy between theory and practice.

Many accepted the rules of the game and for years the gulf between words and deeds was a normal part of everyday life. Others were disturbed, even shocked, by this change in theory, regarding it as a departure from Party spirit, class principles and a socialist world outlook.

Not long ago Aron Rakhlin, a history scholar and retired colonel, sent me a copy of the letter he wrote to 'dear Comrade Stalin' on 14 November 1949. He accused Vyshinsky of revisionism, of alienating the law from politics and of making a fetish of the letter of the law instead of putting its 'revolutionary spirit' into practice, and he suggested that the unassailable Academician's 'bourgeois school' should be exposed immediately.

As one goes through his correspondence, the many letters he received give one some idea of the amount of work and diversity of the problems he had to face.

Celebrities in high offices always receive piles of correspondence in the form of requests, appeals and pleas for help. More often than not they have a team of secretaries, assistants and assessors working on them and protecting them from an excessive work load. Vyshinsky was different in that he read all his correspondence himself, if only in the form of detailed reports compiled by his assistants. You can see his personal jottings and instructions everywhere, and in many cases he replied to the letters himself, with a thoroughness quite uncharacteristic of today.

Some of the letters are noteworthy if only because they take us back to the tense atmosphere of those days and help us to feel the timbre and pace of his daily life.

He particularly enjoyed reading letters from foreigners, from so-called 'ordinary people'. More often than not, these letters are full of adoration and love.

An American from Ohio by the name of Jack Videmeo informed Vyshinsky that he prayed for him every day and knew for sure that 'some kind of superior force has been prophetically and favourably guiding the remarkable actions' of this 'outstanding man ... all through his long and wonderful life'.

The editor of the New York journal *Rubicon*, Luigi Criscuolo, expressing his admiration for Molotov, Vyshinsky and Gromyko, asked 'most gracious and highly-revered Andrei Yanuarievich' to take note of the people 'who represent us Americans at the UN: they're just a heap of politicians, and they don't carry any more weight than the food merchants in Madison Avenue, they're all just a load of haberdashers, if not worse.'

Appealing to 'Mr Vyshinsky's world-famous humanity', Lucille Voyard of Tennessee hoped that he would help her and her children leave 'hateful America for a country where everyone breathes freely' – the Soviet Union, where she 'could open a small business, doing what she could to contribute to the struggle for peace throughout the world.'

Vyshinsky always wrote back, thanking them and sending them his greetings. He even gave instructions to send Mrs Voyard a signed photograph as a consolation for, 'much to his regret', not being able to satisfy her request.

A separate file contains verse, odes and cantatas dedicated to him. They include not only amateur compositions, like those, say, of Ruth Hall of Iowa, but professional ones by the Californian writer and composer Harvey Henderson and many of his colleagues. All these writings are kept in archives, and I hope one day someone will take the trouble to organize a concert for connoisseurs: the repertoire will be monotonous but the tragi-comic angle on life would merit it.

His domestic correspondence also gave him considerable pleasure. He received rapturous letters from admirers, ranging from a Vyshinsky

Collective Farm worker by the name of Anastasia Lukina who 'got up and went to bed with Andrei Yanuarievich's dear name on her lips' to renowned figures in the arts such as the Chairman of the Arts Committee, Mikhail Khrapchenko, who shared his innermost thoughts with him: 'The Soviet artistic intelligentsia knows your constant attention to leading creative ventures, your profound interest in new phenomena of art.'

Who did not know about Vyshinsky's 'interest in new phenomena'? Everyone remembered what had happened to Meyerhold. And that was not all: just then the theatre of his friends Alisa Koonen and Alexander Tairov – the world-famous Chamber Theatre – was under attack. But it would be pointless to search in Vyshinsky's enormous archive for a single line, word or even hint of an attempt to intervene, help and defend the theatre. A year later the persecuted Tairov would die and his 'friend' would not attend his funeral or even write a terse formal note, a single word of condolence, to the great actress who had been bereaved.

But this certainly did not mean that his 'constant attention to ... creative ventures' had slackened at all. At the request of the then chairman of the Film Committee, I. G. Bolshakov, he personally studied the script of the feature film *We Defend Peace* and gave several very valuable pieces of advice. Firstly, 'everything concerning Comrade Stalin and Comrade Molotov must be carefully honed'. Secondly, 'the reply of one of the characters, "I am not afraid of death, I embrace it in my sleep", is completely unacceptable. Embracing in one's sleep – will give rise to undesirable associations among the viewers.' And thirdly, 'Although the action takes place in some imaginary country, the impression is that it is Yugoslavia. At this moment in time, however, it is not expedient to depict Yugoslavia in a script.'

Letters, letters ...

Some invisible force (perhaps the one which, according to the American Jack Videmeo, had been guiding his 'remarkable actions' 'all through his long and wonderful life'?) was making various people appeal to him, when they had no obvious need to, in the faint hope of a reply. Perhaps they were collecting valuable autographs.

Alexandra Kollontai's letters caught my eye[4]. By that time she was well-advanced in years and peacefully enjoying her retirement. She did not take the liberty of writing to Vyshinsky direct – he was far too senior. Instead, she wrote to Boris Podtserov, the Foreign Ministry's General Secretary: 'Respected Boris Fedorovich, Would you be so kind as to pass the enclosed letter on to deeply-respected Andrei

298

Yanuarievich.' Her request was answered and her letter soon reached 'deeply-respected Andrei Yanuarievich'.

So what was she so impatient to communicate to this person who had been involved in the destruction of nearly all her old friends? That her grandson had been absolutely delighted by Vyshinsky's visit to the Institute of International Relations and by the lecture he had given.

Perhaps her grandson really had been delighted: Vyshinsky was so strikingly different from the swarms of mediocrities everywhere, so witty, ingenious and erudite, that he could quite well have made a favourable impression on the young student. But what possessed the seventy-nine-year-old pensioner who was no longer in any danger, a genuine member of the intelligentsia who knew the worth of the person she was writing to, what possessed her to write him such an ecstatic and servile letter?

Something must have made her do it.

Letters, letters ... Requests for help. He used to respond readily, it seems. At any rate, he always did. Especially if they were from people who had once lived in Baku. If, that is, they succeeded in proving they had been involved in the revolutionary actions that he had taken part in himself – really and truly, without any of the usual falsifications trumped up at a later date by people eager to please. He would see that they got good pensions, Moscow residence permits, living accommodation. He would corroborate their 'revolutionary service record'. It is easy to imagine what his corroboration meant in the provinces.

Many asked for others and not themselves. For instance, he was approached by friends of Ivy Litvinova, the widow of Maxim Litvinov, who had died in disgrace leaving her without a means of subsistence. Vyshinsky signed her petition for a special pension, but bloodthirsty Shkiryatov, who ruled supreme – in this realm as well – not only refused to take pity on the old woman but would apparently not even listen to the powerful Vyshinsky either. And so Vyshinsky stopped trying.

Nor was there any shortage of denunciations. A. G. Goikhbarg, who had repeatedly been destroyed by the press but had so far avoided execution and the Gulag, was denounced to Vyshinsky with particular relish, if the archive materials are anything to go by. While working at the Academic Institute of Law, Goikhbarg had dared speak out publicly against Stalin's memorable decree of 8 July 1944 which had been cribbed off Hitler's law 'on the German mother', a decree degrading women and putting children born out of wedlock virtually outside the law. This criticism cost Goikhbarg his job but not, however, his freedom, and he even continued visiting the institute's library every now and then.

Here he talked to various scientific researchers 'using expressions', wrote the institute's vice-director, A. A. Karp, in his denunciation,

> that were insulting to the Party and the Government. For example, at one time he declared to everyone he met that the resolution on the courts of honour had been 'palmed off' on the government[5] ... He uses insulting expressions about certain high-ranking comrades ... The other day an institute teacher, A. A. Askerov[6], said that he was amazed how long Professor Goikhbarg would be allowed to go on talking all sorts of harmful insulting nonsense about individual members of the Government and Party with such impunity'.

Vyshinsky pricked up his ears. Who were they, these 'individual members' whom the professor was insulting in public? He requested more precise information. It was forthcoming: 'In keeping with your instructions I am sending you some statements by Professor Goikhbarg ... He declared: "All Vyshinsky's and Gromyko's actions at the UN General Assembly and Security Council were incorrect, they do not know international law."'

His intuition had not failed him: he, Vyshinsky, had been among these 'individual members'. The information was passed on to Beria. But no consequences followed: Goikhbarg lived safely until 1962. The luck of the draw? Special deserts? Or was he simply pronounced insane and given up as a waste of time? Who knows? But Vyshinsky collected together all the materials on Goikhbarg in a separate file and carefully kept them. Just in case...

Two letters with the notes – obviously written by assistants – with the words 'No reply to be sent' stuck to them are also noticeable. One is on an international topic, the other a domestic one, but both were destined to remain unanswered, and they can help us recreate the atmosphere of those years and add new shades of colour to the portrait of the country's top lawyer and diplomat.

One is from Anna-Louise Strong, a well-known American journalist at the time. Caught up in the Revolution, Leninism, the pathos of the social reforms, she had gone to Moscow as a young woman and worked on Soviet newspapers and in Soviet publishing houses, specializing in Oriental issues, and writing profusely about China and the processes taking place in that part of the world. She had always heartily approved all the policies of the Party led by Comrade Stalin. This, however, did not prevent her from suddenly being arrested after the war, declared a foreign spy and then deported from the Soviet Union.

After her return to the USA she remained as staunch a Communist as ever. The letter of 26 August 1950 addressed to 'dear Comrade Vyshinsky' comes with a copy of her book *In North Korea: An Eye-Witness Account* in which she enthusiastically writes about the 'great reforms in the Country of Morning Freshness', about Stalin, about Kim Il Sung:

> I am enclosing my latest work, dear Andrei Yanuarievich, for you to see that the entry visa to North Korea you gave me in 1947 has been of benefit and that I am continuing to struggle just as before, and as always, for our common cause. The charge levelled by Moscow and the boycott which has made nine tenths of my American friends believe that this charge is true have, of course, been heavy blows for me. Neither in Moscow nor here have I ever been told exactly what I have done. Nor have I been given the chance to reply to the charges. I make bold to point out to you as an ex-prosecutor that this is unlawful and unjust, that this is an unwarranted attack against a person who has worked hard and beneficially over forty years.
>
> But even cripples have to do everything in their power when such a titanic struggle for peace is being fought as the one you, Andrei Yanuarievich, are leading with admirable energy. Although I had neither a publisher nor access to the book shops, nor my notebook which was confiscated in Moscow, I still have managed to write, print and distribute over 8,000 copies of my 'eye-witness stories'. . . .
>
> Should it ever become possible to inform me what I have done against the USSR, and permissible to reply, I shall be very pleased. . . . None of the officials at your Embassy in the USA will see me, and no official in the USSR I have written to has replied. . . . And even so I continue working with faith in the triumph of the peace cause under the leadership of great Stalin.

Because of the secretary's instruction one can be sure that Vyshinsky read the letter. What did he make of it, I wonder? What impression did the last lines make on him? Did he recall the victims of the 'Great Moscow Trials' whose remains were now buried in unmarked graves? The 'mad dogs', 'stinking carrion', 'hyena', 'jackals' and 'typhus-infected lice' who, after listening to the Procurator's insults, humbly got up from their places and, ecstatically beating their breasts, praised great Stalin to the skies. After being crushed and 'worked over' there was nothing else they could do. But what about slandered and humiliated Anna Louise, desperately pleading for justice from her distant California home, did she have no alternative either?

Now a different letter on an entirely different subject, from P. Konovalov of the town of Velikiye Luki. His letter is short but eloquent. And most telling:

> In your book *Issues of the Theory of State and Law* (1949) on page 334, citing V. I. Lenin's work *State and Revolution*, you assert that in *State and Revolution* Lenin wrote about one remarkable measure of the Paris Commune – the 'abolition of all the monetary privileges of officials and the introduction of a pay scheme for state officials on a level with workers' wages'. Why then does something which was abolished by the Paris Commune exist in our socialist state? I put this question to the local lecturers of the regional committee of the CPSU at the monthly courses of propagandists and lecturers of the Velikiye Luki regional committee of the CPSU who replied that this principle is not applied in our country and will not be either. Is this so? I, of course, doubt it.

Everything is remarkable here: his cunning doubts, the directness of his question when only now is it being asked aloud and widely discussed everywhere, even at the Congress of People's Deputies, and the dismaying cynicism of the reply of the 'local lecturers of the regional committee', and the completely obvious charge of hypocrisy and duplicity levelled against the book's author (to whom the letter was also addressed).

The letter ends as follows: 'Will you, Comrade Vyshinsky, or your assistants, be so kind as to comment on this position.'

Of course, neither Comrade Vyshinsky nor his assistants were so kind. And, anyway, what comments could they make? And how?

Of course, he enjoyed privileges. Who didn't at this level of power? Quotations from Marx, Lenin, and even Stalin were all good for speeches, lectures and seminars. They were a convention but not real life. Nobody took these quotations seriously, nobody made them guidelines for life. The naïvety of the provincial propagandist who had exposed the rulers' hypocritical moral code with such sublime candour did not, I think, infuriate or surprise Vyshinsky but made him laugh.

It is unlikely they generally thought of privileges as such. To them luxury and prosperity were simply a normal part of life, their well-earned right. It is well known that when Molotov, Kaganovich and other of their associates were given the status of ordinary citizens in the mid-fifties, they were amazed to discover that bread, tea, shirts, sheets, cinema and Underground tickets all had to be paid for. For the first time in a great many years they actually saw money and at first could not work out how much everything cost. So, the propagandist Konovalov had not pinpointed the problem properly – it was not *monetary* privileges they enjoyed but *non-monetary* ones, and in this way the Russian 'problem' was different from the one facing the Paris Commune.

A relatively recent rebel, revolutionary, and fighter for social justice, party purity and class intransigence, did Vyshinsky really think about privileges when he was living in the lap of luxury in his town and country abodes, eating delicacies, and washing them down with imported wine, lounging in foreign mansions and the suites of the ss *Queen Elizabeth*, his favourite liner, riding in an open limousine through the streets of New York to and from the Waldorf Astoria Hotel in a cavalcade of cars escorted by a fleet of motorcyclists? No, he regarded all these blessings as natural deserts for his talent, loyalty, labour and risk.

To make up for it, though, whenever necessary in the intrigues and internal strife that were an integral part of life, he (and he was not the only one, surely?) could also produce this particular trump card from the pack to deal an incontestable blow. Thus, for a short while he succeeded in gaining the upper hand over the last of his main rivals – Andrei Gromyko.

Unlike Vyshinsky, and especially the other slightly higher-ranking members of the same team, Gromyko in the early days did not display a need for ostentatious chic, and was quite content with the most basic comforts that went with his official position. Among these basic comforts was a *dacha* in the village of Vnukovo near Moscow which was badly in need of reconstruction and repair. However, as is well known, it is impossible to get repair work done in the Soviet Union in the usual, normal way – by paying for it. And so Gromyko resorted to the usual way of doing things in our society (as did everyone else who could): he borrowed some of the Ministry's building materials and got the workmen from the Ministry's construction unit to work for him. Nobody would have taken any notice of this innocent venture, which had long since become normal practice, but Vyshinsky did.

And not by chance either. He knew that Molotov's position was weakening, that any convenient cause for attacking the people in Molotov's circle would be quite favourably welcomed by the Leader. Vyshinsky would never have ventured to lift his hand against Molotov's closest associate if he had not been confident of success.

So he spoke of Bolshevik modesty, of the need to 'guard purity', of 'Lenin's struggle against privileges' and the equality of one and all before the law, regardless of merits, which 'Comrade Gromyko undoubtedly has and, what's more, they are great'. He secured a discussion of 'Communist Gromyko's action' at a Party committee meeting, and as a suitable punishment Andrei Andreyevich was sent off to London as Ambassador, and Andrei Yanuarievich won a point for his team. This long-forgotten episode is unique to Gromyko's career, which was marked by a slow and steady rise up the ladder: never before or afterwards, until his retirement, was he to take another step backwards. His short exile in London was the only blot in an otherwise fortunate career. And Vyshinsky had a hand in it.

It was then that Vyshinsky himself prepared for his final step upwards – the moment of glory of his unparalleled career. On 16 October 1952, at the first plenum of the Central Committee elected by the 19th Party Congress, he, along with Brezhnev, the unforgettable Professor Yudin and other 'loyal' and 'most loyal' colleagues, became a candidate-member of the Presidium, that is, rose at last to the penultimate step (for he was still only a candidate-member and not a full one) of the ladder of power. He was nearly at the very top.

He was to remain at the top of the Party – formally rather than practically – for one hundred and forty days.

14

Vyshinsky was destined to spend just under five months at the top of the Party ladder. This was also how long he was to keep his ministerial portfolio. These months were pervaded by a terrifying atmosphere in which new catastrophes were anticipated on a far more nightmarish scale than anything that had gone before. They could hardly be more nightmarish, it would seem. But the progressively more insane dictator's fantasy knew no bounds. This time Stalin had got ready to annihilate his last 'closest comrades-in-arms', and this was to entail not only meetings with the accursed 'enemies' and songs of praise to the Father and Genius but also medieval street executions at the hands of an enraged crowd unable to control their righteous wrath.

In his posthumously published *Notes: Through the Eyes of a Man of My Generation*, the writer Konstantin Simonov, who had become a Central Committee candidate-member at the 19th Party Congress, records an incident he once witnessed. This account gives one an idea of the events the country was on the verge of.

The entire plenum [he is referring here to the Central Committee plenum which took place after the 19th Congress on 16 October 1952] lasted ... two or two and a half hours, of which Stalin's speech took up approximately an hour and a half ... First, he attacked Molotov with ... a list of accusations and suspicions, accusations of cruelty, insufficient firmness, suspicions of cowardice, capitulation ... He spoke mercilessly of Molotov for a long time ... with anger so intense it seemed to be posing a direct danger to Molotov, a direct threat to come to the final conclusions, which, remembering the past, could be expected of Stalin ... There was a similar pattern to the next part of his speech devoted to Mikoyan, more succinct but because of some of its nuances perhaps even more malicious and disrespectful....

Molotov's and Mikoyan's faces were white and lifeless. They were still just as white and lifeless when Stalin finished, went back to the table and sat down, and then they – first Molotov and then Mikoyan – ... tried to explain their actions and deeds to Stalin, and justify themselves...

Both speakers seemed like accused men in the dock making their final statements, who, while denying all the blame that had been heaped on them, could hardly hope for a change in their fates which had already been decided by Stalin ... He wanted to humiliate them, especially Molotov, to destroy the halo which Molotov still had, despite the fact that for the past few years he had actually been discharged from his duties to a considerable extent, despite the fact that for several years now Vyshinsky had been directly in charge of the Foreign Ministry, despite the fact that his wife was in prison ... He was destroying the notion that Molotov was the firmest, staunchest follower of Stalin. While doing so, he was accusing him of capitulation, of possible cowardice and capitulation, that is, precisely what 'nobody had even suspected Molotov of'.

It is highly probable that the next 'band of foreign hirelings', 'terrorists' and 'conspirators' were going to be Molotov, Malenkov, Voroshilov, Kaganovich and Mikoyan. Would Beria be included as well? If so, who would Stalin get to carry his plans through? If not, who would Beria side with – the 'terrorists' or the 'Leader'? All we can do today is guess.

Vyshinsky could not have failed to notice the new wave of arrests. The doctors from the Kremlin hospital and clinic where he and his family were treated were disappearing, one after another. Among them were doctors from the commission of experts at the Bukharin-Rykov trial, like Professor Vladimir Vinogradov and Professor Nikolai Shereshevsky, who had been ready in the name of science to corroborate any absurd indictment and who had been privy to other falsifications. But there was nothing else they could do, except, perhaps, commit suicide. 'In all elements man is a tyrant, traitor or captive' – Pushkin understood this long before Stalin and Beria appeared on the scene.

Shall I ever be able to forget that dreadful day – 31 December 1952? It is hard to explain exactly what made it so dreadful. A foreboding of disaster turned New Year's Eve, the liveliest of all festive occasions, into a day of anxiety and sorrow. We, of course, had no information to go by but we had intuition – one could sense it in the air, in the very texture of life – we were on the brink of a disaster: the Apocalypse of the Twentieth Century. I am not exaggerating in the slightest – you see, what I am referring to here is a sensation, nothing more, and it can only be subjective. However, it does not simply appear out of the blue – something somehow causes it to appear.

Friends had invited me to various parties, and Mother raised no objections but I ended up going nowhere. She, of course, stayed in as well. So, there we were, just the two of us sitting at the table with nothing on it except a bottle of wine and a cake. But neither of us felt like eating anything.

Close to midnight the telephone rang. It was a woman friend of Mother's, the lawyer Horvitz, whom I mentioned in my introduction. Mother only listened but I could tell by her face that something terrible had happened. 'We must send a telegram to Vyshinsky,' she finally said. 'It would be better, of course, to go and see him but perhaps it's too late.' She listened again for a minute or so. 'And ring at once!' She put down the receiver. There was a dreadful look on her face. 'Three days ago Valentin Lifshits was sentenced to death', she just managed to say as she slumped onto a chair.

Valentin Lifshits was one of the most promising young academic lawyers and criminal trial specialists of the day; his teachers, who included Professor Strogovich, believed he was destined to become a leading figure in jurisprudence. Not long before he had brilliantly defended his thesis but had then been unable to find work in Moscow. After considerable difficulty he had got a job in Gorky but made frequent visits home. I scarcely knew him as there was a fairly large gap in our ages, and, besides, I had nothing to do with the Institute of Law, where he had done his postgraduate studies. Mother, however, was good friends with his mother – Professor Sofia Yevseyevna Kopelyanskaya, who in those days was the top specialist in defending minors. In the twenties Kopelyanskaya had worked in the People's Commissariat of Education, where there was a special department dealing with the protection of mothers' and children's legal rights. Vyshinsky was a Deputy People's Commissar at the time and one of his functions was to keep an eye on this department. Kopelyanskaya met him on mutual business matters nearly every day. In those days – at the end of the twenties and beginning of the thirties – impenetrable barriers had not yet been set up between superiors and subordinates, ways were simpler and more democratic, and, what's more, the Deputy People's Commissar and his colleague had 'blood' as well as work in common – they were both half-Polish. Indeed Vyshinsky called her by her Polish name – 'Zossya'.

We did not notice it turn midnight. We clinked glasses an hour late but without drinking a drop. A plate crashed onto the floor and broke.

'That means good luck,' I exclaimed foolishly. The door bell rang. It was Dora Vladimirovna Horvitz with the text of the telegram to Vyshinsky she had written for Kopelyanskaya, who was in a state of shock. The text was immediately edited and typed out, and then I had to take it down to the telegraph office. I raced across the frozen, strangely deserted, almost dead city, which was busy seeing in the New Year, all the way to Gorky Street, at least three kilometres away, clutching the sheet of paper in my hand which just might – one so wanted to believe it – bring hope of salvation.

But there was no hope at all. Valentin had been charged with no more, no less than an attempt upon the life of Comrade Stalin: he had allegedly intended to kill the Leader as he was driving along Arbat Street to his *dacha*. Valentin was going to drag a heavy machine-gun up to the roof-top of the building which now houses the Prague restaurant and fire a round at the limousine. So how could Vyshinsky, who was expecting to become the next spy and terrorist at any moment, possibly raise objections?

Zossya did not receive a reply. Vyshinsky's silence was his reply.

Valentin was executed in February, only a matter of weeks before the tyrant's death. He was one of the last in the endless row of victims and one of the first in the endless row of posthumous rehabilitations. In her stoic fight to restore her son's good name Professor Kopelyanskaya discovered the truth: Valentin had been slandered by his close friend, Professor Serafim Pokrovsky, who turned out to be a vile provocateur and, thus, virtually an assassin.[1]

The country meanwhile was living in an atmosphere of fear and hatred; fear of the unknown and hatred for the 'assassins in white coats'.[2] Thousands of people requiring urgent medical attention refused to be treated. The murky wave of anti-Semitism, the surest sign of a deep political crisis and economic instability, soared up, threatening to grow into an all-destructive storm. It was at this time that in his wisdom the Leader contrived to award the International Stalin Peace Prize to Ilya Ehrenburg, and the celebrations to mark this occasion were widely covered by the press. Foreign Minister Vyshinsky was able to pacify anxious foreign statesmen and diplomats by passionately refuting this 'recurrent anti-Soviet slander' and referring to the prize that had been awarded to 'such an outstanding public figure as the deputy of the Supreme Soviet of the USSR and renowned writer Comrade Ehrenburg'. It was unlikely, however, that these denials could have had an impact on anyone reasonably experienced and still in full command of their mental faculties. Especially seeing that

308

everyone still had memories of 'Kristallnacht', the laws on the 'purity of the Aryan race' and other acts of the unforgettable Nazi leader who had also simultaneously bestowed gifts on Jews who were 'useful to the state' as tokens of appreciation. Albert Einstein was one of the many to send a telegram to Vyshinsky expressing his concern and indignation. However, even he was not deemed worthy of a reply.

Nevertheless, Vyshinsky could not hide from Stalin the West's reaction to the trial being prepared and its inevitable repercussions. Einstein's telegram acted as a pretext to justify this disturbing report. There is no documentary evidence to support the view that Vyshinsky suggested this trial be dropped or at least postponed, and, besides, there was no way Vyshinsky could recommend anything of the sort to Comrade Stalin. Expounding facts that one knew would not be to his liking was very dangerous. He may have calculated on the Leader's wrath being directed against Molotov and not him, as Molotov's wife was still languishing in Vladimir Prison for her links with the despicable Zionists.

Every morning millions of people opened their newspapers, expecting reports on the 'Doctors' Trial' that was underway. However, the preparations were literally for a massacre, not a trial. Academician Vyshinsky was also making preparations – to give theoretical substance to this new method of 'popular justice'. But he did not have to in the end: fate decreed otherwise.

5 March 1953 marked a turning point not only in the life of the world and the Soviet Union but also in the lives of millions of people. How did Vyshinsky feel losing the man who had swept him up to great heights, and from whom for thirty-five years he had, at any moment, expected a stab in the back? The leader he had served with servile loyalty and who had, at the same time, filled him with indescribable terror?

Vyshinsky did not commit his true feelings to paper but we can guess that one fear must have inevitably been replaced by another. He understood that a new era was now taking over from the old one, and that exposures were bound to follow. And suppose Beria and his cronies were to get the upper hand, why should they need Vyshinsky as an accomplice and witness? They might as well put all the blame on him; on the Leader and his Prosecutor . . .

Stalin's death brought Vyshinsky's career at home to an end. The very same day the 'leading group' – Malenkov, Beria, Molotov, Bulgarin and Kaganovich – dismissed him from the Central Committee's

Presidium and simultaneously stripped him of his ministerial portfolio. The post of First Deputy Minister was split between him and Yakov Malik,[3] and he was sent into honourable exile to New York as the Soviet Union's permanent delegate to the United Nations. Incidentally, it was at this time that Leonid Ilyich Brezhnev was also removed from the Central Committee's Presidium and Secretariat 'in view of his transfer to the post of head of the political directorate of the Naval Ministry' – not a very fine transfer.

The doctors' release, Ryutin's arrest, Beria's liquidation – the obvious, visible signs of the start of a new phase in Soviet history all happened when Vyshinsky was already well settled in New York. He watched the momentous events taking place in the country from afar, taking no part in them whatsoever, and gaining satisfaction from contemplating the results.

But did they really give him 'satisfaction'? Beria was his curse, his eternal nightmare – under him nobody felt safe. But there were few, except perhaps his closest subordinates, who were bound by such unbreakable chains to him. Not for long, perhaps, but very much hand-in-hand, they had worked on their joint 'project' together, smearing each other with their countless victims' blood. Beria's elimination liberated him but it also marked the inevitable beginning of his own end.

Just then, in the summer of 1953, a new book by Vyshinsky – a successive edition of his collected articles, reports and speeches – was due to appear. It was saturated not only with adoration of Stalin but also flattering admiration for his 'punitive sword', the Leader's loyal comrade-in-arms and favourite pupil, dear Comrade Beria. Of course, the vigilant editors and censors would have removed these expressions of admiration themselves but Vyshinsky managed to forestall them by taking even more drastic measures: he ordered the type-setting to be smashed. His political intuition had not deceived him, and his reactions were just as quick as ever.

Very, very timidly and unsurely a rehabilitation campaign began. At first it was only provisional but the trend was quite clear. Here, too, Vyshinsky was in the lead; he quickly saw which way the wind was blowing and turned the same way.

One episode, to my mind, tells more about this man in the final stage of his life and career than any general discussions.

Among the top lawyers whose arrest Vyshinsky had sanctioned in 1937 was Chief Transport Procurator of the USSR Gherman Mikhailovich Segal, who was then forty years old. In his address at a general staff meeting in the Procurator's office, to mark the twentieth anniversary of the October Revolution, Vyshinsky had appealed to his audience for increased vigilance 'not to permit infiltration into our midst, for the supervision of lawfulness and the administration of justice on such spies, Trotskyite-Bukharinite agents, double-dealers and counter-revolutionaries as ...' Segal was among those he had then proceeded to list.

The Chief Transport Procurator was charged with the rarest of crimes: 'establishing contact with his father'. I have come across a great many bizarre charges in the documents of those years but never anything to match this. True, Segal's father was not an ordinary father, but a 'German spy'. He specially had 'contact' with his son at breakfast or supper to improve preparations for sabotaging the railways. One of the Procurator's friends, Polonsky, a Deputy People's Commissar for Communications, used to visit them, and the father would sit at the table while the son purposely started discussing 'official matters'. Through the father and son people in Berlin then found out about these 'matters'.

In November 1937 the family was shot, but in the spring of 1954 an inquiry was launched, following a complaint by the Procurator's widow, Lyudmila Vasilievna Segal, who had just returned from a labour camp. While the case had been fabricated in a matter of days, the inquiry was conducted slowly and thoroughly. The Military Procurator, Lieutenant Colonel of the Justice Proshko, decided to ask Segal's colleagues to write testimonials on him. Vyshinsky was at the top of his list.

Andrei Yanuarievich was not in the least surprised by this request and swiftly submitted a brief, low-key but totally unequivocal official reply. 'Gherman Mikhailovich Segal,' it states on the official writing paper of the First Deputy Foreign Minister of the USSR, 'was a man devoted to the Communist Party and a capable lawyer'. The fact that he had also been down on Vyshinsky's list of names was not mentioned in the reply.

There is no doubting it, this outstanding lawyer and outstanding diplomat always kept pace with the times, detecting any sudden twists and turns with exceptional subtlety.

Whenever he spoke at a session of the UN General Assembly or at its committee meetings, Vyshinsky's colleagues from various countries, as always, flocked to listen to him. The auditorium was always full when Vyshinsky was due to speak. And it was not only because these occasions always turned into lively political shows. After Stalin's death and the changes in the Kremlin, his audience expected to hear new proposals each time from the Soviet Union's delegate, and so listened most carefully to every word, trying to detect between the lines new tendencies in the foreign policy of one of the great powers. And, evidently, they did detect a difference; the speaker's vocabulary changed before their very eyes, the abusive sobriquets and coarse epithets gradually diminished and then completely vanished, and his vocabulary became more civilized and decorous.

It was here, in New York, among his family and closest colleagues, that Vyshinsky modestly celebrated his seventieth birthday. News came of yet another Order of Lenin. The sixth and last. Congratulatory telegrams poured in from Moscow – most of them official but also a few from individual well-wishers, mainly writers, such as Arkady Perventsev, Alexander Korneichuk and Leonid Sobolev. The writer Lieutenant General Alexei Ignatiev sent particularly warm and heart-felt greetings: 'It is not sufficient to admire you, one should be inspired by you.'

And quite a few really were inspired by him; many of his foreign colleagues, especially from the socialist countries, also sent their con-gratulations. It was expected that a small reception would be held at least for the select few whom he referred to as 'comrade' in his official duties to enable these 'comrades' to express their lofty feelings for the former Procurator in an informal atmosphere. But no reception was held.

Instead Vyshinsky gave a dinner party 'for his family and close friends' in the residence of the Soviet delegation to the UN in the New York suburb of Glen Cove. But was there really anyone in the world close to him besides his daughter and wife? Genuinely close in real human terms?

Kapitolina Isidorovna and Zinaida Andreyevna were beside him, which was the main thing, and he knew the true worth of the others perfectly well. The toastmaster at the birthday dinner table was Pro-fessor Amazasi Arutyunyan, later Ambassador to Canada, an Armen-ian from Baku, whom Vyshinsky had taken under his wing and patronized, receiving filial concern and loyalty in return. One of the few to have free access to his high-ranking patron, he adroitly dem-onstrated his readiness to carry out at all times any whim he might have.

'You know, dearly beloved Andrei Yanuarievich,' he began his introductory speech,

I am a straightforward man, and I always speak the truth boldly, no matter how much it might hurt. That is why I say with all the directness I am capable of: you are a great lawyer, Andrei Yanuarievich, a great diplomat, a great speaker. The whole world admires you. You captivate hearts. You yourself are able to understand the full power of your charm – when you speak you cannot help but experience tremendous, absolutely incomparable satisfaction.

'Yes,' interrupted Vyshinsky, who was used to speaking for hours himself, but disliked others doing so, and could never miss a chance to crack a caustic joke. 'You're right as always – when I finish a speech, I feel just like I'm having an orgasm.'

That's how he joked – after all, he was entitled to relax and have a good time among family and close friends at his birthday party. But I doubt he was in a mood for jokes. By a symbolic twist of fate his birthday coincided almost to the day with the trial of Beria and his cronies. The execution of the main henchman of the Stalin era with whom he was indissolubly linked must have made Vyshinsky ponder what the future inevitably held in store for him. He must have understood that Molotov, still in power, would be only too happy to demonstrate his long-standing 'love' for him and try and avoid taking the blame by heaping it all on his First Deputy. He must have understood that the other 'comrades-in-arms' – Malenkov, Kaganovich, Voroshilov and so on – also feverishly clinging to power, were cowards and that they would not lift a finger to support him. But under the circumstances what could he do? Nothing but put his trust in fortune again.

There were, however, substantial grounds to suppose that fortune would smile on him again. At the next elections to the Supreme Soviet he got back his deputy's mandate.

Fortune's scenario was truly brilliant: instead of representing the Saratov province, he was now the deputy for Latvia's capital. But this was quite appropriate: could the people of Riga have forgotten his good deeds fourteen years ago? The only annoying part was that he had very little time left to represent their interests in 'parliament'.

He still managed to enjoy all the blessings that life showers upon Fortune's favourites. A five-storey house on Park Avenue, the most luxurious district of New York, was purchased from a millionaire, and Vyshinsky, his family and his suite of colleagues, secretaries, chef and doctors all moved into its apartments. In 1954 Vyshinsky chose to return home for his summer vacation – not by plane but on the fashionable transatlantic liner, the ss *Queen Elizabeth*, accompanied by his wife and daughter. Reporters and photographers flew in from practically all the world's top newspapers and magazines to see him off in a blaze of flashlights: the rumour spread that he would not be returning to New York.

But it was only a rumour. In the autumn, when the General Assembly and UN committees resumed their work, Vyshinsky, suntanned and refreshed, took up his usual place at the head of the Soviet Union's delegation, as though nothing was amiss. Just as before, his wife and daughter were there with him in his New York apartment. With his constant smile and self-confident air he seemed to be saying to those who were hoping for or predicting something that he was back in favour again – as always.

The UN political committee was continuing its discussions on the international monitoring of the use of atomic power. At the centre of the debate was the issue concerning whether the International Atomic Energy Agency should be independent and autonomous or, as the Soviet Union argued, accountable to the UN and the Security Council. The reason for the amendment was perfectly clear: its acceptance would enable any of the great powers (and, thus, the Soviet Union) to use its right of veto whenever necessary. Vyshinsky defended this position convincingly and calmly, without resorting to his usual lexicon. The speech he made at the political committee on 17 November caused many delegates to waver in their support for the draft resolution put forward by the United States, Great Britain, France, Australia, Belgium, Canada and the South American Union. Vyshinsky's next speech was set for Monday, 22 November; in between times efforts had to be made to find a compromise and try and draw the sides together.

On Saturday, 20 November, the entire Soviet delegation set off for Glen Cove where Vyshinsky was to prepare his speech. On the Sunday morning a ciphered message suddenly arrived from Moscow with new instructions: the whole speech had to be reworked. And then suddenly the UN Secretary General, Dag Hammarskjöld, decided to hold a Sunday luncheon party for a Latin American foreign minister who was passing through New York. There could be no question of turning the invitation down, but this lost time made Vyshinsky tense; he was the first speaker the next day.

The Polish delegate, Stanislaw Krzeszewski, was among the guests at the luncheon, and Vyshinsky managed to warn him about the new instructions so that his speech the next day did not take him totally by surprise. Evidently, Krzeszewski was not exactly delighted by the news: according to eye-witnesses, they spent a long time heatedly wrangling with each other in Polish. Instead of going out to Glen Cove, Vyshinsky decided to stay on in his Park Avenue apartment, where he also had an office. He called for his shorthand secretary, Valentina Karaseva, dictated and corrected her shorthand copy and then dictated some more: he could work indefatigably, without sparing himself or, indeed, others.

During the night he felt unwell. The delegation's doctor on duty came and gave him a sedative and sleeping draught. After they had all gone away, Vyshinsky stayed in his office and went to sleep on the sofa. He woke up early in the morning, feeling better. Once again he was in a cheerful and buoyant mood – he just had to put the finishing touches to his reworked speech, and then he would be ready to mount the rostrum that very minute if needs be. He asked his cook, Ivan Illarionovich, to make him some extra strong coffee, and that made him feel even more refreshed. He started dictating to Karaseva again and then suddenly stopped short and whispered, 'I feel ill!'

Karaseva's hysterical cry for help roused the whole household. His personal doctor came rushing down from his apartment on the next floor, followed by all the other members of the small Soviet medical team. They found him sitting on his swivel chair, his shirt buttons undone and his head thrown back. When they carried him over to the sofa he kept wheezing but did not speak. His wife and daughter were urgently sent for. Hearing the news, Zinaida Andreyevna screamed: 'They've killed him!'

Panic broke out. All the means at the medical team's disposal had been used up. He was dying right before their eyes.

The telephone rang. A diplomat on duty picked up the receiver. It was the US permanent delegate to the UN, Henry Cabot Lodge. 'What's going on?' he asked immediately. 'Nothing, Mr Ambassador,' the diplomat on duty hurriedly replied. 'Are you sure?' Lodge retorted in an ironic tone. 'Maybe you need some medical aid?' 'No, thank you, Mr Ambassador.' 'All right . . . If you should, ring this number at once.' (Much later when the delegation's building was being decorated, some workmen would discover a bug in one of the legs of Vyshinsky's writing desk.)

The office was meanwhile filling up with people. Vyshinsky had stopped wheezing: he was dead. It had turned 9 a.m. In forty or fifty minutes' time he was due to make his speech: people were waiting for him. There could be no more stalling. An ambulance was called merely to certify the death. However, the guards, mindful of their instructions, refused to let the 'unauthorized persons' inside the delegation's grounds, even doctors. The wrangling continued. Time ticked on.

By walkie-talkie they managed to track down the Soviet Ambassador, who had already arrived for the speech and was waiting inside the UN building. Ambassador Zarubin then ordered the doctors to be let in. 'This is your personal responsibility,' the chief guard warned him gravely. A coded telegram was sent off to Moscow while a protocol was being composed. Vyshinsky's wife stood by, stony-faced, while his daughter sobbed bitterly. There were no other mourners.

Before his body was carried through into the conference hall for the farewell ceremony, an urgently organized commission was instructed to remove, collect together and seal all the papers, documents, drafts and even personal letters he had left. The safe was opened. The first articles to come into view were a small Browning (found to be loaded)[4] on top of a large red file.

The file contained only one document: a letter beginning, 'Dear and deeply respected Iosif Vissarionovich!' I have not managed to find the original or even a copy of this letter. For this reason I shall recount its contents from the words of the people who actually held it in their hands at the time, read it through several times and memorized it well.

What struck them most were the instructions written diagonally across the left corner. The handwriting was terribly familiar – facsimiles of it had appeared in the press umpteen times: 'For Comrade Vyshinsky. I.St. [Stalin's way of signing his name]'

The letter was from Dmitry Zakharovich Manuilsky, a well-known Comintern activist and member of its executive committee until its dissolution in 1943. As Foreign Minister of the Ukraine he had headed its delegation to the UN General Assembly for many years in succession, sitting next to Vyshinsky and making speeches, it goes without saying, in support of him. They were comrades in a common cause, in a common struggle.

What was Comrade Manuilsky writing to Comrade Stalin about? He was asking, begging, imploring him not to believe Comrade Vyshinsky under any circumstances. Under none whatsoever. I have not got long to live, Manuilsky wrote, but I do not want a secret, which you, of course, do not know, to go with me to the grave. Otherwise you might trust this deceitful man who would gladly betray you if the situation changed.

This, or roughly this, is what Stalin was told by one of the few Bolsheviks who had served in the Party since before the October Revolution, survived the brutal purges, remained in the upper echelons of power, and, what's more, had been able to prove his boundless loyalty on numerous occasions. At the tragic February-March Central Committee Plenum of 1937 it was he who had supported Yezhov's motion along with Budionny, Shvernik, Kosarev and Yakir to have Bukharin and Rykov put on trial and shot. At a sitting of the Comintern's executive committee in May 1937 it was he who had crushed Bela Kun 'for showing disrespect to great Stalin' and accused him of ties with the Rumanian Secret Police in 1919. Nobody had come to Bela Kun's defence. Palmiro Togliatti and Klement Gottwald, Otto Kuusinen and Wilhelm Pieck had sat there in silence, their heads bowed . . . 'I swear,' Bela Kun had shouted out, 'I did not want to insult Comrade Stalin. I want to explain everything to Comrade Stalin.'

Comrade Stalin telephoned the 'offender' himself but not to listen to his explanations. 'Rumours have been spread,' he said, 'of your arrest. The usual lies and slander of bourgeois propaganda! Would you refute these vile rumours to the foreign press.' Bela Kun, of course, did as he was asked. Then he was arrested. The operation had been accomplished.

Now Manuilsky was making a similar accusation against Vyshinsky. He wrote that the latter had been in contact with the Tsarist secret police and had betrayed several Baku Bolsheviks to them. He cited four or five names but, because they were not well-known, the people who read the letter did not commit them to memory.

The letter also contained something along the following lines: Vyshinsky is a man without principles; he is ready to serve any leader and any ideas as long as this gives him total security and a life of luxury. He is chronically afraid, and so hates everyone around him . . . Let us also not forget that in 1917–18 Manuilsky had been a board member of the People's Commissariat of Food and had worked alongside Vyshinsky. Most likely, therefore, he knew him better than many others.

There is no reason to doubt the authenticity of the eye-witnesses' evidence, or that they memorized this document well. It is not in the least surprising that Stalin with the sadism he had perfected to an art forwarded the denunciation to the person it was directed against, deriving pleasure from his confusion, and thus keeping both the informer and the possible victim on the hook. Without instructions

Vyshinsky could not let on that he even partly knew. And Manuilsky, waiting for the reply which never came, could not let on what he had written about him or whom to. Such was the dramatic conflict, such was the plot that was made even more intense by the fact that the two met nearly every day at meetings, sittings, conferences and receptions. Day after day, year after year.

The letter was dated 1947 or 1948. Maybe even 1949. That means it had been in the safe for somewhere between five and seven years. It is a well-known fact that at the end of the forties, Vyshinsky suddenly fell ill while holidaying at the spa resort of Karlovy Vary, but his illness had nothing to do with the one he had gone there to receive treatment for. Foreign journalists found out about his nervous stress, and sensational articles appeared in the press on the famous diplomat's mysterious ailment. In the end the news agency TASS was forced to print a denial. This was always regarded as circumstantial evidence proving that the denied rumours were even partially true. And they spread like wild fire when Vyshinsky suddenly broke off his course of treatment and went back to Moscow. But the reason he went back was to carefully go through some archive documents. What and who was he searching for? Wasn't it for the people whom Manuilsky had named in his letter? Wasn't it for the reasons for their arrest by the Tsarist secret police? Wasn't he trying to destroy the evidence that might establish his guilt? Stalin was almost bound to have known these people in Baku. So, what had become of them afterwards? Whatever way you look at it, it makes an intriguing puzzle. But then how many other puzzles, no less intriguing, has this age produced for us?

There was one other document in the safe besides the file and the Browning. Written in capitals in bright violet ink on thick writing paper. It was unsigned and what you would call a poison-pen letter:

Vyshinsky!
Everybody knows you're a Menshevik. Stalin, when he has done with you will bump you off because you know a lot. Beat it before it's too late. *Memento Moris*. Look at Yagoda....

Its contents are not particularly interesting. The only really interesting part of it is why and, what's more, where and how Vyshinsky kept it. And how long he had had it for.

More likely than not, the note was sent to Vyshinsky (or surreptitiously left for him) in America and not in the Soviet Union. Possibly, by one of the 'displaced persons'. The grammatical mistakes give its author away. Not his name, of course, but his 'social origin'. But the psychological riddle we are posed is why Vyshinsky kept it, knowing as he did that wherever he went, he was always under strict surveillance, and always had been and always would be, and that even the most sophisticated of safes would not prevent it from being examined.

Was it a case of habits dying hard, of the prosecutor in him dreaming of catching the culprit and uncovering yet another nest of terrorists and wreckers, and then handing them over to someone new but just as efficient as Yezhov? Or was he simply used to not throwing anything away – just in case? Or was he drawn to this 'text' like a magnet and, while subconsciously dreading the very thought of it, turning over and over in his mind the various ways in which his fate might be decided? He hardly wanted to end up the same way as Beria, but who could definitely say then, in 1953 or 1954, how quickly and how much the bands were going to be loosened?

All one can do is hazard a guess. But this document existed and had remained intact. And it became the property of a very small circle of people only after its original owners had ceased to be under any threat.

The official statement of the Central Committee and Soviet of Ministers announcing the 'eminent statesman's sudden death' appeared in all the central Soviet newspapers. According to the published obituary, he had been 'a loyal son of the Communist Party, self-effacing in his work, exceptionally modest and self-exacting.' And it ended with the words: 'Soviet people will keep the blessed memory of Andrei Yanuarievich Vyshinsky in their hearts forever.'

It was only part of a ritual, and there is no need to find fault in it. But what is interesting is that in the obituary (at the end of 1954) not a word was said about the role of the deceased in the struggle against enemies of the people and about his crushing speeches in court. Not a word.

In New York meanwhile the General Assembly gathered for a plenary sitting. A state of mourning was announced at the UN. The session's Chairman, Van Cleffens, announced the loss that the UN had suffered, and everyone present rose to their feet. Speeches in commemoration of Vyshinsky were made by the delegates of the United Kingdom, France, the USA, Iran, Greece, Poland, New Zealand, Pakistan, Finland, Thailand, Czechoslovakia, the South American Union, Burma, Canada, Egypt, Yugoslavia, Saudi Arabia, Indonesia, Liberia, Afghanistan, Yemen and Ethiopia.

'We are deeply saddened,' said India's delegate Menon, 'by the sudden death of Mr Vyshinsky, an outstanding representative of a great country ... The United Nations has lost one of the strongest participants of its debates, a man of high intellect, an outstanding statesman.' The Syrian delegate spoke of the 'treasure troves of vast knowledge' which the deceased's intellect had enjoyed. Iraq's delegate mourned 'a charming colleague – the epitome of originality, sportiveness and lofty parliamentary discipline.' A Turkish diplomat considered him 'a real gentlemen' while a Lebanese one hailed him as 'one of the greatest men the United Nations has ever seen or will indeed ever see within its walls.' Israel's delegate recalled his 'truly wonderful voice – smooth, resonant, full of deep concern for the tasks and procedure of our organization. This was not simply a man, not merely an individual,' declaimed the diplomat from Tel Aviv in the best traditions of magniloquent oratory, 'but an entire institution, he has become a legend in our midst.'

Speaking on behalf of the Scandinavian countries, the Danish delegate compared Vyshinsky's death to the fall of a mighty tree in a forest: 'The forest is in mourning – it has been orphaned.' Representing twenty countries of Latin America, Ecuador's delegate said, 'Mr Vyshinsky interpreted the legal and ideological significance of the Revolution.... As a speaker, there was none like him.... His death will stir us to forget our differences and unite.'

Condolences on the Deputy Foreign Minister's death were also received by the Soviet Embassy in Washington. The French Prime Minister and Foreign Minister Mendès-France, the UN Secretary General Hammarskjöld, the Chairman of the General Assembly's 9th Session Van Cleffens went there to pay their last respects. Paul Robeson lowered his head onto his massive hands, and sobbed by the black-framed portrait of Vyshinsky.

The coffin containing his mortal remains was flown to Moscow, escorted by Ambassador Zarubin, and farewell ceremonies were held at the airports of Paris and Berlin on the way. Late in the evening Molotov met his friend's body at Moscow's Vnukovo Airport. Gromyko was at his side.

The following day five doctors – none of whom had been 'involved' in the so-called 'Doctors' Trial' – published their report: Vyshinsky's death had been caused 'by a sharp interruption in the coronary circulation of the blood'. Delegations from enterprises and institutions, academic establishments and public organizations went to pay their last respects to Vyshinsky in Trade Union House's Hall of Columns, the scene of many an historic event. How many people were there in this mourning procession whose mutilated lives or those of their loved ones were linked with the name of this man? With this man whose death, after Stalin's and Beria's, had finally brought an era to a close.

His colleagues came to pay their last respects to the great orator: Molotov, Khrushchev, Malenkov, Kaganovich, Voroshilov, Mikoyan, Suslov, Bulganin, and Kosygin. And Marshal Zhukov, who had been forced to share the joy of victory with him at the table in Karlshorst. And Academicians and diplomats. The six Orders of Lenin lying on small satin cushions at the foot of the coffin, almost drowned in a sea of flowers, called to mind the good services Vyshinsky had rendered the country.

The following day Vyshinsky was buried by the Kremlin wall in Red Square. The entire Politburo gathered on the rostrum of Lenin's Mausoleum. Molotov was the first to speak. 'We who worked beside him,' he pronounced falteringly in a mournful voice 'have lost a close person, a discerning comrade, a dear friend.' Pharisaism continued to lead its solitary existence, and words were spoken which had no contact with reality. Party and state etiquette still dictated that a loathed enemy should be called a dear friend.

'His great abilities,' continued Molotov,

versatile knowledge, which he was continually adding to, and exceptional energy found their beneficial application in various spheres of Soviet construction.... His brilliant speeches in the defence of Soviet legality and speeches for the prosecution, which we all remember, against the enemies of the Soviet state, against wreckers and subversive foreign agents, against treacherous groups of Trotskyites and Rightists ... his great and unforgettable service to the Soviet people.... He is renowned as a discerning and high-principled comrade.... He has left behind many friends who will always remember him and his glorious deeds with love and respect.

Next to speak was the President of the Academy of Sciences, Nesmeyanov: 'Andrei Yanuarievich enjoyed great prestige among Soviet academics, they valued him ... as a man of integrity.'

An artillery salute was fired and a military unit marched by, stepping out. The life of a man who had left, whether one liked it or not, memories of himself and his deeds for all times was crowned with the highest honours the funeral rites in our country could provide.

The gold letters on the black marble slab – 'Andrei Yanuarievich Vyshinsky' – engraved his name on the Kremlin wall.

Since then nearly thirty-five years have gone by and more than one new generation has appeared. Over half the people living in the Soviet Union were born after Vyshinsky's death. For two thirds of the population, including those who were children at the time of his death, he is no more than an historical exhibit. That is why I did not expect my short profile on him in *Literaturnaya Gazieta* to cause much of a reaction. Especially after the shameful pages of our more recent history, which had just come to light and, indeed, continue to do so.

But it caused a storm. A squall. A tornado. Never in all my many years as a journalist had I received so many letters from readers. How this name and the actions connected with it had sunk into the minds of millions of people. With what volcanic wrath they wrote and what a gamut of feelings was reflected!

The profile ended with the following passage, which caused a particularly heated reaction:

> Recently a reader – an old Communist, war and labour veteran – sent me a letter suggesting a demand should be made for the criminal procurator's ashes to be removed from the Kremlin wall. In my opinion, this should not be done. Not only because it is generally better to leave ashes, no matter whose they are, well alone. The place in the wall, the titles, the awards, his speeches and actions – they are all landmarks of that era, an ineffaceable sign of their times, and it is there, in this time of his, that he should remain, just as he was.

Now this was something practically nobody wanted to agree with. I do not remember another occasion when readers disagreed with me with such astonishing unanimity. Emotion triumphed over reason. The tragedy of a whole people, the tragedy of millions indivisibly bound with the name of this monster, the natural and ineradicable need to settle scores with him in memory of all his victims, make a sober analysis of the arguments 'for' and 'against' impossible. While this unappeased wrath is seething, and the cries of guiltlessly executed victims are still coming from graves, the time is not right for debates.

I am still opposed to the pagan method of symbolically punishing the ashes. And I still think the terrible line of black slabs in the Kremlin wall where, just as in life and in history, henchmen are found alongside victims, and heroes alongside villains, says far more about that time in the past and about the nightmare that befell a great country and a great people.

But, of course, it is not a matter of choosing a place for the Inquisitor's ashes. It is a matter of learning – if only some day in the future – a lesson from our unfortunate history.

Is the saying 'History's only lesson is that one learns no lessons from it' really not a bitter joke but the sad truth?

Notes

Introduction

1. This 'friend' is still alive and well. He had a very hard time acquiring his doctorate and then quietly slipped into a job at some undistinguished institute. He did not get far in his career; my mother had apparently ruined his chances. No, it was more likely Vyshinsky who did that. He had done a good turn. The department my 'friend' had worked so diligently for dislikes deciphered agents. As the Russian saying goes 'Don't dig someone else's grave or you'll end up falling in it yourself.' Alas, it did not come true very often. This time it did.

2. Konstantin Petrovich Gorshenin, the fifth consecutive Procurator-General of the USSR. Two of his predecessors – Mikhail Pankratiev and Viktor Bochkov – like Gorshenin himself and Georgi Safonov who replaced him, were ignominiously consigned to oblivion. Like many other functionaries, Gorshenin also longed to become an academic. His official position facilitated this. A sinecure was found for him, and he was made a professor and department head of labour law at Moscow University. In this capacity he did not give a single lecture or seminar, finding colleagues to do them for him. Once or twice a year he would appear at meetings of the students' union. I once read a paper in his presence. After five minutes he started fidgeting and glancing at his watch, and ten minutes later hurried off on important business.

Chapter One

1. From 1901 onwards legal 'revolutionary' organizations intended for 'letting off steam' and transforming political demands into economic ones were put under police surveillance by the head of the Moscow secret police department, Sergei Zubatov. This type of 'police socialism' was referred to as 'Zubatov's socialism' after its initiator.

2. Grigory Ordzhonikidze, better known by his Party pseudonym of 'Sergo', was considered Stalin's friend before the Revolution, and later became one of his closest associates as a Politburo member and the People's Commissar of Heavy Industry. He was firmly against the escalation of the repressions. On the eve of the Central Committee plenum at which

Bukharin's and Rykov's fate was to be decided, he died under mysterious circumstances. He was either forced to commit suicide or was shot: the truth has yet to be established.

3. P. N. Malyantovich's life is a ready-made documentary drama with extraordinary twists and turns, so typical of this era of our history.

Lenin did not attach to Malyantovich's instructions on his arrest the same importance as historians and lawyers of the Stalinist school were to thrust upon future generations. He knew him not only as an outstanding political counsel for the defence and public figure, expelled at one time from the university and banned from residing in Moscow and the Moscow province by the Governor-General of Moscow; not only as the author of speeches, which had caused a sensation nationwide, against the Tsarist government's policies and in support of the workers and their rights; not only as the defending counsel of the renowned Bolshevik Vatslav Vorovsky and the celebrated Piotr Zalamov, who was to become the prototype of Pavel Vlasov, the hero of Maxim Gorky's novel *Mother*. But he knew him also as the lawyer who had appeared in the case in which the legacy of the millionaire Savva Morozov had been contested, and as the lawyer who had won one hundred thousand roubles for the Bolshevik Party. And as the man who had saved the well-known Bolshevik Virgily Shantser (Marat); after the latter's arrest Malyantovich had taken in two of his children.

On Lenin's suggestion the Petrograd Soviet decided to release Malyantovich immediately from the fortress. Subsequently, to avoid possible misunderstandings, the Commissar of Justice, Kursky, and the Commissar of Education, Lunacharsky, provided him with suitable mandates guaranteeing his immunity. Three years later, on Lenin's orders, Malyantovich was given a post on the Main Board of Political Education, and a year later Dzerzhinsky invited him to run the legal affairs of the Supreme Economic Council, of which he was in charge. In other words, neither Lenin nor his closest colleagues held him responsible for the order on Lenin's arrest.

However, 'the accursed thirties' came along and everything changed. On 1 November 1937 Malyantovich shared the same fate as millions: after being thrown into the Lubyanka, he was taken to the torture chamber of Lefortovo Prison and then to Butyrka Prison. He was to be denounced as the leader of a 'conspiracy' in the Moscow Indiana Collegium, of which he was then a member. Judging by their imposing signatures on the investigation's documents, it looked as though highest-ranking NKVD officials had a hand in Malyantovich's 'case': Lev Vlodzimirsky, Solomon Milshtein and Vsevolod Merkulov. Seriously ill and by then aged sixty-eight, the prisoner heroically withstood torture and pleaded not guilty. He was tortured for another two years, but all in vain. Here is an excerpt from the report on the interrogation proceedings of 14 January 1939:

Investigator Mironovich: 'Do you intend giving evidence today on your counter-revolutionary activity?'

Malyantovich: 'I intend saying today what I shall say tomorrow and the day after: that I was never engaged in counter-revolutionary activity, and never took part in, or led any counter-revolutionary organizations.'

Investigator: 'Your wiles, Malyantovich, will not help you.... Don't wait, Malyantovich, for further convictions.'

And so Malyantovich took his advice, believing that his former assistant, whom he had once helped out of grave trouble, and who had gone on to become the head of the country's legal profession, as he himself had once been, would not let this punishment be carried out. He wrote to Vyshinsky himself from prison, as did his blind and bedridden wife, Angelica Pavlovna Kranikhfeld-Malyantovich, whose hand twenty or so years before Vyshinsky had kissed as he thanked her for her delicious tea and cream buns, and who, as a well-known Moscow dentist, had looked after his teeth free of charge. And so, too, did his daughter Galli Pavlovna Malyantovich-Shelkovnikova.... On the orders of Procurator-General A. Ya. Vyshinsky these letters were left unanswered. For nearly a year Malyantovich was not called to an interrogation session and simply awaited his turn to stand trial before the Military Board of the Supreme Soviet. On 22 January 1940, after a fifteen-minute hearing of his case, Malyantovich was shot. So were his two sons, his brother and his brother's family.

Immediately after Stalin's death Malyantovich's daughter and sole survivor began campaigning for his posthumous rehabilitation. Vyshinsky showed no desire to help restore the good name of his rescuer and patron. Among the many who petitioned for the restoration of justice were the old Bolsheviks A. S. Kurskaya, V. P. Antonov-Saratovsky, P. I. Voevodin, Gorky's first wife, Yekaterina Pavlovna Peshkova, the writer Samuil Marshak, the well-known lawyer and correspondent member of the Academy of Sciences, Aron Trainin, and some of Moscow's most celebrated lawyers. It took five years to overcome the conservatism of the Procurator's office. His formal rehabilitation took place in 1959, but the name of this outstanding figure of Russian democracy is still taboo to this day.

4. The subsequent fates of Rykov and Kamenev are generally well known, but that of Khalatov far less so. This eminent statesman did not have any particular narrow speciality but like a loyal soldier went everywhere he was sent. He held prominent posts on the railway and in public catering; he headed the central commission on improving academics' working and living conditions, and the All-Union Society of Inventors. However, his main claim to fame was as the head of the association of

state publishing houses, where he became on close terms with Gorky and other outstanding writers.

On 27 June 1937 he was arrested. Two weeks later the same fate befell his wife. His mother, Yekaterina Gerasimovna, was immediately dismissed from work (she had headed the Lenin Library's book fund) and expelled from Moscow. As a young lad Vyshinsky had tucked into her delicious homemade doughnuts at the Khalatov's hospitable Baku home. But now he did not reply to her letters in which she, of course, did not say a word either about their times in Baku or how indebted the Procurator-General was to her son. Nor did he reply to the letters of Artiomy Khalatov's wife, Tatyana Pavlovna Khudyakova. Nor, for that matter, did Stalin, whom their daughter, Svetlana, wrote to from exile: 'I am writing to you as both everyone's friend and as a father. I am an excellent pupil, I am in the seventh year, I have four certificates of merit.... Save my Mummy and Daddy.' By that time her daddy had already been shot as a spy and terrorist, and as one of the closest associates of that 'enemy of the people', Rykov. After seventeen years of labour camps and exile, his mother and wife lived to see his posthumous rehabilitation, which was energetically petitioned for by Yekaterina Pavlovna Peshkova, Academician Krzhizhanovsky and the well-known producer and actor Nikolai Okhlopkov.

5. Incidentally, this biting aphorism could quite possibly be the source of a legal joke I once heard as a student. Investigator to prisoner: 'Witness "X" alleges you conducted anti-Soviet agitation!' 'He's lying!' objects the prisoner. 'That you were preparing a terrorist act against Comrade Stalin!' 'He's lying.' 'All right, on such and such a date were you with "X" at your mutual comrade's birthday party?' 'Yes, I was.' 'Did you have a drink?' 'Yes.' 'Did you eat a herring tail with it?' 'Yes, I did.' 'If the witness's evidence is correct about the herring's tail, why should he lie about all the rest? So let's write, "I confirm the evidence of Comrade 'X'."'

6. It is unlikely that Vyshinsky forgot this commendable report or the sneer with which the Tula executive committee's chairman greeted him. The People's Commissar of Health of the USSR and Central Committee candidate member Grigory Naumovich Kaminsky was arrested on 25 June 1937, four months after he had dared to speak out openly at a Central Committee plenum, albeit very cautiously, against the reprisals being prepared against Bukharin and Rykov. He was denounced as a wrecker, a terrorist and the leader of a counter-revolutionary group. A large gang of NKVD investigators worked on his 'frame-up' – Kogan, Vizel, Skurikhin, Matusov and Pateleyev. Grigory Roginsky, Procurator-General Vyshinsky's assistant and favourite, signed the indictment – most probably, with his superior's knowledge. A fifteen-minute trial was held under the chairmanship of the henchman, Ulrikh. On 10 February

1938 Kaminsky was executed – a month before Bukharin, whom he had tried to save.

7. In the past Ivan Mikhailovich Maisky (1884–1975) had been an eminent Menshevik, and a member of the Menshevik Party's Siberian, Samara and Saratov committees. Under Stalin he was Ambassador to Finland and Britain, and a Deputy People's Commissar of Foreign Affairs. He was also a prominent historian and member of the Academy of Sciences.

8. A Menshevik and a member of the Bund Central Committee ('The General Jewish Workers' Union'), David Iosefich Zaslavsky (1880–1965) studied at the law faculty of Kiev University at the same time as Vyshinsky. In 1917 he conducted a malicious campaign against Lenin, denouncing him in printed articles as a German spy. There were few whom Lenin attacked so vehemently as Zaslavsky, calling him a rogue, a notorious slanderer, a gossip and a scoundrel, and berating anyone who shook his hand. Later Zaslavsky became an official Soviet journalist, and *Pravda*'s chief satirical writer, gaining the unlimited right to tear honest people to shreds. Hundreds of politicians and a great many people from the arts and sciences, who, unlike Zaslavsky, had faithfully served the Bolshevik cause all their lives, fell victim to his malicious satire. This turncoat's name and venomous pen struck terror into people's hearts. I myself saw two sentences imposed: in the first, someone got ten years for calling Zaslavsky a filthy person in the company of friends; in the second, someone who had shown his colleagues Lenin's articles on Zaslavsky was given eight years. Vyshinsky appealed against this second sentence on the grounds that it was 'too lenient', and had the judge dismissed: 'Comrade Zaslavsky embodies all that the Party stands for, his defamation is a vile enemy attack against the Soviet Union.' He was, I believe, quite the most ruthless and murderous bastard in the world of journalism in those days.

Chapter Two

1. At the end of the twenties Krylenko was to leave Yelena Fedorovna Rozmirovich for another woman, and this, most likely, saved her life. She survived the insanity of the arrests, torture and executions in her post as director of the Lenin Library, retired very quickly and died in total obscurity in the same year as the People's Father. Her first husband, Alexander Troyanovsky, a Menshevik who only went over to the Bolsheviks in 1923, also avoided the Terror. He was later ambassador to Japan and the US. He died in 1955. At the party trial in Poronin he had supported Yelena Rozmirovich, also convinced that Malinovsky was a police agent.

2. The judicial board which sentenced Malinovsky to death consisted of Otto Karklin, the prominent Latvian Communist who was shot in 1937;

Mikhail Tomsky, the old Bolshevik, long-standing Central Committee and Politburo member, and close associate of Bukharin and Rykov, who had been in charge of the trade unions for many years; viciously persecuted and facing inescapable arrest at any moment, he committed suicide on 22 August 1936; and Ivan Zhukov, the worker, old Bolshevik and People's Commissar of Local Industry of the RSFSR, who was charged in connection with Bukharin, Rykov and Tomsky, arrested in 1937 and executed in 1938.

3. Pomgol – the abbreviated title of the Commission in Aid of Famine Victims in the RSFSR, Ukraine, Byelorussia and the Trans-Caucasian Federation which operated in 1921–2. While helping many thousands of families to survive, it also became a refuge for speculators and marauders, who lined their pockets at the expense of others.

4. From the beginning of the Revolution leather jackets had been a sign of a person's association with the commissars' corps: they were usually worn by representatives of the new authorities – from people's commissars to local managers. Some of the latter were immediately corrupted by the power and wealth concentrated in their hands.

5. Aron Solts was not the chairman, as the author of the memoirs asserts, but a member of the Central Control Commission, the Party's highest court. Alexander Galkin, one of the most prominent lawyers of the twenties and thirties, was then working as the chairman of the Board of Appeal of the Supreme Court of the RSFSR. He was shot in 1937. Boris Berman gained fame as one of the chief investigators in the Zinoviev-Kamenev case. He held high posts in the NKVD Foreign Department, and raged around Byelorussia. He was awarded the Order of Lenin for his special services, and in 1937, along with many other executioners, was even given the honour of becoming a deputy of the Supreme Soviet of the USSR for the Polotsk electoral district in Byelorussia. He was then recalled to the central apparatus. After Lavrentii Beria's arrival at the NKVD he was thrown into the Lubyanka's prison cellars and executed in 1939.

6. Vera Zasulich was an activist in the Russian revolutionary movement, and a Narodnik (populists who set up discussion circles for workers and peasants in the 1870s in an attempt to make a better society). In 1878 she tried to assassinate the Governor of St Petersburg, Trepov, and was brought to trial and then acquitted, thanks mainly to the great Russian lawyer Anatoly Kon, who presided over the trial. In 1903 she joined the Menshevik Party and was highly critical of the October Revolution. She died in 1919.

7. Mendel Beilis, a simple Jewish worker at a Kiev brick factory, was brought to trial in 1913, charged with the ritual murder of a Russian boy. Despite the tremendous pressure of reactionary political and religious circles and the incredible efforts of members of the 'Black Hundred', he was still found not guilty.

329

8. There is very convincing corroboration – from a psychological rather than a legal viewpoint, of course – of the story about Stalin taking revenge for the medical diagnosis, and one containing a fact which had been totally authenticated. A quarter of a century later, Stalin's personal doctor, Academician V. N. Vinogradov (an 'expert' at Bukharin's trial, who signed the indictment against his comrades and colleagues), pre-scribed 'complete rest and a total break from any work' for his patient, who had a stroke and was suffering from nervous exhaustion. Stalin, seeing in this an attempt to overthrow him with the help of medicine, started yelling furiously: 'Put him in irons, put him in irons!' After being put in irons and suffering even worse ordeals (on Stalin's instructions he was beaten as well), Vinogradov survived the tyrant's death, and was released and rehabilitated.

9. Bekhterev's grand-daughter, Natalya, who was three at the time of his death, was to follow in his footsteps and become an outstanding physiologist, Academician, important public figure. She is presently a People's Deputy of the USSR.

10. To illustrate my point I shall quote two anecdotes relating to the same period. In his memoirs, the great Russian actor Mikhail Chekhov, then head of the second Moscow Art Theatre, wrote:

> I visited ... Procurator Krylenko. The fate of the man for whom I was then petitioning was entirely in his hands. The door opened, and there appeared a small, stocky man with a shaven head and round, artificial-looking white eyes. 'What do you want?' he bellowed in a hysterical rage, still standing in the doorway of his office, his right hand clutching and tugging at his left. He leapt towards me and, deafening me with shouts, started pounding the air around my shoulders with his fists; he was craning his neck as though he was going to butt me and then dive through the door, and the whites of his empty eyes were rolling wildly. Without discovering the reason for my visit, he roared, 'No!' and, tugging at his left hand again, rushed at another petitioner. Before I had time to come to my senses and leave, I noticed that Krylenko had suddenly stopped shouting and was now whispering. The pale petitioner, also stammering in a whisper, was trying to explain something to him. I left before I could see how the insane procurator behaved with his third and fourth visitors.

The second excerpt is from the notes I made in 1969 during a con-versation with the lawyer Lidya Izrailevna Rozenblum. She looked much younger than her age, despite the persecution she had undergone, and had an astounding memory. The only woman counsel for the defence at the Shakhty Trial, she made a speech which many people were to remem-ber – and to which Krylenko, according to Mikhail Koltsov, responded with the remark: 'It would have been better if you had been a prosecutor.'

This is what Lydia Rozenblum told me about Vyshinsky:

> I remember my two visits to him well. The first was directly to do with
> the Shakhty Trial. I needed to look at some volume about the case, and
> in the recess I went into the room next door, which had been turned
> into the judges' lounge and meeting place. Such things weren't encour-
> aged, but there was nothing else I could do. I expected to be shouted
> at but he greeted me in a very cordial manner and invited me to sit
> down. There were tea and biscuits on the table, and he refused to let
> me leave until I had had at least one biscuit and a cup of tea. He
> inquired whether the counsels for the defence had been provided with
> adequate working conditions. He asked if they had any complaints
> about the trial. 'I'm not pressurizing you, am I?' he asked and roared
> with laughter. I was amazed how courteous he was. Before I left he
> stood up and kissed my hand. The second time I had occasion to meet
> him was in my capacity as a lawyer for Zhurgaz [the Journal and
> Newspaper Association] when, a short time later, he had again been
> transferred to the Procurator's office. His secretary had warned me
> that he was in a great hurry, but he talked in a leisurely manner,
> listening attentively and responding to all my requests, and was
> extremely polite. Once again – and this has remained very firmly in
> my memory – he escorted me to the door and kissed my hand. I can't
> forget the scent of the expensive eau de Cologne he was wearing, it
> was really good and, believe you me, I know what I'm talking about
> when it comes to perfumes.

11. At a plenum of the Central Council of Academic Workers the well-known
Marxist historian and Bolshevik Party member since 1905, Academician
Mikhail Nikolayevich Pokrovsky, criticized short business trips abroad
thus: 'It is not knowledge that they bring back from trips like these but
new suits, and they come back dazzled not by their industrial experience
but by the bright shop windows.' He suggested organizing trips for
'genuinely serious people' for one and a half to two years so that they
could 'enrich themselves with ideas and work skills'. Vyshinsky, who
had never been abroad himself and well knew how Stalin regarded such
trips, defined Pokrovsky's suggestion as 'nostalgia for all things foreign'.

12. Andrei Sergeyevich Bubnov joined the Bolshevik Party in 1903. In
October 1917 he became a Politburo member of the Central Committee
and of the Petrograd Military Revolutionary Committee, along with
Stalin, Sverdlov and Dzerzhinsky. A longstanding Central Committee
member, he was also the People's Commissar of Education of the RSFSR
until his arrest. The 'indictment' was approved by Vyshinsky, and he
was shot in 1940.

13. Several years later, at the 17th Party Congress (February 1934), Krupskaya was to join in the rapturous praise of the great leader who had

once loutishly insulted her and provoked Lenin into writing the last letter of his life – in his wife's defence. 'Everyone knows,' she exclaimed, 'what a massive role in this victory [over the 'Leftists' and 'Rightists'] has been played by Comrade Stalin [at this point the delegates began applauding wildly], and it is for this reason that the feelings experienced by the Congress have come pouring out in the form of such ardent greetings, in the strong applause which the Congress has given Comrade Stalin.' She also bitterly attacked not only the so-called 'New Opposition', of which she herself was a member, but all the others and all her comrades and friends.

In August 1938, towards the end of his short and stormy career, Yezhov went to a sitting of the Party Control Committee, of which she was still a member, with the express purpose of destroying her. Without mincing his words, he declared that she was Trotsky's accomplice, and this, he claimed, had hastened Lenin's death. He then added that 'it was only respect for the memory of Lenin that prevented [him] from turning her over to Vyshinsky and Ulrikh, as he had other traitors.' Krupskaya fainted, and she was immediately sent off 'to be treated' at a NKVD sanatorium near Moscow. She died (naturally, or with someone's help?) on her seventieth birthday, on 26 February 1939.

Chapter Three

1. M. N. Ryutin was born into a Siberian peasant's family in 1890. He studied at a teachers' seminary, and then worked in a village school. In 1914 he joined the Bolshevik Party, and in 1917 was made chairman of the Soviet of Workers' and Soldiers' Deputies in Harbin, and then commander-in-chief of the troops of the Irkutsk Military District. Later he became the secretary of the Irkutsk and then Dagestan regional committees of the Party, and of the Krasnopresnya district committee in Moscow. He was elected to the Central Committee and was a delegate at four Party congresses and several all-union conferences. After being dismissed from Party work, he became a vice-editor of the newspaper *Krasnaya Presnya*, a member of the Supreme Economic Council, and the chairman of the Film Industry Board. For the last eighteen months before his arrest he worked as an economist in the Soyuzelectro Trust.

2. Ryutin's 'Manifesto' should not be confused with his 'Platform', which is widely known from historical literature. The 'Platform' (dating from the late twenties) was an alternative programme for building socialism in the USSR, and the two hundred or so pages of its text were quite widely discussed. The fourteen-page 'Manifesto' (published for the first time in the journal *Yunost*, November 1988) is essentially a proclamation calling for the overthrow of Stalin and his clique (1932).

3. As the deputy head of the secret political department of the Main Direc-

torate of State Security of the NKVD of the USSR under Molchanov, Genrikh Samoilovich Lyushkov helped him, along with Boris Berman and others, to prepare the Zinoviev-Kamenev trial. He was a 'Yagoda man', and his chief's fall from grace could have cost him his life. However, his friendship with Yezhov saved him for a while. Lyushkov was sent to the Soviet Far East as the head of the regional department of the NKVD. He was personally responsible for tens of thousands of deaths. As the 'best and most deserving' operative he represented the Kolyma area in the Supreme Soviet of the USSR. But not for long. Two high-ranking cut-throats – Lev Mekhlis and Mikhail Frinovsky – arrived in the Far East to 'establish order' among the local NKVD operatives. Deciding not to tempt fate any longer, and making use of the fact that he also officially commanded the local border troops, Lyushkov slipped across the Manchurian border on 13 June 1938 and began feverishly giving the Japanese all kinds of secret intelligence. And he knew a lot. He was interned and put in Harbin prison where he safely survived until August 1945. When the Soviet army began to attack Harbin, he was shot by the Japanese.

4. All the original investigation and court materials comprising the 'Ryutin Case' have remained intact. They include the record of the proceedings of the preliminary hearing by the Military Board of the Supreme Soviet of the USSR on 9 January 1937, 'in which Procurator-General of the USSR Comrade Vyshinsky participated'. The judges, after referring to 'Comrade Vyshinsky' three times, announced that they totally agreed with the indictment, which covered three-quarters of a sheet of typed paper and had Vyshinsky's signature scrawled across it in red pencil, and that they were ready to pass judgement on Ryutin without the participation of a prosecution and defence and without calling witnesses.

The trial took place next day. The record of the proceedings covers only six lines of one page and the sentence less than a page, with wide gaps and margins.

The 'court' examined the case the following day, on 10 January. The hearing began at 11.35 and ended at 12.15: in other words, it took forty minutes – a long time in those days. According to the records of the proceedings, 'The accused declared that he did not wish to reply to the question of whether he pleaded guilty and in general refused to give any evidence on the charges brought against him.... The accused was given his final word in which he said nothing.' The sentence was obvious. A few minutes later Martemyan Ryutin was dead.

'Immediately after my grandfather was killed,' Ryutin's grand-daughter, Yulia Zakharovna Zhukovskaya, wrote to me,

his sons Vasily, an engineer of the Tupolev Construction Bureau, and Vissarion, also an aircraft engineer, were killed, the wife of one of the sons went mad, and my grandmother was arrested. Back in 1932, after Grandfather's first arrest, Mother (who was then twenty) went to Vyshinsky. He knew her and had visited her home and eaten Siberian meat dumplings there. He used to call her "Lyubochka" but now without even looking up, he simply said, "There is nothing I can do to help you." We were thrown out onto the street without any of our things.

Ryutin's act of martyrdom shows that even during the most desperate times there were still people who stuck to their principles, people for whom these principles did not become small change in the struggle for survival – or, especially, in their struggle for promotion. It also shows that not everyone in those days was blind, or subject to optical illusions, or so confused that they lost all ability to reason.

5. This Council, the 'Rada', was a parliament organized by the Ukrainian nationalist Simon Petliura in part of the Ukrainian territory which periodically came under his control in 1917–20.
6. According to the historian Robert Conquest, in his book *The Great Terror*, all trace of Sukhanov was lost after 1934. Information on him, however, may be gathered from his case dossier. He spent five years in prison. On 20 March 1935 the Presidium of the Central Executive Committee of the USSR commuted the remainder of his sentence to exile in the Siberian town of Tobolsk, where he worked as an economist for a regional fishery enterprise ('Obrybtrest'), and then as a German language teacher in a Tartar school. On 19 September 1937, on the orders of the Tobolsk prosecutor, Rapoport, he was rearrested – most probably as part of the programme to liquidate 'socially dangerous elements' – and charged with having 'contacts with German spies', and also with anti-Soviet agitation after serving his time in exile. He spent a year in Tobolsk Prison and was then transported to Omsk, where the local henchman Saenko subjected him to his own special brand of torture.

In a letter to A. I. Mikoyan on 10 September 1939 – in other words, after he had been sentenced to death by the Tribunal of the Siberian Military District – he described what he had been subjected to:

> It was suggested to me that I set forth my 'crimes' against the Soviet authorities myself – in other words, invent them. My investigators backed up their demand with a whole arsenal of coercive measures, gradually set into motion and slowly increased. . . . A major role in my behaviour was played by the threats to put my wife, a sick old woman, in a similar position to myself. I knew from a precedent that these were by no means empty threats. I had to save my wife from such a fate at any price. I gave way to the demands of the Omsk authorities. . . . The statement of 19 November 1938, which I signed, is the price I paid for . . . saving my wife. However, this price did not seem excessively high, or my compromise excessively great. For through my inves-

334

tigators' incompetence the statement was full of incongruities, and absurd both in general and in detail. No well-informed reader could regard it as plausible or based on what I had said during the normal conditions of an investigation.

Further on in his letter to Mikoyan (it is hard to say why he particularly chose him to write to) he says:

> And there is always every possibility of organizing a purely political act, but not in such a crude and primitive manner; and in such an instance the case should have been put in more capable hands, especially as it had to do with people of some historical repute. Finally, as far as I am concerned, it is impossible to understand what political purpose my execution could serve ... Doubtless, this is being correctly evaluated by the government's leadership.

Sukhanov and the 'government's leadership' were, however, at odds as far as the 'political purpose' of his execution was concerned. On 21 June 1940 the Presidium of the Supreme Soviet of the USSR confirmed the correctness of the sentence, and Sukhanov was executed. All attempts by his wife and son to have Sukhanov rehabilitated during the Khrushchev thaw failed. The Central State Special Archive of the Ministry of Internal Affairs of the USSR (now the KGB archive) reported that 'according to information of the French police, in April 1929 Sukhanov ... was being kept by the Bulgarian ambassador to Berlin', that his acquaintance, Hilger, 'as a counsellor of the German Embassy in Moscow, was in charge of a special department there, and another acquaintance, Scheiffer, the Moscow correspondent of the *Berliner Tageblatt* newspaper, served in the Intelligence Service and was a personal agent of Lloyd George.' This 'testimonial' was enough to confirm that the two sentences in the Sukhanov case were well-grounded. He has still to be rehabilitated.

7. Sheinin instantly made an impression on Vyshinsky, who could not stand dimwits, by being quick on the uptake and energetically carrying out the task at hand. He was also totally loyal, as Vyshinsky rightly sensed. He was to take part in the investigation of all the cases brought to a public trial. What's more, in his speeches Vyshinsky found a way of mentioning in passing Sheinin's participation in the preliminary interrogations – although a great many NKVD operatives worked on the so-called investigation, they all remained anonymous. For his part, the popular writer and official of the Procurator's office gave the investigation cogency and respectability.

Sheinin remained totally loyal to Vyshinsky to the very end, carrying out his most intricate instructions even after he had left his post as Procurator-General. But when Sheinin underwent the same fate as his numerous victims, Vyshinsky did not lift a finger to help him.

Sheinin's downfall began in 1948. After being given the responsible task of 'investigating' the case of the death of the producer and actor Solomon Mikhoels, he took the mission seriously and quickly uncovered the threads which led to the real assassins – whereas he had been given to understand in fairly transparent terms that Mikhoels had been the subject of revenge by Zionists for his 'loyalty to internationalism'. Had this version won the day, Mikhoels would have been canonized and the nationalists would have been destroyed in his name. Sheinin was removed from the investigation – something that had never happened before. In 1950 he was awarded the Stalin Prize as one of the authors of the screenplay of the deceitful, time-serving film *The Meeting on the Elbe*, and then immediately dismissed from the Procurator's office. He was without work for a whole year, not daring to appeal to his kind genius for help. However, he got some work in the end: on 19 October, as he was returning to Moscow by train from Sochi, two men in civilian clothes stepped into his carriage and suggested he get out of the train and travel the rest of the way by car. He was accused of being connected with a nationalist terrorist group, and the warrant for his arrest was signed by the Minister of State Security, Ignatiev, and the Procurator-General of the USSR, Safonov. Well-acquainted with the Lubyanka's secrets, Sheinin manoeuvred, denouncing in the process many well-known writers and figures in the arts. Attempts were made to involve him in the massive case of the European Anti-Fascist Committee, and later in the Doctors' Plot. These attempts would most probably have proved successful had Stalin not died. Sheinin was kept in prison for another eight months and finally released in November 1953. He did not work in the legal profession again and died fourteen years later without sharing his recollections of events which only he knew about and only he could retell, and in this way at least make a clean breast of them. He respected Vyshinsky to the end. After being released from prison, on Vyshinsky's seventieth birthday he sent a congratulatory telegram to him in New York, full of love and admiration. He also let him know that he was at liberty and that he was still just as devoted as ever to the mentor who had turned his back on him. Vyshinsky did not reply.

8. The son of a Latvian revolutionary, Ulrikh was the chairman of the Military Board for over twenty years in succession, and a delegate of the Supreme Soviet of the USSR. He was awarded numerous orders, and on lists at official gatherings his name always came directly after the Central Committee secretaries and deputies of the Council of People's Commissars. A thick-set man with a clean-shaven head, inflamed pink eyes, a square moustache and a huge fleshy nose, he inspired revulsion and fear in everyone with whom he came into contact. In 1948 he was suddenly dismissed and appointed to the insignificant post of course manager at the Military Academy of Law. He was by then a colonel-general, while

his superior at the academy was only a colonel. He never had an apartment of his own, and lived in a fairly modest room at the Metropole Hotel, where towards the end of his life he used to take representatives of the oldest profession, trembling with fear; after getting drunk, he used to regale them with stories about the executions he had attended. (So great was his love of the art that he sometimes carried out the death sentences himself.) He died of a heart attack in his new office in 1951, and was buried without honours at the historic Novodevichii Cemetery.

9. I got to know Ilya Davidovich Braude well during the last year and a half of his life when I served my apprenticeship as a barrister in his practice. He spoke to me on numerous occasions about the *Notes* he was working on, and, plucking up courage, I once asked him if he was going to describe the Pyatakov or Bukharin cases. 'I have not lost possession of my faculties yet, my dear man,' he replied and then added, 'Nobody ever forgives someone who knows a lot.' Only once, when we were returning late one evening from a trial he had successfully conducted, did he suddenly give vent to his feelings and tell me about an incident which I shall recount slightly later on.

10. Let us note that this law (Decree of the Central Executive Committee of the USSR 'On the Procedure of Conducting Cases on the Preparation or Perpetration of Terrorist Acts') was only published in *Izvestia* on 5 December. Thus, it is difficult to state with absolute certainty exactly when the great Leader dictated his text, and Kalinin and Yenukidze countersigned it.

Chapter Four

1. In a letter to me a doctor of the Leningrad Ambulance Service, Mikhail Borisovich Goloshchekin, described how in the fifties he had met Vulfson's widow, Doctor Gita Feldman, in Moscow's Botkin Hospital, where she was working at the time. Although Vyshinsky had lavished praise on this 'delicate but heroic woman', she was none too flattering about him. During conversations with her before and after the trial, she said that he had been rude and insulting. This once again corroborates the speculative element of the trial. The Procurator was not in the least concerned about the fate of a particular individual: he needed to carry out a psychological assault on the population by creating the 'image' of an incorruptible guardian of lawfulness for himself just before the first of the three 'trials of the century'.

2. Birobidzhan is the 'capital' of the so-called 'Jewish Autonomous Region' which was created by Stalin in the Soviet Far East by the Manchurian border. Subsequently it was intended to send all the Jewish population of the European part of the USSR to this dreadful region.

3. Lazar Kaganovich, one of Stalin's closest associates, who was noted not

337

only for his exceptional illiteracy but also for his equally exceptional brutality, is still alive today. At the time this book went to print, he was going on ninety-six. Long since retired, he continues to remain proudly silent.

4. But how can one determine which of the defendants was more willing? In the naïve hope of saving himself from arrest Pyatakov had written to Stalin asking, in return for his life and freedom, to be allowed to shoot all those condemned to death, including his ex-wife. Even Yezhov 'pointed out the absurdity of the suggestion to him' (the quotation is from one of Yezhov's short reports to Stalin). After this was there anything Pyatakov could deny Vyshinsky as they made preparations together for the imminent judicial farce?

5. In some recent accounts this telegram's contents and meaning have been misinterpreted. 'Stalin did not forgive Bukharin for the telegram,' asserts one author. He 'did not forgive' him for 'asking for the sentence not to be executed'. Bukharin was not, however, coming to the convicted men's defence: he was merely afraid that Zinoviev and Kamenev would be hastily executed, and their testimony against him would be left as irrefutable evidence. He had nothing against the sentence itself.

6. Mikhail Petrovich Tomsky joined the Bolshevik Party in 1904 and was a delegate to the London Party Congress. He took part in the February and October revolutions. For many years he was a Central Committee and Politburo member, and in charge of the Soviet trade unions. From 1932 until the day of his death he ran the State Publishing House. After the Revolution he became a member of the Revolutionary Tribunal at the All-Russian Central Executive Committee, and he participated, in particular, in the case of the Left SRs who had been involved in the assassination of the German Ambassador Mirbach and had organized an uprising. The tribunal passed extremely mild, almost symbolic sentences, and, what's more, not even these were served: the All-Russian Central Executive Committee saw fit to amnesty the convicted prisoners.

7. Grigory Yakovlevich Sokolnikov joined the Bolsheviks in 1905, and took an active part in the October Revolution. After living as an émigré with Lenin, he returned to Petrograd from Switzerland with him in April 1917. He worked closely with Stalin editing *Pravda*. He was the People's Commissar of Finances, the Soviet Ambassador to London and a Deputy People's Commissar of Foreign Affairs.

8. In a recorded telephone conversation Vyshinsky's daughter, Zinaida Andreyevna, insisted that it was the NKVD who had forced her father to take over the Serebryakovs' *dacha*. After all, there was nothing to stop this all-powerful department from handing out palaces as easily as it did death penalties, depending on how it saw fit! Let us only note that, unlike those who received death penalties, Vyshinsky did not object much to his 'punishment' and in fact, if the truth be known, did his best to make

338

himself as comfortable as possible in his palace. Just like everything else in his life, he managed very successfully.

9. These are sad, cynical lies for the benefit of Vyshinsky and all the other organizers of the trial: the defence had read no 'materials on the case' and could not have 'leafed through' documents because there were none. S. K. Kaznacheyev, who was even less inclined than Braude to recall this dark chapter, remarked only once in conversation with me that the lawyers prepared for the trials (for this one and the one after) 'in keeping with the text of the indictment'. This may be corroborated by the fact that in the speeches of all three lawyers there is not a single concrete reference to any case materials.

10. Ten of the twenty who signed the main obituary mourning the 'sudden' death of 'dear Sergo' were later to be liquidated. A similar fate was to befall Doctor Lev Levin, who signed the false medical report on the causes of Ordzhonikidze's death: less than a year later he would be sitting in the dock next to Bukharin as the 'assassin' of Gorky, Gorky's son Maxim, the OGPU Chairman Nenzhinsky and Politburo member Kuibyshev.

11. Among the award-winners was a senior inspector of the Military Board, Alexander Batner, who was to be the court secretary at the Bukharin trial. After the war he would be implicated in criminal official abuses of a by no means disinterested nature, and would be dismissed from the Supreme Court and brought to trial. After his release from prison he would take to drink and become a troublemaker and public menace. When he got drunk he would start swearing and kicking up a fuss, attacking his family and neighbours and yelling that he would 'liquidate' them all as he already had hundreds of enemies of the people.

12. The life of Lev Matveyevich Subotsky (1900–1959) is also the stuff novels are made of. From an early age he was a hard-working tribunal official, pronouncing death sentences by the dozen. In his spare time he taught himself to operate several pieces of factory machinery simultaneously. His second career, which he pursued quite separately, was as a literary critic. His two careers possibly coincided in an entirely different official department which was to shape the rest of his life. In January 1931 he became the Chief Military Procurator's assistant, and in 1934, while still in the same post, he became one of the founders of the Soviet Writers' Union and received Membership Card No. 72. In the morning he would conduct interrogations at the Military Procurator's office, and in the afternoon he would edit the journals *Krasnaya Nov* and *Novy Mir*. Or, perhaps, it was the other way round. From 1935 to 1937, again without leaving his post at the Military Procurator's office, Colonel of the Justice Subotsky was editor-in-chief of the weekly literary newspaper *Literaturnaya Gazieta*. It took Subotsky a whole day to interrogate Tukhachevsky and his comrades, and so the newspaper was without its editor-in-chief for at least twenty-four hours.

After the military commanders had been executed, he remained at liberty (and in his official posts) for another three months. He was then arrested and spent the next three years under investigation. His former subordinates and pupils applied the same 'persuasive methods' to him that he himself had used. His appeals to Vyshinsky were to no avail. We do not know what drama was enacted behind the securely locked dungeon doors, but in 1940 he was suddenly released, and the case against him dropped. He did not go back to the Procurator's office, but for two years was a secretary of the Writers' Union of the USSR, finally relinquishing the post to Anatoly Safronov. When the campaign began against 'stateless cosmopolitans', Subotsky again found himself in the role of victim, not henchman. He was not put behind bars again, but was given a severe Party reprimand 'for harbouring ideologically alien views'. In his numerous autobiographical notes he did not write a single word about his part in the Tukhachevsky case.

13. This revenge for refusing to take part in the show which the henchmen had prepared was, unfortunately, quite real and not fabricated. This is precisely what the best pupils of Vyshinsky, Yezhov and Beria did later to the prominent Bulgarian revolutionary Traicho Kostov, for refusing to slander himself in a public trial in Sofia and for denying the testimony which had been beaten out of him. Unlike Krestinsky, he stood firm to the very end. In this way he saved the lives of his co-defendants. As an example to future victims he was condemned to death while the others, who had not broken the rules, received prison sentences. They lived to see the tyrant's death and were released. But Traicho Kostov was not merely executed, he was killed in such a sadistic and painstaking manner that I cannot bring myself to go into the details. Before he died he was still forced (they could break anyone) to write a letter in which he slandered himself in a quite unthinkable manner – the text of this 'act of penitence' was published in the press.

14. Boris Kamkov and the other witnesses in this case, Valerian Osinsky and Vladimir Karelin, were killed immediately after the trial ended, and Vasily Mantsev, a year later. Varvara Yakovleva died in a labour camp during the war. The most prominent of the Left SRs, Maria Spiridonova, was not even summoned to the court because they knew full well that neither torture nor threats would make her comply with the 'Citizen Prosecutor'.

15. Vladimir Ivanov joined the Bolsheviks in 1915, and fought in Moscow during the October Revolution. He was a secretary of the Yaroslavl Provincial Committee and the Northern Caucasian Regional Committee, and the First Secretary of the Central Committee of Uzbekistan. At the 17th Party Congress he was elected to the Central Committee. Just before his arrest he was appointed the People's Commissar of the Timber Industry of the USSR.

16. Rakovsky's life was spared and he was sentenced to twenty-three years

of imprisonment. He was then sixty-five. He served his sentence in the notorious Orel Central Prison, which was just the same twenty years after the overthrow of Tsarism as it had been under the Tsars. Even the nature of its prisoners' crimes had not changed; they were still convinced enemies of autocracy. It was from there that Rakovsky was to write letters to Stalin, Molotov, Kalinin and Vyshinsky, demanding that the trumped-up charges against him be withdrawn.

In 1956 Aronson, an investigator in the Krylenko 'case' and many others, was questioned. Along with many hundreds of his colleagues he had later become a victim and been sent to Oriol Prison, where he met and often talked to Rakovsky. According to Aronson, in May 1941 Rakovsky said to him:

> I have decided to change my tactics. So far I have only asked for mercy and not written about the case itself. Now I am going to write a statement requesting a review of my case and revealing all the secrets of Soviet investigation. So that at least the people who handle all the statements such as mine will learn how cases and trials are trumped up in our country for reasons of political revenge. I may be about to die, I may be a corpse, but remember ... some time or other even the corpses will start speaking.

War broke out and Rakovsky never managed to carry out his intention. On 8 September Beria signed a list bearing the names of 154 prisoners who were to be annihilated. A death sentence of the Military Board of the Supreme Court of the USSR was drawn up for each of them *in absentia* for 'counter-revolutionary agitation' in prison. They were accused of convincing one another of the triumph of Fascism and thereby creating a 'defeatist mood'. One of the people on the list was Rakovsky. He was executed on 11 September 1941.

17. Two of the five experts – Professors Vladimir Vinogradov and Nikolai Shereshevsky – were to become 'doctor assassins' themselves fourteen years later, and were to be saved only by Stalin's death. Vinogradov would sign the medical report on Andrei Zhdanov's natural death, and then be accused of taking part in his premeditated murder on British Intelligence's instructions. They would be released while Vyshinsky was still alive and Vinogradov would even treat him medically.

18. Doctor Rozenblum confirmed this when questioned in connection with the same case: 'I was summoned to the Internal Prison to attend to Blyukher: one of his eyes had been beaten out.' There is another telling detail in this testimony:

> I was in the same prison cell as Yekaterina Ivanovna Kalinina [the wife of the Soviet Union's 'President'], Kosarev's wife [a Central Committee member and the head of the Komsomol], Maria Naneishvili, Blyukher's wife – Galina Kolchugina and others.... Kalinina used to tell me to

stop tormenting myself and confess to everything [to being an English spy] as they were going to beat a confession out of me just the same.

19. For some reason or other Stalin particularly loathed Rozengolts. In *The History of the All-Union Communist Party (Bolsheviks)* (Short Course) he even wrote Rozengolts's name several times with a small letter – a sign of contempt – putting him in the same league as Bukharin and Rykov. Did Stalin really believe that Rozengolts wanted to assassinate him? Vyshinsky came to such a conclusion only because Rozengolts had asked Stalin to receive him. For Vyshinsky this was 'ample and incontrovertible' evidence: why should a People's Commissar ask to see the General Secretary if not to assassinate him?

    Just as the final curtain was about to come down, knowing Stalin's mood, Vyshinsky decided to have a really good go at Rozengolts. This had absolutely nothing to do with the case at hand, but Vyshinsky entertained the hall by mockingly reading out the text of Rozengolts's 'talisman' – the sixty-eighth and ninety-first Psalms.

20. After the death of her husband and father-in-law and Yagoda's execution Nadezhda Alexeyevna Peshkova decided to lead a quiet life at long last and married the talented young philosopher and writer Ivan Luppol. In 1939 he became an Academician and his future looked highly promising, but then Stalin once again remembered the family of his 'friend' Maxim Gorky and decided to grace it with his attention. Luppol was arrested, tried and sent off to Saratov Prison, where he served his sentence with the great biologist Academician Nikolai Vavilov. It was there that they were both killed in 1943.

21. In those days Chkalov was known all over the world as the first pilot to fly non-stop from Moscow to the United States across the North Pole. 'Chkalov,' recalls his son Igor, 'went to all the court sessions. A man of exceptional honesty and forthrightness, he did not doubt the innocence of the revolutionaries and comrades-in-arms of Lenin, and said as much to Vyshinsky. The Procurator merely laughed and retorted in an offhand manner: 'Naïve, that's what you are, Valery Pavlovich.' The pilot's son believes that his father's tragic death on 15 December 1938 was definitely not the result of an accident, as it is generally considered to this day. Most likely, this secret will also be disclosed one day.

22. Davies was to stand by this fanatical idea of his in the future as well: he wrote a book entitled *Mission to Moscow* in which he became an active promulgator of Stalin's policies. A film was then made from the book which Davies took to Moscow with a personal message from Roosevelt in which the President referred to ex-ambassador Davies as his 'old friend'. Davies personally showed the film to Stalin, who then purchased it, and it was shown on Soviet cinema screens throughout the war. In the film version Vyshinsky little resembled himself – physically, that is. In spirit, he came across exactly as he intended: as the inflexible exposer

of traitors and terrorists. In his public speeches and published writings Davies endeavoured to defend Stalin's position as much as possible: 'It is quite clear,' he declared in one of his speeches, 'that all these trials, purges and liquidations which at the time seemed so harsh, and shocked the whole world so much, were part of a decisive and energetic effort on the part of Stalin's Government to protect itself not only from a *coup d'état* from within but also from an attack from without. The purge established order in the country and freed it from treason.'

Davies' energetic efforts did not pass unnoticed. Immediately after the war, on 18 May 1945, he was awarded an Order of Lenin, the only foreign diplomat in the entire history of the Soviet Union to be deemed worthy of such an honour, and, what's more, with the short but expressive formulation – 'for successful activity'. To mark the presentation of the award the Soviet Embassy in Washington held a sumptuous reception in his honour on 21 November of the same year.

23. I remember Denis Pritt well from his addresses at the Sofia Congress of the International Association of Democratic Lawyers (1960), which he chaired for many years. The audience gave him a rapturous ovation, and quite rightly, too. You see, he and his colleagues had played a prominent role in preventing Georgi Dimitrov from receiving a harsh sentence at the Leipzig trial. They had organized an international campaign in his defence as well as the so-called 'London counter-trial' which turned into a trial on Fascism. What possessed this eminent lawyer who, undoubtedly, set store by his reputation to second Vyshinsky and help him crush his innocent and defenceless victims? His efforts were fittingly rewarded after Stalin's death: in 1954 he was awarded the International Lenin Prize.

Chapter Five

1. Vladimir Pavlovich Milyutin, a Bolshevik from 1910, became a member of the first Soviet government which was formed on the night of 25–26 October 1917, and the People's Commissariat of Agriculture. In 1917–18 he was a member of the Central Committee. Right up to his arrest he held key Party and state posts.

2. I remember Yakov Naumovich Matusov well. He had been a captain of State Security, and the holder of several decorations awarded for his valiant service in the Lubyanka dungeons. After being honourably retired with a special pension and other perquisites, he set his sights on the Moscow Judicial Collegium, where his credentials immediately got him the post of director of a legal consultation office; his steady salary and the equally steady stream of gifts from subordinates enabled him to enjoy life without any particular cares or worries. Imposing and immaculately turned out, he was remembered by his colleagues for his good manners

343

and jovial disposition. He preferred not to speak of his military deserts, merely smiling in a telltale manner. Many other Lubyanka experts also found shelter at the Judicial Collegium. I remember, for instance, Lev Ilyich Novobratsky, who was already a major-general of the Ministry of State Security when he became a lawyer defending the downtrodden and oppressed. He and his ex-colleagues were particularly revered, and it was with ill-disguised envy, not horror, and in an undertone that people used to speak about their past.

3. Marina Simonyan was Krylenko's daughter by his first marriage. At that time she was living with her mother apart from him. She was not there during the conversation but pieced it together from relatives' stories. However, her recollections are undoubtedly authentic, and corroborated by other testimonies.

4. Nikolai Kirillovich Antipov, a Bolshevik from 1912, played an active role in the October Revolution in Petrograd and went on to become a secretary in various Moscow and Leningrad regional and district Party organizations. From 1924 onwards he was repeatedly elected to the Central Committee and was subsequently the People's Commissar of Postal and Telegraph Offices, the chairman of the Commission on Soviet Control, and the vice-chairman of the Soviet of Peoples' Commissars of the USSR. He was arrested on 21 June 1937, and only eleven days later, on 2 July, handed in a statement saying he was ready to 'expose all his accomplices', which he then proceeded to do, naming dozens, if not hundreds of people who had already been arrested or were about to be, and others still for future use. According to the records, his investigators were justified in claiming in their final statements that Antipov was 'ready for anything'. Condemned to death on 28 July 1938, he was not, however, executed; such a valuable witness as he was saved 'just in case'. He was transferred to the death cell of Orel Prison, where he spent two years, and was then shot with its other inmates on 11 September 1941.

5. Daniil Yegorovich Sulimov joined the Bolshevik Party in 1905. From 1921 he was repeatedly elected to the Central Committee. He became the President of the Soviet People's Commissariat of the RSFSR. In 1936 the Northern Caucasian town of Batalpashinsk was named after him. However, a few months later it lost its new name when Sulimov lost his life. It was then, incidentally, presented to Yezhov and became known as Yezhovo-Cherkessk, but again only for a year. Now it is simply called Cherkessk.

6. Andrei Sergeyevich Bubnov became a Bolshevik in 1903. In October 1917 he was a member of the Politburo of the Central Committee and the Petrograd Military Revolutionary Committee along with Stalin, Sverdlov, and Dzerzhinsky. For many years he was the People's Commissar of Education of the RSFSR.

7. Varvara Nikolayevna Yakovleva joined the Bolshevik Party in 1903, and

played an active part in the 1905 Revolution, and the February and October Revolutions. She was a secretary of the Moscow Committee and the Siberian Bureau of the Central Committee; in 1929–37 she held the post of People's Commissar of Finances of the RSFSR. In 1918 she sided with the 'left Communists', and in 1923 with the Trotskyites. She was shot in the yard of Orel Prison on 11 September 1941.

8. Valentin Andreyevich Trifonov was the father of writer Yuri Trifonov, who described him in his book *Camp-Fire Reflections*. He joined the Bolsheviks in 1904, and took part in the October Revolution in Petrograd. He was one of the founders of the Red Army, a board member of the People's Commissariat of Military Affairs and Frontline Revolutionary Military Councils, the first chairman of the Military Board of the Supreme Court of the USSR (1923–1925), and subsequently chairman of the Soviet of People's Commissars of the USSR.

9. Ioann Ilyich Shneiderman's laudable service was interrupted shortly after Antonov-Ovseyenko was killed. He was arrested in November 1938, and charged in connection with 'enemy of the people' Kozlova. The crime of this woman about whom we know nothing was that, 'according to agents' information', she had formerly been Pilsudski's mistress. As the laconic but substantive certificate of the Special Department of the NKVD states, 'the charge in question was dropped in view of her exceptional physical unattractiveness', and she was released. But Shneiderman continued to serve time although, it would seem, his connection with a 'non-enemy of the people' was not in itself a criminal offence. Exceptional physical unattractiveness, in the investigators' opinion, had prevented Pilsudski from making amorous advances but not Shneiderman. He survived until the thaw and gave evidence against his former colleagues. All trace of him was then lost.

10. Stanislav Stanislavovich Pilyavsky was a lawyer, diplomat and politician. After serving in the Polish Bureau of the Central Committee of the Workers' and Peasants' Party (Bolsheviks), he went on to work successively as the department head of Justice at the Revolutionary Committee of Poland, the head of rear organizations of the 1st Cavalry Army under the command of Semion Budionny, the Chairman of the Polish delegation on repatriation, a member of the Soviet delegation in Genoa (1922), an assistant Procurator of the RSFSR, and the Deputy Chairman of the Supreme Court of the USSR.

11. Iosif Stanislavovich Unshlikht joined the Bolshevik Party at the beginning of the century, and took part in the Revolution in Poland (1905–7), and then in the October Revolution in Petrograd as a member of the Military Revolutionary Committee. He worked as the vice-chairman of the All-Russian Special Commission for combatting counter-revolution, sabotage and speculation (the Cheka) and the State Political Directorate (OGPU). Later he became the Deputy People's Commissar of Military and Naval

Affairs. His last responsible post was as head of the Main Directorate of Civil Aviation. For many years he was a member of the Central Committee.

12. Yan Karlovich (also known as Pavel Ivanovich) Berzin was the pseudonym of Kuizis Peteris. He became a Bolshevik in 1905, and took part in all three revolutions. For many years he was the head of Soviet military intelligence. He was shot in 1938.

13. Yakov Ivanovich Alksnis, a Bolshevik from 1916, a second-ranking army commander, the Deputy People's Commissar of Defence and Commander-in-Chief of the Red Army's air force. A member of the judicial board which condemned Tukhachevsky, Yakir and other military leaders to death, he was arrested and shot a few months afterwards.

14. Robert Petrovich Eideman was a corps commander, the commanding officer of several fronts during the Civil War and military districts afterwards. Directly before his arrest he was the chairman of the Central Council of the Society for Organizing Anti-Aircraft and Chemical Defence, a semi-military mass organization exerting considerable influence in the thirties. He was shot after being sentenced to death at the Tukhachevsky-Yakir trial.

15. Fedor Mikhailovich Nakhimson was the brother of the renowned Bolshevik, Semion Nakhimson, after whom Leningrad's Vladimirsky Prospekt was at one time named. Semion Nakhimson was the Chairman of Yasoslavls District Executive Committee. He was seized during the White Guard Rebellion and executed. His brother, Fedor, died of a heart attack after hearing the death sentence passed on him.

16. Ivan Adolfovich Teodorovich joined the Russian Workers' Party in 1895, and became a Central Committee member in 1907. He took part in the October Revolution. He was a member of the first Soviet government, working in the People's Commissariat of Food. He was shot in 1937.

17. As an undergraduate I attended Professor Amfiteatrov's lectures on civil law and later, as a postgraduate, I often met him at the All-Union Institute of Law, where he worked as a senior researcher. Short, impeccably dressed, emphatically polite and formal, he gave the impression of being in a world of his own. His quiet voice, the weary and indifferent look in his eyes behind his pince-nez, the constant stern expression on his face and the terse, colourlessly glib replies he sometimes allowed himself when reluctantly drawn into a conversation did not make him easy to communicate with. We knew that he had been in prison and this inevitably gave him a stigma as far as we were concerned. He must have sensed this, of course. So, how could he be expected to smile and get on easily with other people?

Chapter Six

1. Avvakum was the ideologist and head of the Russian ecclesiastical schism in the 17th century. As a result of his conflict with the official Church he suffered persecution and deportation numerous times. He spent fifteen years in a dungeon. By a Tsarist decree he was condemned to the cruelest form of execution: he was burnt at the stake. Was it not this possible outcome Vyshinsky was alluding to when he compared Strogovich to Avvakum?

2. A year later, however, another geniune academic would join this close circle of honorary members – the octogenarian microbiologist and epidemiologist Nikolai Gamaleya. For nearly ten years the profoundly-moved new honorary member did not know how to express his gratitude to his dearly beloved leader and, finally, in his ninetieth year he applied to join the Party.

Chapter Seven

1. Beria, who was then Yezhov's deputy, moved into Chubar's *dacha* a few days after the latter's arrest. The takeover by major and minor officials of the apartments and *dachas* of people awaiting execution is a tragic and profoundly symbolic page in the history of that time. It became a widespread phenomenon. Even Iosif Pyatnitsky, the oldest Bolshevik, 'Iskra' agent, and ex-secretary of the Executive Committee of the Comintern, even he, a man renowned for his impeccable moral reputation, took over the apartment of his comrade Karl Radek. It was not long before Pyatnitsky's turn came too.

2. The fate of Tserpento, that minute 'cog' in the massive machinery of destruction, is remarkable and dramatic. Of Polish descent, he studied at the Stalingrad Pedagogical Institute, where he interpreted the appeals everywhere to expose enemies with naïve fervour and 'exposed' his fellow students as he saw fit. This was appreciated by the people he made his denunciations to, and he was immediately recruited into the secret service. No sooner had he turned professional than he was called to Moscow. He was then twenty-six years old. After being appointed head of operations of the 4th department of the NKVD, he naturally took part in the falsification of several cases, only gradually becoming aware of what the holy war against the spies and terrorists was really all about.

   He was particularly shaken by two cases. The 'Trotskyite' Goryachev, who had been arrested in Georgia, told him during the investigation that Beria was a leading agent of the Mussavatist secret service in Azerbaijan. Tserpento immediately reported this to Yezhov's secretary, Shapiro, and then handed an official report to Yezhov personally. He received a severe warning 'to mind his own business' but, as we can see, he did not follow this advice. It is hard to say what prompted his reports – impetuous courage or the naïvety of a person who had still not registered the truth. Whatever the case, these reports are extraordinary and point to the fact that even among those directly involved in the falsification of cases in the NKVD, there were some who refused to put up with the lawlessness and terror.

'There are people working in the NKVD who are trumping up cases against honest people,' Tserpento wrote to Stalin, Zhdanov, Andreyev and Malenkov from prison. His letters were simply attached to his dossier.

> Someone who is perishing at sea tosses a fragile bottle into the waves – a cry for help. He still hopes! But isn't his hope futile? After all, there are so many rocks under the surface of the sea, and the breakers by the shore are ruthlessly cruel! Aren't my statements like these bottles? Many of them have perished in the bottomless sea of paper, dashed against the indifference of paper souls – against these underwater rocks of public life.

'Citizen Vyshinsky,' he wrote to the Procurator-General, 'you are the conscience and hope of our law. Intervene, investigate, help!' However, Vyshinsky did none of these things. Tserpento's case dragged on for three years; they kept searching for a 'spy organization' whose mission he had been on. No such organization could be found, but Tserpento was still shot – two weeks after the outbreak of war. He has still to be rehabilitated.

3. When he was being tortured, did Kosarev remember his part in the work of the commission of the Plenum of the Central Committee of the All-Union Communist Party (Bolsheviks) in the Bukharin-Rykov case, in which he had seconded Yezhov's proposal to bring them to trial and execute them?

4. There is a very old Odessan anecdote which goes like this: 'Zhora, fry the fish!' shouts one neighbour out of the window. 'But where is the fish?' asks Zhora in surprise. 'Just get on with the frying and the fish will come later.' This shows the way in which the charges were compiled.

5. After marrying Zinaida Nikolayevna Raikh, who had once been Sergei Yesenin's wife and then became the leading actress of his theatre, Meyerhold, as a token of love for this outstanding woman, joined his own surname to hers and officially became Meyerhold-Raikh, and Zinaida Nikolayevna changed hers to Raikh-Meyerhold. Zinaida Nikolayevna's children from her marriage to Yesenin, whom Meyerhold adopted, kept their father's surname.

6. Aron Alexandrovich Solts joined the Workers' Party in 1898, and took part in the 1905 February and October Revolutions. He was a member of the Supreme Courts of the RSFSR and the USSR. Well known for his many years of work in the Central Control Commission of the All-Union Communist Party (Bolsheviks), Solts was referred to as 'the Party's conscience'. He also took an active part in the work of the Comintern.

Somehow he escaped arrest but was removed from all his posts, refused all manner of work and declared insane. He died in total obscurity just before the end of the war in May 1945.

7. Isaak Abramovich Zelensky was one of the main accused in the third 'Moscow Trial' (the Bukharin-Rykov case). He became a Bolshevik in 1906 and took an active part in the October Revolution. He was a member of the Central Committee for many years, a secretary of the Party's Moscow Committee, the Central Asian Bureau, and the Central Committee.

8. Ivan Terentievich Golyakov headed the Supreme Court of the USSR after zealous and productive service as a member of the Military Board. He was personally responsible for sentencing hundreds of innocent people to death and thousands to hard labour. I remember him well in the post of Director of the All-Union Institute of Law where I did my postgraduate studies. There he found a quiet haven after years of stormy work in the courts. Benevolent, quiet-mannered, attentive to his subordinates, he enjoyed the touching affection of some of the country's top law scholars who had won European acclaim even before the Revolution. They simply adored him. When it was suddenly rumoured that Golyakov was leaving his director's post, the other venerable professors sent a delegation to him, begging their favourite pastor not to forsake his faithful flock. And it worked. This institute's leading researcher was none other than Vyshinsky's daughter, Zinaida Andreyevna, who, unlike her father, was tall and well-built with a charming school-girls' fringe and a permanently kind and friendly smile on her face. Her career deterioriated somewhat after her father's death. She is now retired and lives in the same apartment in Granovsky Street and the same *dacha* in the village of Lutsino near Moscow that once belonged to the eminent statesman Academician Vyshinsky.

9. Nikolai Mikhailovich Tulaikov was an active member of two academies: the Academy of Sciences and the All-Union Lenin Academy of Agricultural Sciences. He was a prominent agronomist and soil specialist, the author of many works in which, in particular, methods were developed to combat drought. He was shot in 1938.

Chapter Eight

1. 'I have certain grounds to suppose,' writes Yevgeny Gnedin of Bessonov further on,

> that when he was in Berlin, he sent information through the Ambassador to V. M. Molotov. And, incidentally, it happened more than once that people who were carrying out confidential missions for Molotov were got rid of, possibly with Molotov's assistance, possibly as a 'lesson' to the latter. To sum up, S. A. Bessonov, talented, intelligent and

educated as he undoubtedly was, came into excessively close contact with the hellish state machinery, and it exterminated him.

2. Boris Yefimovich Shtein, a doctor of historical sciences, professor, and diplomat, attended many international conferences and was the Soviet ambassador in a number of countries. In 1952 he was dismissed from diplomatic work but charges were not brought against him.

3. During an inquiry in 1955 Leonid Bashtakov, one of Beria's most savage executioners, described Robert Eikhe's last moments:

> One day I was summoned to Beria's office in Sukhanovskaya Prison. There I saw our operatives, Rodos and Esaulov, and also Eikhe. In my presence, on Beria's instructions, Rodos and Esaulov brutally beat Eikhe with rubber rods; he fell but they picked him up and went on beating him. Beria kept asking him the same question, 'Will you confess to being a spy or won't you?' Eikhe kept replying, 'I won't confess'. Then the beating began although the day before Eikhe had already been sentenced to death. One of Eikhe's eyes had been beaten out and blood was streaming out of it but he went on repeating, 'I won't confess'. When Beria had satisfied himself that he could not get a confession out of him, he ordered them to lead him away to be shot.

4. The ex-editor-in-chief of *Literaturnaya Gazieta*, Alexander Chakovsky, told me a story he had heard from Alexander Fadeyev. One day Stalin summoned Fadeyev, put two volumes of the 'Koltsov Case' down in front of him and suggested he read them there and then in his office. Fadeyev started reading, making a mental note of the numerous pencilled comments Stalin had put in the margins. Going by his comments, Stalin had been particularly struck by the fact that Koltsov had been recruited as a 'spy' by André Malraux, who, judging by the evidence, had been an agent of French Intelligence for a long time. Noticing that Fadeyev was reading this part of the evidence, Stalin exclaimed, 'There's your celebrated intelligentsia for you! They refuse to collaborate with the NKVD, but Malraux here and other Western members of the intelligentsia for some reason don't. Think upon it, Comrade Fadeyev!'

5. *Bezhin Meadow* is the title of a well-known short story by Turgenev. Eisenstein's *Bezhin Meadow*, however, had nothing at all to do with Turgenev except, perhaps, for the bitter inner confrontation. It recounts the infamous story of Pavlik Morozov, a Young Pioneer, more likely invented than real, who denounced his father and became the hero of numerous 'textbook' poems and plays. The legend helped spread the denunciation mania. From his father's conversations at night with *kulaks*, the film's hero, Stepok, learns about plans to set fire to the building of the village Soviet and the collective farm's crops, and informs the collective farm's management. The conspirators are arrested, but the boy's father manages to overcome his escort of guards and escapes. He finds

his son and shoots him, and Stepok dies in the arms of the political commissar, Vassily. The *kulaks*, however, are still punished – they are found in a church which has been turned into a club. Stalin ordered all the copies of this film to be destroyed.

6. Maria Alexandrovna Spiridonova was one of the most famous Russian women revolutionaries and leaders of the Social Revolutionary Party. For the murder of a Tsarist punitive expedition member in 1906 she was given a life sentence of hard labour. She opposed the Brest Peace Treaty and was among the organizers of the Leftist Social Revolutionary revolt in 1918.

Chapter Nine

1. I remember very well one of the criminal cases my mother worked on at the end of the 1940s, which was in fact directly linked with the signing of the German-Soviet pact. The very next day, 24 August 1939, all the highly popular anti-Nazi films started to be removed from the cinema screens everywhere. They included *Professor Mamlok*, whose screenplay had been written by Lion Feuchtwanger (I wonder what this enthusiastic admirer of Stalin and Vyshinsky thought when he read about the Molotov-Ribbentrop pact?) and *The Oppenheim Family*, whose screenplay was by Friedrich Wolf. In September 1939, at the very start of the school year, a group of schoolchildren from near Moscow, not very well versed in the intricate workings of foreign policy, ordered these two films from their local club for a school showing. The two 'ring-leaders' – a boy and girl both aged sixteen – were immediately arrested and sentenced for anti-revolutionary agitation. When they were released from their respective labour camps and living in exile at the end of the war, they and their parents tried to get the sentence repealed. But they got nowhere; just as before they were told that they had 'acted against the Soviet government's foreign policy'. After unsuccessfully appealing to the Procurator's office and the Supreme Court, my mother decided to write to Vyshinsky, one of the pillars of Soviet foreign policy, to draw his attention to the fact that 'such an interpretation by the bodies of justices actually discredited Soviet foreign policy'. A reply to this letter again came from the Procurator's office but this time 'on Comrade Vyshinsky's instructions'. Among other things, it stated that 'the lawyer's arbitrary interpretation ... testifies to his inadequate political maturity.' This could have meant the lawyer was to be prosecuted, but she was lucky this time. This formulation, which was unusual for an official reply from the Procurator's Office, was very reminiscent of Vyshinsky's style. It seems to me (I have no evidence, of course) that the reply was simply a copy of what he had written on the lawyer's letter.

2. Bubnov's arrest was preceded by a denunciation of him which Nadezhda

351

Konstantinovna had made to the leader: 'Dear Iosif Vissarionovich,' she had written on 5 July 1937, 'I want to tell you about what I have had to think about recently.' So, what had Lenin's faithful companion had to think about in the summer of 1937, immediately after the execution of Tukhachevsky and Yakir and after Bukharin's and Rykov's arrests which she had actually witnessed? 'The power of the People's Commissar in the People's Commissariat is limitless ... The Party committee ... must not be allowed to turn into a simple weapon for carrying out the People's Commissar's will ... All this has a pernicious effect on the cause.' (The letter's author had underlined this whole passage.)

Undoubtedly, People's Commissar Bubnov was no different from any of the other people's commissars and had unlimited power in his department. But could Krupskaya not know what fate awaited him after such a denunciation? A few days later Bubnov was arrested. However, he would have ended up the same way even without the denunciation, and so we shall not lay the blame for his downfall on his deputy.

3. Rudolf Kirkhenshtein joined the Bolshevik Party in 1907. He took an active part in the October Revolution, and was awarded the Order of the Red Banner for heroism. He was a close friend of Y. Berzin, a Chekist and one of the most experienced Soviet intelligence officers, who worked under the code name of 'Prince'. He had a superb command of several foreign languages. In particular, he was the go-between of the famous intelligence officer Lev Manevich, who died in an Italian prison and was made a Hero of the Soviet Union twenty years later.

4. Ivan Andreyevich Chichayev was a leading Chekist who worked in many countries. When, as a result of the purges, the professional diplomats' posts were taken over by poorly qualified officials who had been promoted, Chichayev was on hand to give them helpful advice. This is also what he did with Derevyansky's predecessor, the Soviet Ambassador to Latvia, I. Z. Zotov, an ex-teacher of political economics who had been promoted to diplomatic work in 1937. After Latvia Chichayev worked in Sweden as Alexandra Kollontai's counsellor and then assisted Alexander Bogomolov, the Soviet Ambassador at the Union of Emigré Governments in London. He met de Gaulle and Beneš. He used to be summoned to Moscow to report to Vyshinsky. His last important diplomatic posting was as a senior counsellor in Czechoslovakia.

5. 'Smersh', an abbreviation of the Russian phrase 'death to spies', was the name given to NKVD special sub-divisions whose task during the war was to capture German wreckers and spies.

6. Years later one of the victims of the deportations sent Vyshinsky this poignant note from the heart of the Krasnoyarsk region. It is short but highly telling:

In 1940 I personally listened to you in Riga and was charmed by your speech which was full of such conviction and truth. I felt confident that all would be well for us under the protection of the strong Soviet Union. In 1941 my family and I were deported to Siberia, where I am now. My husband was sentenced to ten years, and for seven years I have had no news of him.

Maria Konstantinovna Ozol

Vyshinsky did not reply to this letter, just as he did not to many others like it. But he kept it in his archive.

Chapter Ten

1. Valentin Mikhailovich Berezhkov, a writer, scholar and doctor of historical sciences, took part in Molotov's talks with Hitler and Ribbentrop in Berlin in 1940. He acted as interpreter at the Tehran, Yalta and Potsdam conferences. Until recently he was the editor of the journal *USA: Politics, Economics, Ideology.*
2. Vladimir Georgievich Dekanozov, a Kartalin by birth (one of the ethnic groups within Georgia), was one of Beria's closest associates. He worked with him in Tbilisi and later followed him to Moscow. He became the head of the foreign department of the NKVD, and in 1939, after being appointed to the post of Deputy People's Commissar of Foreign Affairs, under Molotov, led the 'purge' of diplomats of the Chicherin-Litvinov school. From 1940 until the start of the war he was the Soviet Ambassador in Hitler's Germany. Along with Soviet Embassy personnel and a Soviet army column he was exchanged at the Bulgarian border town of Svilengrad for the German Embassy personnel and German Ambassador, Schulenburg – at the same time as Turkey was handed over to the Nazis in exchange for the Caucasus. He remained a Deputy People's Commissar of Foreign Affairs until the end of the war when a scandal involving young women brought his career to an abrupt end. He had a particular weak spot for young typists and shorthand secretaries and usually encountered no resistance, but one day he met his match. The girl in question rejected his advances and complained to her influential father. The latter made the matter known to Molotov, who detested loose conduct. Beria washed his hands of the affair and Dekanozov was forced to work as a deputy to the chairman of the Radio Committee for several years. Then Beria's second-in-command, Merkulov, who was head of a new department – the Main Directorate of Soviet Property Abroad (GUSIMZ) – took Dekanozov on as his deputy. After Stalin's death when Beria embarked upon his euphoric 'hundred days', he sent Dekanozov to his native Georgia as the Minister of State Security. Not long afterwards

he was arrested there. In December 1953 he was shot along with Merkulov, Kobulov and other top-ranking executioners.

3. Members of the Red Army's Supreme Command, Avgust Ivanovich Kork and Ieronim Petrovich Uborievich were executed with Marshal Tukhachevsky.

4. I talked to Yakov Matveyevich Raitses for several hours in August 1988. I had been informed by at least twenty readers that this man who had been actively involved in the top Soviet military commanders' massacre was alive and well and living in Kaluga, a mere three-hour train ride away from Moscow. I immediately set about arranging to meet him. But could one call the strange dialogue we had a 'talk'? There he was, this living eye-witness – a well-fed and well-groomed man of seventy odd who looked much younger than his age with four rows of decoration ribbons, and a file full of letters of thanks and certificates of merit. 'Tell me about Loktionov's interrogation,' I began. 'I don't remember.' 'Then, how about Maria Nesterenko's?' 'I don't remember.' 'Then, about the last minutes of her life.' 'I don't remember.' 'Well, about anything at all.' 'I don't remember, I don't remember. I don't remember...' We parted. Then he caught me up in the courtyard outside: 'Believe me, I'm an honest man.' Those were his last words to me. I wonder what he and the likes of him mean by the word 'honesty'?

5. Many of the people who worked with Vyshinsky or used to meet him recall that he tried hard to make out that he did not know Polish and even saw fit to stress this point. Evidently, his Polish really was not very good or certainly not as good as it should have been, considering his Polish origin. He usually chose to understate this origin although, when he needed to, he still remembered how to speak Polish – not very brilliantly, perhaps, but it still helped him out of more than one tricky situation.

6. The 'Antonovites' were followers of the Social Revolutionary A. S. Antonov, who mounted an unsuccessful uprising against the Bolsheviks in the Tambov Province in 1920–21.

7. Before the Revolution Alexander Nikolayevich Vertinsky became popular with his 'little Piero arias', songs of his own composition which he used to perform in an exquisite and brilliantly original manner. Essentially, he was the 'father' of the modern Russian ballad. He emigrated in 1919 at the age of thirty and toured many countries of the world. Upon his return to the USSR he gave tremendously successful concerts all over the country and acted in films. For his part as the cardinal in the film *The Conspiracy of the Doomed* – screenplay by Nikolai Virta (based on the Hungarian Cardinal Mindszenty) – Vertinsky was awarded the Stalin Prize. However, he never lived to see himself totally recognized by the authorities as a unique artist and the founder of an entire genre in art.

Chapter Twelve

1. Matvei Fedorovich Shkiryatov was one of Stalin's vilest henchmen whose name was quite rightly ranked alongside those of Yezhov and Beria. He became a Bolshevik in 1906, and took an active part in the October Revolution. For many years he worked in the highest control bodies of the Party, and took charge of the Party purges and beatings of Party officials. He worked hand in hand with the NKVD and Ministry of State Security, and had his 'own' prison where he personally interrogated important prisoners. He died almost at the same time as Vyshinsky before any form of judgement could be passed on him.

2. This was preceded by torture of such amazing subtlety that it makes one wonder whether its 'inventors' were not only the greatest executioners of all times and peoples but also totally insane by then. Kuznetsov, Voznesensky, and the others were, among other things, literally trampled on and burned with white-hot irons – not in the 'usual' torture chamber but in the railway carriage of a train circling round and round Moscow. The performance in court was surrounded by a ritual which made the fantasies of the last Caesars of the Roman Empire seem positively dull: after the sentence was passed, white shrouds with fools' caps were immediately thrown over the prisoners who had been sentenced to death, and officers carried them out of the courtroom feet first, chained and bound. Even if one interprets this as some insane kind of medieval mystery play put on by brutal thugs who had forced their way into power, it still defies all reason.

3. A. Lozovsky was the party pseudonym of Solomon Abramovich Dridzo.

4. Lina Solomonovna Shtern was a top physiologist and a member of the Academy of Sciences and the Academy of Medical Sciences. At the time of her arrest she was seventy. After her release she continued with her scientific work until her death at the age of ninety.

5. Ryumin was shot in 1954, Grishayev escaped punishment and became a professor and doctor of law. Until recently he was working in the Department of Criminal Law at the All-Union Open Institute of Law.

6. Alexander Alexandrovich Fadeyev was a well-known novelist, the General Secretary of the Writers' Union, and a Central Committee member. Besides being a high-ranking official and a very close associate of Stalin, he was also a writer of considerable standing. He gave his sanction to the arrest of scores of writers. In 1956, after the 20th Congress had set about exposing Stalin's crimes, and a campaign began to rehabilitate the victims, he committed suicide.

7. The Kerch landing, a 'New Year's present' to the Leader organized on the orders of his envoy, the vile Lev Mekhlis, was a pointless venture from a military viewpoint and needlessly cost the country thousands of lives. To make up for it, the Supreme Commander was thus able to demonstrate yet again his inexhaustible supply of humour.

Chapter Thirteen

1. Nikolai Grigorievich Alexandrov was a notable figure among his colleagues. He worked at the same time in two very different professions – law and music – and did very well in the second, becoming the chief conductor of Moscow's Operetta Theatre at the end of the thirties. A sybarite, *bon vivant* and delightful wit, he became very friendly with Vyshinsky's daughter, and it was partly her influence that made him leave the theatre to devote himself to academic study, where he quickly advanced to become a leading theorist in labour law. Unfortunately, even Zinaida Andreyevna's patronage did not prevent him from falling victim to the wrath of her father, who, as one can see, did not always share her sympathies.

2. During a visit to Paris at the end of November 1951 Vyshinsky went to see Molière's *Le Bourgeois Gentilhomme* at the Comédie Française and left an inscription in the special guest book. At last the public had access not only to his autograph – a flourish over an official document – but also to a sample of 'original writing', and the latter was immediately handed over to the renowned French graphologist Henri Rocourt to be analysed. His conclusion was as follows: 'To accomplish his ends this person is capable of resorting to anything, even cunning; he subordinates his entire life, including his personal life, to the task at hand.'

   It is quite probable that the opinion formed of Vyshinsky had influenced the analysis of his handwriting. This just goes to show that such an opinion already existed.

3. In the international arena Vyshinsky became renowned as a staunch defender of the victims of racial persecution. His archive contains a letter from the chairman of the executive committee of the World Jewish Congress, Nahum Goldmann: 'We are grateful to Your Excellency for understanding our proposals regarding the fact that the definition of "citizens of the United Nations" in Mikhail Dogorov's economic articles should include victims of racial, Nazi and Fascist discrimination or persecutions and thus provide the Jews in former enemy countries who have suffered as a result of the embezzlement perpetrated by the Nazi and Fascist regimes, with the opportunity of regaining their property.

   'We were particularly heartened by the fact that Your Excellency approved our proposals regarding effective measures for rooting out anti-Semitism by punishing racial propaganda and acts inciting racial hatred and discrimination.'

4. Alexandra Mikhailovna Kollontai (1872–1952) joined the Bolshevik Party in 1915. During the October Revolution she was a Central Committee member, and then government member in the People's Commissariat of Social Security. She took part in several opposition movements, including the so-called 'Workers' Opposition'. She was the world's first woman ambassador, representing her government in

Norway, Mexico, and Sweden. She was fortunate enough to escape the terror as she presented no danger to Stalin and her influence in the West could have proved useful to him.

5. The 'courts of honour' were introduced by a secret decree signed by Stalin, who had decided to deal with professors N. G. Klyuyeva and G. I. Roskin in a more humane manner than the NKVD 'Troikas'. Through Academician V. V. Parin these academics gave their American colleagues the manuscript of their book *The Biotherapy of Malignant Growths*, which was being published in a Soviet publishing house.

6. I remember senior lecturer Alexander Alexandrovich Askerov well. He taught a strange subject for those days at Moscow University – 'Soviet Construction'. However it was not his teaching that has stuck in my memory, or even his dreadfully lugubrious appearance – the dark glasses on a square face, wide-brimmed hat pulled down over his forehead, black glove on the end of his artificial arm which did not bend at the elbow – it was his speech at a 'court of honour'.

A student was standing trial for committing the horrific crime of having a picture of the American film actress Deanna Durbin on his bedside table in his hostel. She had won the hearts of Soviet cinema audiences in films such as *One Hundred Men and a Girl* and *His Butler's Sister*. A public 'trial' was held in the main assembly hall at which Askerov appeared in the role of prosecutor. Thumping his artificial arm down on the rostrum, he bombastically exclaimed: 'I accuse the blind man who failed to see behind the film actress's charming smile the savage snarl of American imperialism.' Askerov was then followed by a student who really was blind. Poor soul, he had never seen Deanna Durbin, but he could conjure up her savage snarl in his imagination and it had enraged him. He demanded that the 'traitor who has given up our wonderful girls for a foreign wrecker' be immediately expelled from the university. And he was.

What could one do to help the pariah? Remembering my recent experience, I suggested writing to Vyshinsky: who could figure out the snarl of American imperialism better than he? Vyshinsky did not reply to the letter, but his assistant let us know through the rector's office that, unfortunately, Andrei Yanuarievich did not consider himself sufficiently competent where matters of art were concerned.

Chapter Fourteen

1. Serafim Alexandrovich Pokrovsky, a professor of history and Russian law, was a man of brilliant intellect and versatile knowledge, a superb conversationalist, a wonderful lecturer, a music and ballet-lover. I attended his lectures at the Institute of Foreign Trade, met him more than once and was always under the spell of his charm. In the twenties

he had dared argue with the Peoples' Leader by venturing to express his own point of view, and had been given a boorish 'thrashing' by his opponent, and in public, what's more: in two 'replies to S. Pokrovsky' in the ninth volume of Stalin's collected works. Arrested for such 'anti-Soviet activity' at the beginning of the thirties, Pokrovsky was sent off to a labour camp where he was recruited by the NKVD. From 1934 he became a paid provocateur, and after his release was allowed to return to his academic post where his new work got fully underway and virtually took over as his main occupation. He carried it out with sincere enthusiasm and indubitable pleasure, being paid a very large bounty 'by the job', for each of his victims.

I saw him dining with Valentin Lifshits several times in the courtyard of the Central Journalist's Club, where there used to be a summer restaurant. He was always cheerful, vivacious and moderately 'tanked up', and there was a wily glint in his small eyes. On the night of 5–6 March 1953, a few hours after Stalin's death, he was arrested along with many other more important NKVD agents (evidently, they were all listed to be placed under arrest on 'Day X', straight after Stalin's death), and spent nearly the rest of the year in prison. Upon the insistence of Sofia Kopelyanskaya and Valentin's colleagues from the Institute of Law of the Academy of Sciences a thorough inquiry was conducted, which resulted in Pokrovsky being expelled from the Party. During the course of the inquiry he gave a detailed explanation of how he had traded in people over many years. His account is horrifying to read.

2. It is well known that one of the doctors who treated Maxim Gorky, Maxim Yulianovich Belostotsky, who later appeared at the Bukharin-Rykov trial to expose his accomplices, was 'found' by Yezhov, and called as a witness for the prosecution by Vyshinsky. Fifteen years later there was no need to search for anyone: the school of Beria and Vyshinsky worked without a hitch, and an informer came forward without even being asked to. She was Doctor Lydia Fedoseyevna Timashuk, whose feat was rapturously extolled by top journalists Olga Chekotkina, Yelena Kononenko and other of their colleagues. On 20 January 'for assistance rendered to the government in exposing the doctor assassins' Timashuk was awarded the Order of Lenin. But before she had the time to wear the order on the lapel of her best suit, it was taken away again: on 4 April the 'doctor assassins' were rehabilitated and the doctor informer disgraced. However, the lapel of her suit did not stay bare for long: a year later – without any fanfare – she was awarded the Order of Lenin again, this time for irreproachable, long-standing service to the glory of Soviet medicine. She was thus compensated for her moral losses. I wonder if the second order was the same one with the same number as the first? A question of no consequence but interesting all the same.

Lydia Timashuk remained in charge of the electrocardiology department of the No 1 Kremlin Clinic for a long time. Later on colleagues noticed the total inadequacy of her conclusions. When she used to attend meetings of cardiologists, nobody wanted to sit next to her. (This did not happen in her own clinic, of course – the 'official' doctors there could not afford to make such demonstrative gestures.)

3. This in itself was a great demotion for Vyshinsky. Malik had been his subordinate for many years, and he had been constantly taunted by his chief. He had difficulty with his pronunciation and tended to speak thickly, and was certainly no match for our great orator. Indeed, Vyshinsky used to tease him in public by saying things like: 'Why do you keep saying blah-blah-blah?' or 'Spit your porridge out and stop bleating.' Now they were on equal terms.

4. I do not know whether it is this fact or simply a weakness for controversial conjectures that has given rise to the legend of Vyshinsky being called back to Moscow to give some kind of explanations for the unlawful repressions and deciding that the best way out was to shoot himself. In his article 'The Theatre of Joseph Stalin' (journal *Theatre*, August 1988) Anton Antonov-Ovseyenko retells this legend as though it were indisputable fact, instead of specifying that it is only a rumour. And that is what it certainly is. Nobody summoned Vyshinsky to Moscow 'for explanations'. He died in front of two dozen people, some of whom are still alive today.

Index

365

Tukhachevsky papers, 103; interrogates military commanders, 104; and alterations to law, 105; and Krestinsky, 110–12; on poison threat, 116; identifies Bukharin's corpse, 121; and confessions, 124–5; and Krylenko, 131–4, 136, 139, 145; chess-playing, 138–9; condemns Meren, 148; protects assistants, 152; public image, 155–9, 290; attacks Bukharin, 159–60; elected to Academy of Sciences, 160–1; as member of Central Committee, 170–1; visits Stalin, 172, 175–7; as Deputy Chairman of Soviet People's Commissariat, 177–8, 186; at 1st Theatre Conference, 179–81; Meyerhold appeals to, 181; and world of arts, 186–7, 192; and foreign affairs, 193–5; and Western Ukraine, 204; and Russian language and educational reforms, 204–5; mission in Latvia, 208–15; eczema, 212; as Deputy People's Commissar of Foreign Affairs, 215, 241; and outbreak of war, 217–18, 221; evacuates to Kuibyshev, 226–32; returns to Moscow, 234; and publication of Bible, 234–5; readmits Vertinsky, 236–7; absent from Tehran conference, 239–40; fluency in dictating, 240; relations with Beria, 240–1; on Allied control council for Italy, 242–5; and repatriations and displaced persons, 243–4, 283–4; at Yalta conference, 245; 1945 mission to Rumania, 245–6; working methods and views, 247–9; diplomatic skills, 250–1; languages, 250, 252; 1945 mission to Berlin, 251; described by Roberts, 252–4; waltzing, 254; as international public figure, 255; and Rumanian peace treaty, 256–7; and Bulgaria, 257–8; and Nuremberg trials, 258–61; Shawcross on, 260–1; receives appeals for help, 274–5, 296–7; diplomatic uniform, 278, 293; appointed Foreign Minister, 279–80; witticisms and sayings, 281; diplomatic invective and bombast, 282–7; ill-treats colleagues and associates, 288–90; charm and human qualities, 290–3; and women,

290–1; and alcohol, 291–2; remains active in jurisprudence, 293–6; on individual responsibility in law, 295; response to personal correspondence, 296–301; privileges, 302–3; as candidate member of Presidium, 304; and 'Doctors' Trial', 308–9; dismissed on Stalin's death, 309; as permanent delegate to UN, 310, 314; 70th birthday, 312–13; life in New York, 313; death, 315–16, 320; and Manuilsky's letter of denunciation, 316–18; obituary, tributes and reactions to, 319–23; *Essays on the History of Communism*, 39, 46; *From Prisons to Educational Institutions*, 71; 'The head of the Soviet government' (article), 206; *The Theory of Legal Evidence in Soviet Law*, 160–1, 190–2

Vyshinsky, Yanuarii (V's father), 14

Welles, Sumner, 218
Willie, Wendell, 234
Wrangel, F. P., 30
Wrangel Island, 75

Yablochkin, Alexander, 178
Yagoda, Genrikh, 68, 70–1, 74, 100, 119–20, 138, 177
Yakir, Iona, 103, 106, 147
Yakovlev, Commissioner, 77
Yakovlev, Artillery Marshal Nikolai, 262
Yakovleva, Varvara, 138, 140, 202
Yakubovich, Mikhail, 60
Yalta conference, 1945, 239, 245
Yaroslavsky, Emelian, 57, 162, 228
Yasensky, Bruno, 98
Yaunzem, Irma, 214
Yelagin, Yuri, 180, 202
Yemilyanov, Ananii Pavlovich, 22
Yenukidze, Abel, 57, 68, 138, 146
Yerefeev (Molotov's subordinate), 252
Yermansky (Menshevik), 29
Yesenin, Sergei, 185
Yesenina, Tatyana Sergeyevna, 185–6
Yevkodimov, Yevgeny, 42, 77
Yezhov, Nikolai: replaced by Beria, 2; exiles author's uncle, 9; and Kirov murder, 68; in Special Security Commission, 70; on RSFSR Constitution commission, 77; and Bukharin-Rykov trial, 84–5, 106, 118; Serebryakov intends killing, 95;